THE MEAT COOKBOOK

NICHOLA FLETCHER

Recipes by Christopher Trotter, Elena Rosemond-Hoerr, Rachel Green

**LONDON, NEW YORK,
MUNICH, MELBOURNE, DELHI**

DK UK
Senior Editors Bob Bridle, Vanessa Daubney
Senior Art Editors Lucy Parissi, Sara Robin
Editorial Assistant Elizabeth Clinton
Managing Editor Dawn Henderson
Managing Art Editor Christine Keilty
Senior Jacket Creative Nicola Powling
Pre-Production Producer Raymond Williams
Senior Producers Oliver Jeffreys, Jen Scothern
Art Director Peter Luff
Publisher Peggy Vance

DK INDIA
Senior Art Editor Balwant Singh
Project Editor Neha Samuel
Editor Manasvi Vohra
Art Editor Anjan Dey
Assistant Editor Arjun Pereira
Assistant Art Editor Pallavi Kapur
Managing Editor Alicia Ingty
Managing Art Editor Navidita Thapa
Pre-Production Manager Sunil Sharma
Senior DTP Designer Tarun Sharma
DTP Designers Anurag Trivedi, Satish Chandra Gaur

WARNING: Please take care when following the instructions in this book, especially when using knives and saws, and when handling animal carcasses and heavy sections of meat. Neither the author nor publisher can accept responsibility for any accidents that may result from following instructions contained in this book.

NOTE: The author and publisher advocate sustainable food choices, and every effort has been made to include only sustainable foods in this book. Food sustainability is, however, a shifting landscape, and so we encourage readers to keep up to date with advice on this subject, so that they are equipped to make their own ethical choices.

First published in Great Britain in 2014 by
Dorling Kindersley Limited
80 Strand, London WC2R 0RL

2 4 6 8 10 9 7 5 3
001 – 192992 – Sep/2014

Copyright © 2014
Dorling Kindersley Limited
A Penguin Random House Company

All rights reserved. No part of this publication may be reproduced, stored in a retrieval system, or transmitted in any form or by any means, electronic, mechanical, photocopying, recording or otherwise, without prior permission of the copyright owner.

A CIP catalogue record for this book is available from the British Library.

ISBN 978-1-4093-4502-2

Colour reproduction by Alta Image
Printed and bound in China by South China Printing Co. Ltd

Discover more at **www.dk.com**

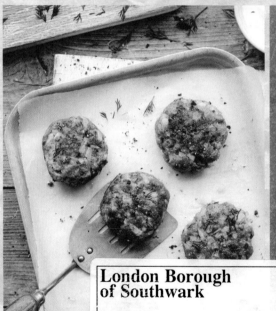

London Borough of Southwark	
CW	
SK 2458388 X	
Askews & Holts	09-Sep-2014
641.66 FOO	£25.00

CONTENTS

FOREWORD

Meat is a truly fascinating subject. I have been privileged to have worked with it for over forty years. My interest in the subject has given me a multi-faceted career that combines food writer, teacher, food historian, farmer, and meat processor. On top of that, living in the country has taught me much about wild creatures. This book will, I hope, allow me to share some of these insights.

As a food historian, farmer, and meat processor, I have learnt that eating meat can produce powerful emotions more complicated than the simple pleasure of sharing and eating it. I have never shied away from the reality that if you eat meat, an animal has died to produce it. In today's ever more virtual and urban world it is hard for people to understand the interaction we had with animals in our historic roles as hunters, nomads, herders, and small farmers. If you work closely with animals, whether it is studying what distresses or calms them, or marvelling at a carcass being skilfully prepared, you can, and do, truly respect them. As a society we have lost that intimacy and this loss can produce mystery, confusion, and even fear.

But there is nothing to fear when we prepare animals in a respectful way. It is possible to farm and despatch animals in such a way that they don't suffer, and wild animals now need management in a world whose balance of nature can be so easily tilted the wrong way. A growing shortage of land means we must make best use of our environment – "Meat matters" (see pp10–11) explains how some places will only produce vegetation that humans can't eat. Animals convert this efficiently into meat. With a world population as large as ours to feed, there is no utopian food production method; even vegan food production harms insects, wild creatures, and the environment. So if we choose to eat meat it is up to us to find out how it is produced, to waste none of it, and to use it respectfully and proportionately. Then we will eat it joyously.

As a food writer and teacher I have explored just how meat works when it is prepared and then cooked. What is it that makes one piece of meat better than another? And what does "better" mean anyway? One person's "impeccable" may be another's over- or undercooked. But once you understand the basic structure of meat – what makes it and what changes it – the mysteries that perplex so many people become simple background knowledge that can be used to buy, prepare, and cook any meat. So before rushing straight to our sumptuous collection of recipes, do read these important parts; they are as essential as any of the ingredients. Even if you don't feel up to having a go at home butchery, do study these pages and you will gain a deeper understanding.

Meat has formed an integral part of the culture of nearly every country. Signifying luxury and sometimes power, regarded as a gift from God, and appreciated as a joyous privilege, meat is an important food that should be celebrated. I hope you will feast on these pages.

Nichola Fletcher

MEAT
KNOW-HOW

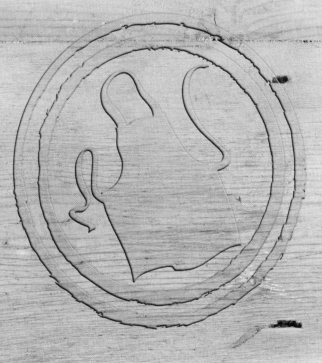

MEAT MATTERS

MEAT – SUCH A MOUTH-WATERING WORD. FOR MANY PEOPLE, A MEAL IS NOT A PROPER MEAL IF THERE IS NO MEAT. MOST EMERGING COUNTRIES WANT TO EAT MORE OF IT, AND CONSUMPTION HAS NEVER BEEN SO HIGH. BUT IT CAN ALSO BE EMOTIVE – THERE ARE MANY REASONS WHY SOME PEOPLE CHOOSE NOT TO EAT MEAT. SO SHOULD WE EAT IT OR NOT? PERHAPS THE ANSWER IS "BOTH". WE CAN EAT MEAT AND ENJOY IT WHERE WE FEEL COMFORTABLE ABOUT THE WAY IT IS PRODUCED, BUT WE SHOULD PROBABLY AVOID IT WHERE WE DON'T.

Critics often say that feeding grain and oil seeds to animals is not a sustainable way to produce food. People should eat the grain themselves. There is some truth in that argument, but it applies mainly to intensively farmed meat such as feedlot cattle (see p142) and intensive pig and poultry production. These systems rely on crops to produce meat quickly and at a price to satisfy the world's demand for cheap meat. Hens are the most efficient converters of grain into food, followed by pigs, cattle, and sheep.

GRASS-FED MEAT

Many areas of the world, however, cannot grow crops sustainably. Think of arid scrub or cold countries; mountains or forest regions. Grasses grow most efficiently in these places. Humans can't digest grass, so the most sensible thing to do is to allow animals to turn it into nutritious meat, which they do admirably.

And then there are wild animals – lots of them. This is meat at its most natural. Yet there are so few hunters nowadays that some populations are out of control. Pigeons raid crops; wild boar dig up vineyards; roe deer nibble young trees; elk lumber across roads into vehicles – they have become pests and have sometimes started to destroy their own environment. Are rabbits eating your vegetable garden? Why not eat the rabbit and enjoy the flavour of the wild combined with your carrots?

THE GRAIN DRAIN

Crops such as wheat, barley, soya, oil seeds, beans, and peas are crops that humans can eat. But these same crops are used to make animal feed (known as "concentrates"). Our planet needs its forests desperately, so to cut them down to grow crops creates ecological problems, no matter who eats the crop. To cut them down to feed livestock is certainly questionable in the long term. So what an animal or bird has been fed on is ethically important, too.

MEAT AND NUTRITION

Meat is a good source of protein, iron, and other nutrients and vitamins, but we are all warned not to eat too much animal fat as this can lead to obesity and heart problems.

Given the environmental problems of feeding animals on grain, it is interesting, but perhaps not surprising, to discover that ruminants (grazing animals such as cows, sheep, deer, and goats) – which munch their way slowly through a natural diet of grasses and vegetation instead of being fed with concentrates – are nutritionally far better for us. It is concentrated, high-energy diets that change meat from having "good" fat to having "bad" fat.

THE MEAT TO EAT

Pigs and poultry are rather more problematic. They have been reared for centuries in peoples' back yards on a varied diet of scraps and whatever else they can forage in the fields and woodlands. Some are still raised like that for private consumption. But apart from slow-grown Iberian pigs living on acorns, commercial production almost always relies on concentrated feed. The best systems combine concentrates with an outdoor life. So free-range hens and geese that can scratch about or graze grass, and outdoor pigs that can wallow in mud and root about for insects, produce the best-quality meat.

However, the vast majority of pigs and poultry are contained in buildings. They rarely experience the outside world, and are fed not only on concentrates, but in many countries on antibiotics and growth promoters as well. Intensive feedlot cattle are also given these and other medications. They make meat cheaper. But how sensible is it to use antibiotics in food production? Do we really want to feed our children on meat produced with growth promoters?

PROVIDING CONDITIONS THAT ARE CLOSEST TO AN ANIMAL'S NATURAL HABITAT AND BEHAVIOUR IS THE BEST HUSBANDRY A FARMER CAN OFFER HIS STOCK.

IT'S IN THE BREEDING

All over the world animals have adapted to cope with local conditions and to make remarkably good use of available food. Goats thrive in near-desert conditions and climb trees to nibble thorns and leaves. To survive long, arctic winters, reindeer lay down 15cm (6in) of fat in the short summer. Island sheep survive on salt grass and seaweed washed up by winter gales. In dry climates, cattle developed fatty humps to tide them over lean periods. In addition, different breeds have been carefully selected over hundreds of years to produce something extra that farmers want. In the past, domestic animals were selected to produce lots of fat. Nowadays, the reverse is true. Sheep are bred to produce more than one lamb. Some beef breeds now have an extra leg muscle. Pigs and poultry are bred to survive, and even be content,

under the most intensive conditions. It is worth noting, however, that most animal diseases are the result of animals being bred for a special characteristic.

HAPPY MEAT

In many countries, consumer pressure has led to a vast improvement in animal welfare, although in other countries animals fare much worse. Research into animal behaviour helps farmers understand how their livestock can live contented lives and how they can be transported and slaughtered more humanely. This is in everyone's interest because contented animals are more profitable.

Good animal welfare is the art of balance. Too much stress (excitement) produces fear; too little brings boredom with its own problems. Overcrowding is bad for any animal, but equally most are happiest living

together in flocks or herds. Too much food is just as bad as too little, and for an animal to experience extreme heat or cold can be as bad as not being able to experience any weather at all. Above all, providing conditions that are closest to an animal's habitat and suit its natural behaviour is the best husbandry a farmer can offer his stock.

QUALITY NOT QUANTITY

We can feel comfortable about the meat we eat when we have chosen it carefully, thought about how it was produced, and not wasted any. It was only in the 20th century, when people started to eat such large amounts of meat, that obesity became a major problem. So perhaps many of us would lead healthier lives if we chose our meat more carefully, but ate a little less. Perhaps our natural world would be a better place if less meat was raised intensively.

ASK THE BUTCHER

GOOD-QUALITY MEAT COMES FROM A VARIETY OF SOURCES. HOWEVER, AS POOR-QUALITY MEAT CAN COME FROM THESE SAME SOURCES IT IS IMPORTANT TO FIND A SUPPLIER THAT YOU TRUST, WHERE YOU CAN ASK QUESTIONS AND RECEIVE HONEST ANSWERS.

SHOPPING AROUND

• **Supermarkets** In the West, the majority of meat is bought in supermarkets. These giant conglomerates are highly aware of the need for customer trust and some are proactive in working with their suppliers to ensure good quality at keen prices. But where costs are cut and supply chains are complicated, unpleasant practices can, and do, creep in.

• **Markets and farmers' markets** It is tempting to assume that when food is purchased in the open air from a cheery vendor, it will be of superior quality. Usually it will, especially where producers sell their own meat and poultry. But some vendors simply sell on anonymous mass market meat. Even producers selling their own meat may have sausages manufactured for them by a central plant that uses many additives. But increasing numbers of enthusiastic producer–manufacturers are usually found at these specialist local markets and they are well worth seeking out.

• **Butchers' shops** The best ones are family businesses rather than chains. Some have been in the same family for generations and have built up a reputation and a clientèle prepared to pay for excellence. Family butchers know where their meat comes from and are likely to have facilities for dry-ageing it. They will be able to obtain even the most obscure cut for you (though you may need to order it in advance).

• **Online** As with all online shopping, a good website can disguise a low-grade business. But direct selling with overnight courier deliveries has made it possible for countless excellent small businesses to become viable. The many media guides will direct you to good sources.

DRY-AGEING MEAT Cold air circulating around the carcass allows the meat to mature without creating harmful moulds. Harmless moulds often occur, but they are trimmed off.

ASKING THE RIGHT QUESTIONS

The different methods of meat production are described on pages 10–11 and will help you decide what to seek out and ask for when buying meat. Almost always, meat that is produced sustainably and under good welfare conditions will be the most expensive. Here are some other key questions to ask.

WHERE DOES YOUR MEAT COME FROM?

Local meat is of better quality where the butcher can visit the producer and build up a trusting relationship. In areas where the land is unsuitable for free-range and grazing animals, local might mean very intensive, so in this case, the best meat may be brought in from some distance away, even imported. Provided that it is suitably transported and stored, the quality should not be compromised. However, the further away the source is, the more difficult it is to be really certain of how the meat was produced.

HOW IS YOUR MEAT MATURED?

Some meat tastes better if it is matured for a period of time; this practice is more traditional in cold climates. Beef and game meats are usually matured; domestic poultry, lamb, and pork are not. There are two main ways of ageing meat:

• **Dry-ageing or hanging** This produces the best results. The carcass (or a section of the carcass) is hung in cold, airy conditions so that it slightly dries out and also produces enzymes that tenderize the meat. This concentrates and improves the flavour. Dry-aged meat is usually darker.

• **Vacuum-pack maturing** Meat (usually boneless) is packed into strong, vacuum bags and all the air is removed. The meat then matures for several weeks and becomes more tender. However, the improvement in flavour gained by dry-ageing is not achieved using this method.

WHICH BREEDS ARE YOUR BEEF, LAMB, AND PORK – AND WHAT SPECIES IS THE GAME?

Commercial breeds are selected to produce a particular trait. Sometimes this improves quality, but often the reverse is true. Traditional heritage breeds are still reared, but they are usually local specialities. Although more expensive, they are worth seeking out because their producers tend to take special care of these rare animals and their meat. Game animals and birds are different species, not different breeds. A good butcher should know which he is selling.

WHAT ARE YOUR MEAT PRODUCTS MADE OF?

A vast array of meat products (such as burgers, meatballs, satays, sausages, and pies) are made from minced offcuts unsuitable for other forms of cooking. These make efficient use of the whole carcass. However, most commercial products contain additives that help them last longer, or alter their flavour, colour, and texture. Very cheap products often contain mechanically recovered meat (MRM) that is usually marked on the label. Most of these products are easy, quick, and cheaper to make at home and will taste much better when freshly made, so consider buying mince rather than made-up products.

WHAT DOES THE BEST MEAT LOOK LIKE, AND HOW SHOULD IT SMELL?

• **Colour** Each meat has its own natural colour, but exercise, green vegetables or grass, the presence of iron, and dry-ageing make it darker. Oxidized meat becomes a dull brown. Vacuum-packed meat can darken or appear iridescent in the pack, but reverts to its natural colour once opened.

• **Smell** Fresh meat should have a faint, sweet smell, however it is packed. Sometimes, though, vacuum-packed meat that has been stored for some time smells strong when taken out of the pack. Leave it in the open air for about an hour and the smell should disappear. If it doesn't, discard it. Game that has been hung will also have a stronger smell.

WHICH CUTS ARE BEST?

It is tempting to stay with a few "best" cuts that are familiar, but all carcasses produce a range of flavours and textures. Prime (that is, expensive) cuts come from the loin and top of the legs. Shoulders and the lower parts of the legs contain more collagen so need longer cooking. Very often, cheaper cuts have the most interesting flavour and texture.

AGED MEAT Dry-aged meat is deep red but not brown; a dark band around the outside indicates partly aged meat. Brown meat has been oxidized.

NON-AGED MEAT Many people think that bright red meat is better. In fact it has far less flavour than well matured meat.

A CUT ABOVE

THE ENJOYMENT OF MEAT IS MADE UP OF SEVERAL ELEMENTS, INCLUDING ITS TENDERNESS, FLAVOUR, SUCCULENCE, AND JUICINESS. PERSONAL PREFERENCE IS ALSO A FACTOR – ONE PERSON'S OVERCOOKED IS ANOTHER'S UNDERCOOKED; ONE PERSON'S CHEWY IS ANOTHER'S DELIGHTFUL TEXTURE; AND A SUBTLE AND DELICATE FLAVOUR COULD EQUALLY BE REGARDED AS TASTELESS.

TENDERNESS

Tender meat is the aim of every cook and many aspects of meat can affect its tenderness:

• The age of the animal is important; young animals are always more tender. Old ones have thicker sinew and gristle as well. However, a good butcher can greatly improve the meat of older animals such as mutton or wild deer by trimming off these parts.

• Dry-ageing and vacuum-maturing meat (see pp12–13) makes it tender, as does keeping meat in any liquid that excludes the air. So storing meat in oil or in a non-acid marinade will tenderize it.

• Mechanical ways of tenderizing meat, such as beating, mincing, or cutting it across the grain, can shorten the meat fibres to make it feel more tender.

• Some fruit, such as pineapple and papaya, contain enzymes that will break down meat fibres and are used in marinades. Artificial tenderizers contain similar enzymes. Alternatively, Chinese cooks cover tough cuts of meat in a mixture of sodium bicarbonate, sugar, wine, and flour to tenderize them.

• Using the right cooking method for each cut will make sure it becomes tender. Overcooking roasts and steaks makes them tough, while undercooking stews doesn't allow time for the meat to become tender.

FLAVOUR

Good flavour is the second great aim of the cook, whether it needs enhancing or toning down, and it can be achieved by a combination of many things.

The flavour of any fat will be affected by what the animal eats because fats readily pick up flavour, good or bad. So free-ranging and wild animals normally have more interesting

IN THE PINK Juicy meat has a high water content and, since blood is made mainly of water, this is why pink meat can never be dry.

meat. Animals wandering over fields, salt marshes, or heather hills will all pick up nuances of flavour from their varied diet. However, very lean meats such as venison are less affected by diet. On the down side, stress at slaughter, or bruising beforehand, can leave a bitter or sour taste. Intensively raised pigs are especially prone to stress.

Dry-ageing or hanging improves the flavour of many domestic and game meats, whereas meat kept in a vacuum pack for too long will have a sour taste.

Perfectly raised and prepared meat needs little enhancement and its flavour is often best enjoyed in its simplest form. But in the kitchen, other ingredients add flavours. Sometimes they disguise an overpowering taste, but usually they enhance flavour. Spices and herbs as well as vegetables, fruits, and liquids all add complexity of flavour.

SUCCULENCE

This is the slippery texture that makes meat so pleasant to eat; it is usually associated with fat. Although fat is nowadays regarded as a mixed blessing, it transforms the texture as well as flavour, especially if the meat has some intermuscular fat and is well marbled.

Fat on the surface of meat keeps the outside moist, and where it is present within the meat, it melts away during the cooking to keep the interior moist, too. When meat is lean, cooking it past the pink stage by any method will make it dry unless something is added to keep it succulent. This could be fat, introduced by larding or barding (see p232), or it could be minced fat included in sausages, burgers, and pies. A creamy sauce can also make any dry meat feel succulent.

Succulence can be added without using unwanted fat, too. The silky texture of slowly cooked shin, and other cuts with a lot of collagen, make meat feel succulent. Likewise, vegetables that cook down to a slippery texture not only add flavour but also succulence. An alternative for lean meat is to simmer it and then, when it is cooked, plunge it into a mixture of vegetable oil, herbs, and spices until cool. The oil counteracts any dry texture well.

JUICINESS

Juicy meat has a high water content. This is why pink and red meat is more moist than well-done meat – it is impossible for pink meat to be dry. If there is no fat, meat will feel unpleasantly dry if cooked past the pink stage. As mentioned above, cooking meat

VERY LEAN MEAT
Meats such as venison and bison have little or no visible fat, either within the muscle meat itself or between the blocks of muscle.

LEAN MEAT
This steak has a chunk of fat between the muscles, but there is hardly any within the muscle meat.

MARBLED MEAT
This steak has specks of fat evenly distributed within the muscles as well as a generous amount between the muscles.

gently in a liquid and then keeping it immersed until cold will help meat retain moisture and prevent it from drying out.

A HEALTHY DIET

Humans have been eating meat for more than a million years as it contains many beneficial nutrients. Protein is an obvious one, but red meat offers one of the most easily available sources of iron (many Western women are iron deficient). The darker the meat, the more iron it contains, so game meats are especially good.

A healthy diet should not contain too much fat. This is a simple message, but although it is harmful to eat too much saturated fat, some fatty acids (such as Omega-3) are essential for building the brain and repairing our bodies.

For the maximum health benefit, choose meat from wild animals or meat from grass-fed cattle and sheep, or meat from pigs and poultry that live a truly free-range existence.

ASSESSING FAT CONTENT

Fat is distributed throughout the carcass, some species having more than others. The animal's diet will also affect how much fat there is. There are three main types of fat:

• **External fat** This accumulates just under the skin and is thickest along the back and rump of the animal. It is reasonably hard fat and it is easy to trim off any excess. Unless you want more, leave a maximum of 2cm (¾in) of fat to cover a large roast and 5mm (¼in) around small joints, steaks, and chops.

• **Intermuscular fat** This appears between the individual muscles and is most prevalent in cuts from the shoulder and fore ribs. A good butcher will trim most of it off, but pockets of fat will remain.

• **Intramuscular fat, or marbling** When animals are in peak condition, small specks of fat become distributed throughout the muscles of the meat. This lubricates it as it cooks and makes the meat feel succulent.

STAY SHARP

The dos and don'ts of keeping your knives sharp:

- **Do** store knives on a knife rack – either a magnetic or slot type.
- **Do** protect sharp tips by keeping a cork on them.
- **Do** chop onto a wooden or food-grade plastic board.
- **Don't** chop onto hard surfaces such as ceramic, slate, stone, or steel.

CLEAVER
LARGE COOK'S KNIFE
MEDIUM BONING KNIFE
SMALL THIN COOK'S KNIFE

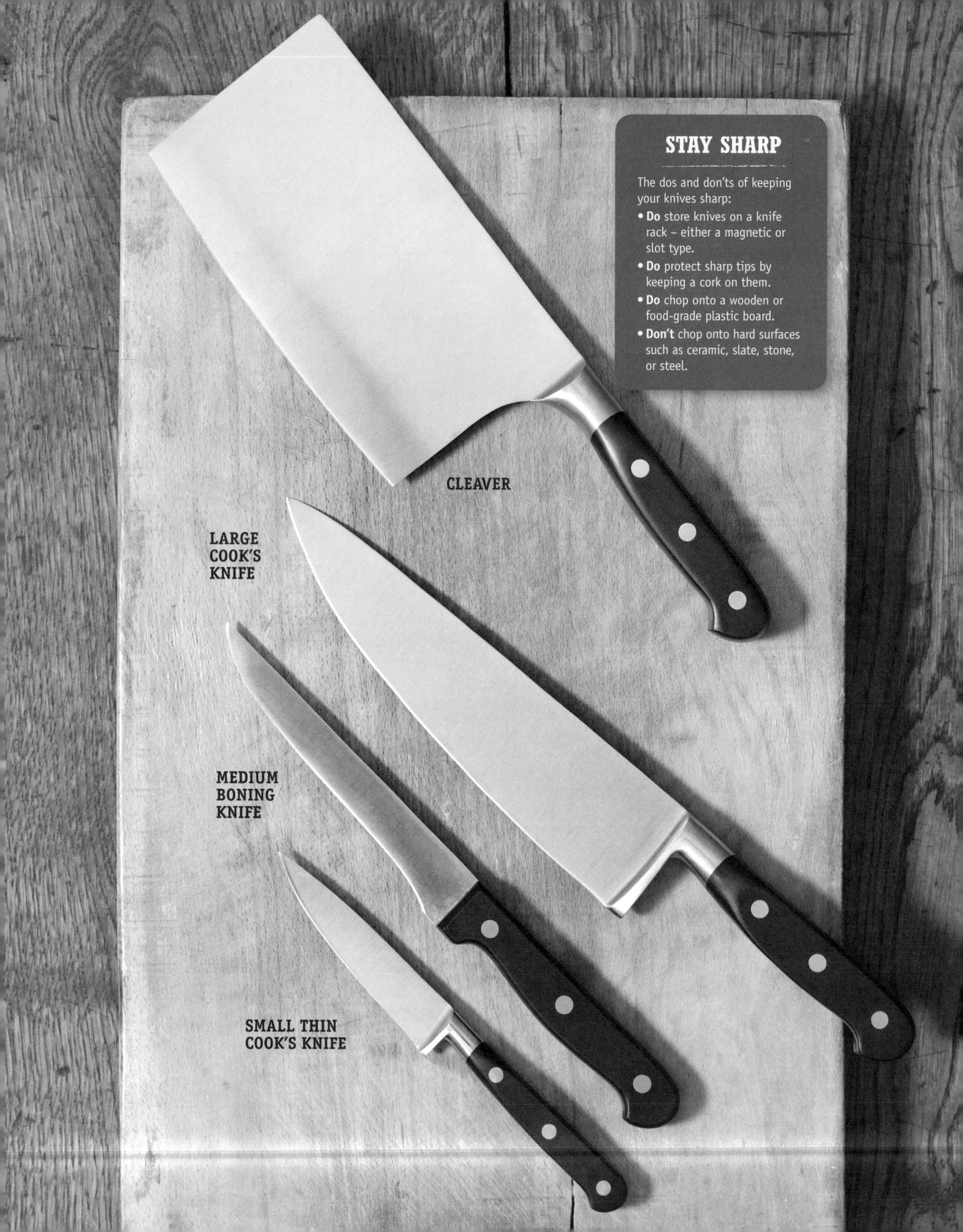

KNIFE STORIES

A COOK'S FAVOURITE KNIFE IS A PERSONAL MATTER. SOME PREFER HEAVY KNIVES; OTHERS FIND LIGHT ONES SUIT THEM BETTER. ONE THING, HOWEVER, IS CERTAIN – THE SECRET TO SUCCESSFUL MEAT PREPARATION IS KEEPING YOUR KNIVES SHARP.

TYPES OF KNIFE

- **Cleaver** Some people prefer to use a cleaver for all kitchen tasks; others never use one at all. Most Chinese cooks use nothing else.
- **Large cook's knife** Use for slicing large pieces of meat and for carving boneless joints. Use long stroking cuts rather than a sawing motion to produce the neatest slices.
- **Medium boning knife** The thin curved blade allows the knife to be manipulated around bones without damaging the meat.
- **Small thin cook's knife** This is invaluable for many tasks, such as boning out poultry or chopping small items.

BLADE MATERIALS

Knife blades are made from many materials, but the most common are:

- **Carbon steel and damasked steel** These are the easiest to sharpen but rust unless oiled. They are unsuitable for dishwashers.
- **Stainless steel** The most common material, it keeps its edge but takes longer to sharpen. Different alloys and ways of tempering them can produce very light, thin blades.
- **Ceramic knives** Although they are very sharp, ceramic knives are expensive, fragile, and need specialist sharpeners.

ADDITIONAL EQUIPMENT

Equipment lists can seem daunting, but each piece is designed for a particular job and many people enjoy collecting these specialist tools. Not everything listed below is essential and many can be used for more than one function.

- **Meat thermometer** Apart from good knives, this is the most important tool for the meat cook (see p29 for more information).
- **Oven thermometer** Useful for checking the temperature of the oven as very few – especially older ones – actually operate at the marked temperature.
- **Chopping boards** Wooden boards used to be thought of as unsanitary, but now they are regarded as better than plastic (which is harder to clean thoroughly when scored by knives) as wood contains natural antibacterial properties.

- **Tongs** Invaluable for turning joints and steaks when browning them, tongs prevent fat from being splashed onto the hand. Use long-handled tongs for barbecues.
- **Gravy skimmer** This jug with a low spout efficiently separates meat juices from fat.
- **Kitchen/Carving fork** Use to lift or turn poultry and large joints in the oven and to hold meat while slicing. The guard prevents the knife from slipping onto your hand while carving towards you.
- **Poultry shears or strong snips** Use for cutting through thin bones, usually poultry. Good quality, strong general-purpose snips may also be used.
- **Trussing needle** A very long, very strong needle that can be threaded with string to truss or tie meat.

POTS AND PANS FOR THE MEAT COOK

- **Stock pot** Stock bones occupy a surprisingly large space, so a stockpot needs to be large (15–20 litres/3½–4½ gallons) and have a lid.
- **Extra large colander or sieve** Use to strain stock into a large bowl or pan. A muslin cloth is useful to strain out fine debris.
- **Cast-iron lidded casseroles** These allow an even distribution of heat. Meat and vegetables can be browned in them before adding liquid and either simmering or oven cooking.
- **Frying pans** Use a large pan for browning many small pieces of meat without overcrowding them. Medium and smaller pans are good for frying steaks or small pieces of meat. Buy pans with the heaviest base possible for the best heat distribution because thin bases can warp.
- **Wok** Good for stir-frying, woks can be used over gas or charcoal. Electric attachments and standalone woks are also available.
- **Deep-fat fryer with basket** Buy one large enough for your needs as deep-fried food must not be crowded or it will absorb the oil.

- **Roasting trays or dishes with racks** Several sizes are useful, including a small dish for two-person roasts. The rack allows excess fat to drain off the meat.
- **Crock pot or electric slow cooker** These use very little energy to slow-cook meat and are ideal for busy people because they can be left to cook all day.

SHARPENING KNIVES

Blunt knives squeeze the juice out of meat, and can make cutting through skin and sinews hard. There are several ways to sharpen knives:

USING A SHARPENING STEEL
Method 1 Hold the steel vertically with its point on a wooden board or folded cloth. Keeping the angle of the knife consistently at about 10–20 degrees, stroke it down either side of the steel to sharpen both edges.

Method 2 Hold the steel in one hand and the knife in the other. Stroke the knife down alternating sides of the steel towards your hand, keeping the angle consistent at all times.

USING DRAW-THROUGH HAND SHARPENERS
Steel blades inside the device sharpen the knife as it is drawn between them. Hand-held and electric (below) versions are available. Press the knife firmly downwards and draw it through the device to sharpen it. Remember to tilt the end as you draw the knife through, to make sure the tip is sharpened.

THE RAW DEAL

PROCESSING MEAT HAS MANY FUNCTIONS. SLICING AND CHOPPING MEAT ALTERS
ITS TEXTURE SO THAT IT CAN EVEN BE EATEN RAW. MINCING ALSO MAKES
USE OF OFFCUTS TO MAKE A VARIETY OF TRADITIONAL PREPARATIONS.

SLICING, CHOPPING, MINCING, AND PROCESSING MEAT

- **Slice meat across the grain** to make it feel more tender, or to prevent it from distorting during cooking.
- **Slice meat with the grain** for stir-fry strips so that they don't break apart when cooked.
- **Chop large pieces of meat** before mincing or processing, or into even-sized pieces for frying and grilling so that they cook evenly.
- **Mince meat that is tough** to cook whole (breaking it into tiny pieces makes it feel more tender), to help it cook quicker, and for terrines, sausages, raised pies, and burgers.
- **Process or pound meat** using a food processor, blender, or pestle and mortar to make a paste for a smooth pâté, stuffing, or quenelles.

HAND-CHOPPING MINCE

Finely chopping meat by hand produces mince that is far juicier than mince ground with a mincer, which can squeeze out moisture. This method is ideal for making gourmet burgers and steak tartare. Aim to chop the meat as close to the cooking and serving time as possible for a fresher tasting dish. You will need a heavy chopping board and two matched heavy knives, which must be exceedingly sharp:

GOURMET BURGERS These are made from good-quality hand-chopped meat with its own natural fat for flavour and succulence. Little else apart from chopped onion is needed.

1 Trim off every scrap of gristle, fat, and sinew from the meat.
2 Cut the meat into 1cm ($\frac{1}{2}$in) cubes and spread it out across the chopping board in a single layer.
3 Using a motion rather like beating two drumsticks, use the weight of the knives to chop the meat with an easy rhythm.
4 From time to time, scrape the meat back to the centre of the board to ensure even chopping. Continue until the desired fineness is achieved.

MAKING CARPACCIO

Typically made from very thin slices of beef fillet cut about 2mm ($\frac{1}{10}$in) thick, carpaccio can be sliced from raw meat or the outside can be quickly seared first. Partially freezing the meat first makes it easier to cut very thin slices. If the slices are too thick, flatten them by beating them between sheets of cling film.

MAKING MINCED MEAT PRODUCTS

Meatballs, burgers, patties, satays, and koftes all use a minced meat mixture. Most meat contains enough of its own natural fat, but lean meats may need extra fat to keep the meat moist.

As a healthier alternative to adding fat to lean minced meat, add finely chopped vegetables instead. Onions, aubergines, sweet peppers, or mushrooms – softened in a very small amount of oil – all work well. Serving minced meat products with a sauce will also help to make them feel more moist when you eat them.

Burger purists use hand-chopped meat (see above) mixed with only salt, pepper, and sometimes a little chopped onion. These burgers can be cooked pink. Most, however, are made from mince and a variety of vegetables, herbs, and spices added to taste. Patties are a flatter version of burgers.

FORMING BURGERS BY HAND

1 Divide the meat into equal portions. Squeeze each one tightly to form a firm ball.
2 Lightly press each ball to flatten the sides. Press harder to make patties.

FORMING BURGERS WITH A BURGER PRESS

1 Line the press with waxed paper or cellophane discs.
2 Fill with meat and press into shape.

FORMING MEATBALLS

Use rubber gloves, or wet your hands to prevent the meat sticking to your fingers:
1 Divide the meat into equal amounts. Make reduced-fat meatballs very small so there is a large surface to be coated with sauce. This makes them seem less dry.
2 Squeeze each portion together firmly and roll it into a ball between your fingertips.
3 Roll the meatballs in flour just before you cook them.

MAKING SATAYS AND KOFTES

Spicy flavoured mince is pressed onto sticks before being grilled or fried. Miniature versions with a dipping sauce make good canapés:
1 Soak wooden sticks in water to prevent the meat from turning on the stick and to allow even cooking – this also prevents the sticks from burning.
2 Press the meat firmly onto the sticks.

COOKING MINCE

Minced meat has a higher risk of contamination due to its large proportion of outer surface. Unless you have prepared your own mince and are confident that it has not been contaminated, all these minced meat products should be cooked until the internal temperature reaches 75°C (165°F).

BEEF CARPACCIO The essence of carpaccio is its ultra-thin slices, which make it seem lusciously tender. Scrupulously clean utensils are needed if meat is to be eaten raw.

GLAZING MEAT A good way of introducing different flavours is to glaze meat. Mustard and honey can help spices and herbs to stick to the meat as it cooks.

UNDER THE SKIN

USING HERBS, SPICES, AND FLAVOURED LIQUIDS WILL TRANSFORM NOT ONLY THE FLAVOUR OF MEAT, BUT SOMETIMES ITS TEXTURE AS WELL. DIFFERENT FLAVOUR PAIRINGS COMPLEMENT DIFFERENT MEATS – SEE PAGES 32–33 FOR SUGGESTIONS.

SPICE AND HERB RUBS

Rubbing spices and herbs onto the surface of meat, or under the skin of poultry, introduces new flavours. Adding salt or oil helps to draw the flavours into the meat. Leave the rub for several hours before cooking to intensify the flavours.

UNDER-THE-SKIN RUBS FOR POULTRY

• Try making a pocket in a small fillet of meat or poultry, then stuff herbs and spices mixed with butter or oil into the pocket. Secure with string or a cocktail stick.
• Lift the skin off the breast meat of a bird and slash the meat underneath. Mix herbs and spices with butter and smear this mixture into the meat. Replace the skin.

HERB CRUSTS

These can be as simple as pressing herbs onto the oiled surface of meat, or using a thicker crust made of herbs and grains bound with egg to add flavour and a crunchy texture. Once you have prepared the crust mixture, press it on firmly so it does not crumble off the meat during cooking. If the crust is thick, allow a little extra cooking time. Note that covering meat with a herb crust will prevent it from browning.

MARINATING MEAT

Marinades flavour meat without preserving it. Acid liquids (such as vinegar, wine, and citrus juice) dry out meat. Oily marinades absorb spice, vegetable, and herb flavours and transmit them to the meat. Depending on its size (a joint or small pieces), marinate the meat for 1–5 hours before cooking.
1 Mix together the marinade ingredients and heat if instructed. If heated, allow to cool before proceeding.
2 Immerse the meat in the marinade. For awkward-shaped pieces of meat, use a strong polythene bag to hold the meat and draw up liquid around it.

SALTING AND CURING MEAT

Using salt to cure meat is an ancient technique. It is simple, because just salt, flavoured with spices, is used to draw out some of the meat's moisture, but it is also complicated because only trial and error will produce the effect you want to achieve. Experiment, and keep notes of all your weights and timings.

TYPES OF SALT

Curing salt prevents bacteria forming and maintains the meat's red colour.
• **Pickling or kosher salt** A fine salt that dissolves quickly, but does not contain iodine or anti-caking agents that can turn brine cloudy. Good for brine-curing.
• **Coarse salt** Free of iodine or anti-caking agents, it is cheaper but takes a little longer to dissolve. Good for dry-salting.
• **Curing salt, or Prague powder no. 1** Often coloured pink, this contains sodium nitrite that helps to preserve meat and keeps it red.
• **Dry-curing salt, or Prague powder no. 2** Similar to Prague powder no. 1, but contains sodium nitrate as well. Highly recommended for home dry-salting in place of saltpetre.

HOW LONG DOES IT TAKE?

Meat that is to be fully preserved will need longer to cure than meat that will be cooked afterwards. The thinner the meat, the more quickly it will cure.
• **Pork belly** Dry-salt or brine for 1 week to make bacon.
• **Whole pork leg** Dry-salt for 4–6 weeks to make ham ready to cook. After salting it can take 6–12 months to dry fully.
• **Rolled beef brisket** Brine for approximately 1 week to make salt beef ready to cook (see p150). If salted for longer, soak the meat for 12–24 hours before cooking.

DOS AND DON'TS

• Never use old-fashioned saltpetre, which contains potassium. Use modern curing salt.
• Never use metal dishes for salt cures; they will corrode.
• Boneless meat preserves better than meat on the bone.
• Lightly cured meat has an enhanced flavour, but will not be preserved; it must be cooked.
• Due to the risk of food poisoning, do not attempt to preserve poultry. It should always be cooked after being cured.

DRY-SALTING MEAT

Use salt for small pieces, or two parts salt to one part sugar for larger joints. Add spices if wished. Allow approximately 1.5kg (3lb 3oz) salt mix plus 30g (1oz) dry-curing salt for every 3kg (6½lb) meat. Work in a cool place.

Dry-cured meat is ready when it has lost about 30 per cent of its weight, but test it for taste and give it longer if needed.

Adding sugar or honey to the salt prevents the meat from becoming hard. If the meat is very hard after curing, soak it before cooking.

BRINE-CURING MEAT

A more gentle way of curing than salting, the brine can be made of water, wine, cider, or other liquids, plus spices and herbs to add flavour. The strength of brines varies, but start with 5 litres (8¾ pints) of liquid for every 1kg (2¼lb) of salt. Add 30g (1oz) of curing salt for a full cure.

Brine meat for 8–12 hours if it is to be cooked or smoked, or for at least 1 week if being fully cured.

CURING SALT

SMOKING HOT

HOT-SMOKING YOUR OWN MEAT OPENS UP A WHOLE WORLD OF FUN, AND THERE ARE AS MANY DIFFERENT WAYS OF SMOKING AS THERE ARE TYPES OF SMOKER. HOT-SMOKING INVOLVES BUILDING A FIRE AND DAMPING IT DOWN WITH MOISTENED WOOD TO PRODUCE SMOKE, WHICH FLAVOURS THE MEAT WHILE IT GENTLY COOKS. THE MEAT IS USUALLY FIRST MARINATED OR RUBBED WITH SPICES, AND THEN GLAZES ARE BRUSHED ON DURING THE SMOKING PROCESS TO GIVE A RICH, STICKY CRUST.

IN HOT-SMOKING, the meat should be much further away from the open fire than when grilling, as it needs to cook for several hours. To make sure the meat does not cook too quickly, build the fire on one side of the grill and place the meat on a rack on the opposite side, then close the lid. Charcoal separators make sure the fire remains in place.

WHAT EQUIPMENT DO I NEED?
The Internet is bursting with suggestions, which range from instructions for building a pit in the ground, or a brick grill, to a professional smoker costing well over £1,000. They will all produce good results. Manufacturers will provide detailed instructions on how to use each one. Three of the most popular types of smoker include:
• **Charcoal kettle grill or bullet smoker** An economical smoker, this type can be used with briquettes or wood charcoal as well as more specialist woods. It can be powered by gas or electricity.
• **Electric wood pellet grill** An electric spark ignites flavoured wood pellets that trickle down an auger to the fire. The pellets will have the correct amount of moisture and the temperature can be regulated.
• **Ceramic grill** This uses a very small amount of charcoal in a little firebox. The meat will need spraying with liquid as there is no room for a pan of water.

YOU WILL ALSO NEED:
• **Chimney starter** For lighting the grill, but also for replenishing ready-ignited fuel so the temperature does not drop.

CHARCOAL SMOKING A charcoal and wood mixture is added to the fire; this is dampened to make moist, steamy smoke.

• **Grill thermometer** For measuring the temperature in the grill as the food smokes. The ideal temperature for hot-smoking is 110–120°C (225–250°F).
• **Meat thermometer** For checking if the meat is cooked.
• **Brushes** For applying glazes to the meat as it cooks. Long-handled paintbrushes or cotton mops can be used.
• **Plastic spray diffuser** For spraying the meat while it cooks.
• **Tongs** For turning the meat (preferable to using a fork, which pierces the meat).
• **Insulated gloves** Recommended for protecting your hands and wrists from spitting fat.

WHICH WOOD SHOULD I USE?
You can use any type of wood provided it has not been treated with chemicals. Small logs, chunks of wood, woodchips, shavings, and sawdust are all suitable. Wood pellets are made from compressed sawdust. Unless you are experienced at hot-smoking, it is best to start with a charcoal fire, then add a mixture of charcoal and your chosen wood so the smoke is not too intense and bitter.
• **Pine and mesquite** These woods give the strongest, most resinous smoke.
• **Oak, pecan, walnut, and hickory** These give a deep, richly flavoured smoke.
• **Alder, maple, and vine** These woods give a subtle light to medium smoke.
• **Fruit woods** These give a sweet, aromatic smoke.

HOT-SMOKING IN THE OVEN
This is a simple way of hot-smoking without the need for specialist equipment. The meat benefits from being marinated in oil and herbs

first, and should be browned before being smoked. Try this with a piece of meat about 5cm (2in) thick. Preheat the oven to 230°C (450°F/Gas 8):
1 Cover the base of a flat-bottomed roasting tin with 1cm (1/2in) of smoker's sawdust. Add flavourings, such as herbs or fruit tea, and cover with foil. Pierce holes in the foil.
2 Put the meat on top of the foil and cover with a lid or additional foil. Place the tin over a high heat until it starts to produce smoke, then cook in the oven for 6 minutes.
3 Remove from the oven and allow it to cool under the foil. When cold, wrap in cling film and refrigerate. Slice thinly and serve with spiced fruit jelly.

HOT-SMOKING A CHICKEN
Use a sweet, mild wood to smoke chicken and sit a pan of hot water beside the meat to make steam. Prepare the chicken by splitting it in half, then brine or marinate (see p21) it for 5 hours using some fruit juice in the liquid. Then rinse, and pat it dry:

1 Lift the breast skin and rub spices, herbs, and butter into the meat.
2 Light the smoker and bring it to 120°C (250°F). Place the chicken halves skin-side up on a rack, well away from the fire with the thighs closest to the heat, and close the lid.
3 Keep checking the temperature and the smoke. Every hour, brush or spray the skin with a flavoured liquid. Make sure it does not get too hot and burn.
4 The chicken will take about 4 hours and is cooked when the internal temperature of the thigh meat reaches 75°C (165°F).
5 Once cooked, shred all the meat, mixing all the spices and the glaze from the skin into the meat, and then serve.

SLOWLY DOES IT

LOW TEMPERATURES, LIQUIDS, AND LONG COOKING TIMES ENSURE THAT MEAT STAYS MOIST AS IT COOKS ALL THE WAY THROUGH. SLOW-COOKING IS PERFECT FOR CHEAPER CUTS OF MEAT THAT MAY BE TOUGH OR SINEWY; THEY COST BARELY HALF AS MUCH AS PRIME CUTS. THESE DISHES LEND THEMSELVES TO "GETTING AHEAD" AS THE FLAVOURS IMPROVE WITH KEEPING.

BROWNING THE MEAT

Most slow-cooking methods start off by browning the meat. Although it is not essential, it always adds lots of extra flavour and colour to the dish.

Make sure the meat is completely dry so that it browns quickly. If meat takes too long to brown, it becomes tough.

Fry the pieces in small batches, making sure they have plenty of space so the outside browns very quickly. If crowded they will release water, which makes them boil rather than brown.

DEGLAZE THE PAN

The frying pan will accumulate a lot of caramelized bits during the browning process. Add a little water to dissolve them and add this delicious browning to your dish, otherwise it may burn onto the pan and taste bitter.

COOKING METHODS

• **Stewing** Small pieces or slices of meat are browned, covered with liquid and cooked in a lidded dish in the oven or on the stovetop. Where there is plenty of gravy, dumplings can be cooked in the stew once the meat is cooked. Electric slow-cookers (or crock pots) use very little electricity and can be left to cook all day.

• **Braising** Cuts or joints are cooked to well done in a covered dish in a slow oven. Braising uses less liquid than in a stew, but the steam produced keeps the meat moist. Fatty cuts cook really well this way; very lean joints benefit from larding. This method is especially good for poultry pieces or slices of pork and lamb shoulder, which cook in about an hour.

• **Pot roasting and slow roasting** Prime cuts can be cooked pink; tougher cuts are cooked to well done. Place the meat in a deep tray

BEEFY DISH A deep, rich gravy surrounding meltingly tender pieces of beef; this is the epitome of the perfect stew.

or dish with some vegetables, if desired. Pot roasts usually have some liquid, too. The meat is browned first at a high temperature, then loosely covered and cooked slowly for several hours at around 140°C (280°F/Gas 1).

• **Simmering and poaching** The meat is not browned, so no extra fat is used. A joint or whole bird is completely immersed in liquid (usually water) that is brought slowly to the boil. The temperature is immediately reduced to a very low heat so that the water is barely bubbling. Cool the meat in its liquid before straining it off to prevent it from drying out. Reduce the stock and use it to make a sauce for the meat. Simmering is especially good for meat on the bone as the stock is rich and silky.

• **Steaming** Thin strips or small pieces of very tender meat can be cooked in a steamer for very low-fat dishes. Care must be taken to cook the meat enough, but at the same time not to toughen it by overcooking. A meat thermometer shows when it is just cooked. The cooked meat is quite bland so benefits from added flavourings. See also sous vide and steam "roasting" on page 29.

Minced meat preparations, such as covered terrines, are placed in a dish of water (known as a bain marie) and cooked in the oven – the water ensures that the meat is cooked gently and evenly throughout.

• **Pressure cooking** Meat is prepared in the same way as for stewing or braising, but when the lid and pressure cap are put on and the temperature raised, the pressure in the pan cooks the meat extremely quickly, so this is a very economical way of cooking meat. Make sure the pan is cooled before opening the pressurized lid.

• **Slow barbecue** Perfect for cooking meat slowly so it falls off the bone; it can also be shredded. The process is the same as for hot-smoking (see p22), except that damp wood is not used since no smoke is required.

TASTE AND TEXTURE

• Never try to speed up slow-cooked dishes (except when pressure cooking); if they get too hot, the moisture is squeezed out of the meat leaving it tough and dry.

• Only dust meat in flour if you want a flour-thickened gravy. Make sure the meat is almost dry and use only a very light dusting or the gravy will be too thick.

• Don't use flour if other starchy ingredients, such as potatoes, are included in the dish.

• If there is flour in the dish, don't cook it on top of the stove as it will stick to the base of the pan. Cook it in the oven.

• If a broth is too watery at the end, strain off the meat, reduce the broth, and return it to the meat. Don't boil the meat in the broth or it will fall to pieces.

• Adding vegetables improves the texture and flavour; they are especially helpful for dishes containing lean meat, and also make the dish go further so reducing the cost.

• Snippets of bacon add flavour to a stew.

• Although herbs and spices are cooked with the meat, only add salt near the end of cooking otherwise the dish could be too salty.

EXCESS FAT

If a stew produces too much fat during cooking, skim off any excess from the top with a spoon or ladle. Start at the centre of the dish and depress the spoon, but do not let any liquid enter it. Using a circular spiral motion, move the spoon to the edge of the dish where the fat will have accumulated. Allow the fat to trickle into the spoon and remove it. Repeat the procedure until you have removed as much excess fat as possible.

FAST AND FURIOUS

FRYING AND GRILLING MEAT IS AN EXCITING METHOD OF COOKING THAT REQUIRES SKILL TO MAKE SURE THE MEAT DOESN'T OVERCOOK. A COMBINATION OF FIERCE HEAT FOLLOWED BY GENTLE RESTING PRODUCES THE BEST RESULTS.

WHEN GRILLING OR FRYING MEAT, the aim is to produce a brown, flavoursome outer surface with moist flesh inside. Many cuts of meat can be cooked this way, as well as burgers, sausages, kebabs, and satays.

For rare and medium-rare meat, prime cuts are usually recommended, although many of the cheaper cuts can also be used. For those who like their meat cooked to well-done, only the prime cuts will stay tender enough.

How well cooked the meat should be is a matter of personal preference, although poultry and minced meat products should be cooked until the juices run clear, and have an internal temperature of 75ºC (165ºF). In some countries, the same applies to pork (see the cooking charts on pages 40–45).

Ideally, meat should be brought to room temperature before cooking so there is less contrast between the outside and inside temperatures during cooking. In reality, most meat is cooked straight from the fridge and needs a little extra time to cook.

PERFECTLY PINK

Some people like meat with a cooked band surrounding an undercooked centre. Others prefer the colour to be uniformly distributed so the juices and flavours are distributed throughout the meat. To do this requires three stages, especially if the piece of meat is more than 2cm (³⁄₄in) thick. For pieces under 1cm (¹⁄₂in) thick, just follow steps 1 and 3.
1 Brown the outside of the meat as quickly and thoroughly as possible – 2 minutes per side is the minimum for a steak.
2 Lower the heat and partially cook the meat.
3 Rest the meat in a warm place for 2 minutes for every 1cm (¹⁄₂in) of thickness to finish its cooking and distribute the juices.

ON THE HEAT When cooking meat on the barbecue, make sure there is a warm place to one side of the heat to rest thick steaks or roasts.

SEARING OR BROWNING MEAT

Grilling or frying at a high temperature caramelizes the surface of meat and gives it its delicious flavour. Heavy-bottomed frying pans produce the best results. Thin pans overheat easily and often warp, which causes uneven browning.

Apply a thin layer of pure lard, beef dripping, or oil that can be heated to high temperatures – such as grapeseed, rapeseed, or groundnut. Heat the pan until it starts to smoke. Lay the meat in it and do not touch it for a minute or two. Then check the meat and when it is well browned, turn it over. If you turn the meat before it is really brown, some liquid will be pushed out and the meat will boil, not brown.

SHALLOW FRYING AND GRILL PANS

Use a heavy frying pan, or a ridged cast-iron grill pan, which uses less fat and produces a striped effect on the meat. Brown the meat as above, using butter if wished, then reduce the heat. Turn the meat a few more times until cooked. Large pieces of meat need more fat to cook than thin ones.

STIR FRYING AND SAUTÉING

Use a wok or deep-sided frying pan over a high heat. Slice everything thinly beforehand, so it cooks evenly. The meat is put in first, then any vegetables, moving the food around quickly all the time. Liquid is added at the end. The whole process takes only minutes and the food is served at once.

CHARCOAL AND BARBECUE GRILLING

This is usually done outside, although indoor artificial charcoal grills are available. Wait until the coals have subsided to a grey ash before cooking. If possible, have a cooler area to rest large pieces of meat after grilling. Very fatty cuts can cause flames to flare up so turn them frequently to avoid a burnt coating.

DEEP-FAT FRYING

Large, uneven pieces of meat that do not sit easily in a flat frying pan, or are coated in

BROWNING MEAT If using butter to fry, wait until it stops foaming before placing steaks into the frying pan. This helps the meat to brown more quickly.

batter, can be cooked in a deep-fat fryer. Half fill the pan with oil or fat and heat it to 180–190°C (350–375°F). If the oil is not hot enough, it gets absorbed into the food.

GRILLING UNDER A TOP (OVEN) GRILL

Meat is placed under a fierce heat that cooks it from above. Good for reduced fat cooking as only a spray of oil is needed to brown the meat. Best for thicker pieces of meat as anything thinner than 2cm (¾in) is easily overcooked.

TANDOOR OVEN

A heavy, cylindrical clay oven built to retain and reflect the fierce heat from a charcoal fire. Meat is covered in a marinade or paste, threaded on metal skewers, and lowered into the oven; it cooks very quickly and keeps the meat juicy.

DOUBLE-SIDED GRILLS

These grill on both sides at once under a closed lid. Surplus fat drains into a tray. Fatty meats cook well but lean meats steam rather than grill and don't brown.

ROASTING MEAT

A PERFECTLY ROASTED JOINT OF MEAT TURNS ANY MEAL INTO AN OCCASION, WHETHER IT IS A HUGE CELEBRATION JOINT, A MEDIUM-SIZED FAMILY ONE, OR A TINY ROAST FOR TWO PEOPLE. UNDERSTANDING WHAT HAPPENS TO THE MEAT WHILE IT COOKS GIVES YOU GREATER CONTROL.

CHOOSING THE RIGHT CUT

Roasts are good on or off the bone, although bone-in joints look very impressive. When cooking roasts to well-done, bones lubricate the meat. In rare joints, however, they are less important. Bone-in cuts (with the exception of loin cuts) contain several different muscles, some of which cook at different times and whose grain lies in different directions. This can make timing and carving more awkward.

The best roasting joints come from the middle part of an animal (ribs, saddle, and loin), or the hind leg, although tender lamb and veal shoulders make excellent, more informal joints. Tougher cuts can be slow roasted successfully.

If the meat is marbled with fat, it will stay succulent from rare to well done; very lean meat, such as most game, is not successful roasted to well done. Very small joints (less than 5cm/2in thick) are rather like a thick steak (see pp174–5).

OVEN ROASTING: THE THREE STAGES

1 Brown the meat This is what makes roasted meat taste so good. Extra small joints and birds will not be roasted for long enough to brown the outside so should be browned all over in a frying pan first (see p27) and then only given 5–10 minutes in the hot oven. For larger joints, start them off for 20–30 minutes in a hot oven at 220°C (425°F/Gas 7) for fan ovens and 230°C (450°F/Gas 8) for standard ovens. Very large joints, such as turkey and goose, will need 45–50 minutes to brown and may need turning round in the oven midway.

2 Partly cook it The oven is then turned down to 180°C (350°F/Gas 4) to nearly (but not quite) cook the meat. This is where a meat thermometer is invaluable because the number of variables (temperature of the meat when

PERFECTLY COOKED This joint has been rested, so the juices in the meat are evenly distributed, making it moist all the way to the edge.

it started, its thickness and fat cover, oven variations, and degree of doneness required) make it impossible to give exact timings. The meat must come out of the oven when it is 3–5°C (5–8°F) below the desired finished temperature to avoid it overcooking. For dark game meats, taking the meat out 10°C (16°F) below is even better.

3 Rest the meat This crucial stage completes the cooking and makes the meat more tender. It also distributes the juices evenly because the heat continues towards the centre of the meat while the less-cooked juices in the centre are drawn back to the edge. This is the secret to perfectly roasted meat. All you need do is keep the meat warm – it must not be cooked any more. The ideal temperature is 80°C (175°F). A plate-warming drawer is perfect, otherwise put the joint over a warm stove or radiator. Cover it with foil and a thick cloth to keep in the heat. Make sure the joint does not get cold. The meat thermometer should show the temperature rising until the meat is cooked to your liking.

SPIT ROASTING

This is how all meat used to be roasted and gives arguably the best results of all. Browning, cooking, and resting are combined in one process. The meat is slowly turned in front of a hot fire, held in a cage, or on a metal skewer. Spit roasts work best when the meat has a good covering of fat, so lean meat should be barded (see p232). A drip tray catches the fat and juices. Some ovens have electric spits – use a meat thermometer to check how it cooks.

LOW TEMPERATURE "ROASTING"

This slow method cuts out the second stage of roasting. Meat is cooked rare but there is no danger of overcooking if a meal is delayed slightly. Brown the joint all over, in a pan or a hot oven. Open the oven door afterwards and fan out the intense heat. Then cook it very slowly at a temperature of 80–100°C (175–200°F) for several hours. A thin joint – less than 5cm (2in) thick – will cook in about an hour. Large joints take 2–3 hours or more; use a meat thermometer to show how it is cooking. This method is not suitable for domestic poultry.

SOUS VIDE AND STEAM "ROASTING"

Meat is sealed into a vacuum pack (sous vide) that is immersed in a bath of water kept at a tightly controlled temperature. The process is slow but utterly reliable, although not everyone likes such uniformity of cooking. Steam cooking is similar, but the meat cooks in moist steam rather than a water bath. The meat is quickly browned before serving to improve flavour and appearance.

PIT COOKING

This is popular in the Pacific Rim, especially New Zealand. A fire is lit in a sizeable pit containing large stones. The meat and other food is prepared beforehand and packed into a metal basket. This is placed onto the hot stones and immediately covered in wet matting or leaves to produce steam. It is then covered with earth and left to cook for about three hours using the heat stored in the pit.

MEAT THERMOMETERS

A meat thermometer is the best piece of equipment for successful roasting. It is more reliable than any cooking chart because it tells you exactly what stage your meat has reached, whatever its size, weight, or shape, and however inaccurate your oven controls might be. Never submerge any part other than the metal probe in water. Clean the thermometer carefully, and use a disinfectant wipe before storing. Avoid touching any bones in the meat, as this distorts the reading. There are two main types:

Clock dial thermometer These are made of metal and sometimes silicone, and are robust and cheap to buy, with no batteries to run out. They use markers or colours to indicate the doneness of the meat and are easy to read at a glance. Insert the probe into the thickest part of the meat, ideally into the surface facing the oven window so that it can be read without having to move the meat. Leave it in the joint throughout the cooking and resting time.

Digital probe thermometer The sharp tip makes it easy to probe the thickest part of the meat and quickly read the temperature from time to time. This type can also be used while frying to check the temperature of steak, poultry breasts, and burgers. Longer handled versions with folding probes are also available; these are ideal for the barbecue.

FINISHED INTERNAL TEMPERATURE OF MEAT AFTER RESTING
(Take-out-of-the-oven temperature should be 3–5°C/5–8°F below this.)

BEEF, VENISON, LAMB, GOAT

Blue	50°C (120°F)
Rare	55°C (130°F)
Medium	60°C (140°F)
Well done	65°C (150°F) (not recommended for dark-fleshed game)

PORK

Medium	70°C (160°F)
Well done	75°C (165°F)

DOMESTIC POULTRY

75°C (165°F)

GETTING SAUCY

HOWEVER PERFECTLY COOKED IT IS, ADDING A SAUCE TO DRY-COOKED (ROASTED OR GRILLED) MEAT MAKES IT FAR MORE ENJOYABLE. SOME SAUCES TAKE TIME TO PREPARE SO MAKE THEM IN ADVANCE TO PREVENT THE MEAT FROM OVERCOOKING WHILE WAITING FOR THE SAUCE TO COOK.

MAKING STOCK

Keeping small tubs of reduced stock in your freezer makes cooking any kind of sauce simple. Stock that is not reduced makes a good base for soup. Every time you have spare bones, wrap and freeze them until you have enough to make stock. Or buy some from the butcher. Use a mixture of meaty bones and scraps (for flavour) and bones with cartilage (for texture).

1 Brush the bones with oil and roast them until they are really brown. Don't let them burn though, or the stock will taste bitter.

2 Pack the bones tightly into a large pan with vegetables, if desired, and completely cover with water. Bring to the boil and reduce to a low simmer, or place in a low oven heated to 160°C (325°F/Gas 3). Poultry bones should not be allowed to boil, however, or the stock will become cloudy.

3 After 2–3 hours, strain the stock through a fine sieve or muslin cloth. When it is completely cold, skim off any fat.

4 Return the stock to the clean pan. Add wine, if desired. Boil until it has reduced to between one half and one third of its original volume. This will concentrate the flavour.

5 Cool and pour into small tubs or ice-cube trays and freeze for later use.

MAKING JUS

These clear sauces, made by boiling off the meat juices after cooking, work best where there is plenty of flavoursome caramelized browning left in the pan or roasting tin. Add concentrated jellied stock for a savoury, syrupy texture, or a little fruit jelly for a sweet, syrupy texture.

THICKENING SAUCES

A variety of textures can be added to a dish by adding a thickened sauce. Creamy sauces, for example, are good for well-done meat.

ADDING FLOUR

• Add a few teaspoons of flour to the roasting tin, stir to absorb the juices, then add liquid gradually and let it cook.

• Make a thin white sauce using flour with stock or milk, and add to the roasting tin. This is good for large amounts of gravy.

• Make *beurre manié* ("kneaded butter") by mashing together 30g (1oz) each of butter and flour. Whisk small amounts into a thin sauce and simmer for 10–15 minutes.

ADDING EGG, CREAM, AND BUTTER

• Whisk butter and lemon juice into egg yolks in a bain marie. Then add complementary herbs.

• Use double cream to thicken sauces. It can be safely boiled and will readily absorb flavours.

• Whisk small pieces of butter into a thin jus over a low heat just before serving.

ADDING VEGETABLES AND FRUIT

Cook vegetables or fruit until soft, then rub them through a sieve or blend to a purée. Add this to the roasting tin or sauce.

CREAMY SAUCE Poultry breasts such as pheasant, chicken, or guinea fowl, can feel quite dry when cooked through, so they benefit from a creamy sauce.

EMERGENCY FLAVOURS

Sometimes a sauce or gravy lacks taste and needs something – fast – to make it interesting. Decide which flavour pairings will go with your meat (see pp32–3), start by adding small amounts, and don't add too many. Tiny amounts of stock cube can also be used.

Acid flavours: orange, lemon and lime juice, wine, wine vinegar, yogurt.
Sweet, fruity flavours: fruit jellies, fruit juices, honey, brown sugar, cider, spirits.
Rich, savoury flavours: soy, tea, mustard, coffee, cocoa powder, curry paste.

BÉARNAISE SAUCE

Makes 200ml (7fl oz)

Prep: 10 mins **Cook:** 5 mins

INGREDIENTS

2 small shallots, finely chopped

1 tbsp chopped tarragon

2 tbsp white wine vinegar

2 tbsp white wine

1 tsp peppercorns, crushed

3 egg yolks

200g (7oz) unsalted butter, softened and cubed

salt and freshly ground black pepper

1 tbsp lemon juice

1 Put the shallots, tarragon, vinegar, wine, and peppercorns in a heavy non-metallic saucepan and boil for 2 minutes, or until reduced by at least half. Strain through a sieve, and set aside to cool.
2 Put the egg yolks and 1 tbsp water in a heatproof bowl, set over a pan of barely simmering water. The bowl must not touch the water. Whisk in the cooled liquid, then whisk in the butter, one cube at a time, until it has melted and combined. Season to taste with salt, pepper, and lemon juice.

BLUE CHEESE SAUCE

Makes 250ml (9fl oz)

Prep: 15 mins **Cook:** 15 mins

INGREDIENTS

50g (1¾oz) unsalted butter

2 shallots, finely diced

4 tbsp dry white wine

1 tbsp brandy

2 tbsp rich beef stock

200ml (7fl oz) double cream

100g (3½oz) Roquefort cheese, crumbled

1 tbsp finely snipped chives

salt and freshly ground black pepper

1 Heat half the butter in a small frying pan over a low heat. Add the shallots, and cook for about 5 minutes, until softened. Then add the wine and brandy, and bring to the boil.
2 Add the stock and cook until reduced by half. Then add the cream, mix well, and reduce the heat to a simmer. Cook for about 5 minutes, then whisk in the remaining butter and the cheese. Remove from the heat and strain through a sieve. Stir in the chives and season to taste.

HOLLANDAISE SAUCE

Makes 200ml (7fl oz)

Prep: 10 mins **Cook:** 5 mins

INGREDIENTS

1 tbsp white wine vinegar

juice of ½ lemon

3 large egg yolks

salt and ground white pepper

175g (6oz) butter

1 Put the vinegar and lemon juice in a small saucepan. Bring to the boil and remove from the heat.
2 Meanwhile, place the egg yolks in a food processor or blender, season with a little salt and pepper, and blend for 1 minute. With the motor running, slowly add the lemon juice and vinegar mixture.
3 Put the butter in the same pan and leave over a low heat until melted. When it begins to foam, remove from the heat. With the food processor running, gradually add the butter to form a thick sauce. Serve immediately.

CRANBERRY SAUCE

Makes 300ml (10fl oz)

Prep: 5 mins
Cook: 15 mins

INGREDIENTS

250g (9oz) fresh or frozen cranberries

1 small shallot, finely chopped

100g (3½oz) light muscovado sugar

zest and juice of 1 orange

4 tbsp red wine or port

1 Put the cranberries in a sauce pan with the shallot, sugar, orange zest and juice, and red wine or port. Bring to the boil, stirring, until the sugar is dissolved.
2 Simmer gently for 10–12 minutes, or until the cranberries are beginning to break up.
3 Leave to cool, then transfer to a serving dish or storage jar. (This sauce can be kept refrigerated for up to 1 week.)

BÉARNAISE SAUCE

HOLLANDAISE SAUCE

BLUE CHEESE SAUCE

CRANBERRY SAUCE

FLAVOUR PAIRINGS

A whole world of ingredients is now available to the cook. Although some are common partners to all meat, others go particularly well with certain meats. Sometimes it is the flavour combinations that excite us, sometimes a texture complements the meat. Here is a brief guide to start you off.

POULTRY

With their delicate flavour, turkey, chicken, and poussin make a good background for a variety of flavours. Duck and goose benefit from stronger flavours that counteract the flavoursome layer of fat.

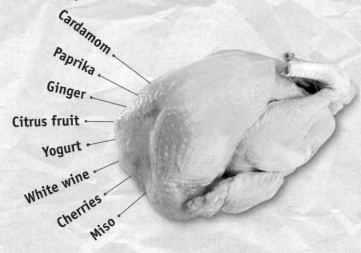

Cardamom
Paprika
Ginger
Citrus fruit
Yogurt
White wine
Cherries
Miso

PORK

With its slightly fungal overtones, combined with its fat, pork can absorb complex and powerful flavours. Where fat is trimmed off, it is more delicate and some poultry flavours apply.

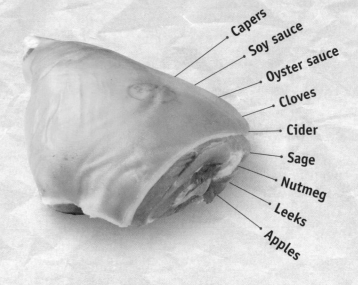

Capers
Soy sauce
Oyster sauce
Cloves
Cider
Sage
Nutmeg
Leeks
Apples

VEAL

Being such a pale and delicately flavoured meat, veal is traditionally paired with delicate seasonings, although occasionally a small amount of something piquant accentuates its subtle flavour.

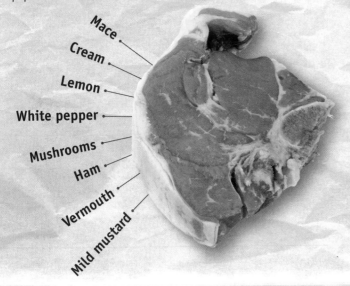

Mace
Cream
Lemon
White pepper
Mushrooms
Ham
Vermouth
Mild mustard

BEEF

One of the most robustly flavoured of meats, beef delights in powerful flavours, but use these sparingly. If the beef is very lean, use slippery textures to avoid it feeling dry.

Black pepper
Tarragon
Chilli
Coriander
Horseradish
Red wine
Truffles
Mustard

LAMB AND YOUNG GOAT

Even though lamb is leaner than mutton, it can still carry an amount of fat, so choose ingredients that cut through this. Young goat is leaner, so pairs with delicate flavours.

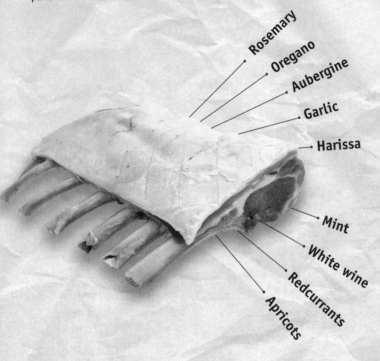

Rosemary
Oregano
Aubergine
Garlic
Harissa
Mint
White wine
Redcurrants
Apricots

MUTTON AND OLD GOAT

Both dark and powerfully flavoured, mutton and old goat meat work well with punchy flavours and moist textures. Try also some of the recommendations for dark game.

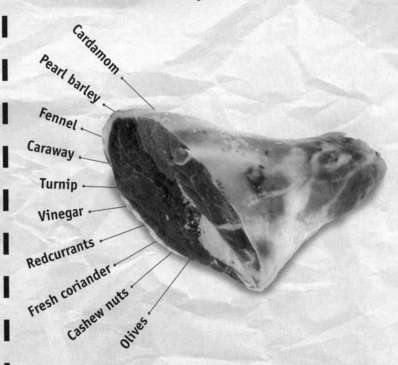

Cardamom
Pearl barley
Fennel
Caraway
Turnip
Vinegar
Redcurrants
Fresh coriander
Cashew nuts
Olives

LIGHT GAME

From pheasant, partridge, woodcock, and quail to rabbits, light-fleshed game meat has a huge range of complex and delicate flavours that may be enhanced by hanging and are complemented by the pairings below.

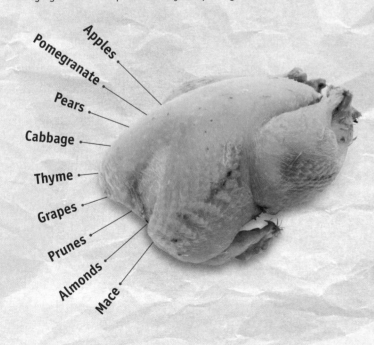

Apples
Pomegranate
Pears
Cabbage
Thyme
Grapes
Prunes
Almonds
Mace

DARK GAME

Hanging dark game meat, such as venison and hare, can make it taste powerful, but when fresh it has a concentrated meaty taste. These meats go well with fruity flavours and succulent textures.

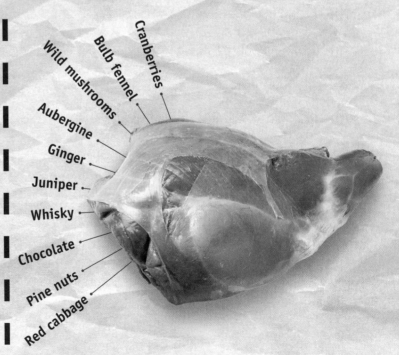

Cranberries
Bulb fennel
Wild mushrooms
Aubergine
Ginger
Juniper
Whisky
Chocolate
Pine nuts
Red cabbage

MORE FOR LESS

MEAT CAN BE AN EXPENSIVE INGREDIENT AND SHOULD NEVER BE WASTED. OVER THE CENTURIES, THE MANY WAYS OF MAKING A MODEST AMOUNT OF MEAT STRETCH TO FEED A FAMILY HAVE EVOLVED INTO A WHOLE RANGE OF TASTY DISHES.

REDUCING THE COST

- Use the whole beast. Prime cuts are an expensive luxury and are best enjoyed only occasionally. Use cheaper cuts more often.
- Explore the world of minced meat dishes. This is one of the least expensive forms of meat, but makes countless tasty dishes, from meatballs to satays.
- Try cooking some offal (see pp270–87 for recipes). You might be amazed at how delicious and cheap it can be.
- Cook several portions at once and freeze some for another time. This also makes the best use of the oven or hob, and your time.

STARCHY SIDES

Many cuisines have traditional ways of making a small amount of meat feel satisfying. This often involves serving some delicious form of starch either just before the meat or alongside it.

PASTRY

Pastry can transform a small amount of meat into a delicious pie or pudding.
- Dish meat pies are topped with a filling crust of shortcrust or flaky pastry.

PASTA SAUCES A creamy sauce coats pasta, such as spaghetti, well and requires only a small quantity of meat.

- Raised meat pies are completely enclosed in a strong hot water crust.
- Suet meat puddings are enclosed in a rich pastry and steamed in a covered bowl.

DUMPLINGS

Made with flour, fat, baking powder, and seasoning, dumplings are made by forming balls and dropping them into a bubbling stew or broth. Many contain herbs and vegetables.

PASTA AND NOODLES

These filling, starchy sides – made from flour, egg, and water – require only a small amount of meat sauce to taste good.

BATTER

- Yorkshire pudding is batter that is oven cooked in very hot fat. Traditionally served with gravy before the meat, it is now usually served with roast beef.
- Spätzle are made from a thick batter forced through holes into boiling water to make small irregular shapes. Sometimes they are fried in butter afterwards.

FORCEMEAT

This is a mixture of breadcrumbs, seasoned with onions, herbs, and spices, all bound together with egg.
- Small balls of forcemeat can be fried and served with meat dishes.
- Forcemeat can be baked in a dish and served alongside poultry or meat.
- Forcemeat can be used as stuffing for birds, either in the cavity or under the skin.

VEGETABLES

Serving a variety of interesting vegetables makes the meat go further.
- Serve them in a sauce to add a creamy texture for fried or roasted meat.
- Scatter lots of fresh herbs or lemon juice on them just before serving.
- Boil root vegetables and add them to a vinaigrette and serve warm with fresh herbs.
- Dip them in batter or egg-and-breadcrumbs and fry them as a great contrast to stews.

- Roast root vegetables alongside roasting meat for added colour and flavours.
- Add layers of soft vegetables such as tinned tomatoes, cooked onions, aubergines or sweet peppers to minced meat dishes to bulk them out and add flavours.

USING LEFTOVER MEAT

There are many ways of turning leftover meat into a delicious second meal.

MAKING RISSOLES

If there is a small amount of cooked meat left over, use it to make rissoles:

1 Chop the leftover meat finely. Then cook and mash some potato, parsnip, or other starchy root vegetable.
2 Stir in the meat along with some fresh herbs and seasoning. Roll in breadcrumbs and fry.

MAKING A PIE

After a roast chicken meal, it is surprising how much meat is left on the bird. This is perfect for making a pie:

1 Remove all the meat from the carcass and mix it with leftover gravy or sauce. If there is not enough gravy, make a white sauce from butter, flour, and milk.
2 Add some vegetables, such as cooked onions and mushrooms.
3 Pour the mixture into a dish, cover with pastry, and serve as a delicious pie. (Alternatively, leftover chunks of roast or stewed meat can be made into pasties.)

MAKING PASTA SAUCE

This is a good option when only a small amount of meat is left over:

1 Chop the meat finely, add any leftover sauce, as well as some cooked onion, garlic, tomatoes, and herbs.
2 Moisten with liquid such as water, stock, wine, or cream, and serve with pasta.

SLOW COOKED Cheaper cuts of meat make delicious meals when slowly cooked. Add lots of vegetables such as onions, leeks, and carrots to make it go further.

FREEZING MEAT

As long as raw meat is wrapped tightly in a thick layer of plastic to exclude the air, it will keep for many months in the freezer. Vacuum-packed meat keeps for years.

- Cooked meat that is frozen in its liquid – such as a stew – will freeze well for several months. Ensure it has cooled before freezing.

- Freeze mince or minced-meat products in thin packs so that they defrost quickly and evenly. They will also keep for several months.

Note that the following situations can lead to unpleasant tasting meat, although it will not be harmful:

- Fat eventually changes its flavour and will taste rancid when frozen for too long.

- Cooked products with a high water content – such as terrines and pies – become mushy and wet when frozen for too long.

- If air reaches meat through burst packaging, the surface will become white and dry with freezer burn. This can be cut off.

- Whole poultry is prone to freezer burn in the cavity.

THAWING MEAT

Thaw meat in as cold an environment as possible to avoid the cell walls breaking down and releasing too much moisture.

- If using a microwave to thaw meat, use the lowest possible setting and allow it to stand for a while afterwards to avoid moisture loss.

- Thaw large pieces in the fridge so that the outer surface does not become too warm while the interior defrosts.

- A little liquid is always produced so place meat in a dish in the fridge to prevent moisture dripping onto other food.

- Vacuum-packed meat can be quickly and safely thawed in a basin of cold water. Even a large joint will thaw in about two hours.

CARVING POULTRY

On all poultry, the dark leg and thigh meat is the most succulent. Breast meat is paler and more tender, but can be dry. Remove the wishbone before cooking to make carving the breast easier.

CARVING KNOW-HOW

All meat is easier to carve if it has been rested beforehand. If the meat squeaks as it is being carved, then either it is undercooked, or it has not been rested for long enough.

THE CARVING KNIFE

A carving knife should be thin and flexible but strong enough to cut through joints. Above all, the knife needs to be very sharp to avoid flaking the meat rather than cutting it. A blunt knife will squeeze the juice out of the meat. The carving knife should be long enough to protrude 5cm (2in) either side of the joint to allow large slices to be cut, using a sawing action.

CARVING FORK

A carving fork has a guard to prevent the knife from slipping up the fork when cuts are being made towards the fork. It also has curved prongs so that it can be used to hold the meat in place while being carved.

WHAT TO CARVE ON?

Any meat cooked to well done can be carved on a board that won't blunt the knife. If the joint or bird has a lot of red juices, these will run off a board. In that case, use a warm carving platter that will collect these juices. For informal eating, slow-roasted meat can be carved or pulled off the bone and served in the roasting pan. Pour off any excess fat first, and add a little liquid to dissolve the roasting juices, then carve the meat and allow it to soak up all the juices.

REMOVE STRING AND SKEWERS

Remove any skewers, trussing strings, or elastic bands before carving. If possible, remove any netting, although be aware that sometimes this causes rolled meat to fall apart.

CARVING SMALL BIRDS

Small birds may be served whole or halved, or the legs and breasts may be removed. This is more wasteful, but makes small birds easier to eat with a knife and fork.

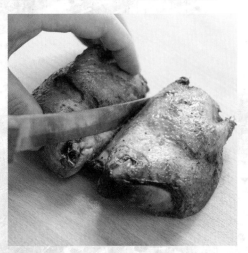

1 Cut the bird lengthways along the breast bone. Open out the bird.

2 Using strong shears or a heavy knife, cut down either side of the backbone to divide the bird in two.

CARVING CHICKEN AND MEDIUM-SIZED BIRDS

All parts of a chicken and domestic duck will be tender. But on some game birds, the legs, and in particular the drumsticks, can be tough and sinewy.

1 Bend the legs outwards and remove them at the joint. Serve whole or divide into drumsticks and thighs.

2 Carve the breast into slices, starting at the thicker (neck) end (see Step 5, opposite). Cut off the wings and serve separately if wished.

CARVING A TURKEY OR LARGE GOOSE

Only carve off as much meat as you will need because the rest of the meat will remain moist on the carcass. Serve the meat with stuffing, either from the cavity or from a separate dish.

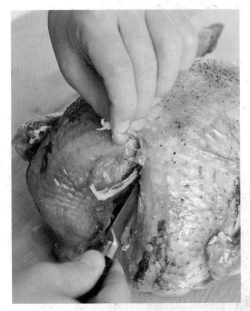

1 Remove the wishbone. To do this, lift up or cut off a small flap of skin from the neck end. Feel for the wishbone with your fingers. Cut round it as closely as possible, then pull it out.

2 Now remove the leg. Pull it outwards using a carving fork and then cut through it at the joint.

3 Divide the leg into drumstick and thigh. Then slice off the leg meat parallel to the bone, including the skin if desired.

4 Cut off the wing at the joint, including a little bit of breast meat. Divide it at the joints and carve the meat as above. Alternatively, reserve the wing for stock.

5 Carve the breast into slices, starting at the thicker (neck) end. Place the back of the fork against the meat as you carve it to hold the slices in place.

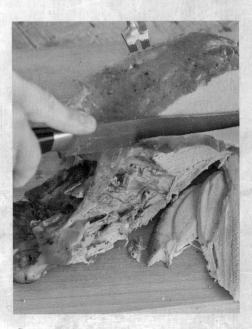

6 Repeat for the other side of the bird, but this time secure it by sticking the carving fork straight down into the carcass of the side without any meat.

CARVING JOINTS OF MEAT

All cuts of meat will feel more tender if carved across the grain of the meat, rather than with the grain. However, very tender cuts, such as loin and fillet, can cope with being cut with the grain. Steaks and tiny joints may be so thin that to cut across the grain would make the slices too small. They should be cut on the slant to make the slices bigger, but always cut across the grain.

CARVING RIB AND LOIN JOINTS

Racks are carved by cutting between the ribs. Beef ribs are usually carved by taking the meat off the bone first. Boneless loin joints are usually carved across the grain.

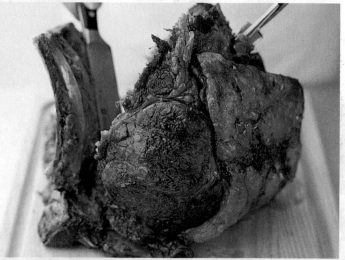

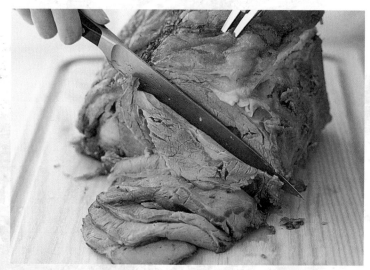

1 Run the carving knife down the inside of the ribs, keeping it flat against the bone. Turn the knife outwards 90°. Cut the meat off the wing bone or rib.

2 Turn the joint over and remove the fillet, if present, using the same procedure. Cut the meat across the grain into slices.

CARVING SADDLE AND RACK JOINTS

If a rack joint has had the chine bone fully removed, then it is simply sliced between the rib bones. If not, carve like a saddle. A young, tender saddle can be carved along the length of the muscles.

1 Place the joint with the fillet/rib side facing downwards. Run the knife down one side of the backbone. There is a small bump at the base; make sure the knife goes over it to avoid cutting into the muscle. Turn the knife outwards 90° and cut the meat off the wing bone or rib.

2 Cut the meat across the grain into slices. Repeat on the other side, if it's a full saddle. Turn the joint over and remove the fillet(s), if there are any. Slice on the slant, across the grain, and serve each person some loin and some fillet.

CARVING A WHOLE LEG ON THE BONE

A whole leg is much easier to carve if the pelvic bone (or aitch bone) has been removed before cooking. If it hasn't, ask the butcher to do this, or follow the instuctions on p293.

1 Cut off a thick slice of the meat from the thinner side of the bone so that the joint sits firmly on its base.

2 With the plump muscle uppermost, start to slice straight across the meat until you hit the bone. Continue to cut slices about 4mm (¼in) thick.

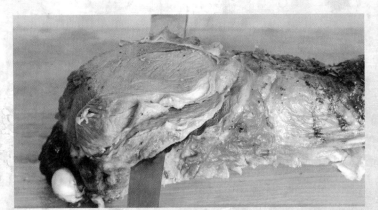

3 Turn the knife and make a horizontal cut along the top of the bone to release the slices.

4 Turn the joint and repeat the exercise. Cut slices on the slant, so that they are not too small.

CARVING A SHOULDER JOINT

Carving a shoulder is similar to carving a leg, except for the curious shape of the bladebone.

1 Turn the shoulder skin-side uppermost. Cut all the way down one side of the bladebone. Tilt the knife 90° outwards to lift the meat off the flat of the bone.

2 Repeat with the other side. Carve both these muscles across the grain into slices. Turn the joint over and carve the meat off the other side, slightly slanting it to make the slices larger.

COOKING CHARTS – POULTRY AND FEATHERED GAME

CUT	GRILL/BARBECUE	FRY/STIR-FRY	ROAST	BRAISE/STEW
NOTES	Internal-temperature reading for all domestic poultry: 75°C (165°F). **For Ostrich, see Venison, Bison, Buffalo and Ostrich, page 45.** **Temperatures** listed are for general cooking, but may vary in recipes.			
CHICKEN AND TURKEY Whole or half chicken, chicken quarter, chicken crown, turkey quarters	**Chicken quarter:** Barbecue at medium heat for 25–30 mins, turning at least twice, or until cooked through. **Half chicken and turkey quarters:** Grill cut side at medium heat for 30 mins. Then turn and grill 15–20 mins until cooked, then brown skin side before serving. Not recommended for whole and crowns or whole turkey.	**Chicken quarter:** Fry in deep fat for 20–30 mins, or until cooked through. Not recommended for whole, half, or crowns or whole turkey.	**Whole or half chicken:** Preheat oven to 180°C (350°F/Gas 4). Roast for 20 mins per 450g (1lb) plus 20 mins, or until juices run clear. **Chicken quarter:** Roast for 30 mins, or until juices run clear. **Turkey:** Slow-roast unstuffed, whole turkey at 160°C (325°F/Gas 3) for 3½–4 hours for 3.5-5.5kg (7–9lbs); 4–4½ hours for 5.5-7kg (12–15lb); and 4½–5 hours for 7–9kg (15–20lb). Do not undercook. Rest for 30 mins.	**Whole or half chicken:** Brown if desired, then add liquid, plus vegetables if required, and cover. Simmer, or stew at 160°C (325°F/Gas 3) for 1–2 hours. **Turkey:** Stew turkey joints as chicken, adding 30 mins to cooking time.
Whole leg, thigh, drumstick	Barbecue or grill whole leg, thigh, and drumstick as quarter.	Fry whole leg, thigh, and drumstick as quarter. Not recommended for larger pieces of turkey.	Roast whole leg, thigh, and drumstick as quarter.	Simmer or stew whole leg as whole or half chicken, but for 1 hour. Also suitable for soup. **Turkey:** Stew turkey joints as chicken, adding 30 mins to cooking time.
Wing	Barbecue or grill chicken wings for 20–25 mins, turning at least twice, or until cooked through.	Fry wing as quarter. Not recommended for larger pieces of turkey.	Roast wing as quarter, but for 20 mins.	Simmer or stew wing as whole or half chicken, but for 1 hour. Also suitable for soup. **Turkey:** Stew turkey joints as chicken, adding 30 mins to cooking time.
Breast fillet	Barbecue or grill breast fillet for 20–30 mins, turning at least twice, or until cooked through.	Fry breast fillet as quarter, but for 10–20 mins, or until cooked through. Not recommended for larger pieces of turkey.	Not recommended.	Simmer or stew breast fillet as whole or half chicken, but for 1 hour. **Turkey:** Stew turkey joints as chicken, adding 30 mins to cooking time.
Goujons, diced and sliced chicken and turkey	Heat barbecue or grill to medium-high. Thread onto skewers and brush with oil. Brown on all sides, then cook for 10–15 mins, or until cooked through. **Turkey:** Grill turkey quarters as half chicken.	Heat oil in a frying pan over a high heat. Brown dice all over, then lower heat and continue cooking for 5–15 mins (3–5 mins for goujons and strips), or until cooked through. Not recommended for larger pieces of turkey.	Not recommended.	Not recommended for goujons or small slices. **Diced and thick slices:** Simmer or stew as whole or half chicken, but for 1 hour.
Minced poultry	Heat barbecue or grill to medium-high. Press mince onto skewers or shape into patties, including some fat. Cook for 10–20 mins, depending on thickness, or until cooked through.	Heat oil in a frying pan over a medium heat. Press mince onto skewers or shape into patties, including some fat. Fry for 10–20 mins, depending on thickness, or until cooked through.	Not recommended.	Brown mince and vegetables, then add liquid and simmer, or cook at 160°C (325°F/Gas 3), for 1–1½ hours.
POUSSIN AND SQUAB	Halve or spatchcock. Cook for 10–15 mins per side, or until cooked through.	Not recommended.	Roast whole at 220°C (425°F/Gas 7) for 20–30 mins.	Brown the bird or joints all over. Add liquid and cook at 160°C (325°F/Gas 3) for 1–1½ hours, or until tender.
DUCK AND WILD DUCK (for example MALLARD)	**Duck:** Grill breast for 2 mins per side, then cook for 8–10 mins with skin side nearest the heat. Rest for 2–3 mins. **Wild duck:** Grill breast 3–5 mins per side until rare or pink, then slice thinly.	**Duck:** Fry breast for 2 mins per side, then cook for 10–12 mins skin-side down. Rest for 2–3 mins. **Wild duck:** Fry breast 3–5 mins per side until rare or pink, then slice thinly.	**Duck:** Roast whole for 30 mins at 220°C (425°F/Gas 7), then reduce to 180°C (350°F/Gas 4) for 1–1½ hours. **Wild duck** (young birds only): Brown by frying, then roast for 30–45 mins at 220°C (425°F/Gas 7). Rest for 5 mins.	**Duck:** stew as chicken. Remove excess fat before serving. **Wild duck:** Brown the bird or joints all over. Add liquid and cook at 160°C (325°F/Gas 3) for 2–2½ hours, or until tender.
GOOSE AND WILD GOOSE	**Goose:** Grill breast for 5 mins per side. Cook for 10–15 mins skin-side down. Rest for 5 mins. **Wild goose:** grill only young wild goose. Serve rare.	**Goose:** Fry breast for 5 mins per side. Cook for 15–20 mins skin-side down. Rest for 5 mins. **Wild goose:** grill only young wild goose. Serve rare.	**Goose:** Roast whole for 45 mins at 220°C (425°F/Gas 7), then at 180°C (350°F/Gas 4) for 2–2½ hours. **Wild Goose** (young birds only): Roast as above, but for 30 mins at 220°C (425°F/Gas 7), then at 160°C (325°F/Gas 3) for 1–1½ hours.	Stew goose pieces as chicken, but for 1½–2 hours. Remove excess fat before serving.
PHEASANT AND GUINEA FOWL	Grill breast for 7–10 mins per side, or until juices run clear.	Fry breasts for 7–10 mins per side, or until juices run clear.	Roast whole birds at 190°C (375°F/Gas 5) for 40–50 mins, or until juices run clear. Rest for 5–10 mins. Do not overcook.	Brown the bird or joints all over. Add liquid and cook at 160°C (325°F/Gas 3) for 2–2½ hours, or until tender.
GROUSE, PARTRIDGE, PIGEON, QUAIL, SMALL WILD DUCK (for example TEAL), AND WOODCOCK	**Grouse, partridge, and pigeon:** Halve or spatchcock. Cook for 10–15 mins per side, or until juices run clear. **Quail, Teal, and Woodcock:** As above, but cook for 7–10 mins per side.	**Grouse, partridge, and pigeon:** Fry breast 2–4 mins per side until rare or pink, then slice thinly. **Quail, Teal, and Woodcock:** Not recommended.	Only roast young birds. Brown the breasts, then roast at 200°C (400°F/Gas 6) for 20–30 mins (up to 40 mins for grouse). Rest before serving.	Brown the bird or joints all over. Add liquid and cook at 160°C (325°F/Gas 3) for 2–2½ hours, or until tender.
SNIPE	Using a hot grill, cook for 10–15 mins, turning twice.	Not recommended.	Roast at 220°C (425°F/Gas 7) for 10–15 mins, then rest for 5 mins.	Brown all over in butter, then simmer for 30–45 mins, or until tender.

PORK

CUT	GRILL/BARBECUE	FRY/STIR-FRY	ROAST	BRAISE/STEW
NOTES **Temperatures** listed are for general cooking, but may vary in recipes.	Timings are for 2.5cm (1in) steaks. Thicker steaks take longer; thinner ones cook quicker.	Timings are for 2.5cm (1in) steaks unless otherwise stated. Thicker steaks take longer; thinner ones cook quicker.	Internal-temperature reading for well-done pork: 70°C (160°F). Remove from heat and rest when thermometer reads 63°C (145°F).	For timing, weight is less important than if meat is sliced, diced, or cooked as a joint.
Leg	**Leg steaks, escalopes, kebabs:** Preheat grill or barbecue to high. Brush meat with oil. Cook escalopes for 3 mins on each side. Cook steaks for 3 mins on each side, then reduce heat and cook for a further 2 mins per side (or longer if thicker). Grill kebabs for 2–3 mins on each side.	**Leg steaks, escalopes, diced leg:** Heat oil in a heavy pan until smoking hot. Fry escalopes for 2 mins per side. Fry steaks for 2 mins per side, then continue cooking for a further 2 mins per side. Rest for 2–3 mins. Stir-fry diced leg until well browned on all sides.	**Leg joint:** Preheat oven to 220°C (425°F/Gas 7). If there is skin, score it and rub with salt. Roast for 30 mins, then reduce heat to 160°C (325°F/Gas 3) and cook for 23 mins per 450g (1lb). Rest for 20–30 mins.	**Leg steaks** (2.5cm/1in): Preheat oven to 160°C (325°F/Gas 3). Brown meat. Add browned vegetables and liquid. Braise for 1½–2 hours. **Leg joint:** Braise as leg steaks, covered, for 3–3½ hours; if skin is on, increase heat to 200°C (400°F/Gas 6) and cook uncovered for final 20–30 mins to crisp skin.
Chump	**Chump chops:** Preheat grill to high. Brush meat with oil. Grill for 2–3 mins on each side, then reduce heat and cook for another 2–3 mins per side.	Fry **chump chops** as leg steaks.	Roast **chump joint** as leg joint.	Braise **chump chops** as leg steaks. Braise **chump joint** as leg joint, but for 2–3 hours.
Whole fillet/ tenderloin, medallions, and Valentine steaks	**Whole fillet and slices thicker than 4.5cm (1¾in):** Preheat grill to high. Brush meat with oil. Grill for 2–3 mins on each side, then reduce heat and grill, turning, for a further 10 mins. Rest for 5–10 mins. Grill **medallions** and **Valentine steaks** as leg steaks.	**Whole fillet and slices thicker than 4.5cm (1¾in):** Heat oil or butter in frying pan until smoking hot. Fry for 10 mins, turning to brown, reduce heat and cook for a further 5 mins. Rest for 5–10 mins. Fry **medallions and Valentine steaks** as leg steaks.	Not recommended.	Preheat oven to 150°C (300°F/Gas 2). Brown meat, then add vegetables and liquid. Braise for 1–2 hours, basting from time to time to glaze.
Loin steaks, joints, and chops	Grill **loin steaks** and **chops** as chump chops. **Loin joints:** Preheat barbecue to medium. Brown on all sides. Move to indirect heat and cook for 1¼–1½ hours, or until cooked. Rest for 10–15 mins.	Fry **loin steaks** and **chops** as leg steaks.	Roast **loin joint** and **rack** as leg joint.	Braise **loin steaks** and **chops** as leg steaks. Braise **loin joint** and **rack** as leg joint, but for 1½–2 hours.
Belly and spare ribs	**Belly slices:** Grill under medium heat for 10–15 mins, turning several times, then raise heat to high to crisp skin if necessary. **Spare rib rack:** See Barbecue Ribs recipe, pp130–31.	**Belly joint:** Pre-cook by simmering for 2 hours, then cool, slice, or cut thickly, and fry in a very hot frying pan for 8–10 mins to crisp and brown. **Belly slices:** Fry over a medium heat for 15–20 mins, turning several times. Increase heat to crisp fat and skin.	**Belly joint:** Preheat oven to 220°C (425°F/Gas 7). Score skin and rub with salt. Roast for 20 mins. Reduce heat to 150°C (300°F/Gas 2) and cook for 3–4 hours. **Spare ribs and slices:** Slow roast at 160°C (325°F/Gas 3) for 1–1½ hours, basting. Increase heat to 200°C (400°F/Gas 6). Roast for 20–30 mins to brown and glaze.	**Belly joint:** Simmer gently for 2–3 hours; slice thinly to serve with or without a glaze. Or brown belly, then braise at 130°C (250°F/Gas ½) for 4–5 hours; cool, slice, and glaze in a frying pan or hot oven.
Shoulder	Grill **shoulder steaks** and **chops** as chump chops.	Fry **shoulder steaks** and **chops** as chump chops.	**Shoulder/hand/blade joint:** Preheat oven to 220°C (425°F/Gas 7). Score skin and rub with salt. Brown for 30 mins, then reduce heat to 150°C (300°F/Gas 2) and continue roasting for 3–3½ hours.	Braise **shoulder steaks** and **chops** as leg steaks. **Shoulder/hand/blade joint:** Preheat oven to 150°C (300°F/Gas 2). Braise with vegetables for 4–4½ hours; baste to glaze. **Diced shoulder:** Prepare as for fillet/tenderloin. Stew for 1½ hours.
Head, cheeks/jowl, neck/collar, shank/ knuckle/hock	Not recommended.	Not recommended.	**Head:** Preheat oven to 190°C (375°F/Gas 5). After braising, protect ears with foil and roast for 30–45 mins to colour the skin; remove foil for the last 15 mins. Not recommended for other cuts.	**Head:** Brown vegetables, add head and liquid. Simmer, or cook in oven at 150°C (300°F/Gas 2) for 3–3½ hours. **Cheeks/ jowl:** Brown with vegetables, add liquid, cover, and simmer, or braise at 190°C (375°F/Gas 5), for 45–60 mins. Braise **neck/collar** as shoulder/hand/blade joint. **Shank/knuckle/hock:** Simmer for 2–3 hours.
Trotters	After cooking and cooling, split in half, brush with butter, and roll in breadcrumbs. Grill for 15–20 mins, or until crisp and golden brown.	Not recommended.	After cooking and cooling, prepare as for grilling. Roast at 200°C (400°F/Gas 6) for 15–20 mins, or until crisp and golden brown.	Simmer gently for 1–2 hours. Then cool, split in half, roll in breadcrumbs, and grill or roast.
Mince	Preheat grill to high. Press mince onto skewers or form into patties. Brush with oil and grill for 10–15 mins, turning frequently until cooked.	Heat oil in frying pan. Form mince into patties. Brush with oil and fry, turning occasionally, for 10–15 mins until cooked.	Not recommended.	Brown mince and vegetables, add liquid, and simmer for 1–1½ hours.
Sucking pig	Not recommended.	Not recommended.	See Sucking Pig recipe, pp106–07.	Cook as for fillet for 3–4 hours. Then increase heat to 200°C (400°F/Gas 6) and cook uncovered for the last 20–30 mins to crisp the skin.

BEEF

CUT	GRILL/BARBECUE	FRY/STIR-FRY	ROAST	BRAISE/STEW
NOTES **Temperatures** listed are for general cooking, but may vary in recipes.	Timings are for 2.5cm (1in) steaks. Thicker steaks take longer; thinner ones cook quicker.	Timings are for 2.5cm (1in) thick **steaks.** Thicker steaks take longer; thinner ones cook quicker.	Use a meat thermometer to check internal temperature. **Thermometer internal-temperature readings:** rare 60°C (140°F), medium rare 63°C (145°F), medium 65°C (150°F), and well-done 75C° (165°F).	For timing, weight is less important than whether the meat is sliced, diced, or cooked as a joint.
GRILLING STEAK: Fillet, sirloin, ribeye, T-bone, rump, topside, silverside, minute steak	Sirloin, ribeye, T-bone, rump, topside, silverside: Preheat grill to high. Brush meat with oil or melted butter. Grill 2½ mins per side for rare; 4 mins per side for medium; 6 mins per side for well-done. Rest 2–3 mins before serving. Do not cook topside and silverside beyond pink. **Fillet steak:** Grill fillet steak for 2 mins per side for rare; 3 mins per side for medium; 4 mins per side for well-done. Rest 2–3 mins. **Minute steak:** Not recommended.	Fillet, sirloin, ribeye, T-bone: Heat oil, or butter and oil, in a frying pan until very hot. Place steak in pan and do not move until turning it over. Fry 2½ mins per side for rare; 4 mins per side for medium; 6 mins per side for well-done. Rest 2–3 mins. **Minute steak:** fry for 1–1½ mins per side and serve at once. **Topside and silverside:** do not cook beyond pink.	Not recommended.	**Rump, topside, silverside steak:** Preheat oven to 160°C (325°F/Gas 3). Brown meat and add liquid. Braise for 1½–2 hours; **Sirloin, fillet, T-bone, and ribeye:** as above, but cook for 1–1½ hours.
FLASH-FRY STEAK: Deckle, top cap, ribeye cap, flank, skirt, tri-tip, cap of rump, flatiron, hanger, point, knuckle cap	Grill as whole pieces or thread slices on skewers. Heat grill to very hot. Brush steak with oil, then grill for 2–3 mins per side and serve immediately. Do not cook beyond pink. Slice whole pieces thinly across grain to serve.	Fry as whole pieces or slice first. Heat pan to very hot with oil and butter. Fry for 2–3 mins per side and serve immediately. Do not cook beyond pink. Slice whole pieces thinly across grain to serve.	Not recommended.	Preheat oven to 160°C (325°F/Gas 3). Brown meat and any vegetables then add liquid. Braise for 2–3 hours.
BONE-IN ROAST: Sirloin, sirloin rib, forerib,	Heat barbecue to 230°C (450°F). Roast for 25 min with lid down. Reduce heat to 190°C (375°F) and roast 12–15 mins per 450g (1lb) for rare; 20 mins per 450g (1lb) for medium; 25 mins per 450g (1lb) for well-done. Rest for 20–30 mins.	Not recommended.	Preheat oven to 230°C (450°F/Gas 8). Roast for 25 mins. Reduce heat to 190°C (375°F/Gas 5) and roast 12–15 mins per 450g (1lb) for rare; 20 mins per 450g (1lb) for medium; 25 mins per 450g (1lb) for well-done. Rest for 20–30 mins.	Preheat oven to 160°C (325°F/Gas 3). Brown meat and add liquid. Braise joint for 2–3 hours.
BONELESS ROAST: Fillet, sirloin, ribeye, rump, topside	Preheat barbecue to 190°C (375°F). Roast 20 mins per 450g (1lb) plus 20 min for rare; 25 mins per 450g (1lb) plus 25 mins for medium; 30 mins per 450g (1lb) plus 30 mins for well-done. Rest for 20–30 mins.	Not recommended.	**Boneless sirloin, ribeye, rump, topside joint:** Preheat oven to 190°C (375°F/Gas 5). Roast 20 mins per 450g (1lb) plus 20 mins for rare; 25 mins per 450g (1lb) plus 25 mins for medium; 30 mins per 450g (1lb) plus 30 mins for well-done. Rest 20–30 mins. **Fillet joints and Châteaubriand:** Preheat oven to 230°C (450°F/Gas 8). Brown meat in hot oil in a frying pan, then place in oven. Roast for 10–12 mins per 450g (1lb) for rare; 12–15 mins per 450g (1lb) for medium; 14–16 mins per 450g (1lb) for well-done. Rest for 10 mins.	Preheat oven to 160°C (325°F/Gas 3). Brown meat and add liquid. Braise joint for 2–3 hours.
BRAISING JOINT: Thick flank (top rump) silverside, topside, chuck and blade, shoulder, clod, leg-of-mutton, brisket.	Barbecue as a slow-roast: Preheat barbecue to 160°C (325°F). Brush joint with oil. Slow-roast away from direct heat for 3–4 hours, or until tender.	Not recommended.	Not recommended.	Preheat oven to 160°C (325°F/Gas 3). Brown meat and add liquid. Braise joint for 3–4 hours, or until very tender.
SLOW-COOK CUTS: All flash-fry steaks plus shin, ossobuco, heel, neck, clod, ribs, runner.	Not recommended.	Not recommended.	Not recommended.	Preheat oven to 160°C (325°F/Gas 3). Brown meat and add liquid. Braise joint for 3–4 hours, or until very tender.
MINCE	Preheat grill to high. Press mince on to skewers or form into patties. Brush with oil and grill, turning occasionally, for 10–15 mins, or until temperature reaches 75°C (165°F).	Preheat grill to high. Press mince on to skewers or form into patties. Brush with oil and grill, turning occasionally, for 10–15 mins, or until temperature reaches 75°C (165°F).	Not recommended.	Brown mince, add liquid, and simmer, or braise at 160°C (325°F/Gas 3), for 1–1½ hours (steak mince) or 1½–2 hours (regular mince).

VEAL

CUT	GRILL/BARBECUE	FRY/STIR-FRY	ROAST	BRAISE/STEW
NOTES Temperatures listed are for general cooking, but may vary in recipes.	Timings are for 2.5cm (1in) thick steaks. Thicker steaks take longer; thinner ones cook quicker.	Timings are for 2.5cm (1in) thick steaks. Thicker steaks take longer; thinner ones cook quicker.	Internal-temperature readings: rare 60°C (140°F), medium-rare 63°C (145°F), medium 65°C (150°F), and well-done 75°C (165°F).	For timing, weight is less important than whether the meat is sliced, diced, or cooked as a joint.
STEAKS: Topside, silverside, escalopes, rump, sirloin, fillet, T-bone, loin chop, cutlet, ribeye	Preheat grill to high. Brush meat with oil or melted butter. Grill 2½ mins per side for rare; 4 mins per side for medium; 6 mins per side for well-done. Rest 2–3 mins. **Escalopes:** Preheat grill to high. Brush meat with oil. Grill for 2 mins per side (not suitable if coated with breadcrumbs). **Kebabs:** Preheat grill to high. Brush meat with oil. Grill for 2–3 mins on all sides. **Minute steak:** Not recommended.	Heat oil, or butter and oil, in a frying pan until very hot. Place steak in pan and do not move until turning it over. Fry 2½ mins per side for rare; 4 mins per side for medium; 6 mins per side for well-done. Rest 2–3 mins. **Escalopes:** Heat 5mm (¼in) lard, oil, or butter and fry breadcrumbed escalopes for 3 mins per side, or uncoated escalopes for 2 mins per side. **Diced leg:** Heat oil, or butter and oil, and brown meat quickly on all sides, then serve; for large dice, rest for 5 mins. **Minute steak:** fry for 1–1½ mins per side and serve at once. **Topside and silverside:** do not cook beyond pink.	Not recommended.	Brown on all sides, then add browned vegetables and liquid, or braise in oven at 180°C (350°F/Gas 4), for 1–1½ hours, or until tender.
FLASH-FRY STEAK: Deckle, top cap, ribeye cap, flank, skirt, tri-tip, cap of rump, flatiron, hanger, point, knuckle cap	Grill as whole pieces or thread slices on skewers. Heat grill to very hot. Brush steak with oil, then grill for 2–3 mins per side and serve immediately. Do not cook beyond pink. Slice whole pieces thinly across grain to serve.	Fry as whole pieces or slice first. Heat pan to very hot with oil and butter. Fry for 2–3 mins per side and serve immediately. Do not cook beyond pink. Slice whole pieces thinly across grain to serve.	Not recommended.	Preheat oven to 160°C (325°F/Gas 3). Brown meat and any vegetables, then add liquid. Braise for 2–3 hours.
BONE-IN ROASTS: Best end (rib), sirloin	Heat barbecue to 230°C (450°F). Roast for 25 mins with lid down. Reduce heat to 190°C (375°F) and roast 12–15 mins per 450g (1lb) for rare; 20 mins per 450g (1lb) for medium; 25 mins per 450g (1lb) for well-done. Rest 20–30 mins.	Not recommended.	Preheat oven to 230°C (450°F/Gas 8). Roast for 20 mins. Reduce heat to 190°C (375°F/Gas 5) and roast 12–15 mins per 450g (1lb) for rare; 20 mins per 450g (1lb) for medium; 25 mins per 450g (1lb) for well-done. Rest 15–20 mins.	Brown on both sides, then add browned vegetables and liquid, and simmer gently, or braise in the oven at 180°C (350°F/Gas 4), for 1½–2 hours or until tender.
BONELESS ROASTS: Silverside, topside, rump, fillet, loin, best end (ribeye)	Preheat barbecue to 190°C (375°F). Roast 20 mins per 450g (1lb) plus 20 mins for rare; 25 mins per 450g (1lb) plus 25 mins for medium; 30 mins per 450g (1lb) plus 30 mins for well-done. Rest 20 mins.	Not recommended.	**Silverside, topside, rump, loin, best end (ribeye) joint:** Preheat oven to 190°C (375°F/Gas 5). Roast 15 mins per 450g (1lb) plus 20 mins for rare; 20 mins per 450g (1lb) plus 25 mins for medium; 25 mins per 450g (1lb) plus 30 mins for well-done. Rest 20–30 mins. **Fillet joints and Châteaubriand:** Preheat oven to 230°C (450°F/Gas 8). Brown meat in hot oil in a frying pan, then place in oven. Roast for 10–12 mins per 450g (1lb) for rare; 12–15 mins per 450g (1lb) for medium; 14–16 mins per 450g (1lb) for well-done. Rest 10 mins.	Brown on all sides, then add browned vegetables and liquid, and simmer gently, or braise in oven at 180°C (350°F/Gas 4), for 1–1½ hours, or until tender.
BRAISING JOINTS: Thick flank (top rump) silverside, topside, chuck & blade, shoulder, clod, leg-of-mutton, brisket	Barbecue as a slow-roast: Prehreat barbecue to 160°C (325°F). Brush joint with oil. Slow-roast away from direct heat for 3–4 hours, or until tender.	Not recommended.	Not recommended.	Brown on all sides, then add browned vegetables and liquid, and simmer gently, or braise in oven at 180°C (350°F/Gas 4), for 1–1½ hours, or until tender.
SLOW-COOK CUTS: flash-fry steaks plus shin, ossobuco, heel, neck, clod, ribs, runner	Not recommended except for flash-fry cuts.	Not recommended except for flash-fry cuts.	Not recommended.	Preheat oven to 160°C (325°F/Gas 3). Brown meat and add liquid. Braise joint for 2–3 hours, or until very tender.
MINCE	Preheat grill to high. Brush burgers, kebabs and so on with oil and brown for 8 mins, turning twice. Reduce heat to medium. Cook and turn for a further 8–10 mins, or until cooked through.	Fry burgers, kebabs and so on in hot oil, lard or butter for 10–15 mins, or until temperature reaches 75°C (165°F), turning from time to time.	Not recommended.	Brown mince and vegetables in a frying pan, then add liquid and simmer gently, or bake at 180°C (350°F/Gas 4) for 1–1½ hours.

LAMB, MUTTON, AND GOAT

CUT	GRILL/BARBECUE	FRY/STIR-FRY	ROAST	BRAISE/STEW
NOTES Temperatures listed are for general cooking, but may vary in recipes.	Timings vary according to thickness.	Timings vary according to thickness.	**Internal-temperature readings:** rare 60°C (140°F), medium 65°C (150°F), and well-done 75°C (165°F).	
LAMB Leg steaks, diced leg, leg joints	**Leg chops and steaks:** Preheat grill to high. Brush meat with oil. Grill for 3–4 mins per side, then rest 5 mins. **Kebabs:** Grill as steaks and chops, but for 2 mins each side. **Leg joint, bone-in or boneless:** Preheat barbecue to 200°C (400°F). Cook for 25–30 mins per 450g (1lb), then rest 5–10 mins per 450g (1lb).	**Leg steaks and chops:** Heat oil and butter in a hot frying pan. Brown meat for 2 mins each side, then reduce heat and cook for 2–4 mins per side. Rest before serving. **Kebabs:** Fry for 2 mins each side, then serve immediately. Not recommended for leg joints.	**Leg steaks and chops** (2.5cm/1in thick): Preheat oven to 200°C (400°F/Gas 6). Brush meat with butter or oil and roast for 30–45 mins. **Leg joint, bone-in or boneless:** Preheat oven to 200°C (400°F/Gas 6). Roast for 25–30 mins per 450g (1lb), then rest 5 mins per 450g (1lb).	**Leg steaks and chops** (2.5cm/1in thick): Brown meat, then add liquid and simmer, or cook in the oven at 190°C (375°F/Gas 5), for 1 hour. **Diced leg:** Braise as steaks and chops, but for 1–1½ hours. **Leg joint, bone-in or boneless:** Brown all over, then add liquid and cook in oven at 180°C (350°F/Gas 4) for 3–3½ hours.
Saddle and loin	**Fillet:** Preheat grill to high. Brush meat with oil. Grill loin and Barnsley chops and noisettes as leg steaks and chops. Grill butterfly steaks as kebabs. **Loin joint:** Brown 2 mins per side at top heat, then reduce heat to half and grill for 3–4 mins per side; rest 5–10 mins. Grill 2 mins on each side, then rest for 5 mins.	**Loin or Barnsley chops** and **loin steaks:** Cook as leg steaks and chops. **Butterfly steaks:** cook as kebabs. **Loin joint:** Brown meat for 2 mins each side, then reduce heat and cook for 3–5 mins per side; rest 5–10 mins. **Saddle joint:** Not recommended.	**Saddle:** roast as leg joint. **Loin or Barnsley chops:** roast as leg chops. **Butterfly steaks:** Not recommended. **Loin joint:** Preheat oven to 220°C (425°F/Gas 7). Brown joint on all sides, then roast for 8–10 mins, then rest for 5–10 mins.	Braise saddle as leg joint, but for 2–2½ hours. Braise loin and Barnsley chops and noisettes as leg steaks and chops. Not recommended for butterfly steaks. Braise loin joint as leg joint, but for 1–1½ hours.
Best end of neck (rack)	Grill cutlets and neck fillet as leg steaks and chops. **Rack joint:** Preheat barbecue to 200°C (400°F). Cook for 25–30 mins per 450g (1lb), then rest 5–10 mins per 450g (1lb).	Fry neck fillet, cutlets, and best end of neck joint as leg steaks and chops. **Rack:** Not recommended.	Roast neck fillet and cutlets as leg steaks and chops. Roast rack of lamb as loin joint. Roast crown roast, Guard of Honour, and best end joints as leg joint.	Braise neck fillet and cutlets as leg steaks and chops. Braise best end of neck, rack of lamb, and crown roast as leg joint, but for 1–1½ hours.
Forequarter, flank, and breast	Grill shoulder steaks and chops as leg steaks and chops. Not recommended for the other cuts.	Fry shoulder steaks and chops as leg steaks and chops. Not recommended for the other cuts.	**Shoulder joint, bone-in or boneless:** Preheat oven to 200°C (400°F/Gas 6). Roast for 20–30 mins per 450g (1lb) plus 30 mins. Rest for 30 mins. Not recommended for the other cuts.	**Shoulder steaks and chops:** Braise as leg steaks and chops. **Diced shoulder:** Braise as leg steaks and chops, but for 1½–2 hours. **Shoulder joint:** Braise as leg joint. **Shank, breast, scrag end:** Brown, then add liquid and simmer, or cook in oven at 160°C (325°F/Gas 3) for 1½–2 hours.
Minced lamb, mutton, and goat	Preheat grill to high. Press mince on to skewers or form into patties. Brush with oil and grill 2 mins on each side, then rest for 5 mins.	Brown mince, then add liquid and simmer for 45 mins–1 hour. Or, form into patties or balls and cook for 3–5 mins per side.	Not recommended.	Brown, then add liquid and simmer, or cook in oven at 160°C (325°F/Gas 3), for 1½–2 hours.
MUTTON AND GOAT Leg	Not recommended for old mutton and goat. **Leg chops and kebabs:** Cook as lamb chops and kebabs. **Young goat and mutton joints:** cook as lamb leg.	**Leg chops and kebabs:** Heat oil and butter in a frying pan. Fry chops for 3–5 mins per side, according to taste. Fry kebabs for 2–4 mins per side.	**Leg joint:** Preheat oven to 230°C (450°F/Gas 8). For pink meat, roast for 12 mins per 450g (1lb), then rest for 12 mins per 450g (1lb). For well-done, lower heat to 180°C (350°F/Gas 4) for a further 15–20 mins per 45g (1lb), then rest for 5–10 mins.	**Leg chops and diced leg:** Brown meat, then add liquid and simmer, or stew in oven at 180°C (350°F/Gas 4) for 1–1½ hours. **Leg joint:** Brown all over, then add vegetables and liquid, cover, and simmer for 2–3 hours until tender.
Loin and rib	Grill loin chops and cutlets as leg chops. Not recommended for saddle.	Fry loin chops and cutlets as leg chops. Not recommended for saddle.	Roast saddle and loin joints as leg joint. Not recommended for rib.	**Loin chops:** Braise and stew as leg chops. **Loin joint:** Preheat oven to 150°C (300°F/Gas 2). Brown joint all over, add liquid, and cook in oven for 50 mins; reduce heat to 130°C (250°F/Gas ½), baste well, and cook for 45 mins longer.
Forequarter	Not recommended.	Not recommended.	Not recommended.	**Shoulder joints, neck/scrag end and flank:** Braise as leg chops, but for 2–2½ hours. **Diced shoulder:** braise for 1½–2 hours. **Shin/shank:** Braise or stew as leg chops, but for 2½–3 hours.

FURRED GAME AND OTHER ANIMALS

CUT	GRILL/BARBECUE	FRY/STIR-FRY	ROAST	BRAISE/STEW
NOTES Temperatures listed are for general cooking, but may vary in recipes.	Timings vary according to thickness.	Timings vary according to thickness.	Internal-temperature readings: rare 60°C (140°F), medium 65°C (150°F).	
GRILLING AND FRYING: Venison haunch steak, loin steak, fillet, T-bone steak, chops. Ostrich breast steak, leg steak. Bison and buffalo leg steak, T-bone, fillet, sirloin and ribeye steak.	**Haunch/leg/breast steak (only from young animals):** Preheat grill to high. Brush meat with butter or oil. Grill to brown on both sides, then reduce heat and continue grilling, turning once: 1½ mins per 1cm (½in) for rare; 2 mins per 1cm (½in) for medium. Do not overcook; undercook steaks thicker than 2.5cm (1in). Rest for 3–5 mins. **Diced haunch/leg/breast (only from young animals):** Thread on to skewers and brown on all sides. Serve immediately.	**Haunch/leg steak (only from young animals):** Heat pan with butter and/or oil. Brown steak on both sides. Reduce heat and continue frying, turning once; rest to finish cooking. For rare: brown 3 mins, cook 1 min per 1cm (½in), and rest 1 min per 1cm (½in). For medium: brown 4 mins, cook 1½ mins per 1cm (½in), and rest 1½ mins per 1cm (½in). **Diced haunch/leg/breast (only from young animals):** Cook loose or thread meat on to skewers. Brush with butter or oil. Brown on all sides in a very hot pan. Serve immediately.	Not recommended.	**Haunch/leg/breast steaks (only from young deer):** Brown meat, add liquid, and, **for young animals**, braise at 190°C (375°F/Gas 5) for 1½–2 hours. If steaks are from **older animal**, braise at 180°C (350°F/Gas 4) for 2–3 hours. **Diced haunch/leg/breast:** Preheat oven to 160°C (325°F/Gas 3). Brown meat, then braise for 1½ hours, or 2–3 hours for older animals.
BONE-IN JOINTS: Venison saddle, rack, haunch; bison and buffalo sirloin, rib, forerib.	**Only barbecue joints from young animals.** Preheat barbecue to 230°C (450°F). Brown joint all over, then for rare, cook for 2½ mins per 1cm (½in), then remove from the heat, cover, and rest for 2 mins per 1cm (½in). For medium, cook for 3 mins per 1cm (½in), then rest for 3 mins per 1cm (½in).	Not recommended.	**Only roast joints from young animals.** Preheat oven to 230°C (450°F/Gas 8). Brown joint all over. For rare bone-in joint, roast for 2½ mins per 1cm (½in), then reduce heat to 80°C (170°F/Gas ¼) and rest in oven 2 mins per 1cm (½in). For medium bone-in joint, roast for 3 mins per 1cm (½in), then rest for 3 mins per 1cm (½in).	Preheat oven to 190°C (375°F/Gas 5). Brown meat, add liquid, then braise for 1½–2½ hours, or until tender. Braise joints from **older animals** at 180°C (350°F/Gas 4) for 2½–3½ hours, or until tender.
BONELESS JOINTS: Venison rolled haunch, loin; Ostrich breast, leg; bison and buffalo, fillet, sirloin, ribeye, rump, topside.	Barbecue as bone-in joints.	Not recommended.	Preheat oven to 230°C (450°F/Gas 8). Brown joint all over. For rare boneless joint, roast for 2 mins per 1cm (½in), then rest for 2–3 mins per 1cm (½in). For medium boneless joint, roast for 3 mins per 1cm (½in), then rest for 2–3 mins per 1cm (½in).	Preheat oven to 190°C (375°F/ Gas 5). Brown meat, then braise for 1½–2 hours, or 2½–3½ hours if from **older animals**.
BRAISING CUTS: Venison shoulder, haunch; Ostrich breast, leg; bison and buffalo leg and shoulder.	Not recommended.	Steaks must be flash-fried and served pink to avoid toughening.	Not recommended.	Preheat oven to 160°C (325°F/Gas 3). Brown meat, add liquid, then braise for 2–3 hours, or 3–4 hours if from older animals.
SLOW-COOK CUTS: Venison shin, shank, neck, flank. Bison and buffalo shin, ossobuco, heel, neck, clod, ribs, and runner.	Not recommended.	Not recommended.	Not recommended.	**Shin:** Simmer, or stew at 160°C (325°F/ Gas 3), for 4 hours, or 4–5 hours if from older deer. **Other cuts:** Preheat oven to 160°C (325°F/Gas 3). Brown meat, then braise/stew for 2–3 hours, or 3–4 hours if from **older animals**.
MINCE: All meats.	Preheat grill to high. Press mince on to skewers or form into patties. Brush with oil and grill, turning occasionally, for 8–10 mins.	Brown mince, then add liquid and simmer for 45 mins–1 hour. Or, form into patties and cook for 3–5 mins per side.	Not recommended.	Brown, then simmer, or braise at 160°C (325°F/Gas 3) for 1–2 hours.
WILD BOAR	Grill only young wild boar. Grill as venison.	Fry only young wild boar. Fry as venison.	Roast only young wild boar. Roast as venison.	Braise wild boar as venison from older deer.
HORSE AND KANGAROO	Grill as venison. Grill only young kangaroo.	Fry as venison. Fry only young kangaroo.	Roast only horse cuts or kangaroo joints if young, then roast as venison.	Braise as venison.
HARE	Not recommended.	Not recommended.	Hare saddle. Roast as venison bone-in joints.	Braise as venison bone-in joints.
RABBIT AND SQUIRREL	Grill only joints of domestic rabbit. Marinate in oil, then grill for 15–20 mins on a medium heat.	Fry only joints of domestic rabbit. Marinate in oil, then grill for 15–20 mins on a medium heat.	Roast saddle and legs from domestic rabbit; saddle only from wild rabbit. Brown joints in a frying pan, then roast at 220°C (425°F/Gas 7) for 5–10 mins. Rest for 5 mins before serving.	Immerse in liquid, then simmer very slowly for 1½–2½ hours, or until tender.
GUINEA PIG	Halve or spatchcock, then grill on a medium heat for 20–30 mins until juices run clear.	Halve or spatchcock, then fry slowly in a covered pan for 20–30 mins until juices run clear.	Stuff the cavity, then cover with butter or oil and roast at 200°C (400°F/Gas 6) for 30–40 mins; less if not stuffed.	Immerse in liquid, then very slowly simmer for 1½–2½ hours, or until tender.

RECIPE CHOOSERS

SLOW-COOKED

OSSO BUCO
page 287

POT ROAST SMOKED HAM
page 136

CHOLENT
page 92

CAJUN ANDOUILLE GUMBO
page 139

WILD BOAR CURRY
page 239

BRAISED SHIN OF BEEF IN RED WINE
page 177

HUNGARIAN GOULASH
page 113

TAJINE BIL MISHMISH
pages 200–201

VENETIAN DUCK RAGÙ
page 91

BRAISED OXTAIL WITH CLEMENTINE
page 286

PORK WITH CLAMS
page 114

DAUBE OF BEEF WITH PRUNES
page 155

ALSO TRY...

ROASTS

ROAST GROUSE
page 248

HERBY ROAST CHICKEN
page 80

MAPLE AND MUSTARD CRUSTED RIB OF BEEF
page 160

SLOW-COOKED PORK SHOULDER WITH CIDER GRAVY page 112

PARMA HAM-WRAPPED PORK TENDERLOIN page 121

TURDUCKEN
page 83

ROAST POUSSIN WITH PRESERVED LEMONS page 95

SCANDINAVIAN LEG OF MUTTON WITH HONEY MUSTARD AND ROOTS page 218

FAISAN NORMANDE
page 245

FIERY BEEF FILLET WITH ROASTED VEG
page 165

PORK BELLY PORCHETTA
page 127

RACK OF LAMB WITH CELERIAC GALETTES page 205

FRANGO PIRI PIRI
page 79

BAVARIAN ROAST PORK
page 110

FRIED

VEAL SCALOPPINE WITH SALSA VERDE
page 179

VEAL SCHNITZEL WITH FRIED EGG, CAPERS, AND PARSLEY page 180

FILLET STEAK WITH BLUE CHEESE SAUCE page 163

BUTTERMILK CHICKEN WITH BISCUITS
page 64

FRIKADELLER
page 109

VENISON STEAK WITH BLACKBERRIES
page 238

ON THE GRILL

CUBANO
page 137

DRY-RUBBED STEAK WITH CHIMICHURRI SAUCE page 159

LAMB KEBABS WITH YOGURT AND POMEGRANATE page 196

OSTRICH BURGERS
page 257

CAJUN-SPICED CHICKEN
page 74

CLASSIC BURGERS
page 153

MOROCCAN SKEWERED LIVERS AND HEARTS page 272

ALSO TRY

POULTRY

POULTRY

POULTRY IS ONE OF THE MOST UNIVERSALLY LOVED MEATS. DELICIOUS AND TENDER, IT READILY ABSORBS A RANGE OF FLAVOURS. THIS VERSATILITY, COUPLED WITH THE FACT THAT POULTRY IS EASY TO COOK AND RELATIVELY INEXPENSIVE, MEANS THAT IT IS ENJOYED IN EVERY COUNTRY OF THE WORLD.

SUCH POPULARITY MEANS that the demand for poultry of all sorts is enormous. Around the world, the production of chicken alone is approaching 100 million tonnes per year, and most of this comes from birds raised using a variety of intensive methods of production.

PRODUCTION METHODS

There are many different ways of rearing poultry. The main types of production are described below – although some of these methods overlap.

• **Domestic free-range** Domestic fowl are free to scratch about outside – sometimes in a yard, sometimes with access to fields and scrubland. With a varied diet and adequate exercise, their flesh has the best flavour and texture of

all. Most of these birds are reared for home consumption by their keepers, but a few are sold locally and are well worth seeking out. **Diet:** varied, but often includes concentrated feed or concentrates, (see opposite).

• **Commercial free-range** With fresh air and exercise, free-range birds grow slowly. The best systems for rearing chickens provide outdoor space with plenty of vegetation so that the birds can roam about and exhibit natural flock behaviour. A building is available for shade, shelter, and for protection at night. **Diet:** concentrates, plus vegetation.

• **Intensive free-range** These free-range birds go outside by day, but under such crowded conditions that, although they benefit from fresh air, their enclosures have little or no vegetation left. In the most intensive systems, large flocks are housed in huge, deep-litter sheds, with their access to outdoor conditions limited to one or two small exit doors that few birds ever find. **Diet:** concentrates.

• **Intensive deep-litter** Thousands of birds live in large, climate-controlled or ventilated sheds with no access to the outside. They are at liberty to walk about

AROUND THE WORLD, THE PRODUCTION OF CHICKEN ALONE IS APPROACHING 100 MILLION TONNES PER YEAR – MOST OF WHICH COMES FROM INTENSIVELY RAISED BIRDS.

and have perches to roost on, but conditions are crowded. Ammonia build-up from their droppings can cause the birds to develop health problems and deformities.
Diet: concentrates.

• **Caged production** Mostly restricted to egg-laying birds (or layers) – although birds bred for meat can be caged, too – these birds cannot fly or perch. Even walking about is difficult. While in some countries such very cramped conditions are outlawed, in other countries they still exist.
Diet: concentrates.

• **Organic poultry** There are many different organic production marks, but generally an organic label is likely to indicate low stocking densities under good, free-range conditions with organic feed. Many organic birds are also reared in intensive free-range units. The organic system works on the assumption that a well-managed flock will need little medical treatment, although drug use is still permitted.
Diet: organic concentrates, plus vegetation.

POULTRY FEED

All species of poultry are omnivores, except for ducks and geese, which are predominantly herbivores (vegetarians). Virtually all methods of poultry rearing use concentrated feed that contains proteins such as soya, grain, fishmeal, or animal protein. These feeds also contain vitamins and the necessary trace elements to keep the birds healthy (see pp12–13 for more about grain production and the seeds used in concentrated feed).

HEALTH AND SAFETY

In many countries, birds are fed growth promoters to speed up production. These can include antibiotics, growth hormones, and arsenic-containing chemicals. Some of these (growth hormones, in particular) are banned in some countries but still used in others.

Because of the risk of Salmonella and E. coli food poisoning from raw and undercooked poultry, it is always recommended that you cook poultry meat to an internal temperature of at least 75°C (165°F). Always wash equipment that you have used to handle raw poultry thoroughly in hot water. All poultry should be sold and stored properly chilled.

BUYING POULTRY

For poultry to be cheap, compromises have to be made. Production methods (see opposite) will affect the price. It is also common practice in the trade to inject poultry breasts with water, salts, and flavourings to make them cheap and appear plumper. Highly processed products made of reformed poultry, such as nuggets and sausages, often come from old laying hens – the most intensively raised birds – or from ground up bones, skin, and fat. Few of these facts will appear on packaging. Where good practices are kept, they will be promoted, so always check the label carefully before buying.

SPECIES AND BREEDS

Any poultry show will exhibit hundreds of different breeds, each having been bred for a specific purpose: egg-laying, meat production, dual-purpose, or even for fighting. Most commercial birds are hybrids, fine-tuned to thrive and be productive under very specific conditions.

• **Turkey** Modern turkeys are descended from the small, wild, Mexican turkey. Nowadays, they are industrially reared and far bigger than their ancestors, but there are also a number of premium free-range birds available, such as the bronze turkey, which has a better texture and flavour.

• **Chicken** Domestic chickens evolved from the Indian jungle fowl. Modern commercial chickens are hybrids, not breeds, but domestic chicken-keepers have kept alive many local heritage breeds such as the Dorking or Plymouth Rock. There are several different categories of chicken:

Broilers are about 12 weeks old and are reared for roasting.

Capons are castrated males that are fattened to produce tender, plump breasts.

Boiling fowl are older, often ex-laying, hens that need stewing but have an excellent flavour.

Poussin are young chickens sold at 4–6 weeks old, as are Cornish Game Hens, which are slightly larger; despite their name, they are neither game birds nor necessarily female.

• **Duck** Having been domesticated for more than 4,000 years, nowadays most ducks are intensively reared. Most breeds are descended from the wild mallard, with the most common being White Pekin and Aylesbury. The colourful Rouen duck grows more slowly, while the larger, leaner Muscovy is technically of the goose family.

• **Goose** Domestic breeds, such as the Toulouse goose, are descendants of the wild Greylag goose; Asian and African domestic geese are descended from the white Swan Goose. Geese are grass-eaters and rarely housed, so tend to be a seasonal treat. They may be fed on grain for short periods.

POULTRY CUTS

POULTRY MEAT IS ENDLESSLY VERSATILE with cuts for every dish; marinating adds extra flavour to grills and roasts. It should be plump and firm, without dry patches, tears or bruising. It should have a clean, fresh smell; if not, discard it as the meat will not be safe to eat.

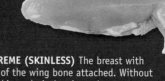

DRUMSTICK Rarely boned or skinned and less meaty than thighs, drumsticks are popular with children and also as finger food, especially when marinated or coated in a sauce.

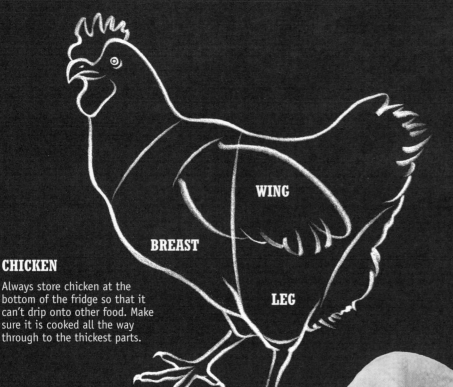

BREAST

WING

LEG

CHICKEN

Always store chicken at the bottom of the fridge so that it can't drip onto other food. Make sure it is cooked all the way through to the thickest parts.

SUPREME (SKINLESS) The breast with part of the wing bone attached. Without the skin and nicely trimmed, a supreme makes an elegant cutlet. It can be coated in breadcrumbs before frying.

WHOLE WING Made up of three parts. Most of the meat is on the breast end, so the bony tip is often removed. Great for buffalo wings, finger food or making stock.

BREAST FILLET Skinless breast is the leanest cut. However, the skin can be stuffed and keeps the meat moist. Breasts are grilled, steamed, baked, simmered, beaten into escalopes or stir-fried.

LEG QUARTER This is the whole leg plus a section of the backbone. It is a cheaper cut because of the high bone content. However, it makes tasty stews and can also be grilled and barbecued.

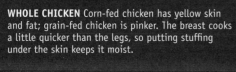

WHOLE CHICKEN Corn-fed chicken has yellow skin and fat; grain-fed chicken is pinker. The breast cooks a little quicker than the legs, so putting stuffing under the skin keeps it moist.

THIGH, SKIN-ON AND BONE-IN Thigh meat is dark and succulent and makes excellent casseroles as well as grills as the skin crisps nicely, keeping the meat moist. Thighs are also sold skinless and boneless.

DICED CHICKEN Lean and tender, diced chicken is useful for casseroles and kebabs for grilling, while strips and **GOUJONS** (the small fillet under the breast) are best for stir-frying.

TURKEY

Turkey meat is leaner than chicken. The average size of a turkey is 5.5kg (12lb); smaller birds are supplied outside the festive seasons.

WHOLE TURKEY The ultimate festive bird. Make sure it is at room temperature 1 hour before cooking.

TURKEY CROWN OR SADDLE The whole bird without legs and back, so easy to cook and to carve.

BONELESS TURKEY ROLL May be breast or leg meat, or a combination. A easy-to-carve joint.

MINCE Lean turkey mince can be used as a beef substitute for healthy eating.

POUSSIN

This is a young chicken sold at 4–6 weeks old. Because these birds are immature, there is a high proportion of bone to meat.

WHOLE Tender and succulent, these young birds have little fat, so brush them with oil.

SPATCHCOCKED Opened out and spatchcocked, poussin roast or grill very quickly and evenly.

GOOSE

The proportion of meat to bone is low, so goose is an expensive treat; however, the light fat is superb for frying and other cooking.

WHOLE GOOSE Prick the fat before cooking so that it drains off. Allow 650g (1½lb) per person.

GOOSE BREAST, SKIN-ON Cook with the skin downwards (upwards if under a grill) to keep meat moist.

DUCK

With all duck, the ratio of meat to fat and bone is low, but the meat is very tasty and rich. The fat is also sold separately for cooking.

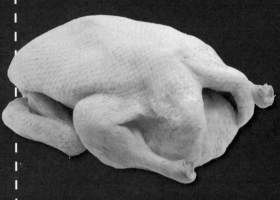

WHOLE DUCK The fat is delicious, but avoid birds with too much. Allow 650g (1½lb) per person.

WHOLE DUCK LEG Delicious grilled, roasted or made into confit. Score fat before cooking.

DUCK BREAST, SKIN-ON If the fat layer is very thick, score it before cooking, and fry fat-side down.

DUCK GOUJONS These are slices of the main breast muscle and are good for marinatimg and stir-frying.

PRESERVED POULTRY

PRESERVED POULTRY IS LESS COMMON than preserved meat, partly because of the dangers of contamination. However, where ducks and geese are produced in large numbers, a range of preserved products has evolved. Chinese cuisine also uses a number of fully or partly dried poultry products.

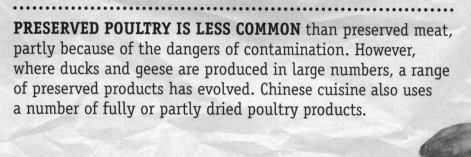

GUANGDONG SAUSAGES A salty sweetness characterizes these dried sausages from China, which are made from coarsely chopped duck or chicken. They are air-dried and usually steamed over rice, or sliced and stir-fried.

SAUCISSON SEC DE CANARD From the great duck-producing areas of France, this saucisson sec is well laced with duck fat. The flavour is best when the sausage is sliced paper-thin.

SALAME D'OCA Goose fat, liver, and fatty pork are stuffed into a skin or goose neck to make this Italian sausage. It is then dried and cooked. Soft and mottled pink, it is served with mostarda.

ALHEIRA DE BARROSO-MONTALEGRE A Portuguese sausage originally made by Jews from any white meat other than pork, alheira can be made from any kind of poultry flavoured with garlic. It is lightly smoked.

JAMBON DE CANARD AUX HERBES Thick strips of duck are rolled in herbs, bound with string and then immersed in dry salt until cured into a firm ham. The dark meat has an intense flavour.

CASSOULET A speciality of southwest France, cassoulet is a stew of beans studded with generous pieces of conserved duck or goose. The Toulouse version also includes sausage.

KIEŁBASA TORUNSKA From the medieval town of Torun in eastern Poland, this is a slim sausage, normally made with pork but sometimes with chicken instead. The traditional long loops are hot smoked.

Confit d'Oie
sous la graisse

MILHAC·OIE
EN PÉRIGORD

1 membre
=
2 parts

CONFIT D'OIE Joints of goose are dry-salted then very slowly cooked in their own fat. This is put into glass jars or tins and sealed to preserve it for many months.

MAGRET DE CANARD SECHÉ AU POIVRE Whole duck breasts are rubbed with cracked black peppercorns, then dry-salted and hung up to dry. The meat has a rich covering of fat on one side.

MAGRET DE CANARD AU FOIE GRAS Duck breasts are stuffed with a core of foie gras, then brined and air-dried. The creamy foie gras contrasts with the dark rich magret. This lightly preserved product has a limited shelf life once sliced open.

MAGRET DE CANARD FUMÉ Similar to the Italian prosciutto below, this French version is smoked after curing, which lends a complementary tartness to the rich duck fat.

PROSCIUTTO D'ANATRA Duck breasts are brined and air-dried until the meat is rich, dark, and powerfully flavoured with a succulent layer of fat.

PRESERVED **POULTRY** **59**

DEBONING A BIRD

Deboned poultry makes eye-catching dishes such as Turducken (see p83). Keep the knife edge tilted towards the bone to avoid cutting the meat. To sever the joints, bend the limb backwards until it cracks.

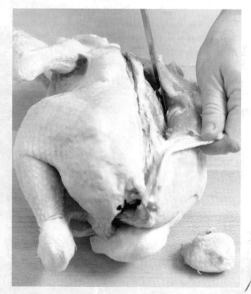

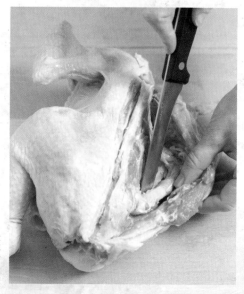

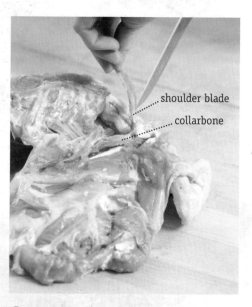

shoulder blade
collarbone

1 Turn the bird breast-side down. Cut off the Parson's nose. Then cut the skin along the backbone. Pulling the skin up and away from the carcass, scrape the meat off one side of the flat back part.

2 At the thigh joint, remove the meat around the ball and socket joint to expose it. Scrape off the meat from the thighbone. Sever the drumstick joint at the ball and socket joint and at the drumstick joint and remove the thighbone.

3 Moving up the bird, continue to scrape the meat off the ribcage and around the thin shoulder blade lying over it. This bone, the collarbone, the wing bone and wishbone all converge in one place.

wing bone

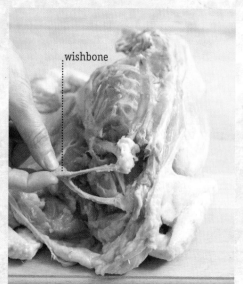

wishbone

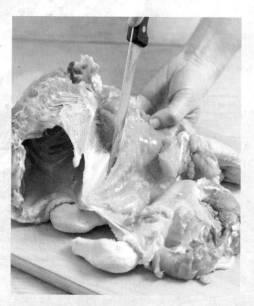

4 Sever the shoulder blade and collarbone from the wing bone, leaving the wing attached by the connecting flesh to the rest of the chicken. The wing bone will be removed later.

5 Scrape off the meat from around the wishbone, bend it backwards and remove it. Now repeat steps 1–5 with the other side of the bird.

6 Scrape the meat off either side of the breastbone. Keeping the knife close to the ridge of the bone, carefully cut off the boned meat, then remove the skeletal frame.

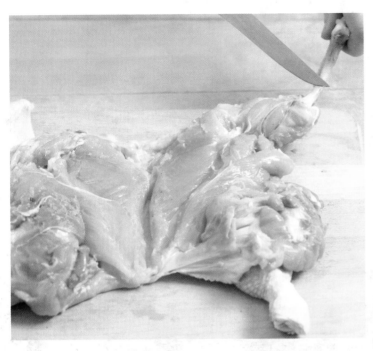

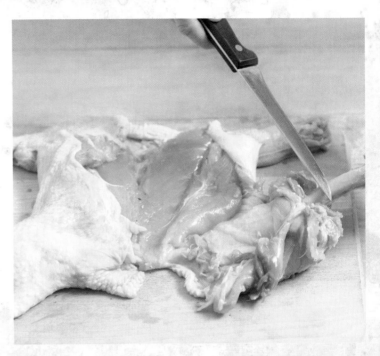

7 To remove the wing bone, cut off the wing tips. Scrape the meat off the bone inside the wing (accessing it either from the main carcass end, or the wing tip end) and pull out the bone.

8 To remove the remaining drumsticks in the legs, cut round the scaly end of the drumstick skin. Scrape the meat off the drumstick (accessing it as for the wing bone) and pull out the bone. The bird is now completely deboned. Cover and store in the fridge until ready to stuff or use in a recipe.

SPATCHCOCKING A BIRD

Spatchcocking involves flattening a bird (of any size) that is to be cooked on a grill or smoked on a barbecue. It avoids the risk of burning thinner parts while leaving thicker parts undercooked.

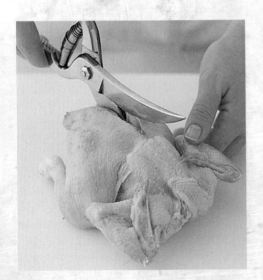

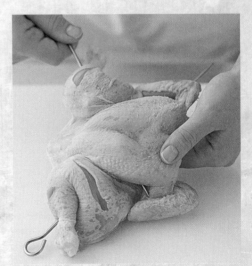

1 Turn the bird upside down. Using poultry shears, cut along one side of the backbone, then cut along the other side and remove the backbone completely. Open out the bird and turn it over.

2 Flatten the bird by pressing down sharply on the breast with the palms of your hands, making it as evenly flat as possible. Where the muscles are of different thicknesses, slash the plumpest parts to ensure even cooking.

3 Push a skewer diagonally through the drumstick, thigh, lower breast and wing as shown. Repeat with another skewer on the other side and press down again to ensure it is flat. If wished, marinate before cooking.

MATZO BALL SOUP

A simpler version of the traditional Passover dish, the matzo balls are judged to be good if they float in the broth.

 **Chicken stock**

SERVES 4–6
PREP 10 mins, plus chilling   **COOK** 1 hr

FOR THE MATZO BALLS

150g (5½oz) matzo meal

60ml (2fl oz) chicken stock

4 eggs

1 tsp baking powder

4 tbsp vegetable oil

salt and freshly ground black pepper

FOR THE BROTH

2 litres (3½ pints) chicken stock

150g (5½oz) carrots, thinly sliced into rounds

2 tbsp chopped dill

1 Mix the matzo meal, chicken stock, eggs, baking powder, vegetable oil, and salt and pepper in a bowl to make a batter. Stir well until fully combined. Cover with cling film and chill for 1 hour.

2 In a medium stock pot, combine the chicken stock, carrots, and dill. Bring to the boil, then reduce the heat to medium-high, and cook for 15 minutes.

3 Take the matzo batter out of the fridge. Using a spoon, form the batter into 6 even-sized balls, about the size of a lime. Drop the balls, one at a time, into the hot soup. Allow them to cook for 2–3 minutes, then use a spoon to flip the balls. Cover the pot, reduce the heat, and simmer for 30–40 minutes, until fully cooked and puffed. Serve hot.

NO PEEKING!

Keep the matzo balls firmly covered as they simmer – lifting the lid to peek inside may cause the balls to fall apart.

TANDOORI CHICKEN SAMOSAS

With roots in Northern India, these spiced meat pastries have been a favourite appetizer across the Middle East for centuries.

 **Cooked chicken**

SERVES 16–20
PREP 30 mins, plus chilling   **COOK** 35 mins

FOR THE DOUGH

300g (10oz) plain flour, plus extra for dusting

1 tbsp ground turmeric

1 tbsp curry powder

1 tsp salt

200g (7oz) vegetable fat

1 egg, beaten, to glaze

FOR THE FILLING

150g (5½oz) cooked chicken, shredded

300g (10oz) sweet potato, peeled and mashed

1 tbsp tandoori paste

250g (9oz) white onion, finely chopped

1 tbsp ground turmeric

1 tbsp curry powder

1 tbsp garam masala

3 garlic cloves, crushed

75g packet frozen peas

juice of 1 lemon

1 Sift the flour, spices, and salt in a large bowl. Rub in the fat until the texture resembles breadcrumbs. Stir 250ml (9fl oz) cold water into the flour mixture, a little at a time, until a loose ball of dough has formed. Wrap in cling film and chill for 1 hour.

2 For the filling, combine all the ingredients in a large bowl. Stir well, ensuring the chicken mixes evenly. Preheat the oven to 180°C (350°F/Gas 4) and line a baking sheet with baking parchment.

3 On a lightly floured surface, roll out the pastry as thinly as possible. Use a pastry knife to cut the pastry into 10cm (4in) wide strips. Cut the strips crossways into 10cm (4in) squares, then in half to make triangles. Place a tablespoon of filling in the centre of each, then bring the points of the triangle together, and use your fingers to pinch the sides closed. Repeat until all of the filling and pastry is used.

4 Place the samosas on the baking sheet and brush with the beaten egg. Bake the samosas in the oven for 30–35 minutes, or until golden brown. Cool slightly before serving.

CHICKEN JAMBALAYA

A traditional southern American dish from Louisiana, it combines the summer flavours of peppers, peas, and herbs with a little heat from the cayenne pepper.

THE CUT Chicken thigh and breast

SERVES 4–6
PREP 15–20 mins   **COOK** 1½ hrs

2 tbsp olive oil

salt and freshly ground black pepper

6 boneless chicken pieces (thighs and breasts), about 700g (1lb 8oz) in total, cut into large chunks

2 tbsp chopped oregano

2 tsp cayenne pepper

1 red onion, finely chopped

3 garlic cloves, finely chopped

1 green pepper, deseeded and finely chopped

1 red pepper, deseeded and finely chopped

200g (7oz) thick slices cooked ham, roughly chopped

900ml (1½ pints) hot chicken stock

175g (6oz) easy-cook, long-grain rice

140g (5oz) shelled fresh peas

small handful of coriander, finely chopped (optional)

1 Heat half the oil in a large, flameproof casserole or Dutch oven over a medium-high heat. Season the chicken pieces, toss them in the oregano and cayenne pepper, and add to the casserole. Do this in batches to avoid overcrowding the pan. Cook for 6–10 minutes until golden brown. Remove and set aside.

2 Heat the remaining oil in the casserole over a medium heat. Add the onion, garlic, and peppers and cook for 5–8 minutes, stirring, until soft. Return the chicken to the casserole and stir in the ham. Pour in the stock and bring to the boil. Then reduce to a simmer, season well, partially cover with the lid, and cook gently for about 40 minutes. Check occasionally and top up with a little hot water if it's drying out.

3 Stir in the rice, turning it so it absorbs all the stock, and cook for about 15 minutes or until the rice is cooked, topping up with more stock if necessary. Add the peas for the last 5 minutes.

4 Taste and and season, if needed, and stir in the coriander, if using. Serve with a green salad and plain yogurt or soured cream.

CHICKEN AND PESTO MEATBALLS

Pesto, with its fresh basil and nutty olive oil, adds a complex flavour to these moist meatballs.

THE CUT Minced chicken

SERVES 4
PREP 25 mins   **COOK** 45 mins

100g (3½oz) pine nuts

100g (3½oz) basil

3 garlic cloves

50g (1¾oz) freshly grated Parmesan

salt and freshly ground black pepper

5 tbsp olive oil

450g (1lb) minced chicken

150g (5½oz) breadcrumbs

1 egg

1 shallot, finely chopped

450g (1lb) packet dried penne pasta

1 In a dry frying pan, lightly toast the pine nuts until golden and set aside to cool. In a food processor, place the basil, garlic, Parmesan, pine nuts, and salt. Pulse to combine. Turn the processor on high and add 4 tablespoons of the oil in a thin drizzle, until a sauce is formed.

2 Preheat the oven to 180°C (350°F/Gas 4). Line a baking tray with baking parchment. In a large bowl, combine the chicken, breadcrumbs, egg, salt and pepper, shallot, and half of the pesto. Stir well to incorporate.

3 Form the chicken mixture into evenly sized balls, approximately 5cm (2in) in diameter. Place on the lined baking tray. Bake for 30–40 minutes, or until the meatballs turn golden.

4 Meanwhile, cook the pasta according to the packet instructions. Drain and toss in the remaining pesto along with the remaining oil. Top the pasta with the cooked meatballs and serve hot.

VARIATION

Beef meatballs Make beef meatballs by combining 450g (1lb) minced beef, 2 eggs, 50g (1¾oz) freshly grated Parmesan, 150g (5½oz) breadcrumbs, and 2 teaspoons each of dried oregano, basil, thyme, and rosemary. Season the mixture well, form into evenly sized balls, and bake as above. Serve the meatballs with shop-bought chunky tomato sauce.

MARINATED CHICKEN FAJITAS

A classic crowd pleaser, this Tex-Mex dish gets its name from the Mexican term for "little meat strips".

 **Chicken breast**

SERVES 3–4
PREP 15 mins, plus marinating **COOK** 15 mins

FOR THE MARINADE

2 tbsp olive oil

1 tbsp lime juice

2 tsp ground cumin

1 tsp smoked paprika, plus extra for the onions

1 tsp dried oregano

1 tsp cayenne pepper or chilli powder

salt and freshly ground black pepper

FOR THE FAJITAS

300g (10oz) skinless boneless chicken breasts, sliced

2 tbsp sunflower oil

1 red onion, cut into 1cm (½in) slices

1 red pepper, deseeded and cut into 1cm (½in) slices

1 yellow pepper, deseeded and cut into 1cm (½in) slices

8 tortillas

soured cream or plain yogurt, chilli sauce, guacamole, and classic tomato salsa, to serve

1 Place the chicken in a large bowl. Whisk together the marinade ingredients and pour over the chicken. Cover and chill in the fridge for at least 30 minutes, or up to 4 hours.

2 Preheat the grill on its highest setting. Grill the chicken slices for 3–5 minutes on each side, until golden and cooked, or chargrill for a smoky flavour.

3 Meanwhile, heat the sunflower oil in a large frying pan or wok over a high heat. Fry the onion and peppers for 5–7 minutes, or until cooked through and coloured on the edges. Season with a little salt and pepper, and smoked paprika.

4 Warm the tortillas in a microwave or a low oven, according to packet instructions. Divide the vegetables and the chicken into 8 equal portions. Place 1 portion of the vegetables on 1 tortilla, top with 1 portion of the chicken, and roll the tortillas to make the fajitas. Serve alongside a choice of soured cream, chilli sauce, guacamole, and tomato salsa.

BUTTERMILK CHICKEN WITH BISCUITS

This popular southern American dish is a delicious combination of hot, fried chicken and flaky, buttery biscuits or savoury scones.

 **Chicken breast**

SERVES 4
PREP 30 mins, plus overnight marinating
COOK 35–40 mins

FOR THE CHICKEN

4 skinless boneless chicken breasts, about 600g (1lb 5oz) in total

250ml (9fl oz) buttermilk

1 tbsp cayenne pepper, plus 1 tsp for the marinade

3 tsp salt, plus extra for the biscuits

oil, for frying

200g (7oz) fresh breadcrumbs

200g (7oz) self-raising flour

2 tsp chilli flakes

FOR THE BISCUITS

200g (7oz) plain flour, plus extra for dusting

½ tsp baking powder

1 tsp bicarbonate of soda

1 tsp cayenne pepper

6 tbsp vegetable fat

150ml (5fl oz) buttermilk

runny honey, or mayonnaise to serve (optional)

1 In a large bowl, combine the chicken breasts with the buttermilk, 1 teaspoon cayenne pepper, and 1 teaspoon salt. Cover with cling film and chill in the fridge overnight.

2 For the biscuits, sift the flour, baking powder, bicarbonate of soda, cayenne pepper, and a pinch of salt into a large bowl. Rub in the fat until the mixture resembles breadcrumbs. Then stir in the buttermilk, a little at a time, until a ball of dough is formed. Preheat the oven to 180°C (350°F/Gas 4).

3 On a lightly floured surface, roll out the pastry to 5mm (¼in) thickness. Fold the pastry in half and roll it out again. Repeat this process 3–4 times, then roll it out to 1cm (½in) thickness. Use a biscuit cutter to cut 10–12cm (4–5in) wide biscuits. Transfer to a baking sheet and bake in the oven for 15 minutes, or until raised and golden brown.

4 Meanwhile, heat the oil in a frying pan to 180°C (350°F). Combine the breadcrumbs, 100g (3½oz) flour, 1 teaspoon chilli flakes, ½ tablespoon cayenne pepper, and ½ teaspoon salt in a bowl. In a second bowl, combine the remaining flour, chilli flakes, cayenne pepper, and salt.

5 Remove the chicken breasts from the marinade. Dip each one first in the flour mixture, then in the marinade, and then the breadcrumb mixture. Shallow fry the chicken breasts for 7–8 minutes, flipping them over, if necessary, until golden brown and cooked through. Remove with a slotted spoon and drain on a plate lined with kitchen paper. Serve the chicken and biscuits alongside each other or in the form of a sandwich, with some runny honey or mayonnaise, if preferred.

VARIATION

Turkey sausage biscuits Combine 600g (1lb 5oz) turkey sausagemeat with 1 tablespoon chilli flakes and 50g (1¾oz) freshly ground Parmesan cheese. Season the mixture with salt and pepper and form into thick burger-like patties. Chill in the fridge for about 1 hour to help them retain their shape. Coat the patties in the breadcrumb and flour mixtures and fry as above. Serve the turkey with the buttermilk biscuits and runny honey.

PAD THAI

A popular Thai street food, this easy stir-fry is a delicious combination of savoury, mildly sour, and sweet flavours.

THE CUT Chicken breast

SERVES 8
PREP 15 mins **COOK** 15 mins

550g (1¼lb) medium or thick dry rice noodles

3 tbsp sunflower oil

4 eggs, lightly beaten

1 tsp shrimp paste (optional)

4 hot red chillies, deseeded and finely chopped

6 skinless boneless chicken breasts, about 900g (2lb) in total, cut into 5mm (¼in) slices

2 bunches of spring onions, finely chopped

splash of Thai fish sauce, such as nam pla

juice of 2 limes

2 tbsp demerara sugar

salt and freshly ground black pepper

300g (10oz) unsalted peanuts

handful of coriander leaves, finely chopped

lime wedges, to garnish

1 Place the noodles in a large bowl, cover with boiling water, and leave for 8 minutes, or until soft. Drain and set aside. Heat 1 tablespoon of the oil in a large wok over a high heat. Swirl it around the wok, pour in the beaten eggs, and tip the wok to spread them around. Cook the eggs for about 1 minute, or until they begin to just set, but don't let them set completely. Remove from the wok, chop, and set aside.

2 Add the remaining oil, shrimp paste (if using), and chillies to the wok, and stir to mix. Then add the chicken and stir vigorously for 5 minutes, or until cooked through and no longer pink. Add the spring onions, fish sauce, lime juice, and sugar, and toss well. Cook for 1–2 minutes, until the sugar has dissolved, then season well with salt and pepper. Return the chopped eggs to the wok.

3 Add the noodles to the wok and toss to coat with the sauce. Then add half the peanuts and half the coriander and toss again. Transfer to a large, shallow warmed serving bowl. Scatter over the remaining peanuts and coriander, garnish with lime wedges, and serve hot.

WALDORF CHICKEN SALAD

This contemporary take on a classic dish, with yogurt in the dressing for lightness, is a great way to use up leftover roast chicken.

THE CUT Chicken breast

SERVES 6
PREP 25–30 mins, plus chilling
COOK 25–35 mins

4 celery sticks

1 onion, quartered

1 carrot, quartered

10–12 black peppercorns

1 bouquet garni, made with 5–6 sprigs of flat-leaf parsley, 2–3 sprigs of thyme, and 1 bay leaf

salt and freshly ground black pepper

750g (1lb 10oz) skinless chicken breasts

125g (4½oz) walnuts

500g (1lb 2oz) tart, crisp apples

juice of 1 lemon

175ml (6fl oz) plain yogurt

175ml (6fl oz) mayonnaise

1 Trim the tops from the celery. Place the trimmings and sticks in a wide saucepan. Add the onion, carrot, peppercorns, and bouquet garni. Season with salt and bring to the boil. Then reduce the heat to a simmer and cook for 10–15 minutes. Add the chicken and cook for a further 10–12 minutes, turning once, until the juices run clear when the meat is pierced at its thickest point.

2 Remove from the heat and leave the chicken to cool in the poaching liquid for 10–15 minutes, then drain on kitchen paper. Use a fork to shred the chicken into slivers about 5cm (2in) long.

3 Preheat the oven to 180°C (350°F/Gas 4). Spread the walnuts on a baking sheet and bake for 5–8 minutes until crisp, turning occasionally.

4 Meanwhile, take the celery sticks out of the poaching liquid and slice them. Set aside. Cut the top and bottom ends from the apples. Halve and core them, then dice the flesh. Place in a large bowl, pour the lemon juice over, and toss to coat.

5 Add the chicken, celery, yogurt, mayonnaise, and two-thirds of the walnuts. Season, stir to combine, and chill for 1 hour. Roughly chop the remaining walnuts. Spoon the salad onto 6 plates, sprinkle the chopped nuts on top, and serve.

CHICKEN PARMESAN

Nothing says classic comfort food like parmesan breaded chicken, aromatic sauce, and melted mozzarella.

THECUT Chicken breast

SERVES 4–6
PREP 30 mins   **COOK** 1 hr 40 mins

1kg (2¼lb) skinless chicken breasts

75g (2½oz) plain flour

2 tsp garlic powder

1 tsp white pepper

75g (2½oz) breadcrumbs

100g (3½oz) freshly grated Parmesan, plus 30g (1oz) extra for the topping

2 eggs, beaten with 1–2 tbsp water

3 tbsp olive oil, for frying

200g (7oz) mozzarella cheese, cut into slices

FOR THE SAUCE

1 tbsp olive oil

150g (5½oz) onion, diced

3 garlic cloves, crushed

800g (1¾lb) tomatoes, diced

250ml (9fl oz) chicken stock

1 tbsp rosemary

1 tsp basil

1 tsp dried oregano

1 tsp dried thyme

salt and freshly ground black pepper

1 For the sauce, heat the oil in a large saucepan over a medium heat. Add the onion and garlic and cook for 5 minutes, stirring, until caramelized. Add the remaining ingredients, season to taste, and reduce the heat to a simmer. Cook for 45 minutes, stirring occasionally. Taste and season, if necessary.

2 Place the chicken between two pieces of cling film and flatten with a meat tenderizer or rolling pin. Mix the flour, half the seasonings, and 1 teaspoon salt in a shallow dish. Combine the breadcrumbs, Parmesan, and remaining seasoning in a second dish. Place the beaten eggs in a small bowl. Heat the oil in a heavy-based pan. Dust the chicken with the flour mixture, dip in the beaten eggs, then coat with the breadcrumb mixture. Fry the chicken for 4 minutes on each side.

3 Set the grill to its highest setting. Transfer the sauce to a casserole and add the chicken, partially covering it with sauce. Top with both lots of cheese and grill for 15 minutes, or until the mozzarella is bubbling. Serve hot over pasta.

JAMAICAN JERK CHICKEN

Serve this spicy chicken with mango salsa, Jamaican rice, and peas for a truly Caribbean feast.

THECUT Chicken drumstick and thigh

SERVES 4
PREP 10 mins, plus marinating
COOK 30–40 mins

4 spring onions, roughly chopped

1 garlic clove, chopped

2cm (¾in) piece of fresh root ginger, finely chopped

1 red chilli, deseeded and finely chopped,

4 tbsp sunflower oil

2 tbsp soy sauce

1 tbsp cider vinegar

juice and finely grated zest of ½ lime

½ tsp dried thyme

½ tsp ground allspice

¼ tsp ground nutmeg

¼ tsp ground cinnamon

1 tbsp soft, dark brown sugar

salt and freshly ground black pepper

8 skin-on bone-in chicken drumsticks, or thighs

1 For the sauce, place all the ingredients except the chicken in a food processor and season well. Pulse to a thick, smooth sauce, scraping down the sides with a spatula during the process. Transfer to a large bowl.

2 Cut 2–3 slashes on each side of the chicken pieces, where the meat is thickest. Add to the sauce, and mix to coat. Cover and marinate in the fridge for at least 2 hours, turning over once halfway through to ensure they are evenly coated.

3 Set the barbecue or grill to its medium setting. Grill the chicken – 30 minutes for drumsticks, 40 minutes for thighs – turning over frequently, and basting with the leftover jerk sauce as it cooks.

4 The meat will separate slightly where it has been slashed, which enables it to cook right through and gives a bigger surface area for the sauce. The chicken is cooked through if the juices run clear when the meat is pierced at its thickest point.

CHICKEN ADOBO

This celebrated Filipino dish brings together the saltiness of soy sauce, the tang of vinegar, and the fragrance of bay leaf.

THE CUT Chicken thigh

SERVES 8
PREP 20 mins   **COOK** 1 hr

1 tbsp olive oil

1.5kg (3lb 3oz) skin-on bone-in chicken thighs

500g (1lb 2oz) white onion, sliced into rings

4 garlic cloves, crushed

1 tbsp freshly ground black pepper

1 tbsp arrowroot

125ml (4¼fl oz) white wine vinegar

125ml (4¼fl oz) soy sauce

juice of 3 limes

1 bay leaf

1 Heat the oil in a saucepan. Add the chicken and cook for about 5–6 minutes on each side, until well-browned all over. Do this in batches to avoid overcrowding the pan. Remove with a slotted spoon and set aside.

2 Add the onions, garlic, pepper, and arrowroot to the pan. Toss to coat the onions. Then return the chicken to the pan. Pour in the vinegar, soy sauce, and lime juice, and add the bay leaf.

3 Reduce the heat to a simmer and cook uncovered for 45 minutes, or until the chicken has cooked through. Remove the bay leaf. Serve hot spooned over white rice.

CHICKEN AND DATE EMPANADAS

First mentioned in a 16th-century Catalan cookbook, empanadas have since become popular across the globe. The chipotle paste in this recipe is an American influence.

THE CUT Chicken thigh

MAKES 10–12
PREP 40 mins, plus chilling   **COOK** 1 hr 20 mins

FOR THE PASTRY

300g (10oz) plain flour, plus extra for dusting

1 tbsp cayenne pepper

salt

100g (3½oz) vegetable fat

200g (7oz) butter, chilled and diced

1 egg, beaten to glaze

FOR THE FILLING

750g (1lb 10oz) skin-on bone-in chicken thighs

2 tbsp olive oil, plus extra for greasing

100g (3½oz) dried dates, finely chopped

100g (3½oz) honey

½ tbsp cayenne pepper

½ tbsp chipotle paste

½ tbsp ground cinnamon

1 For the pastry, sift the flour, cayenne pepper, and half a teaspoon of salt into a large bowl. Rub in the fat and butter until the mixture resembles breadcrumbs.

2 Preheat the oven to 180°C (350°F/Gas 4). Stir 250ml (9fl oz) water into the flour mixture, a little at a time, until a loose ball of dough has formed. Wrap in cling film and chill for 1 hour.

3 For the filling, place the chicken thighs on a baking tray and drizzle with oil. Roast in the oven for 35–40 minutes, or until cooked through. Remove from the oven and let cool. Leave the oven on and lightly grease a baking sheet with oil.

4 Remove the skin and bones from the chicken, lightly shred the meat with a fork, and transfer it to a bowl. Add the dates, honey, and spices to the chicken. Season with salt and stir to combine.

5 On a lightly floured surface, roll out the pastry to a thickness of 5mm (¼in). Use a biscuit cutter to cut 10–12 circles, about 10cm (4in) in diameter. Place 1 tablespoon of the filling in the middle of each circle and fold the pastry over to create a semicircle. Dampen the edges with a little water and press them together to seal.

6 Place the empanadas on the baking sheet and brush with the beaten egg. Bake for 35–40 minutes, or until golden brown. Arrange on a plate and serve hot.

CHICKEN TAJINE

An easy-to-make North African dish, this crowd-pleaser shines with the flavour of the preserved lemon.

THE CUT Chicken thigh

SERVES 4
PREP 10 mins   **COOK** 2 hrs 15 mins

2 tbsp olive oil

1.5kg (3lb 3oz) skin-on bone-in chicken thighs

2 garlic cloves, crushed

300g (10oz) white onions, sliced into thick rings

2 tbsp ground turmeric

2 tbsp curry powder

1 tbsp paprika

1 tbsp mustard powder

1 tbsp ground cinnamon

salt and freshly ground black pepper

100g (3½oz) black olives

1 preserved lemon, sliced

500ml (16fl oz) chicken stock

1 Heat the oil in a tagine, flameproof casserole, or Dutch oven. Add the chicken and cook for about 5–6 minutes on each side, until well-browned all over. Do this in batches to avoid overcrowding the pan. Remove with a slotted spoon and set aside.

2 Add the garlic to the pot and sauté for 5 minutes, until browned. Then add the onions and spices and season to taste. Toss to coat the onions. Spread the onions evenly over the bottom of the pot.

3 Place the chicken on top of the onions along with the olives and preserved lemons. Then pour in the stock and bring to the boil.

4 Reduce the heat to a simmer, cover, and cook for 2 hours. Check the sauce occasionally, making sure it does not get too dry or stick to the pot. Add more stock, if necessary. Remove from the heat and serve hot with couscous.

COQ AU VIN

A classic French dish, this makes a comforting winter meal. The alcohol cooks off, leaving only a rich taste.

THE CUT Chicken thigh or drumstick

SERVES 4
PREP 10 mins **COOK** 1 hr 10 mins

4 tbsp olive oil

100g (3½oz) bacon lardons

150g (5½oz) small button mushrooms, rinsed, dried, and halved, if necessary

12 small pickling onions or shallots

4 tbsp plain flour

salt and freshly ground black pepper

8 skin-on bone-in chicken thighs, drumsticks, or a mixture, about 1kg (2¼lb) in total

4 tbsp brandy (optional)

300ml (10fl oz) red wine

300ml (10fl oz) chicken stock

1 tbsp redcurrant jelly

bunch of bouquet garni

1 Heat 2 tablespoons of oil in a large, lidded saucepan over a medium heat. Fry the bacon, mushrooms, and onions for 5 minutes, until golden brown. Remove from the heat.

2 Heat the remaining oil in a separate pan. Place 1 tablespoon of the flour in a small bowl and season with salt and pepper. Dust the chicken with the flour, shaking off any excess. Fry the chicken for 3–5 minutes, on each side, until golden brown. Do this in batches to avoid overcrowding the pan. Remove from the heat, add the brandy (if using), and ignite with a match to cook off the alcohol.

3 Remove the chicken from the pan and add to the vegetables and bacon. Stir in the remaining flour and cook for 1 minute. Add the wine, stock, redcurrant jelly, and bouquet garni. Return to the heat and bring to the boil. Then reduce to a simmer, cover, and cook for 40–45 minutes, until cooked through. Remove the bouquet garni and serve hot.

ONE-POT SPANISH CHICKEN WITH RICE

Also known as "arroz con pollo", this hassle-free recipe is packed with warm spicy flavour and is the perfect one-pot meal.

THE CUT Chicken thigh

SERVES 4–6
PREP 20 mins **COOK** 1 hr

4 tbsp olive oil

1 heaped tbsp plain flour

salt and freshly ground black pepper

2 tsp smoked paprika, plus extra for dusting

8 skinless boneless chicken thighs, about 650g (1lb 7oz) in total, cut into bite-sized pieces

1 onion, finely chopped

1 red pepper, deseeded and cut into 2cm (¾in) cubes

1 orange pepper, deseeded and cut into 2cm (¾in) cubes

200g (7oz) cooking chorizo, casing removed and cut into 3cm (1in) slices

2 garlic cloves, chopped

½ tsp cayenne pepper (optional)

800ml (1½ pints) chicken stock

3 heaped tbsp chopped flat-leaf parsley

300g (10oz) long-grain or basmati white rice

75g (2½oz) frozen peas

1 tbsp butter

1 Heat 2 tablespoons of the oil in a large, lidded, heavy-based saucepan. Season the flour with salt, pepper, and a little smoked paprika to taste. Dust the chicken evenly with the flour, shaking off any excess. Fry the chicken for 2–3 minutes on each side over a medium heat, until golden brown all over. Do this in batches to avoid overcrowding the pan. Set aside and keep warm.

2 Heat the remaining oil in the pan and cook the onion and peppers for 3–5 minutes, until softened and turning brown. Add the chorizo and cook for 1–2 minutes, until beginning to turn crisp at the edges. Add the garlic, smoked paprika, and cayenne pepper (if using) and cook for 1 minute, until fragrant.

3 Add the stock and scrape up the meaty residue from the pan. Return the chicken to the pan, add two-thirds of the parsley, and bring to the boil. Reduce to a simmer, cover, and cook for 10 minutes.

4 Add the rice and stir well. Cover and cook over a very low heat for about 15 minutes, until the rice has cooked and absorbed most of the liquid. Stir in the peas, butter, and remaining parsley. Remove from the heat and leave to rest, with the lid on, for 5 minutes. Serve warm.

SOUTHERN FRIED CHICKEN

The trick for keeping this dish crisp, light, and juicy is to maintain the oil at the correct temperature.

 Chicken thigh and leg

SERVES 4
PREP 20 mins   **COOK** 15 mins

500ml (16fl oz) buttermilk

1 tbsp hot chilli sauce

8 skin-on, bone-in chicken legs and small thighs

150g (5½oz) self-raising flour

25g (scant 1oz) cornflour

1 tsp salt

1 tsp garlic powder

1 tsp cayenne pepper

1 tsp paprika

1 tsp black pepper

1 litre (1¾ pints) peanut or sunflower oil, for frying

1 Whisk together the buttermilk and hot chilli sauce, and season well. Put the chicken pieces into a dish in a single layer and pour the buttermilk over them. Cover the dish in cling film and chill for at least 4 hours, or preferably overnight.

2 When you are ready to cook the chicken, put all the dry ingredients together in a large plastic bag and shake well to combine. Take the chicken pieces out of the buttermilk mixture and shake off any excess. Put the chicken pieces into the bag, one at a time, and shake until they are well covered with the coating. Lay them on a wire rack as you work, and allow them to rest for 30 minutes at room temperature (this will help the coating to stick during frying).

3 In a large, heavy-based saucepan or deep-fat fryer, heat the oil to 190ºC (375ºF) and carefully lower the chicken pieces into the oil, without overcrowding the pan. Cook for 5–7 minutes on each side (depending on the size of the pieces), turning them over occasionally so that they brown evenly. The temperature of the oil will dip when the chicken is added, and should be maintained at 150–160ºC (300–325ºF). The chicken is ready if the juices run clear when a skewer is inserted into the thickest part of the meat.

4 Remove the chicken pieces from the pan with a slotted spoon and drain well on kitchen paper. If you are cooking in more than one batch, keep the fried chicken warm in the oven at 150ºC (300ºF/ Gas 2) while you cook the remaining pieces.

KARAHI CHICKEN

This relatively simple dry curry from North India gets its name from the wok, or "karahi", in which it is traditionally prepared.

 Chicken thigh

SERVES 4
PREP 15 mins   **COOK** 1 hr

1 tsp coriander seeds

2 green chillies, deseeded

3 garlic cloves

1 tsp ground turmeric

2 tbsp sunflower oil

salt and freshly ground black pepper

8 skin-on chicken thighs, about 1kg (2¼lb) in total, slashed crossways

1 onion, roughly chopped

6 tomatoes, roughly chopped

900ml (1½ pints) hot vegetable stock

5cm (2in) piece of fresh root ginger, peeled and finely chopped

3–4 green bird's eye chillies

bunch of coriander leaves, finely chopped

1 Place the coriander seeds, green chillies, garlic, turmeric, and 1 tablespoon of the oil in a food processor and pulse to a paste. Season the chicken and coat with the spice paste, pushing it into the cuts. Heat half the remaining oil in a large flameproof casserole over a medium-high heat. Add the chicken and cook for 5–6 minutes on each side, or until it begins to colour. Remove the chicken from the casserole and set aside.

2 Heat the remaining oil in the casserole over a medium heat. Add the onion and cook for 3–4 minutes, until softened. Add the tomatoes and cook for a further 5–10 minutes, until soft. Pour in the stock and bring to the boil. Reduce to a simmer, stir in the ginger and bird's eye chillies, and return the chicken to the casserole.

3 Cover and cook gently for 30–40 minutes. Check the sauce occasionally to make sure it does not get too dry or stick to the bottom, adding a little hot water, if necessary. Remove the bird's eye chillies, season to taste as necessary, and stir in the coriander. Serve with rice or chapatis, and some minted yogurt on the side.

VARIATION

Karahi rabbit Use a whole rabbit, jointed into 8 pieces, instead of the chicken thighs. For the spice paste, add 1 teaspoon toasted cumin seeds and ¼ teaspoon ground cloves to the other spices, then pulse in a food processor. In step 2, add 2 diced red peppers with the tomatoes, and cook as above.

BUFFALO CHICKEN WINGS

Hailing from Buffalo, New York, these sweet and spicy chicken wings are easy to prepare and make excellent finger food, served with a traditional salty blue cheese dressing.

THE CUT Chicken wings

SERVES 6
PREP 20–30 mins, plus chilling
COOK 40–50 mins

130g (4¾oz) plain flour

150g (5½oz) breadcrumbs

1 tsp paprika

½ tsp cayenne pepper

½ tsp salt

500ml (16fl oz) buttermilk

24 bone-in chicken wings

1 litre (1¾ pints) groundnut or sunflower oil, for frying

FOR THE SAUCE

250ml (9fl oz) hot chilli sauce

2 garlic cloves, chopped

2 tbsp honey

115g (4oz) butter

FOR THE DRESSING

50g (1¾oz) mayonnaise

100g (3½oz) soured cream

90ml (3fl oz) buttermilk

115g (4oz) blue cheese, crumbled

30ml (1fl oz) cider vinegar

MAKE YOUR OWN

Instead of using shop-bought buttermilk, you can make it at home by combining 1 tablespoon of lemon juice or vinegar with 250ml (9fl oz) of semi-skimmed milk. Let it stand for 10 minutes before using.

1 Place the flour, breadcrumbs, paprika, cayenne pepper, and salt in a large bowl and mix to combine. Place the buttermilk in a separate bowl. Dip the chicken wings in the buttermilk. Then toss them in the flour mixture, making sure each one is evenly coated, and shaking off any excess. Chill the coated chicken wings in the fridge for at least 1 hour.

2 Meanwhile, for the sauce, place the hot chilli sauce, garlic, honey, and butter in a saucepan over a low heat. Let the butter melt, then reduce the heat to a simmer and cook for about 5 minutes. Remove from the heat, set aside, and keep warm.

3 Heat the oil in a large, heavy-based saucepan or deep-fat fryer to 190°C (375°F). Fry the chicken wings in the oil, for 8–10 minutes, or until golden brown all over. Do this in batches of 4–5 wings to avoid overcrowding the pan. Remove the chicken wings from the pan with a slotted spoon and place on a plate.

4 Dip the chicken wings in the sauce mixture. Turn them through the mixture to ensure that they are evenly coated on all sides. Place on a wire rack to cool. For the dressing, place all the ingredients in a food processor and pulse until combined. Serve the dressing in a small bowl along with the chicken wings.

CAJUN-SPICED CHICKEN

This sweet, spicy marinade is delicious and versatile – it can be used in the oven, on the barbecue, and even on the grill.

THE CUT Chicken thigh or drumstick

SERVES 4
PREP 10 mins, plus marinating
COOK 40–45 mins

2 tbsp olive oil

2 tsp light brown sugar

2 tsp paprika

½–1 tsp cayenne pepper or chilli powder, to taste

1 tsp ground cumin

1 tsp dried thyme

1 tsp ground coriander

salt and freshly ground black pepper

8 skin-on bone-in chicken thighs or drumsticks

1 Place all the ingredients, except the chicken, in a large bowl and mix well.

2 Add the chicken to the marinade and mix to coat. Cover and chill in the fridge for at least 1 hour, or preferably up to 4 hours.

3 Preheat the oven to 200°C (400°F/Gas 6). Arrange the chicken on a roasting tray, spaced well apart and in a single layer.

4 Place the roasting tray in the oven and cook for 40–45 minutes, turning occasionally, until the chicken is golden brown and cooked through. Place on a warm plate and serve with rice or sautéed vegetables.

CHICKEN CACCIATORE

Italian for "hunter-style chicken", this dish is traditionally served with polenta to soak up the juices.

THE CUT Chicken leg

SERVES 4
PREP 20 mins   **COOK** 35–40 mins

1.5kg (3lb 3oz) chicken legs, trimmed

salt and freshly ground black pepper

2 tbsp olive oil

2 garlic cloves, sliced

1 onion, chopped

200ml (7fl oz) dry white wine

1 celery stalk, chopped

200g (7oz) button mushrooms, sliced

400g can chopped tomatoes

150ml (5fl oz) chicken stock

1 tbsp tomato purée

2 tsp chopped rosemary

2 tsp chopped sage

8 black olives, pitted and halved

1 Season the chicken with salt and pepper. Heat half the oil in a large, heavy-based frying pan. Add the chicken legs and fry until well-browned on all sides. Do this in batches to avoid overcrowding the pan. Remove with a slotted spoon, place on a plate lined with kitchen paper, and keep hot.

2 Drain off the excess fat and add the remaining oil to the pan. Add the garlic and onion and fry for 3–4 minutes, until soft but not brown. Then add the wine and boil for 1 minute.

3 Add the celery, mushrooms, tomatoes, stock, purée, rosemary, and sage. Stir to mix and reduce the heat to low. Return the chicken to the pan, cover, and cook for 30 minutes, or until the chicken is cooked through.

4 Then add the olives and cook, uncovered, for a further 5–10 minutes. Remove from the heat and serve hot with soft polenta and a salad of fresh mixed leaves.

CHICKEN TIKKA MASALA

An Indian dish that is loved across the world. The combination of garam masala, tomatoes, fresh coriander, and cream gives the sauce a sweet and spicy flavour.

THE CUT Whole chicken

SERVES 6
PREP 20 mins   **COOK** 1 hr 40 mins

1 chicken, about 1.8kg (4lb)

285g (9³⁄₄oz) plain yogurt

2 tbsp ground coriander

1 tbsp salt

FOR THE SAUCE

2 tbsp ghee or clarified butter

2 tbsp garam masala

1 tbsp curry powder

1 tbsp ground turmeric

1 tsp ground cumin

1 tsp cayenne pepper

1 tsp ground ginger

1 tsp ground coriander

500g (1lb 2oz) white onion, diced

4 garlic cloves, crushed

4 x 400g can diced tomatoes, with juices

250ml (9fl oz) double cream

200g (7oz) chopped coriander leaves, to garnish

1 Preheat the oven to 180°C (350°F/Gas 4). Coat the chicken with the yogurt. Place it on a baking tray and sprinkle with the coriander and salt. Transfer to the oven and roast for 1¹⁄₂ hours, or until the internal temperature reaches 75°C (165°F).

2 Meanwhile, combine the ghee and spices in a large saucepan over a medium heat. Cook, stirring constantly, for 1–2 minutes, or until the spices and ghee have browned. Stir in the onions and garlic, cover, and cook for 5–7 minutes, until the onions have softened. Then add the tomatoes and juices and bring to the boil. Reduce the heat and simmer for 45 minutes, stirring occasionally.

3 Remove the chicken from the oven and leave to cool slightly. Remove the skin and bones and, using a fork, lightly shred the meat. Add the shredded chicken into the sauce and stir well. Then add the double cream and simmer for a further 5–7 minutes. Remove from the heat. To serve, garnish with the chopped coriander and serve hot with basmati rice.

LOCRO DE PAPAS

Variations of this rich and hearty potato soup are found throughout the Andes mountains of South America.

THE CUT Whole chicken

SERVES 6
PREP 15 mins
COOK 1 hr 45 mins – 2 hrs 15 mins

1.5kg (3lb 3oz) waxy white potato, such as Cara or Maris Piper, peeled

1 chicken, about 1.8kg (4lb)

6 garlic cloves, crushed

1 tbsp olive oil

500g (1lb 2oz) onion, chopped

2 tsp dried oregano

1 tsp chilli flakes

500g (1lb 2oz) corn kernels

250ml (9fl oz) whole milk

salt and freshly ground black pepper

200g (7oz) queso fresco or feta cheese

1 Chop 500g (1lb 2oz) of the potatoes in half and set aside. Place the chicken in a large stock pot, add just enough water to cover the meat, and bring to the boil.

2 Add one-third of the garlic and the chopped potatoes to the pot, and reduce the heat to a simmer. Cover and cook for 45 minutes, or until the chicken is cooked through.

3 Remove the chicken, along with the garlic and potatoes, from the pot. Discard the skin and bones and use a fork to shred the meat gently. Return the shredded meat to the pot.

4 Cut the remaining potatoes into cubes. Heat the oil in a frying pan, add the onions and remaining garlic, and sauté for 5–7 minutes. Stir in the potato cubes, oregano, and chilli flakes, and cook for 3–5 minutes, until they turn brown. Then add the corn, stir well, and remove from the heat.

5 Transfer the potato and corn mixture to the stock pot, stir in the milk, and season. Bring to the boil, then reduce the heat and simmer for 35–40 minutes, or until the potatoes are soft. Stir in the queso fresco and cook for another 10 minutes. Remove from the heat, spoon into bowls, and serve hot.

POULE AU POT

Literally meaning "chicken in a pot", this classic French dish served with sauce gribiche, a cold-egg sauce, is a complete meal in itself.

THE CUT Whole chicken

SERVES 4–6
PREP 20 mins   **COOK** 1–1½ hrs

1 onion, trimmed

1 clove

1 chicken, about 2kg (4½lb)

salt and freshly ground black pepper

1 bouquet garni

4 litres (7 pints) chicken stock, plus extra if needed

1kg (2¼lb) leeks, trimmed, cut lengthways, and sliced

375g (13oz) carrots, sliced

375g (13oz) turnips, diced

60g (2oz) vermicelli

FOR THE SAUCE GRIBICHE

2 hard-boiled eggs, shelled

juice of ½ lemon

1 tsp Dijon mustard

2 tbsp dry white wine

250ml (9fl oz) vegetable oil

1 tbsp drained capers, finely chopped

3 gherkins, finely chopped

5–7 sprigs of flat-leaf parsley, finely chopped

small bunch of chives, finely snipped

1 Stud the onion with the clove. Place the chicken in a casserole, season, and add the bouquet garni and onion. Add just enough stock to cover three-quarters of the chicken. Bring to the boil, cover, and simmer for 45 minutes.

2 Wrap the leeks in muslin and tie securely to make a bundle. Repeat with the carrots and turnips in separate muslin. Add to the chicken and pour in more stock to cover. Cover and simmer for 25–30 minutes.

3 For the sauce, separate the hard-boiled yolks from the whites. Cut the whites into strips and chop finely. Sieve the yolks into a bowl using the back of a spoon. Add the lemon juice, mustard, wine, and seasoning and whisk until combined. Gradually pour in the oil, whisking constantly. Add the egg whites, capers, gherkins, and herbs, and whisk to combine.

4 Remove the chicken from the casserole. Carve the chicken, cover the pieces with foil, and keep warm. Remove the vegetables from the broth and keep warm. Strain the broth into a pan and simmer for 10–20 minutes. Skim off the fat and adjust the seasoning. Add the vermicelli and cook according to packet instructions.

5 Unwrap the vegetables, discarding the muslin, and add them and the chicken to the broth. Stir and remove from the heat. Serve in bowls with the sauce gribiche in a separate bowl.

TOM KHA GAI

This authentic Thai soup is full of herbs and spices, with the whole chicken making a rich and flavoursome base.

THE CUT Whole chicken

SERVES 6
PREP 10 mins   **COOK** 3 hrs

1 chicken, about 1.8kg (4lb)

1 turnip, halved

2.5cm (1in) piece of fresh root ginger, peeled

1 tbsp red curry paste

juice of 2 limes

2 tbsp Thai fish sauce

40g (1½oz) galangal or fresh root ginger, sliced into rounds

200g (7oz) straw, oyster, or white button mushrooms, thickly sliced

2 shallots, sliced into rings

3 lemongrass stalks, chopped

2–3 bird's eye chillies, deseeded and diced

6 makrut lime leaves, finely chopped

600ml (1 pint) coconut milk

50g (1¾oz) coriander leaves, roughly chopped

salt and freshly ground black pepper

1 Place the chicken in a large stock pot, cover with water, and bring to the boil. Add the turnip and ginger and reduce the heat. Cover and simmer for 2 hours, or until the chicken is fully cooked.

2 Remove from the heat, take the chicken out of the pot, and discard the turnip and ginger. Discard the skin and bones and lightly shred the meat using a fork. Return the shredded meat to the broth.

3 Add the curry paste, lime juice, fish sauce, galangal, mushrooms, shallots, lemongrass, chillies, and makrut lime leaves to the broth and bring to the boil.

4 Reduce the heat to a simmer and stir in the coconut milk. Simmer for 45 minutes, stirring occasionally. Stir in the coriander and season to taste. Ladle into soup bowls and serve hot.

VARIATION

Shredded chicken and rice soup Cook as above but add 200g (7oz) rice to the soup for the last 15 minutes of cooking. Serve hot.

POT-ROAST CHICKEN

A simple one-pot meal, this dish makes for a succulent and tender variation to the traditional roast.

CUT Whole chicken

SERVES 4
PREP 10 mins   **COOK** 1 hr 45 mins

2 tbsp olive oil

1 large onion, cut into 8 wedges

1 leek, cut into 3cm (1¼in) pieces

1 celery stick, cut into 3cm (1¼in) pieces

4 carrots, cut into 3cm (1in) pieces

2 garlic cloves, roughly chopped

8 skin-on new potatoes, halved

350ml (12fl oz) chicken stock

sprig of thyme

1 bay leaf

salt and freshly ground black pepper

1 chicken, about 1.5kg (3lb 3oz)

knob of butter

1 Preheat the oven to 180°C (350°F/Gas 4). Heat the oil in a large, flameproof casserole. Fry the onion, leek, celery, and carrots for 5 minutes until soft and beginning to brown. Stir in the garlic and potatoes and cook for 2 minutes.

2 Add the stock, thyme, and bay leaf, and season to taste. Then cook for a further 2 minutes and remove the casserole from the heat.

3 Rub the chicken with the butter and season the breast with salt and pepper. Place it on the vegetables. Cover and cook in the oven for 1 hour. If the chicken is too close to the lid of the pan, cover it loosely with greaseproof paper to prevent it from sticking.

4 Remove the lid, increase the oven temperature to 200°C (400°F/Gas 6), and cook for a further 30 minutes, or until the breast is golden brown and the sauce has reduced. Remove the herbs before serving.

SESAME CHICKEN SALAD

Bright flavours and fresh vegetables come together in this light and tangy salad.

CUT Whole chicken

SERVES 4
PREP 20 mins   **COOK** 1–1½ hrs, plus chilling

1 chicken, about 1.25kg (2¾lb)

1 tbsp salt

2 tbsp sesame oil

100g (3½oz) celery sticks, thinly sliced

100g (3½oz) carrots, peeled and grated

200g (7oz) red cabbage, shredded

100g (3½oz) shallots, thinly sliced

3 garlic cloves, crushed

50g (1¾oz) coriander leaves, chopped

50g (1¾oz) spring onions, chopped

1 tbsp sesame seeds

juice of 2 limes

FOR THE DRESSING

3 tbsp sesame oil, plus extra if needed

3 tbsp soy sauce, plus extra if needed

3 tbsp rice vinegar

1 tbsp red chilli paste

1 Preheat the oven to 180°C (350°F/Gas 4). Place the chicken, breast-side up, in a roasting tin and rub with the salt and the oil. Roast for 1–1½ hours, or until the internal temperature reaches 75°C (165°F). Remove from the oven and leave to cool.

2 When the chicken is cool enough to handle, remove the skin and use a fork to lightly shred the meat off the bones. Discard the skin and bones and transfer the shredded chicken to a large bowl.

3 For the dressing, mix all the ingredients in a small bowl and stir until well combined. Taste and adjust the quantity of the oil and soy sauce, if required.

4 Add the celery, carrots, cabbage, shallots, and garlic to the shredded chicken. Add the dressing and toss to coat.

5 Stir in the coriander, onions, sesame seeds, and lime juice. Cover and chill in the fridge for 1 hour, or overnight. Serve at room temperature on its own, in a sandwich, or over a green salad.

CIRCASSIAN CHICKEN SALAD

Smoky paprika flavours blend with a creamy walnut sauce in this dish from the Caucasus mountains.

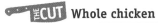 **Whole chicken**

SERVES 6
PREP 15 mins   **COOK** 2 hrs 10 mins

1 chicken, about 1.8kg (4lb)

salt and freshly ground black pepper

100g (3½oz) walnuts

2 slices of bread

500g (1lb 2oz) white onions, chopped

4 garlic cloves

1 tsp cayenne pepper

2 tbsp paprika

500ml (16fl oz) chicken stock

1 tbsp walnut oil

juice of 1 lemon

flat-leaf parsley, to garnish

1 Place the chicken in a large stock pot, cover with water, and bring to the boil. Add a pinch of salt and reduce the heat to a simmer. Cover and cook for 2 hours.

2 When the chicken is cooked through, remove from the water. Set the cooking liquid aside. Discard the skin and bones from the chicken and lightly shred the meat using a fork. Transfer the shredded chicken to a serving platter and, using a fork, spread it on the platter. Set aside.

3 In a food processor, pulse the walnuts until they are finely chopped. Dip the bread slices in the chicken cooking liquid and add to the food processor, along with the onions, garlic, cayenne pepper, and 1 tablespoon each of paprika and black pepper. Pulse until a thick paste forms. Add the stock to the paste, a little at a time, until it takes on the consistency of a sauce.

4 Pour the sauce over the shredded chicken. In a small pan, heat the oil and the remaining paprika. Cook for 2–3 minutes, stirring frequently, until the paprika is toasted. Pour the paprika oil over the chicken, along with the lemon juice. Garnish with parsley and serve at room temperature or chilled.

FRANGO PIRI PIRI

This spicy chicken is a Portugese favourite, ideal for long summer afternoons in the garden. Traditionally it is grilled but this version is roasted in the oven.

 Whole chicken

SERVES 6
PREP 15 mins, plus 24 hrs marinating
COOK 1 hr 10 mins

10 red chillies

115ml (3¾fl oz) olive oil, plus 1 tbsp extra

4 garlic cloves

4 tbsp red wine vinegar

1 tsp sea salt

1 tsp oregano

1 tsp smoked paprika

1 chicken, about 1.8kg (4lb)

salt and freshly ground black pepper

1 Place the chillies and 1 tablespoon of oil in a small bowl. Toss to coat, then grill for 5–10 minutes over a medium-high heat, turning once, until roasted. Remove the stalks.

2 Place the remaining oil, garlic, vinegar, sea salt, oregano, smoked paprika, and the roasted chillies in a food processor and pulse until smooth.

3 Spatchcock the chicken (see p61), using kitchen shears. Place it in a plastic bag with the chilli sauce and marinate for at least 24 hours.

4 Preheat the oven to 200°C (400°F/Gas 6). Remove the chicken from the chilli sauce, arrange in a roasting tin, and season well. Roast for 50 minutes to 1 hour, or until the internal temperature of the meat reaches 75°C (165°F).

HERBY ROAST CHICKEN

Herb butter adds incredible flavour to this roast and helps keep the bird moist as it cooks.

 THE CUT Whole chicken

SERVES 4–6
PREP 10 mins
COOK 1 hr 15 mins – 1 hr 30 mins, plus resting

3 tbsp butter, softened

1 tbsp finely chopped tarragon

1 tbsp finely chopped flat-leaf parsley

1 tbsp chopped thyme

1 garlic clove, crushed

grated zest and juice of ½ lemon

salt and freshly ground black pepper

1 chicken, about 1.5–2kg (3lb 3oz–4½lb)

1 tbsp olive oil

1 Preheat the oven to 230°C (450°F/Gas 8). For the herb butter, place the butter, herbs, garlic, and lemon zest in a large bowl and mash together to combine. Season well with salt and pepper.

2 Place the chicken on a clean work surface. Loosen the skin on the chicken breast and gently separate it from the meat, without tearing the skin, creating a pocket. Spread the herb butter evenly under the skin.

3 Place the chicken in a large roasting tin. Rub the skin with the oil and season. Drizzle over the lemon juice and place the lemon shell in the body cavity.

4 Transfer to the oven and roast for 15 minutes. Then reduce the temperature to 180°C (350°F/Gas 4) and roast for a further 1–1 hour 20 minutes, or until the juices run clear when the meat is peirced with a knife. Rest for 10 minutes, covered with foil. Serve warm.

BEER CAN CHICKEN

This recipe really spices up a barbecue and is well worth the trouble of balancing a chicken on a beer can.

THE CUT Whole chicken

SERVES 6
PREP 20 mins   **COOK** 2 hrs, plus resting

1 chicken, about 1.8kg (4lb)

75g (2½oz) butter, softened

1 tbsp salt

2 tbsp chopped rosemary

1 x 330ml (11fl oz) can of beer, preferably lager

1 Place the chicken on a clean work surface and brush evenly with the butter. Then rub all over with the salt and sprinkle the rosemary over.

2 Preheat the barbecue smoker or oven to 180°C (350°F/Gas 4). Pour out half the beer from the can. Then gently wedge the can in the cavity of the chicken so that the chicken is propped up on the can.

3 Place the chicken, sitting upright on the can, onto the grill. Close the lid and cook for 1½–2 hours, or until the internal temperature reaches 75°C (165°F). Check the chicken occasionally to make sure it is still upright. Remove from the grill and leave to rest and cool slightly. Carve and serve hot.

VARIATION

Herby beer can chicken Sprinkle the chicken with 1 tablespoon of chopped thyme and 2 teaspoons of smoked paprika along with the seasoning in step 1. Cook as above and serve hot.

TURKEY TETRAZZINI

This easy, comforting, and cheesy casserole is the perfect way to enjoy leftover turkey from a big festive meal.

THE CUT Cooked turkey

SERVES 8–10
PREP 10 mins   **COOK** 55 mins

500g (1lb 2oz) dried pasta

3 tbsp butter

4 garlic cloves, crushed

500g (1lb 2oz) onion, chopped

100g (3½oz) button mushrooms, sliced

250ml (9fl oz) white wine

500ml (16fl oz) chicken stock

50g (1¾oz) plain flour

250ml (9fl oz) turkey stock

100ml (3½fl oz) double cream

250ml (9fl oz) milk

400g (14oz) cooked turkey, shredded

1 tsp ground nutmeg

300g (10oz) Monterey Jack or Cheddar cheese

100g (3½oz) freshly grated Parmesan cheese

salt and freshly ground black pepper

225g (8oz) frozen peas

juice of 1 lemon

70g (2½oz) panko breadcrumbs

1 Cook the pasta according to packet instructions. Strain and set aside. Melt the butter in a large frying pan. Add the garlic and onions and sauté for 5–7 minutes, until the onions are tender. Then stir in the mushrooms and cook for 5 more minutes, stirring frequently.

2 Stir in the wine and chicken stock, reduce the heat to a simmer, and allow to reduce for 10 minutes. Then add the flour, stir to incorporate, and pour in the turkey stock a little at a time, whisking into a sauce.

3 Reduce heat to medium-low. Stir in the cream, milk, turkey, nutmeg, and both lots of cheese. Season well, mix to incorporate, and simmer for 15–20 minutes. Then stir in the pasta and the peas. Preheat the oven to 180°C (350°F/Gas 4).

4 Remove the pan from the heat and stir in the lemon juice. Transfer to a casserole dish and top with the breadcrumbs. Bake for 25 minutes, or until golden brown and bubbling. Serve hot.

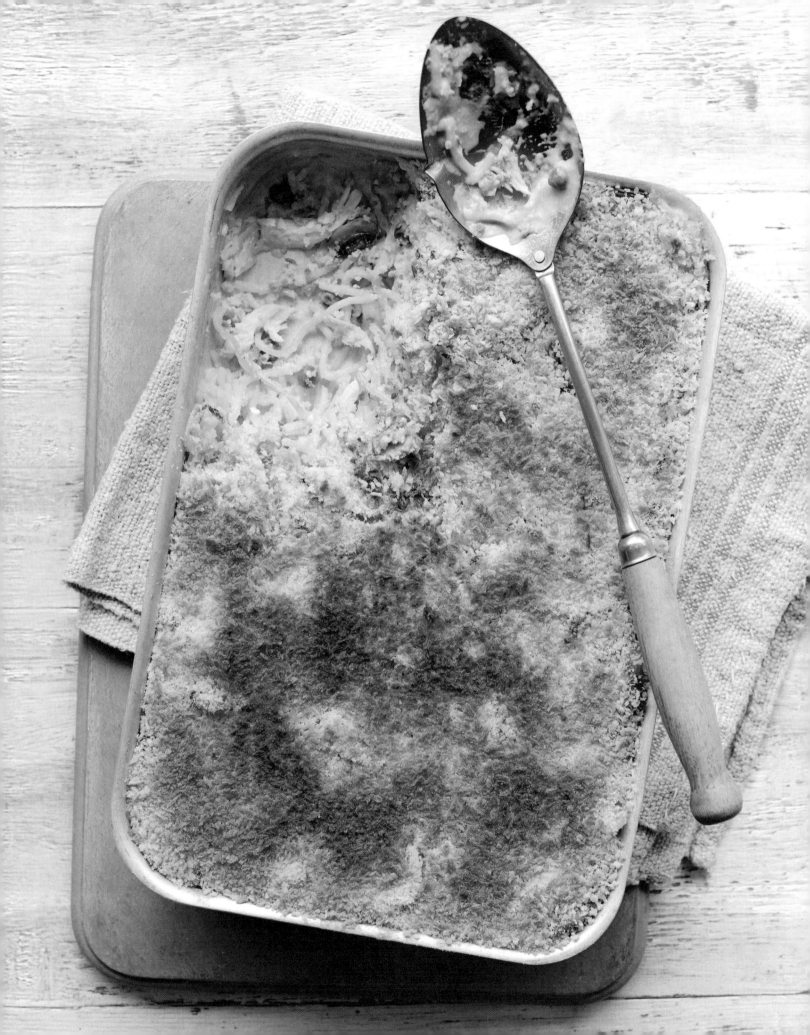

TURDUCKEN

Duck fat bastes the turkey and chicken from the inside, making this dish incredibly moist.

 THECUT Whole turkey, duck, chicken

SERVES 20–25
PREP 2 hrs   **COOK** 3–4 hrs, plus resting

1 turkey, about 6kg (13lb)

2 tbsp cayenne pepper

salt and freshly ground black pepper

2 tbsp garlic powder

250g (9oz) butter, cut into cubes

1 duck, about 2kg (4½lb)

1 chicken, about 1.8kg (4lb)

1 Line a large roasting tin with foil. Debone the turkey, leaving the drumsticks and wings bone-in (see p60). Lay it skin-side down on the roasting tin. Generously sprinkle the cayenne pepper, salt, pepper, and garlic powder over the bird. Top with one-quarter of the butter.

2 Debone the duck, removing the wings entirely and removing the bones from the drumsticks (see p60). Lay the duck skin-side down on top of the turkey, centering the bird. Generously sprinkle with the cayenne pepper, salt, pepper, and garlic powder. Top with one-quarter of the butter.

3 Debone the chicken, removing the wings entirely and removing the bones from the drumsticks (see p60). Lay the chicken skin-side down on top of the duck, centering the bird. Generously sprinkle the cayenne pepper, salt, pepper, and garlic powder over the bird. Top with one-quarter of the butter.

4 Fold the turkey onto itself so that it wraps around the two centre birds. Using butcher's string sew the turkey up where the backbone was. Take care to make sure that the duck and the chicken stay within the turkey cavity. Preheat the oven to 180°C (350°F/Gas 4).

5 Flip the turkey so the bird is seam-side down on the tin. Top generously with the remaining spices, seasoning, and butter. Bake for 3–4 hours, or until the internal temperature for the chicken reaches 75°C (165°F). The juices should run clear when the turkey thigh is pierced at its thickest point.

6 Remove from the oven and leave to rest for 30 minutes. Slice across the bird so that each serving contains chicken, duck, and turkey.

TURKEY AND OLIVE QUICHE

A medley of flavours from salty olives, ripe tomatoes, and cinnamon makes this an ideal brunch quiche.

THECUT Cooked turkey

SERVES 6
PREP 15 mins, plus chilling   **COOK** 45 mins

FOR THE PASTRY

150g (5½oz) plain flour, plus extra for dusting

1 tsp ground cinnamon

1 tsp salt

50g (1¾oz) vegetable fat

10g (¼oz) butter, chilled and diced, plus extra for greasing

1 egg, beaten to glaze

FOR THE FILLING

6 eggs

120ml (4fl oz) double cream

3 tbsp milk

200g (7oz) cooked turkey, shredded

100g (3½oz) black olives, pitted and halved

100g (3½oz) cherry tomatoes, halved

50g (1¾oz) fresh spinach

1 tsp chilli flakes

1 tsp ground cinnamon

1 tsp garlic powder

1 For the pastry, place the flour, cinnamon, and salt in a large bowl and mix well. Rub in the fat and butter, until the mixture resembles breadcrumbs. Then pour in 75ml (2½fl oz) water, a little at a time, until a loose ball of dough has formed. Wrap in cling film and chill for 1 hour.

2 Preheat the oven to 180°C (350°F/Gas 4). For the filling, beat the eggs with the cream and milk. Then add the turkey, olives, tomatoes, spinach, chilli flakes, cinnamon, and garlic powder and mix well.

3 Grease and line a 23cm (9in) loose-bottomed flan tin. On a lightly floured surface, roll the pastry out to a thickness of 5mm (¼in) and use to line the flan tin. Lightly brush the edges of the pastry with the beaten egg. Pour in the filling and spread it evenly into the pastry case. Bake for 45 minutes, or until firm. Serve warm.

SPATCHCOCKED AND GRILLED TURKEY

Flattening the bird reduces the cooking time, making turkey a delicious anytime meal.

THECUT Whole turkey

SERVES 8–10
PREP 30 mins   **COOK** 2 hrs, plus resting

1 turkey, about 6kg (13lb)

2 tbsp each salt and freshly ground black pepper

1 tbsp garlic powder

1 tbsp cayenne pepper

230g (8¼oz) butter, softened

1 Spatchcock the turkey (see p61), using kitchen shears or a boning knife. Place the turkey, breast-side up, in a large roasting tin. Spread it out flat and press down hard along the breast bone with your palm until you feel it snap.

2 Preheat a barbecue grill to its medium-high setting. Place the seasoning and spices in a small bowl and mix well. Rub the turkey with the butter and coat evenly with the spice mix. Place on a large roasting tin and grill for 1½–2 hours, or until the internal temperature reaches 75°C (165°F).

3 Remove from the grill and transfer to a large serving plate or tray. Cover with foil and leave to rest for 30 minutes. Carve and serve hot.

VARIATION

Spatchcocked and roasted turkey Try cooking the turkey in the oven instead of grilling it on a barbecue. For the spice mix, reduce the cayenne pepper by 1 teaspoon and add 1 teaspoon paprika in its place. Preheat the oven to 190°C (375°F/Gas 5) at the end of step 2. Place the turkey in a large roasting tin and cook in the oven for 2 hours, basting with the juices every 30 minutes. Remove from the oven and leave to rest for at least 30 minutes. Carve and serve hot.

DEEP-FRIED TURKEY

The perfect Thanksgiving recipe – this whole deep-fried turkey is sure to impress your holiday guests.

 THE CUT Whole turkey

SERVES 6
PREP 15 mins, plus 2 days marinating
COOK 30 mins, plus resting

1 turkey, about 3kg (6½lb)

groundnut oil, for frying

FOR THE BRINE

4 lemons, halved

4 whole garlic bulbs, unpeeled and halved

100g (3½oz) salt

3 bay leaves

100g (3½oz) brown sugar

1 For the brine, begin two days before you plan to make the dish. Place the turkey in a large stock pot and cover with water. Add the lemons, garlic bulbs, salt, bay leaves, and sugar. Cover and keep in a cool place for at least 2 days.

2 Place a colander over a large bowl. Remove the turkey from the brine and place in the colander to drain for about 1 hour.

3 Heat the oil in a large deep-fat fryer to 190°C (375°F). Pat the turkey dry with kitchen paper. Use a turkey hook or large tongs to slowly lower it into the deep-fat fryer, taking care to avoid splashing the hot oil.

4 Cook the turkey, turning occasionally, for 30 minutes, or until it turns a deep, rich brown and the internal temperature reaches 75°C (165°F). Remove from the oil, place it on a plate, and set aside to rest for at least 1 hour. Carve the turkey and serve warm.

SAFETY FIRST!

Set up the deep-fat fryer outdoors and make sure you follow the instructions on the kit. Keep your arms and feet covered and use gloves while handling the turkey.

TURKEY, MINT, AND CHICORY WRAPS

Crisp chicory lettuce, fresh mint, and creamy yogurt come together in these light and refreshing wraps.

THE CUT Cooked turkey

SERVES 4
PREP 15 mins, plus chilling   **COOK** 45 mins

200g (7oz) cooked turkey, shredded

100g (3½oz) Greek-style yogurt

50g (1¾oz) mint leaves, finely chopped

100g (3½oz) red onions, thinly sliced

100g (3½oz) carrots, grated

1 tsp ground ginger

juice of 1 lemon

salt and freshly ground black pepper

8 chicory leaves

1 In a large bowl, mix the shredded turkey, yogurt, mint, onions, carrots, ginger, and lemon juice, and season. Toss until well combined. Chill in the fridge for 30–45 minutes.

2 Arrange the chicory leaves on a platter. Divide the filling into 8 equal portions. Spoon a portion of the filling on top of each of the chicory leaves and serve.

SEARED DUCK BREAST WITH A RASPBERRY CARDAMOM GLAZE

The tangy, slightly tart raspberry sauce perfectly complements the rich flavours of the crisp duck breast.

 **THE CUT** Duck breast

SERVES 4
PREP 20 mins   **COOK** 20 mins

600g (1lb 5oz) skin-on duck breasts

salt and freshly ground black pepper

FOR THE SAUCE

1 tbsp butter

1 tbsp brown sugar

100g (3½oz) shallots, finely chopped

200g (7oz) fresh raspberries, deseeded and roughly chopped

1 tsp cardamom seeds, crushed

1 tbsp red wine vinegar

1 Use a sharp knife to score the skin on the duck breasts. Rub the meat generously with salt and pepper.

2 Place the duck skin-side down in a heavy-based frying pan over a medium-low heat. Allow the duck fat to render for 10–12 minutes. Turn and cook for a further 3–5 minutes on the other side. Set aside to rest. Keep warm.

3 Drain off the duck fat. In the same pan, melt the butter. Add the sugar and shallots and cook until caramelized.

4 Add the raspberries, cardamom, and vinegar. Cook, stirring frequently, for 5–7 minutes. Transfer the duck to a serving plate and serve topped with the raspberry sauce.

VARIATION

Seared pork chops with blackberry glaze Use pork chops in place of duck breasts, blackberries in place of raspberries, and leave out the cardamom seeds. Cook as above, but fry the pork chops for at least 30–35 minutes, until cooked through.

DUCK PÂTÉ

A simple country pâté comes to life with bursts of freshly ground pepper, citrus, and pistachios.

THE CUT Duck breast

MAKES about 900g (2lb)
PREP 25 mins, plus chilling   **COOK** 2 hrs

250g (9oz) skinless duck breasts, cut into cubes

4 garlic cloves, crushed

3 tbsp orange liqueur

1kg (2¼lb) pork shoulder, finely chopped

100g (3½oz) bacon, chopped

200g (7oz) chicken liver, chopped

250g (9oz) shallots, chopped

450g (1lb) pork back fat

3 eggs, beaten

1 tbsp chopped thyme

½ tsp ground cloves

½ tsp ground ginger

1 tsp ground allspice

100g (3½oz) pistachios, shelled

1 tsp sea salt

1 tbsp freshly ground black pepper

450g (1lb) butter

1 Combine the duck breast, garlic, and orange liqueur in a small bowl. Cover and chill for 1 hour. Place the pork, bacon, chicken liver, shallots, and pork back fat in a food processor, in batches if necessary, and pulse to combine. Transfer to a bowl and stir in the eggs, thyme, cloves, ginger, allspice, pistachios, salt and pepper. Add the duck mixture and stir until well combined.

2 Preheat the oven to 160°C (325°F/Gas 3). Melt the butter in a pan, skimming off any foam. Press the meat mixture into a terrine dish, leaving 1cm (½in) space at the top. Spoon the butter over the meat, covering it completely. Place the dish in a roasting tin. Half-fill the tin with boiling water.

3 Transfer the roasting tin to the oven and bake for 2 hours, or until the internal temperature reaches 63°C (145°F). Remove from the oven and allow to cool completely. Slice and serve over toast or bread. The pâté will keep in the fridge in an airtight container for up to 2 weeks.

DUCK CONFIT

Curing and slow-cooking duck legs in their own fat gives
this dish a rich and buttery taste that is unparalleled.

THE CUT Duck leg

SERVES 6
PREP 15 mins, plus 2 days marinating
COOK 3 hrs 10 mins, plus chilling

4 tbsp coarse sea salt

1 tsp freshly ground black pepper

6 skin-on bone-in duck legs, about 1.3kg (2¾lb) in total

4 garlic cloves, crushed

1 litre (1¾ pints) duck fat

LOW-FAT CONFIT

Sear the duck in its own fat by placing
it skin-side down in a frying pan over
a medium heat until one-quarter of
the fat is rendered. Then cover, place
in the oven, and cook as before.

1 Place the salt and pepper in a small bowl and mix to combine. Rub the duck legs thoroughly with the mixture and place them and the garlic in a sealable plastic bag, or a bowl into which the legs fit neatly. Seal the bag, or cover the bowl, and chill in the fridge for at least 24 hours, and up to 2 days.

2 Preheat the oven to 110°C (225°F/Gas ½). Remove the legs from the bag or bowl and wipe them dry to remove the excess salt. Melt the fat in a large flameproof casserole or Dutch oven. Add the legs, skin-side down, and bring to a gentle boil. Cover and cook in the oven for 3 hours or until tender.

3 Remove from the oven and transfer the legs to a deep, lidded, air-tight container. Pour over the fat from the casserole, cover, and chill. Store in the fridge for at least 24 hours, and up to 2 weeks.

4 Remove the legs from the container and scrape away all visible fat. Heat a heavy-based frying pan and cook the legs for 10–12 minutes, until hot and crisp. Serve hot with green beans.

CRISPY DUCK CHAR SIU

Chinese roast duck is tasty, but it is tricky to cook a whole bird. Try this easy version with duck breasts instead.

THE CUT Duck breast

SERVES 4
PREP 5 mins, plus marinating   **COOK** 25 mins

4 skin-on boneless duck breasts

3 garlic cloves, crushed

3 tbsp soy sauce

3 tbsp rice wine

1 tbsp hoisin sauce

2 tbsp clear honey

2 tsp five-spice powder

salt and freshly ground black pepper

1 Place the duck breasts, skin-side up, on a clean work surface. Use a knife to score the skin in a criss-cross pattern, being careful not to cut down into the meat.

2 Place all the remaining ingredients in a wide, shallow dish and whisk to combine. Add the duck breasts to the marinade and mix to coat the meat. Cover the dish with cling film and leave to marinate for 2–4 hours in the fridge.

3 Preheat the oven to 200°C (400°F/Gas 6). Line a baking tray with foil. Place the duck breasts, skin-side down, in a frying pan. Fry the breasts over a medium heat for about 8 minutes. Remove from the heat.

4 Place the duck breasts, skin-side up, on the baking tray. Cook at the top of the oven for 10 minutes. Remove and leave to rest for 5 minutes. Cut the duck breasts into slices on the diagonal and serve with stir-fried noodles or a green salad.

BATCH AND FREEZE

You can cook double this recipe and bag it up in portions for the freezer to produce a near-instant addition to a quick stir-fry anytime.

CASSOULET

This rich dish, originating in France, is named after the earthenware pot in which it was traditionally cooked.

THE CUT Duck leg

SERVES 6–8
PREP 20 mins   **COOK** 3½ hrs

200g (7oz) pancetta lardons, cut into cubes

3 Toulouse sausages, about 200g (7oz) in total

850g (1¾lb) duck legs

salt

1 tbsp olive oil

2 onions, chopped

4 garlic cloves, crushed

200g (7oz) carrots, cut into cubes

1 tbsp chopped thyme

1 tbsp oregano

400g (14oz) tomatoes, diced

250ml (9fl oz) white wine

500ml (16fl oz) chicken stock

400g (14oz) haricot beans, rinsed, soaked in cold water overnight, and dried

75g (2½oz) butter, softened

100g (3½oz) breadcrumbs

1 Place the pancetta, sausages, and duck legs in a large, flameproof casserole or Dutch oven, and season with a pinch of salt. Cook the meat over a medium heat for 10–15 minutes, until well-browned. Remove all the meat with a slotted spoon and set aside. Preheat the oven to 150ºC (300°F/Gas 2).

2 Add the oil to the pot. Then add the onions and garlic, and cook for 5 minutes over a medium heat, until the onions are browned. Add the carrots, thyme, and oregano, stir well to incorporate, and simmer for 2–3 minutes.

3. Stir in the tomatoes, wine, stock, and beans. Return the meat to the pot, bring to the boil, then remove from the heat. Place the butter and breadcrumbs in bowl and mix to combine. Spread the breadcrumb mixture evenly over the contents in the pot. Bake, uncovered, in the oven for 3 hours. Serve hot.

VARIATION

Pork cassoulet Use pork loin in place of the duck legs, and substitute half the haricot beans with red kidney beans. Cook as above and serve hot.

THAI RED DUCK CURRY

This hot curry will keep you warm and satisfied. An unexpected ingredient, pineapple, brings vitality to the dish.

THE CUT Duck leg and thigh

SERVES 4
PREP 15 mins   **COOK** 1 hr 15 mins

850g (2lb) skinless bone-in duck legs and thighs

3 tbsp sesame oil

2 tsp salt

1 tsp freshly ground white pepper

1 tsp chilli flakes

FOR THE SAUCE

400ml can coconut milk

100g (3½oz) Thai red chilli paste

10 makrut leaves, chopped

3 garlic cloves, crushed

1 tbsp finely chopped fresh root ginger

2 tbsp Thai fish sauce

2 tbsp sugar

juice of 1 lime

100g (3½oz) bird's eye chillies, deseeded and chopped

100g (3½oz) fresh pineapple, peeled, cored, and cut into cubes

24 cherry tomatoes, whole

handful of basil, chopped

1 Preheat the oven to 160°C (325°F/Gas 3). Place the duck leg and thighs fat-side down in a cast-iron frying pan. Drizzle in the sesame oil and add the salt, white pepper, and chilli flakes.

2 Roast for 40–45 minutes, or until the internal temperature reaches 75°C (165°F). Remove and let it rest for 10 minutes. Remove and discard the bones, slice the meat, and set aside.

3 Combine 250ml (9fl oz) of the coconut milk and the red chilli paste in a saucepan over a medium-high heat. Bring to the boil, then reduce the heat and simmer for 10 minutes.

4 Add the duck, remaining coconut milk, makrut leaves, garlic, and ginger. Cook for 15 minutes, stirring occasionally.

5 Once the flavours have infused, stir in the fish sauce, sugar, lime juice, bird's eye chillies, and pineapple. Cook for 3–5 minutes, or until the pineapple is tender. Add the tomatoes and basil, stir, and remove from the heat. Serve hot over basmati rice.

CHINESE ROAST DUCK AND PANCAKES

A classic Chinese recipe, this dish is likely to become a favourite with the entire family.

THE CUT Duck leg

SERVES 4
PREP 20 mins   **COOK** 1 hr 10 mins

4 duck legs

1 heaped tsp five-spice powder

1 tsp coarse sea salt

freshly ground black pepper

1 cucumber, peeled

2 bunches of spring onions

2 x 110g packet Chinese pancakes

300g jar hoisin sauce or plum sauce, to serve

1 Preheat the oven to 160°C (325°F/Gas 3). Prick the skin of the duck legs all over with a fork. Mix the five-spice powder, salt, and a good grinding of pepper in a small bowl. Rub the spice mix all over the duck legs.

2 Place the duck legs, skin-side up, on a rack inside a roasting tray and cook in the oven for 45 minutes. Then increase the oven temperature to 220°C (425°F/Gas 7) and cook for a further 25 minutes, until the skin is crisp and the duck cooked through.

3 Meanwhile, prepare the vegetables. Cut the cucumber in quarters, lengthways, then use a teaspoon to scoop the seeds from each piece. Cut each long piece into 4 chunks, then cut each chunk lengthways into thin strips, so that you are left with a pile of thin cucumber batons. Cut the spring onions into thin strips.

4 Place the duck on a chopping board and, using a sharp knife, gently shred the crisp skin and meat off the bones. Discard the bones, transfer the shredded meat and crisp skin to a plate, and keep warm.

5 Heat the pancakes according to the packet instructions. Serve the duck with the vegetables, pancakes, and the hoisin or plum sauce.

VENETIAN DUCK RAGÙ

A Northern Italian speciality featuring a rich meat sauce, the aromatic herbs will ensure you keep coming back for more.

THE CUT Duck leg

SERVES 6
PREP 40 mins   **COOK** 1½ hrs

1.35kg (3lb) skin-on bone-in duck legs

salt and freshly ground black pepper

2 tbsp olive oil, plus extra for drizzling

4 garlic cloves, crushed

500g (1lb 2oz) white onion, chopped

100g (3½oz) celery stick, sliced

200g (7oz) carrots, peeled and sliced

60g (2oz) porcini mushrooms, finely chopped

1 tbsp dried or fresh rosemary

2 x 400g can chopped tomatoes, in juices

250ml (9fl oz) duck stock, or chicken stock

250ml (9fl oz) red wine, such as Chianti

500g (1lb 2oz) packet pappardelle

1 Place the duck legs on a clean work surface and season well with salt and pepper. Heat the oil in a large casserole or Dutch oven. Add the duck legs and cook for 4–5 minutes on both sides until brown.

2 Add garlic and onion to the pan and cook, stirring frequently, for about 10 minutes, or until caramelized. Stir in the celery and carrots and reduce the heat to a simmer.

3 Stir in the mushrooms, rosemary, tomatoes, duck stock, and red wine. Return the duck legs to the casserole, nestling them in the sauce. Simmer, uncovered, for 1 hour.

4 Remove the duck legs from the sauce and set aside until cool enough to handle. Cook the pappardelle according to packet instructions.

5 Remove the skin and, using a fork, lightly shred the meat off the bones. Discard the skin and bones. Return the shredded meat to the casserole and stir well to incorporate.

6 Strain and plate your pasta, drizzling with a bit of olive oil. Top each dish with a generous portion of the ragù.

ROAST GOOSE

This oven-roasted goose, with crisp skin and tender meat, is the quintessential roast bird for your festive meal.

 Whole goose

SERVES 6–8
PREP 30 mins
COOK 3 hrs 15 mins, plus resting

900g (2lb) carrots, peeled and sliced

900g (2lb) red potatoes, peeled and quartered

500g (1lb 2oz) white onions, chopped

5 garlic cloves, crushed

3 tbsp olive oil

2 tbsp balsamic vinegar

2 tbsp salt

1 goose, wings clipped and giblets removed, about 6kg (12lb)

115g (4oz) butter, softened

freshly ground black pepper

4 tbsp chopped rosemary

1 lemon, halved

bunch of thyme

1 Preheat the oven to 190°C (375°F/Gas 5). Place the carrots, potatoes, onions, and garlic in a large roasting tin. Drizzle over the oil and vinegar, sprinkle over half the salt, and toss to coat.

2 Place the goose breast-side up in the roasting tin. Rub generously with the butter and sprinkle over the pepper, rosemary, and remaining salt. Squeeze over the lemon and place the halves in the body cavity, with the thyme.

3 Roast the goose, uncovered, for 45 minutes, or until well-browned. Baste the bird with the drippings, cover with foil, and roast for a further 2½ hours, or until the internal temperature reaches 75°C (165°F). Remove from the oven and set aside to rest for 30 minutes. Carve and serve hot with the roasted vegetables.

GOOSE POT PIE

In this delicious and spicy recipe, a light and flaky crust is paired with a hearty and flavoursome goose stew.

 Cooked goose

SERVES 6
PREP 30 mins, plus chilling
COOK 1½ hrs

300g (10oz) plain flour, plus extra for dusting

1 tsp chipotle powder

1 tsp salt

75g (2½oz) vegetable fat

75g (2½oz) butter, chilled and diced

1 egg, beaten, to glaze

FOR THE FILLING

2 tbsp butter

500g (1lb 2oz) shallots, sliced

4 garlic cloves, chopped

500g (1lb 2oz) carrots, peeled and sliced

500g (1lb 2oz) peas

1 tbsp chipotle powder or smoked paprika

1 tsp cayenne pepper

1 tsp each salt and freshly ground black pepper

800g (1¾lb) cooked goose, shredded

250ml (9fl oz) chicken stock

1 Sift the flour, chipotle, and salt in a large bowl. Rub in the fat and butter until the mixture resembles breadcrumbs. Add 250ml (9fl oz) cold water, a little at a time, until a loose ball of dough has formed. Wrap in cling film and chill for 1 hour.

2 Meanwhile, make the filling. Heat the butter in a large frying pan. Sauté the shallots and garlic until browned. Add in the carrots, peas, spices, and season. Stir in the goose, add the stock, and reduce the heat to a simmer. Cook for 30 minutes, or until the liquid has reduced. Preheat the oven to 180°C (350°F/Gas 4).

3 On a lightly floured surface, roll out half the pastry to a 5mm (¼in) thick circle. Use it to line a 10 x 5cm (4 x 2in) pie dish and pour the filling in. Roll out the remaining pastry and spread it evenly over the pie. Crimp the edges, cut slits across the top, and brush with the beaten egg. Bake for 45 minutes, or until golden brown. Serve warm.

CHOLENT

The perfect slow-cooked Sabbath meal, cholent is allowed to simmer overnight and into the next day.

 Goose breast

SERVES 6
PREP 10 mins   **COOK** 8–12 hrs

3 tbsp olive oil

700g (1lb 8oz) bone-in beef short ribs

500g (1lb 2oz) skinless boneless goose breast

500g (1lb 2oz) skinless bone-in chicken thighs

500g (1lb 2oz) waxy white potatoes, such as Cara or Maris Piper, peeled and quartered

500g (1lb 2oz) onions, thickly chopped

250g (9oz) carrots, peeled and sliced

4 garlic cloves, crushed

100g (3½oz) haricot beans, rinsed, soaked in cold water overnight, and dried

100g (3½oz) kidney beans, rinsed, soaked in cold water overnight, and dried

100g (3½oz) pearl barley

1 tbsp smoked paprika

salt and freshly ground black pepper

1.5 litres (2¾ pints) chicken stock, plus extra if needed

2 tbsp honey

1 Heat the oil in a large casserole or Dutch oven. Add the ribs, goose breast, and chicken thighs and cook for 3–4 minutes on each side, until well-browned. Do this in batches to avoid overcrowding the pot. Remove the meat with a slotted spoon and set aside.

2 Add the potatoes, onions, carrots, and garlic and spread them evenly over the bottom of the pot. Return all the meat to the pot, placing it on top of the vegetables. Top with the beans, barley, smoked paprika, and season well.

3 Pour in the stock and the honey. Cover, bring to the boil, and then reduce the heat to a simmer. Cook the stew for 8–12 hours, stirring occasionally, and adding in more stock, if needed. Remove the bones and discard. Serve hot.

BRAISED POUSSIN OVER POLENTA

Creamy polenta provides the ideal base for sweet, stewed tomatoes, spicy chorizo, and red wine braised poussin.

THE CUT Whole poussin

SERVES 6
PREP 20 mins   **COOK** 2 hrs

3 skin-on poussins, about 500g (1lb 2oz) each

1 litre (1¾ pints) chicken stock

250ml (9fl oz) red wine

1 tbsp ground allspice

1 bay leaf

1 tbsp sea salt, plus 1 tsp extra for the polenta

FOR THE SAUCE

100g (3½oz) butter

1 whole garlic bulb, finely chopped

200g (7oz) white onion, finely chopped

200g (7oz) button mushrooms, stems removed, rinsed, and sliced

100g (3½oz) cherry tomatoes

1 tbsp clear honey

½ tsp chilli flakes

½ tsp paprika

salt and freshly ground black pepper

FOR THE POLENTA

1 litre (1¾ pints) chicken stock

225g (8oz) polenta

250ml (9fl oz) double cream

1 Preheat the oven to 160°C (325°F/Gas 3). Place the poussins in a heavy stock pot or Dutch oven. Add the stock, wine, allspice, bay leaf, and salt. Cover and cook in the oven for 2 hours, or until the meat falls off the bones.

2 For the sauce, heat the butter in a saucepan over a medium-low heat. Add the garlic and onion and cook for 10 minutes, until caramelized. Then add the remaining ingredients, reduce the heat to a simmer, and cook for about 20 minutes.

3 For the polenta, boil the stock in a large casserole. Add the remaining ingredients, season with sea salt, and bring to the boil. Reduce the heat, cover, and simmer for 12–15 minutes, stirring occasionally. Remove the poussin from the pot and take out the bay leaf. Stir a ladleful of the braising liquid into the polenta and place it in a bowl. Top with the poussin and pour the sauce over.

CARIBBEAN JERK POUSSIN

Jerk poussin, with its peppery spice blend and crisp roasted skin, is a favourite among Caribbean nations.

THE CUT Whole poussin

SERVES 4
PREP 10 mins   **COOK** 45 mins, plus resting

2 poussins, about 500g (1lb 2oz) each

75g (2½oz) butter, softened

1 tsp dried thyme

1 tbsp ground allspice

½ tsp ground cinnamon

½ tsp grated nutmeg

1 tbsp cayenne pepper

pinch of salt

1 tbsp freshly ground white pepper

juice of 2 limes

1 Preheat the oven to 190°C (375°F/Gas 5). Place the poussins breast-side up in a small roasting tin and rub evenly with the butter.

2 Place the thyme, spices, and seasoning in a small bowl, mix well, and sprinkle over the meat. Transfer to the oven and roast for 45 minutes, or until the internal temperature reaches 75°C (165°F).

3 Remove from the oven and drizzle over the lime juice. Cover with foil and leave to rest for 10–15 minutes before carving. Serve warm with the cooking juices drizzled over.

ROAST POUSSIN WITH PRESERVED LEMONS

The delicate flavour of the preserved lemons adds an exciting layer of flavour to the classic roasted poussin.

 **Whole poussin**

SERVES 4
PREP 20 mins   **COOK** 45 mins

1 tsp ground cinnamon

2 tsp fine sea salt

1 tsp paprika

1 tsp freshly ground black pepper

1 tsp garlic powder

4 tbsp olive oil

2 poussins, about 500g (1lb 2oz) each

4 preserved lemons, sliced

4 garlic cloves, chopped

1 Preheat the oven to 180°C (350°F/Gas 4). Place the cinnamon, salt, paprika, pepper, garlic powder, and oil in a small bowl. Mix well to combine. Place the poussins breast-side up in a roasting tin and rub evenly with the oil and spice mix.

2 Divide half of the lemons and garlic between the cavities of the birds. Arrange the remaining lemons on top of the birds.

3 Place the roasting tin in the oven and roast for 35–40 minutes, or until the skin is crisp and the internal temperature reaches 75°C (165°F). Serve hot with lemon rice or couscous.

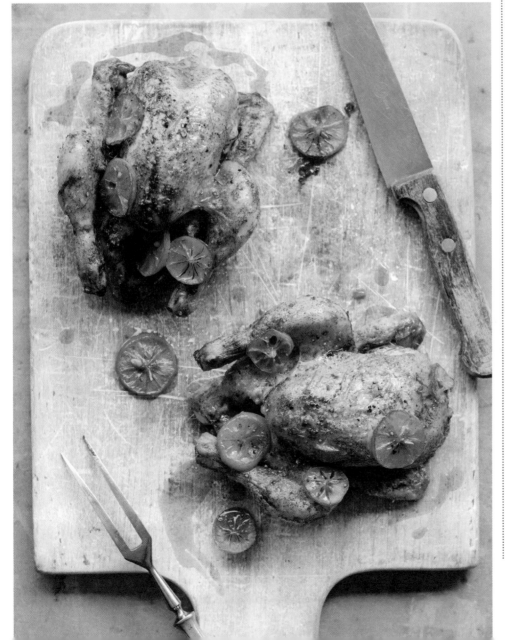

GAI YANG

This traditional Thai-spiced grilled poussin dish is served with a sweet chilli sauce and fresh coriander.

 **Whole poussin**

SERVES 4
PREP 20 mins   **COOK** 35 mins, plus resting

2 poussins, about 500g (1lb 2oz) each

1 tbsp finely chopped coriander stems

1 tbsp light brown sugar

1 lemongrass stalk, finely chopped

1 tbsp ground ginger

1 tsp garlic powder

4 tbsp Thai fish sauce

coriander leaves, finely chopped, to garnish

FOR THE SAUCE

4 garlic cloves, crushed

2 red chillies, deseeded and finely chopped

75ml (2½fl oz) rice vinegar

1 tsp salt

1 tbsp cornflour, mixed with a little warm water

1 Spatchcock the poussins (see p61), using kitchen shears. Spread them on a plate, breast-side up. Preheat the grill to medium-low.

2 Mix the coriander stems, sugar, lemongrass, spices, and the fish sauce in a bowl. Brush the poussin with the spice mix and grill, breast-side up, for 30–35 minutes, or until the internal temperature reaches 75°C (165°F).

3 Meanwhile, make the sauce. Place the garlic, chillies, vinegar, 120ml (4fl oz) water, and salt in a saucepan. Simmer for 10–15 minutes, or until the chillies and garlic have softened. Whisk in the cornflour mixture, a little at a time, stirring constantly. Cook the sauce for a further 10 minutes, until thickened.

4 Remove the poussin from the heat and leave to rest for 10 minutes. Brush with the sweet chilli sauce and garnish with coriander. Serve hot.

PORK

PORK

------- ------- ------- ------- ------- ------- -------

FROM EAST TO WEST, PIGS PROVIDE HUMANS WITH MEAT AND FAT THAT IS EASY TO PRODUCE. PIGS ARE OMNIVORES, ABLE TO THRIVE ON A WIDE RANGE OF PLANTS AND ANIMALS, AND ARE SKILLED AT SCAVENGING FOR FOOD. FOR CENTURIES, THEY WERE THE ONLY SOURCE OF MEAT FOR MANY PEASANTS.

NOWADAYS, PIGS ARE BIG BUSINESS, with nearly two billion animals being produced each year. Asia produces 65 per cent of the world's pigs, with the EU being the second largest producer. Germany, with its thousands of types of sausage, has the highest pig population in the EU, although Denmark boasts three times as many pigs as humans. The US is the third largest pig producer.

While some people regard pigs as dirty, they are in fact intelligent and fastidious animals, but because they have no sweat glands they are prone to heat stress, and their habit of rolling in mud to cool themselves does make them look scruffy. A number of religions forbid the eating of pork, which is something to consider when offering hospitality. Most Jews, Muslims, Rastafarians, and some Hindus do not eat pork, and neither do some Christian sects.

Few people would disagree that the pig's main contribution to our enjoyment of food is the huge range of preserved products (see pp102–5): dried hams, bacon, and cured and smoked sausages of every imaginable shape and size all originated from the need to preserve meat before the invention of refrigeration.

ANIMAL WELFARE

The main welfare considerations in pig farming focus on farrowing (giving birth) and slaughter. In many countries, sows are confined to farrowing crates so they cannot roll over and crush their piglets. Critics argue that pigs are intelligent creatures that are unlikely to squash their offspring when given adequate space to interact with them. Sow crates are banned in the EU and a few US states, but pork is often imported from countries with different welfare laws. Pigs are easily stressed, so careful handling before slaughter is crucial, and some large units slaughter their pigs on site to eliminate transport. As pigs are omnivores, commercial feed consists of a combination of grains, soya beans, and animal protein.

PRODUCTION METHODS

The following are the main commercial pig production methods:
- **Domestic** Although few pigs are raised for sale this way nowadays, across the world, keeping a back-yard pig has been a long-standing tradition, and in many countries people still keep a pig or two for home consumption. Sometimes they live in a pigsty, otherwise in a run or paddock. **Diet:** a mixture of household scraps and grain.

BLACK PUDDINGS, PÂTÉS, TERRINES, AND BRAWN WERE THE DELICIOUS RESULTS OF NOT WISHING TO WASTE A SINGLE SCRAP OF THE ANIMAL.

• **Free-range (outdoor reared)** It is not easy to divide free-range pig production into categories because so many different combinations of systems are used, and there are no legal definitions. Sometimes sows farrow outside in "arcs" (semi-circular sheds) and the piglets may live indoors, more or less intensively, after weaning. Sometimes it is the reverse: the sows farrow inside, but the weaners live outside until ready for slaughtering. Outdoor pigs can turn a damp field into a quagmire. Equally, pigs suffer from sunburn, so they need shelters to protect them from both sun and rain.
Diet: concentrates, roots, and vegetation.
• **Intensive** Most pigs are kept intensively. Sows farrow in crates unless the use of these is banned, and the weaned piglets are reared in large, temperature-controlled sheds, either on slats or with straw on the floor. The units are closely monitored to prevent outbreaks of disease, while vitamins and antibiotics are often administered to prevent disease and encourage fast growth.
Diet: concentrates.
• **Organic** Most organic systems insist on outdoor rearing and sow crates are forbidden. Prophylactic drugs, growth promoters, and antibiotics are not permitted. Medication is only permitted to control disease, and longer than usual withdrawal times are often required before slaughter. All feed has to be organic.
Diet: organic concentrates, roots, and vegetation.

BREEDS AND CATEGORIES
• **Commercial pigs** These are highly specialized hybrids bred to be productive under intensive conditions. American hybrids are based on the Duroc, while Europe uses many Landrace crosses. However, the trend for producing artisanal pork from heritage breeds is growing, and old-fashioned breeds such as the Tamworth or Gloucester Old Spot are raised to produce free-range pork.

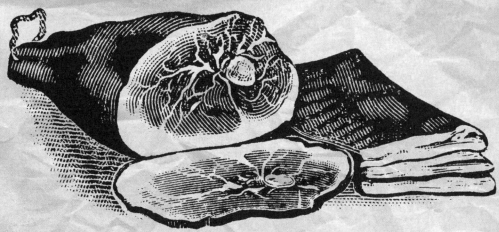

DRIED HAMS, BACON, AND CURED AND SMOKED SAUSAGES OF EVERY SHAPE AND SIZE ALL ORIGINATED FROM THE NEED TO PRESERVE MEAT BEFORE THE INVENTION OF REFRIGERATION.

• **Premium pork products** Products such as hams or salamis often rely on traditional pig breeds. In Spain and Portugal, the Black Iberian pig is greatly prized, as is the woolly Mangalica pig from Hungary, which is bred specially for its superb fat. Many European products using heritage pigs are recognized by symbols, such as PDO (Protected Designation of Origin), PGI (Protected Geographical Indication), TSG (Traditional Specialities Guaranteed), and AOC (*Appellation d'Origine Contrôlée*), that acknowledge the importance of these breeds.
• **Sucking pigs** These are 2- to 6-week-old piglets that are fed on their mothers' milk. Some may be older. The skin is a creamy white and the meat a delicate, pale pink.
• **Pork pigs (porkers)** Most pigs are about eight months old and have a covering of fat, but are otherwise lean. The meat is pink and the fat is white. In contrast, the flesh of many heritage and outdoor pigs is often much darker, due to their diet and the fact that they are slower grown.
• **Processing pigs (baconers)** These pigs are older and fatter and are used for pork products such as bacon, ham, sausages,

and salamis, all of which need a greater proportion of fat to lean meat.

BUYING PORK
Because so much pork is shipped across the world, it is not easy to know how it was produced. Also, there are no legal definitions for "free range" pork. If the method of production is not mentioned, then it is probably intensively raised, as welfare-friendly production is usually promoted at the point of sale.

Some commercial bacon and ham is cured by injecting it with brine. This reduces the cost but makes the meat wetter. It may exude a milky white liquid when cooked and is difficult to brown. Dry-salted products will not do this. Highly processed, cheap products, such as sausages, that have no recognizable pieces of meat in them could be made from mechanically recovered meat (MRM), which could be from any part of the animal. Sometimes this is marked on the label. Some pig diseases are very contagious, so many countries forbid travellers from importing pork, and pork products such as sausages and salami.

PORK CUTS

MORE THAN ANY OTHER MEAT, PORK is used for sausages, hams, and other cured products. Fresh pork, however, offers tasty dishes at affordable prices; it is one of the cheapest of meats. Good pork is pink, not grey, and outdoor pork is darker than intensively raised pork.

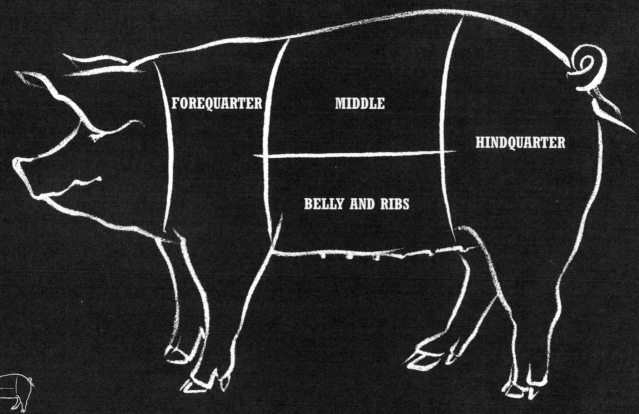

FOREQUARTER   MIDDLE   HINDQUARTER

BELLY AND RIBS

FOREQUARTER CUTS

Pork forequarter cuts have fat running through them so are great for slow-cooking. Spare rib cuts from the neck and ribs are also good for grilling.

SHOULDER MINCE This contains fat and is great for meatballs, meat loaf, and Chinese dumplings.

SPARE RIB JOINT Called "collar" when cured, this bone-in shoulder and neck joint is also sold boned and tied for easier carving.

SHOULDER STEAK With a generous marbling of fat, shoulder steaks are perfect for slow baking.

Additional forequarter cuts

- **ROLLED SHOULDER JOINT** Many parts of the shoulder are rolled and tied for slow roasting.

- **SPARE RIB RACK** These "ribs" are actually the long neck bones. They are cooked in the same way as spare ribs from the flank (see opposite).

- **RIB EYE JOINT** This neat, well-marbled joint is boneless spare ribs. Cook with or without the skin.

- **HAND JOINT** This is a bone-in joint from the top of the leg with the hock removed. Simmer or braise.

- **FOREQUARTER HOCK** Often smoked and useful for soup and stock as it has a high gelatin content.

SUCKING PIG

A whole sucking pig (see pp106–7) makes a spectacular centrepiece and is so tender that, when perfectly cooked, it can be cut with the side of a plate. Make sure your butcher cleans the ears and snout properly.

MIDDLE CUTS

The eye muscle is very lean but the thick layer of fat on the outside can be cut off if wished. Be careful not to overcook these cuts as they can dry out.

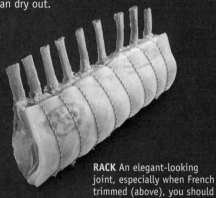

RACK An elegant-looking joint, especially when French trimmed (above), you should ask your butcher to remove the sharp chine bone.

DOUBLE LOIN CHOP Cut from the best end of the bone-in loin, these chops have loin on one side (left) and fillet on the other (right).

LOIN EYE STEAKS From the boneless loin, these can include the outer fat or can be trimmed.

FILLET OR TENDERLOIN The most tender cut of all, a fillet will feed 2–3 people and cooks very quickly.

Additional middle cuts

• **BONELESS LOIN** This tender muscle runs the length of the back so can be cut to any length. Steaks can also be cut from it.

• **CUTLETS** Sliced from the rack, these are usually one rib thick but can be more.

• **LOIN JOINT, BONE-IN SKIN-ON** The skin on this joint provides good crackling but there is often a thick layer of fat underneath.

• **LOIN EYE, TRIMMED** The eye muscle completely trimmed of skin and fat, so a healthy lean joint.

BELLY AND RIB CUTS

These cuts have a large proportion of fat. Whole pieces can be cooked on the barbecue, but it is usually cut into smaller pieces. Bacon is made from the belly.

RACK OF SPARE RIBS Often cooked as a whole piece, individual ribs can be cut to make sticky Chinese spare ribs. Best slow-cooked before being crisped.

BELLY SLICES, BONE-IN These can contain a little cartilage as well as bone, both of which will soften on slow cooking.

Additional belly and rib cuts

• **SHORT-CUT RIBS** A short-cut length of ribs from the rack. Cook as forequarter spare ribs or barbecue.

• **BELLY** A fatty cut, this is delicious when slowly blackened with a sticky sauce. It may be cooked as a whole piece or in slices.

• **ROLLED BELLY** Sometimes stuffed before being rolled and tied, this needs long slow cooking.

HINDQUARTER CUTS

The hindquarter produces some very lean cuts. Whole legs are used to make traditional cured and dried hams as well as cured gammon joints and steaks.

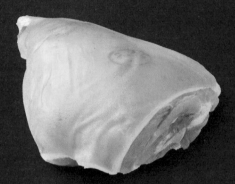

WHOLE LEG A traditional affordable family joint, this is at its best with the skin scored to make crackling. It may also be boned and rolled into smaller joints.

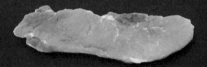

LEG STEAK This lean steak is perfect for grilling and stir-frying. It can also be beaten out thinly to make schnitzels. It is best not to cut them too thickly as they may toughen when cooked.

HOCK Called knuckle when cured and smoked, the hock has a high gelatin content that makes it perfect for soup and stock. It can also be enjoyed as a cheap form of ham.

Additional hindquarter cuts

• **CHUMP ROAST, BONE-IN** This is a plump, tender and meaty joint that includes a little fillet.

• **ROLLED BONELESS LEG ROAST** Useful for making smaller roasts, the meat cooks evenly.

• **CHUMP CHOP** With a distinctive semi-circular shape, this is one of the meatiest types of chop.

• **CHUMP STEAK** As above but without any bone, this is sometimes also referred to as a chump chop.

BACON AND HAM

BACON IS USUALLY BELLY PORK that has been cured with salt and then sliced. The cure may be dry-salt or brine. Often it is smoked afterwards. Ham is usually made from pork legs that are salted and then air-dried; many are smoked as well. Dried hams keep well and most are eaten raw.

SPECK Made in the mountainous region between Austria and Italy, this ham is salted with herbs and spices and very slowly smoked and dried.

PANCETTA Pork belly is dry-salted with herbs, spices, and garlic then dried for three months. It is used by cooks around the world to flavour dishes. *Stesa* is flat pancetta, *arrotolata* is rolled up.

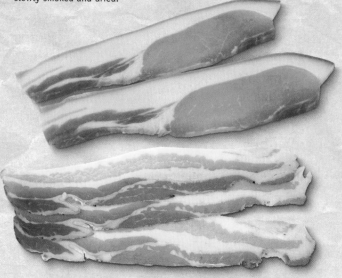

LARDO Thick pork back fat is brine-cured with herbs and spices to make this Italian bacon. With its silky texture and deep flavour, it is enjoyed on toast as an antipasto.

BRITISH AND AMERICAN BACON These are both lightly cured and need to be cooked before eating. Most is made from belly pork (above), but some is made from loin (top). It may be dry-salted or brined, smoked or unsmoked.

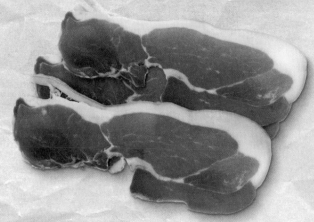

LAP YUK Literally translated as "wax meat", this strongly flavoured Chinese bacon is made from pork belly marinated in Chinese spices and then slowly dried. It is normally chopped to add flavour to other dishes.

JAMBON DE BAYONNE The salt brine for this ham from Bayonne in southwest France includes wine, which gives it its special flavour and moist texture.

COPPA Also called *capocollo*, this ham is made from pork shoulder or neck so has a high fat content. The meat is marinated and salted, packed into casings, and dried.

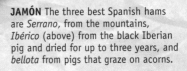

JAMÓN The three best Spanish hams are *Serrano*, from the mountains, *Ibérico* (above) from the black Iberian pig and dried for up to three years, and *bellota* from pigs that graze on acorns.

JINHUA HAM With its cream-coloured fat and dark red meat, this popular Chinese ham is first dry-salted, then soaked before being dried, to develop its distinctive flavour.

ELENSKI A popular Bulgarian ham that is dry-cured for 40 days then air-dried for many months. When dried in the traditional farmhouse kitchen, it acquires a smoky flavour.

CULATELLO From the Parma region of Italy, this ham is made from pigs that are older and fatter than those used for conventional Parma ham.

PRESUNTO This dry-cured Portuguese ham is similar to Spanish *jamón*. The best presunto is also made with pork from the black Iberian pig.

BLACK FOREST HAM A robustly flavoured ham from the Black Forest in Germany. Pork is salted, spiced, and then very slowly cold-smoked over pine. It should be sliced very thinly.

WESTPHALIA HAM This air-dried German ham gets its special flavour from the pigs feeding on acorns in the Westphalian forest. This is enhanced by being smoked over juniper and beech wood.

CURED AND DRIED SAUSAGES

THERE IS A HUGE FAMILY OF PORK SAUSAGES. Some are cured in wine vinegar or curing salts, which gives them a fermented taste. The sausages on these pages have also been dried to preserve them for longer. Other sausages are dried without curing; they have a purer pork flavour.

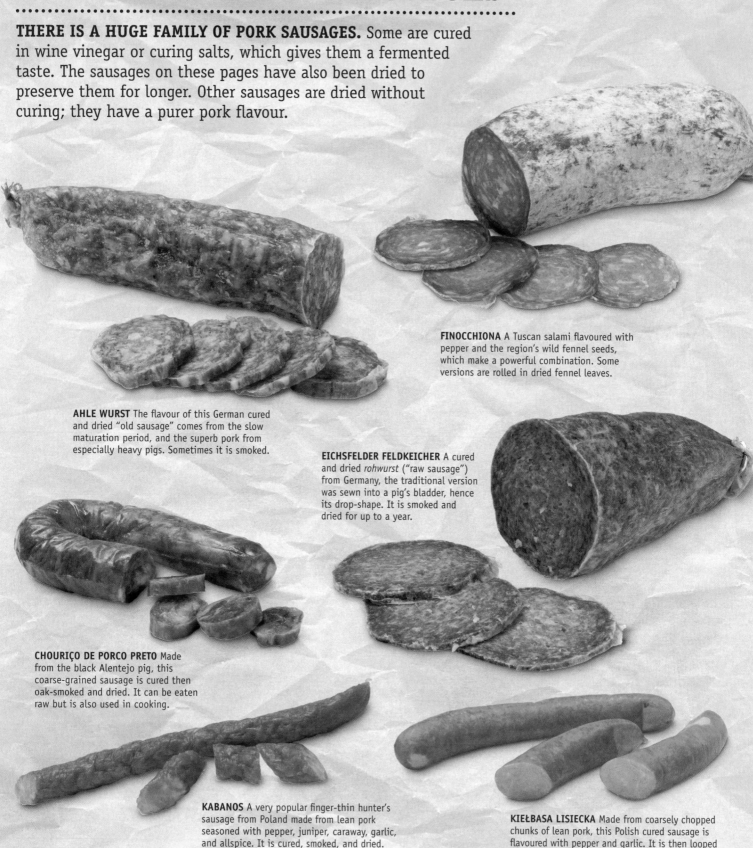

FINOCCHIONA A Tuscan salami flavoured with pepper and the region's wild fennel seeds, which make a powerful combination. Some versions are rolled in dried fennel leaves.

AHLE WURST The flavour of this German cured and dried "old sausage" comes from the slow maturation period, and the superb pork from especially heavy pigs. Sometimes it is smoked.

EICHSFELDER FELDKEICHER A cured and dried *rohwurst* ("raw sausage") from Germany, the traditional version was sewn into a pig's bladder, hence its drop-shape. It is smoked and dried for up to a year.

CHOURIÇO DE PORCO PRETO Made from the black Alentejo pig, this coarse-grained sausage is cured then oak-smoked and dried. It can be eaten raw but is also used in cooking.

KABANOS A very popular finger-thin hunter's sausage from Poland made from lean pork seasoned with pepper, juniper, caraway, garlic, and allspice. It is cured, smoked, and dried.

KIEŁBASA LISIECKA Made from coarsely chopped chunks of lean pork, this Polish cured sausage is flavoured with pepper and garlic. It is then looped onto sticks and smoked and dried over hardwood.

LINGUIÇA A cured and dried sausage common throughout Portugal. Spices include garlic, paprika, oregano, and cumin. This is different from South American linguiça, which is only cured, not dried.

BERGSALAMI From Austria's mountainous regions, this fine-grained *rohwurst* is cured, then hot-smoked over beech and juniper, then dried for up to six weeks to produce its characteristic white mould.

MANGALICA Made from the meat of the curly-coated, fat Mangalica pig, this long Hungarian sausage is bright orange due to sweet paprika. It is cured, cold-smoked, and dried for three months.

SALAME TOSCANO This very salty Italian salami is made to be eaten with unsalted Tuscan bread. The dark red pork is studded with large pieces of fat.

ROSETTE DE LYON The pink meat gives this French sausage its name. The pork is liberally studded with fat. Jésus de Leon is similar and its bulbous shape comes from being dried in a pig's stomach.

SALCHICHÓN DE VIC A hard mountain sausage made from salted pork mixed with cracked black pepper, then lightly smoked and dried. Salchichón is popular throughout Spain and there are many versions.

PREPARING A SUCKING PIG

One of the world's great celebration dishes, roast sucking pig combines a thin, crisp, crackling skin with succulent tender meat. A sucking pig can weigh from 5–15kg (10–34lb). Allow for 450g (1lb) per person.

1 Make sure the supplier has cleaned the feet, ears, and snout. If not already done, remove all traces of hair. Rub salt all over the pig inside and out and leave overnight. Next day, pat the pig dry and stuff the cavity, but not too tightly as the stuffing will expand.

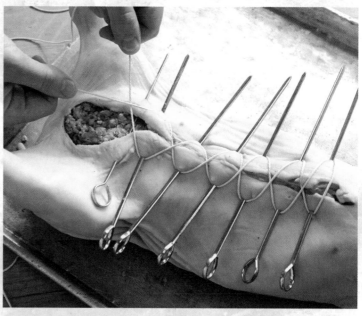

2 Fasten the stuffed cavity loosely with skewers, making sure that you keep them away from the edge of the cavity in case the skin tears. Then use string to pull the skin together as shown, criss-crossing it between the skewers and winding it around the outside as you go.

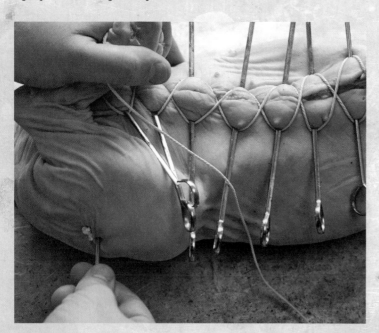

3 Truss the back legs. Thread a trussing needle with string and push it right through the centre of the back legs and the body. Pressing down on the trotters helps to keep the legs in the right position as they are trussed.

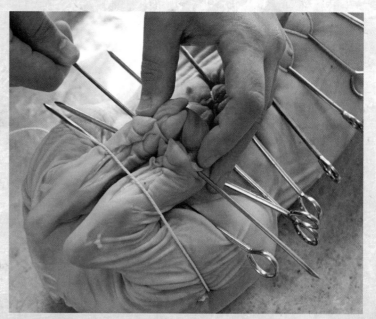

4 Use one hand to hold the trotters together while you pierce through both of them as shown. Pull the ends of the string up fairly tightly and tie them together securely.

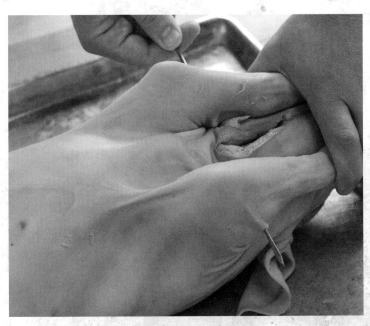

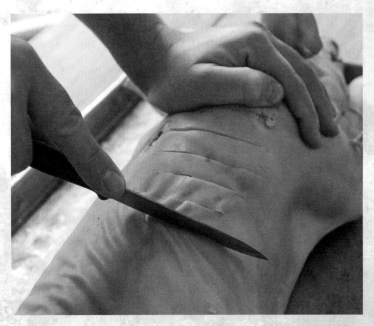

5 Now truss the forelegs. Push the trussing needle through the front legs, chest, and throat and tie. Again, use one hand to hold the legs next to the head, while you push the trussing needle through.

6 Turn the pig the right way up and score the skin across the top of the body using a very sharp knife or scalpel. Make diagonal incisions about 2cm (¾in) apart on either side of the backbone. Do not pierce the meat.

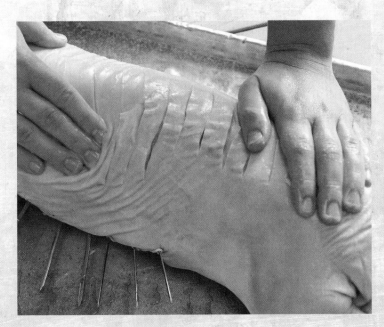

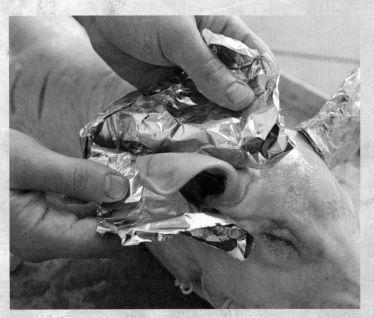

7 Place the pig – still on its belly – in a large roasting tin. Rub it all over with oil and then salt. Heat the oven to 180°C (350°F/Gas 4). When cooking it, allow 45 minutes per kg (20 minutes per lb), and use a meat thermometer to check that the stuffing is cooked through.

8 Before cooking the pig, make some thick pockets of tin foil and cover the oiled ears and tail to prevent them from burning. Place the pig in the oven and baste it every half hour. When cooked, rest the pig in a warm place for 20–30 minutes.

SCOTCH EGGS

A classic British dish and popular picnic snack, these sausagemeat-wrapped eggs are an indulgence like no other.

 Pork sausagemeat

SERVES 6
PREP 20 mins   **COOK** 20 mins

8 eggs

600g (1lb 5oz) pork sausagemeat

3 garlic cloves, crushed

100g (3½oz) spring onions, finely chopped

50g (1¾oz) chives, finely chopped

1 tbsp wholegrain mustard

1 tsp dried chilli flakes

1½ tsp sea salt

1½ tsp freshly ground black pepper

250g (9oz) plain flour

groundnut oil, for frying

250g (9oz) breadcrumbs

1 Bring a saucepan of water to the boil, add 6 of the eggs, and boil for 3–5 minutes for a semi-soft yolk and 5–7 minutes for a firm yolk. Drain, run under cold water, and set aside to cool. Peel the eggs when cool enough to handle.

2 In a large bowl, place the pork, garlic, onions, chives, mustard, one-third of the chilli flakes, and half a teaspoon each of the salt and pepper. Mix to combine. In a separate bowl, place the flour, one-third of the chilli flakes, and another half teaspoon each of the salt and pepper. Mix well.

3 Heat the oil in a deep-fat fryer or a large saucepan to 180°C (350°F). Divide the pork mixture into 6 equal portions. Flatten each portion and wrap it around a boiled egg, making sure the whole egg is covered.

4 Whisk the remaining 2 eggs in a small bowl. Place the breadcrumbs in a shallow dish along with the remaining chilli flakes and seasoning, and mix to combine. Dip each egg first in the flour mixture, then in the beaten eggs, and finally coat with the breadcrumbs.

5 Deep fry the eggs for 4–5 minutes each, turning occasionally, until well-browned. Remove the eggs with a slotted spoon, drain on a plate lined with kitchen paper, and set aside to cool slightly. Serve hot.

SWEDISH MEATBALLS WITH GRAVY

Traditionally served with mashed potatoes and lingonberry jam, these mild meatballs with a rich gravy are the perfect comfort food.

 Minced pork

SERVES 4
PREP 10 mins, plus chilling   **COOK** 20–25 mins

FOR THE MEATBALLS

450g (1lb) minced pork

75g (2½oz) fresh white breadcrumbs

½ onion, finely grated and chilled

1 tbsp whole milk

1 egg, beaten

1 tsp caster sugar

salt and freshly ground black pepper

25g (scant 1oz) butter

1 tbsp sunflower oil

mashed potato, to serve

FOR THE GRAVY

1 heaped tbsp plain flour

250ml (9fl oz) beef stock

1 tsp redcurrant jelly

1 tbsp single cream

1 In a large bowl, mix the pork, breadcrumbs, onion, milk, egg, sugar, and seasoning until well combined. Chill for at least 1 hour. Preheat the oven to 150°C (300°F/Gas 2). 3/4

2 Heat the butter and oil in a large frying pan. With damp hands, shape the pork mixture into walnut-sized balls. Fry the meatballs over a low heat for 10 minutes, turning regularly until browned all over and springy to the touch. Cook them in two batches to avoid overcrowding the pan. Once cooked, transfer them to the oven and cover loosely with foil to keep them warm.

3 To make the gravy, remove the pan from the heat and sprinkle in the flour. Whisk it into the fat in the pan, then gradually whisk in the stock.

4 Return the pan to the heat and cook the gravy until it thickens. Reduce to a simmer, add the redcurrant jelly and cream, and cook for a further 2–3 minutes. Check for seasoning and serve spooned over the meatballs and mashed potato.

STEAMED PORK DIM SUM

This popular light snack has its roots in the ancient Silk Road, where it was served at roadside teahouses.

THE CUT Minced pork

MAKES 20–24 dumplings
PREP 30 mins, plus chilling   **COOK** 15 mins

FOR THE DOUGH

300g (10oz) plain flour, plus extra for dusting

1 tsp salt

1 egg, beaten with 1 tsp water

oil, for greasing

FOR THE FILLING

350g (12oz) minced pork

1 tbsp soy sauce

1 tbsp fish sauce

1 tsp sesame oil

1 spring onion, finely chopped

1 tbsp rice wine

1 garlic clove, crushed

1 tbsp crushed fresh root ginger

1 tsp caster sugar

1 egg

1 tsp cornflour

50g (1¾oz) shiitake mushrooms, chopped

1 Sift the flour and salt into a large bowl. Make a well in the centre, pour in the egg, and mix well to combine. Add 120ml (4fl oz) of water, a little at a time, until a dough forms. Continue to knead the dough until it is smooth, glossy, and elastic.

2 Place the dough on a lightly floured surface and knead for a further 5 minutes. Cover and chill for 30 minutes.

3 For the filling, place all the ingredients in a large bowl and mix well to combine. Turn the dough out onto a lightly floured surface, roll out very thin, and cut into 7.5–10cm (3–4in) squares.

4 To prepare the dumplings, place 1 tablespoon of the filling in the centre of each square. Wet the edges of the dough and pleat it around the sides of the filling. Pinch a "waist" over the top of the dumpling, leaving the centre open to help the filling cook. Gently press the dumpling to flatten the bottom.

5 Place the dumplings on a greased plate and steam over a pan of boiling water for 10–15 minutes, or until the filling has cooked through. Serve hot with soy sauce for dipping.

FRIKADELLER

Originally from Denmark, these moist patties are also popular in Germany. The creamy dill dip adds a lovely fresh note.

THE CUT Minced pork

SERVES 4
PREP 30 mins, plus resting   **COOK** 20–25 mins

FOR THE PATTIES

450g (1lb) minced lean pork

125g (4½oz) fresh brown breadcrumbs

1 onion, finely chopped

¼ tsp ground allspice

1 egg

1 tbsp whole milk

2 tsp chopped dill

salt and freshly ground black pepper

1 tbsp sunflower oil, for frying

FOR THE DIP

4 tbsp soured cream

2 tsp chopped dill

1 Place all the ingredients, except the oil, in a bowl and mix well, making sure the dill and onions are evenly incorporated. Divide the mixture into 12 equal portions, shape them into balls, and gently flatten into patty-like shapes. Place them on a plate and set aside to rest in a cool place for about 30 minutes.

2 Heat the oil in a large, non-stick frying pan over a medium heat. Fry the patties for 5–10 minutes, turning regularly until lightly brown on both sides. Then reduce the heat and cook for 5 more minutes to cook through. Remove from the pan, transfer to a plate, and keep warm. Cook the patties in batches to avoid overcrowding the pan.

3 For the dip, mix the soured cream and dill in a small bowl. Serve the Frikadeller patties along with the dill cream dip and a mixed green salad.

PORK AND BEER STEW

A typical German stew blending savoury beer with spices and thickened with rye bread, this is a rich and intense dish.

THE CUT Pork shoulder

SERVES 4
PREP 30 mins **COOK** 1½ hrs

2 tbsp groundnut oil

600g (1lb 5oz) pork shoulder, cut into cubes

1 large onion, thinly sliced

2 garlic cloves, crushed

2 carrots, cut into thick batons

125g (4½oz) button mushrooms, sliced

¼ tsp ground allspice

1 bay leaf

1 cinnamon stick

300ml (10fl oz) bottle dark beer

200ml (7fl oz) pork or chicken stock

85g (3oz) rye breadcrumbs

salt and freshly ground black pepper

chopped flat-leaf parsley, to garnish

1 Heat 1 tablespoon of the oil in a heavy-based casserole. Add the pork, in batches, and cook for about 10 minutes, until well-browned on all sides. Remove with a slotted spoon and set aside.

2 Add the remaining oil to the casserole, reduce the heat, and add the onion. Cook for about 5 minutes, stirring, until the onion softens. Add the garlic and cook for 1 more minute. Then stir in the carrots and mushrooms, cook gently for 5 minutes, and add the allspice and bay leaf.

3 Return the meat to the casserole and add the cinnamon stick, beer, stock, and breadcrumbs. Bring to the boil and season to taste. Then reduce to a gentle simmer, cover partially, and cook for about 1 hour, until the pork is tender.

4 Remove the bay leaf and cinnamon stick and check for seasoning. Garnish with the parsley and serve with buttered green cabbage or kale.

BIGOS

To make this authentic Polish hunter's stew, it's worth using Polish sausages such as wiejska or kilometrova, but any smoked sausage will work well, too.

THE CUT Pork shoulder

SERVES 8
PREP 40 mins **COOK** 2 hrs

15g (½oz) dried mushrooms, such as porcini

2 x 680g jars of sauerkraut

250g (9oz) streaky bacon rashers, cut into lardons

2 large onions, roughly chopped

1 kg (2¼lb) pork shoulder, diced

10 dried prunes

8 juniper berries

½ tsp ground allspice

3 bay leaves

2 tbsp clear honey

1 tbsp tomato purée

1 litre (1¾ pints) chicken stock

250g (9oz) smoked sausage, chopped into bite-sized pieces

1 Soak the mushrooms in 200ml (7fl oz) boiling water, cover, and set aside. Cook the sauerkraut in a large, flameproof casserole over a low heat for about 5–10 minutes. Meanwhile, fry half the bacon in a large, non-stick frying pan. Once the fat is released, stir in the onions, reduce the heat, and cook for 5 minutes, stirring occasionally, until soft. Add the bacon mixture to the sauerkraut, stir well, and set aside. Preheat the oven to 180°C (350°F/Gas 4).

2 Fry the remaining bacon in the pan for about 5 minutes. Remove with a slotted spoon, leaving the fat in the pan, and add to the sauerkraut. Then cook the diced pork in the pan over a high heat for 5–10 minutes, until well-browned. Add it to the sauerkraut. Then stir in the mushrooms and the soaking water and add all the remaining ingredients, except the sausage. Place the casserole over a high heat and bring to the boil. Then cover and cook in the oven for 1½ hours.

3 Remove from the oven, add the sausages, and stir to combine. Return to the oven and cook for 30 minutes, or until the pork is tender. Remove the bay leaves and juniper berries, and serve with small boiled potatoes.

BAVARIAN ROAST PORK

This German favourite features caraway seeds and a healthy dose of garlic, and is best when served with sauerkraut.

THE CUT Pork shoulder

SERVES 6
PREP 20 mins **COOK** 4 hrs, plus resting

1.8kg (4lb) skin-on boneless pork shoulder

2 tbsp caraway seeds

1 tbsp paprika

1 tbsp each of salt and freshly ground black pepper

4 tbsp olive oil

500g (1lb 2oz) white onion, chopped

500g (1lb 2oz) carrots, sliced

500g (1lb 2oz) waxy potatoes, such as Charlotte or Anya potatoes

4 garlic cloves

250ml (9fl oz) vegetable stock (optional)

1 Preheat the oven to 160°C (325°F/Gas 3). Use a knife to lightly score the skin of the pork. Combine the caraway seeds, paprika, salt, pepper, and half the oil in a bowl. Coat the meat with two-thirds of the spice mixture.

2 Place the onion, carrots, potatoes, and garlic in a roasting pan and toss with the remaining oil and spice mix. Place the pork in the pan with its fat side up.

3 Roast the pork and vegetables in the oven for 3–4, hours or until the internal temperature of the meat reaches 65°C (150°F). Add stock to the roasting pan to prevent the vegetables from drying out, if required.

4 Remove from the oven and leave to rest for at least 5 minutes before carving. Serve alongside the roasted vegetables, if preferred.

VARIATION

Bavarian-style roast beef Use the top rump of beef in place of the pork shoulder. For the marinade, use 2 tablespoons crushed allspice berries instead of the caraway seeds and 1 tablespoon chipotle paste instead of the paprika. Cook as above and serve with the roasted vegetables.

SLOW-COOKED PORK SHOULDER WITH CIDER GRAVY

Pork shoulder is an inexpensive and large cut, and roasts far better than a more traditional (but drier) pork leg. The boozy gravy adds a rich flavour to this simple dish.

THE CUT Pork shoulder

SERVES 6–8
PREP 10 mins, plus chilling
COOK 3 hrs, plus resting

2kg (4½lb) skin-on bone-in pork shoulder

1 tbsp olive oil

salt and freshly ground black pepper

300ml (10fl oz) cider

200ml (7fl oz) chicken stock

1 tbsp plain flour

1 With a sharp knife, make criss-cross slits all over the skin of the pork, being careful not to cut through to the meat underneath. (You can ask your butcher to do this for you.) Rub the skin dry with kitchen paper and leave the meat to rest, uncovered, in the fridge for at least 4 hours, but preferably overnight. This will help the skin crisp on cooking.

2 Preheat the oven to 180°C (350°F/Gas 4). Place the meat skin-side up in a roasting tray, and rub the oil and salt all over the top, being sure to get inside the slits in the skin.

3 Pour the cider and stock into the roasting tray, being careful not to splash the top of the meat. Cover the skin with a piece of greaseproof paper (this will help to stop the skin sticking to the foil), then cover the whole roasting tray with foil, sealing it tightly so that no steam escapes.

4 Roast the pork for 2½ hours, then remove the foil and greaseproof paper, increase the oven temperature to 230°C (450°F/Gas 8), and roast for 30–40 minutes until the skin is crisp. Remove the pork from the oven and separate the crackling. Leave the crackling uncovered in the turned-off oven. Wrap the pork in foil to keep warm while you make the gravy.

5 For the gravy, skim about 4 tablespoons of the pork fat from the top of the cooking juices into a saucepan and set it over a low heat. Whisk in the flour and cook it for 2–3 minutes, whisking constantly, until it bubbles and starts to change colour. Meanwhile, skim off and discard as much of the remaining fat as possible from the cooking liquid. Then pour the liquid into the pan a little at a time, whisking as you go, until you have a thick, rich gravy. Check the seasoning. Bring it to the boil, reduce to a simmer, and cook for 5 minutes before serving with the pork and crackling.

NICE DEVICE

One of the best kitchen devices ever invented is the fat-separating jug, which has a spout at the bottom instead of the top. As the fat floats to the top of any liquid poured in, this jug allows you to use as much of the natural juices as possible from a roast, while leaving the fat behind.

HUNGARIAN GOULASH

This traditional herdsman's supper is made unique by the use of paprika and caraway seeds.

 Pork shoulder

SERVES 6–8
PREP 30 mins **COOK** 2 hrs

3 tbsp vegetable oil

800g (1¾lb) pork shoulder, cut into cubes

1 large onion, roughly chopped

1 garlic clove, crushed

½ tsp caraway seeds

1–2 tbsp paprika

2 ripe tomatoes, blanched, peeled, and diced

3 tbsp tomato purée

1 large red pepper, deseeded and thinly sliced

2 large potatoes, peeled and cut into cubes

salt and freshly ground black pepper

chopped dill, to garnish

1 Heat the oil in a large, flameproof casserole over a high heat. Add the meat, in batches, and cook until well-browned all over. Remove the meat with a slotted spoon, transfer to a plate lined with kitchen paper, and set aside.

2 Reduce the heat, add the onion, and cook for 1–2 minutes, until softened. Add the garlic, caraway seeds, paprika, and 2 tablespoons of water. Stir to mix the flavours and colour.

3 Return the meat to the casserole and stir to combine all the ingredients. Add enough water just to cover the meat and bring to the boil. Then reduce the heat to a gentle simmer, cover, and cook for 1 hour, until the meat is tender.

4 Add the tomatoes and tomato purée, red pepper, and potatoes. Season well and bring to the boil. Then reduce to a simmer for 30 more minutes. Remove from the heat, garnish with chopped dill, and serve hot in deep bowls.

VARIATION

Chicken goulash Use chicken in place of the pork, and green pepper in place of the red pepper. Replace the paprika with smoked paprika, and cook as above. Serve topped with soured cream and chopped fresh dill.

POSOLE

This Mexican stew is traditionally made with dried hominy, which are soaked and enlarged corn kernels.

Pork shoulder

SERVES 8
PREP 20 mins **COOK** 5 hrs, plus resting

1kg (2¼lb) boneless pork shoulder

2 tbsp ground cumin

½ tbsp garlic powder

½ tbsp smoked paprika

salt and freshly ground black pepper

200g (7oz) red onion, sliced

250ml (9fl oz) chicken stock

FOR THE POSOLE

60ml (2fl oz) vegetable oil

4 garlic cloves, crushed

200g (7oz) red onion, chopped

20 cherry tomatoes, halved

2 x 400g can chopped tomatoes, with juices

1.25 litres (2 pints) chicken stock

100g (3½oz) frozen corn, defrosted

50g (1¾oz) dried pinto beans, rinsed and soaked in cold water overnight

1 tbsp dried oregano

1 tsp cumin seeds

50g (1¾oz) coriander leaves, to garnish

100g (3½oz) grated Cheddar cheese, to garnish

250g (9oz) white onion, chopped, to garnish

1 Preheat the oven to 140°C (275°F/Gas 1). For the pork, place the cumin, garlic powder, and smoked paprika in a small bowl and season well. Mix the spices and use to rub evenly on both sides of the pork. Place the pork and red onions in a small roasting tin, pour in the stock, and cover with foil. Transfer to the oven and roast for 5 hours.

2 Meanwhile, make the posole. Heat the oil in a large, heavy-based saucepan. Add the garlic and onions and sauté until tender. Add the remaining ingredients, season well, and stir to combine. Cover and simmer for 2 hours, stirring occasionally.

3 Remove the pork from the oven, leave it to rest for 30 minutes, then use a fork to shred the meat. Add the shredded meat, along with the onions, to the posole. Season to taste. Serve the posole hot, garnished with coriander, cheese, and white onion.

COCHINITA PIBIL

Inspired by the traditional Mexican dish of Mayan origin, which means "sucking pig cooked in a pit", this dish uses slow-cooked pork shoulder.

THE CUT Pork shoulder

SERVES 8
PREP 45 mins, plus overnight marinating
COOK 2½ hrs, plus resting

2.7kg (6lb) skin-on bone-in pork shoulder

3 tbsp garlic, finely chopped

grated zest of 1 orange, plus juice of 3 oranges

1 tbsp dried oregano

1 tbsp ground cumin

1 tbsp each of salt and freshly ground black pepper

225g (8oz) onions, thinly sliced

juice of 1 lime

juice of 1 lemon

120ml (4fl oz) dry sherry

1 Trim the excess fat from the shoulder and score the meat. Place the garlic, orange zest, oregano, cumin, salt, and pepper in a small bowl, and combine to form a paste. Rub the mixture all over the pork, pushing it into the slits.

2 Place the onions in a large bowl and top with the pork. Mix the fruit juices and the sherry and pour over the pork. Cover the bowl and leave in a cool place to marinate overnight.

3 Preheat the oven to 160°C (325°F/Gas 3). Remove the pork from the bowl, reserving the marinade. Pat the pork dry with kitchen paper and set aside for about 2 hours to bring it to room temperature.

4 Transfer the pork and marinade to a roasting pan. Roast the pork in the oven for 2½ hours, basting with the marinade every 30 minutes, until the internal temperature reaches 75°C (165°F). Remove from the oven and allow to rest for 15 minutes before carving. To serve, carve the meat into slices and place on a platter, with the hot juices spooned over.

POTTED PORK

Also known as *rilletes de porc*, this rich and savoury spread is perfect with crusty bread and a spicy mustard.

THE CUT Pork shoulder

MAKES 1.2 litres (2 pints)
PREP 15 mins
COOK 4 hrs, plus resting and chilling

1 tbsp brown sugar

½ tsp dried thyme

½ tsp cinnamon

½ tsp cloves

½ tsp grated nutmeg

½ tsp ground ginger

½ tsp garlic powder

1 tbsp sea salt, plus extra to taste

1kg (2¼lb) pork shoulder

350g (12oz) butter

4 garlic cloves, crushed

100g (3½oz) shallots, finely chopped

50g (1¾oz) sage

freshly ground black pepper, to taste

1 Preheat the oven to 160°C (325°F/Gas 3). Place the sugar, thyme, cinnamon, cloves, nutmeg, ginger, garlic, and salt in a small bowl and mix well to combine. Rub both sides of the pork shoulder with the spice mixture and place in a roasting pan. Cover with foil and cook for 4 hours.

2 Melt the butter in a saucepan over a low heat and skim off the foam. Remove the pork from the oven and set aside to rest for 30 minutes. Roughly shred the meat, and place it in a food processor along with the garlic, shallots, sage, and half the melted butter. Pulse the mixture until it forms a smooth paste. Season to taste.

3 Spoon the mixture into pint glasses, with the remaining melted butter poured over. Seal and chill in the fridge for at least 1 hour. Serve chilled with sliced bread or crackers.

PORK WITH CLAMS

The marriage of pork, shellfish, and cured ham is particularly delicious in this Portuguese dish from the Alentejo region.

THE CUT Pork shoulder

SERVES 6
PREP 30 mins   **COOK** 2 hrs

60ml (2fl oz) olive oil

500g (1lb 2oz) boneless pork shoulder

450g (1lb) onions, finely chopped

6 garlic cloves, chopped

1 bay leaf

¼ tsp chilli flakes

400g can peeled plum tomatoes

240ml (8fl oz) dry white wine

50g (1¾oz) presunto or Parma ham

175g (6oz) chouriço or chorizo sausages

about 300g (10oz) small Venus clams or cockles

1 Heat the oil in a heavy-based casserole over a high heat. Cut the pork into 2.5cm (1in) pieces, add to the casserole, and cook for 10 minutes, until lightly browned on all sides. Reduce the heat and add the onions, garlic, bay leaf, and chilli flakes. Then cook, stirring occasionally, for 5 more minutes.

2 Add the tomatoes, crushing them with the back of a wooden spoon. Stir in all but 2 tablespoons of the wine, bring to the boil, and then reduce to a gentle simmer. Cover and cook for 30 minutes.

3 Chop the presunto into small cubes and add to the casserole. Cover the stew and simmer for 30 minutes. Cut the chouriço into small chunks and add to the stew. Cover and cook for about 15 minutes, until the pork is tender.

4 Rinse the clams under cold running water and spread over the surface of the casserole. Drizzle over the remaining wine and stir it lightly into the sauce. Cover, increase the heat a little, and shake the pan firmly, for about 5 minutes to help open the clams. Discard any clams that do not open. Stir well to mix the ingredients, and remove the bay leaf. Serve with crusty bread and a green salad.

PORK CARNITAS

Slow-cooking the pork tenderizes the meat and adds flavour to this spicy Mexican speciality.

THE CUT Pork shoulder

SERVES 6
PREP 20 mins   **COOK** 3½ hrs

1kg (2¼lb) boneless pork shoulder

1 tbsp chipotle paste or smoked paprika

1 tsp dried oregano

1 tsp ground cumin

1 tsp chilli flakes

1 tsp garlic powder

salt and freshly ground black pepper

500g (1lb 2oz) white onion, thinly sliced

3 garlic cloves, crushed

3 tbsp olive oil

juice of 1 lime

1 Preheat the oven to 160°C (325°F/Gas 3). Rinse the pork and pat dry with kitchen paper. Place the spices and seasoning in a small bowl and mix well. Place the pork on a clean work surface and rub the spice mix over generously.

2 In a large roasting pan, heat the onions and garlic over a medium heat. Place the pork on top and drizzle over 1 tablespoon of the oil and the lime juice. Cover the pan with foil and transfer to the oven. Roast the pork for 2½–3 hours, or until the internal temperature reaches 65°C (150°F).

3 Remove the pan from the oven and set aside to rest and cool slightly for at least 5 minutes. When cool enough to handle, use a fork to shred the pork lightly. Heat the remaining oil in a large frying pan and sauté the shredded pork over a medium-high heat, until crisp. Serve with corn tortillas and salsa.

VARIATION

Slow-cooked chicken carnitas with guacamole
Use boneless chicken breasts instead of the pork shoulder and cook as above. For the guacamole, mash 2 peeled avocados, 100g (3½oz) quartered cherry tomatoes, 1 chopped red onion, 75g (2½oz) chopped coriander, salt, pepper, and the juice of 2 limes in a large bowl. Arrange the shredded chicken on a plate, top with the guacamole, and serve.

CANDIED HAND OF PORK

Based on an inexpensive cut of pork, this simple Chinese recipe imparts classic sweet and sour flavours.

THE CUT Hand of pork

SERVES 6
PREP 20 mins   **COOK** 2½ hrs

1 bone-in hand of pork, about 2kg (4½lb)

10cm (4in) piece of fresh root ginger, peeled and thickly sliced

3 spring onions, halved lengthways

6 tbsp soy sauce

3 tbsp dry sherry

25g (scant 1oz) brown sugar

1 Place the pork in a large, heavy-based saucepan. Cover with cold water, bring to the boil, and boil for 5 minutes. Drain and rinse the pork and return to the pan, skin-side down. Add the ginger, spring onions, soy sauce, sherry, and sugar, and about 1 litre (1¾ pints) water. Bring to the boil, cover, and simmer for 1 hour, moving the joint occasionally to prevent it from sticking to the bottom of the pan.

2 Turn the joint over and add enough water to cover one-third of the pork. Cover and bring to the boil. Then reduce to a simmer and cook for a further 1 hour, moving the joint occasionally.

3 Remove the lid and increase the heat to allow the sauce to cook further. Baste the joint with the sauce as it thickens, making sure it does not stick to the bottom of the pan. When the sauce is of a coating texture, remove the joint from the pan.

4 To serve, carve the joint towards the bone and arrange the meat on a platter. Pour the sauce over and serve immediately.

SHAKE IT UP

To prevent the pork from sticking to the bottom of the pan, the Chinese often place it on a bamboo mat after the initial 5 minutes of cooking. An occasional prod of the meat or shaking of the pan will also work.

PORK AND SPRING GREENS

This quick stir-fry makes the most of leafy seasonal produce and is best served with fluffy rice.

THE CUT Pork fillet or tenderloin

SERVES 4
PREP 10 mins   **COOK** 10 mins

1 tbsp olive oil

350g (12oz) pork fillet or tenderloin, cut into thin strips

4 garlic cloves, sliced

2 heads of spring greens, shredded

2 tsp onion seeds

salt and freshly ground black pepper

1 Heat the oil in a wok over a medium-high heat. Add the pork and stir-fry for about 5 minutes, moving it around the wok as it heats up.

2 Add the garlic and greens and continue to stir-fry over a medium-high heat for 1 minute, or until the greens have just wilted. Add the onion seeds, stir to combine, then season with salt and pepper. Serve immediately.

VARIATION

Pigeon breasts with spring greens and hoisin sauce
Use 8 skinless pigeon breasts, about 350g (12oz), instead of the pork, and sunflower oil instead of olive oil. Stir-fry the strips of meat for 2 minutes, then add 2 tablespoons of hoisin sauce and stir-fry for 1 more minute. Then cook as above and add a dash of soy sauce, to taste, at the end.

WHOLE GLAZED GAMMON

A combination of marmalade and pineapple juice gives this succulent gammon a wonderful sweet, sticky finish and makes it the perfect festive table centrepiece.

THE CUT Whole gammon or ham

SERVES 8–10
PREP 20 mins   **COOK** 2½ hrs

2kg (4½lb) piece of smoked gammon or ham

3 heaped tbsp smooth marmalade

2 tbsp pineapple juice

1 tbsp clear honey

1 heaped tbsp soft light brown sugar

2 tbsp wholegrain mustard

salt and freshly ground black pepper

1 Preheat the oven to 160°C (325°F/Gas 3). Place the gammon, skin-side up, on a rack in a large roasting tin. Pour water to a depth of 3cm (1in) into the tin. Cover tightly with foil and seal to ensure that no steam escapes. Cook in the oven for 2 hours.

2 Meanwhile, place the marmalade, pineapple juice, honey, brown sugar, and mustard in a large saucepan over a medium heat. Season with salt and pepper and bring to the boil. Then reduce the heat to a simmer and cook for 5–7 minutes, until thickened.

3 Remove the gammon from the oven and increase the oven temperature to 200°C (400°F/Gas 6). Remove the skin, leaving a thin layer of the fat. Cut a criss-cross pattern in the fat.

4 Brush some of the glaze over the gammon. Return to the oven for 30 minutes, brushing with the glaze every 10 minutes, until brown and crispy. Remove from the oven and serve hot with mashed potatoes.

LOIN OF PORK COOKED IN MILK

Lactic acid in the milk helps to tenderize the meat, and the lemon sauce enhances the flavour in this classic north Italian dish.

THE CUT Pork fillet or tenderloin

SERVES 4
PREP 15 mins   **COOK** 2 hrs, plus resting

700g (1lb 8oz) boneless pork fillet or tenderloin

sea salt and freshly ground black pepper

2 tbsp olive oil

50g (1¾oz) unsalted butter

675ml (1 pint) whole milk

5 garlic cloves, cut in half

1 tbsp chopped sage leaves

zest of 1 lemon, cut into strips

200ml (7fl oz) full-fat cream

1. Rub the pork with kitchen paper to remove excess moisture and season well. Heat the oil and butter in a large, lidded, heavy-based saucepan. Add the pork and cook until well-browned all over. Meanwhile, heat the milk in a separate saucepan and set aside. Remove the pork from the pan and pour away half of the fat.

2 Reduce the heat and add the garlic and sage. Stir briefly, making sure the garlic doesn't burn. Return the pork to the pan and pour the heated milk over. Add the lemon zest and bring to the boil. Reduce the heat to a simmer, cover partially, and cook for 1½–2 hours. Remove from the heat.

3 Transfer the pork to a serving dish and set aside for 5 minutes. Add the cream to the pan and simmer for 5–10 minutes, until the sauce thickens. Remove from the heat. When cool enough to handle, cut the meat in thick slices and arrange on a serving dish. Scrape the brown bits from the bottom of the pan and add them to the sauce. These have a great flavour. Serve the pork with the milk and lemon sauce spooned over.

HERB APPEAL

If sage is not readily available, you can use fresh oregano or marjoram in its place.

MOLE SHREDDED PORK ENCHILADAS

Mole, a traditional Mexican sauce flavoured with chilli and dark chocolate, adds a deep, rich taste to this popular recipe.

THE CUT Pork fillet or tenderloin

SERVES 4
PREP 20 mins   **COOK** 1½ hrs

900g (2lb) boneless pork fillet or tenderloin

225g (8oz) grated Monterey Jack or Cheddar cheese

4 large tortillas

FOR THE SAUCE

1 tsp olive oil

1 onion, finely chopped

3 garlic cloves, crushed

30g (1oz) plain or dark chocolate, broken into pieces

2 x 400g can chopped tomatoes

1 tsp chipotle paste

pinch of cayenne pepper

pinch of ground cinnamon

pinch of sugar

salt and freshly ground black pepper

1 For the sauce, heat the oil in a large saucepan over a medium heat. Add the onion and sauté for 4 minutes, until soft. Then add the garlic and sauté for a further minute. Stir in the chocolate, tomatoes, chipotle, cayenne pepper, cinnamon, and sugar. Season well. Reduce the heat to a simmer.

2 In a frying pan, seal the pork for about 30 seconds, on each side, over a high heat. Add the pork to the sauce, turning once to coat, and simmer for 1 hour, stirring occasionally. Remove the pork from the sauce and shred the meat with a fork.

3 Preheat the oven to 180°C (350°F/Gas 4). Divide the meat and half the cheese between the tortillas. Roll up the tortillas tightly. Spoon half the mole sauce into a large flameproof casserole or baking dish. Lay the stuffed tortillas, seam-side down, in a row over the sauce. Top them with the remaining sauce and cheese and bake for 25 minutes. Serve hot with refried black beans and pico de gallo.

PARMA HAM-WRAPPED PORK TENDERLOIN WITH SAUSAGE AND GORGONZOLA STUFFING

A favourite at the holiday table, this dish features the most popular cuts of pork – the fillet or tenderloin, salty Parma ham, and spiced sausage.

THE CUT Pork fillet or tenderloin

SERVES 4
PREP 30 mins   **COOK** 2 hrs, plus resting

2 tbsp butter

3 garlic cloves, crushed

50g (1¾oz) shallots, sliced

150g (5½oz) sausagemeat

1 tsp dried mixed herbs

1 tsp dried oregano

1 tsp dried rosemary

½ tbsp crushed chilli flakes

salt and freshly ground black pepper

75g (2½oz) kale, roughly chopped

25g (scant 1oz) crumbled Gorgonzola

300g (10oz) boneless pork fillet or tenderloin

100g (3½oz) Parma ham

250ml (9fl oz) chicken stock

1. Melt the butter in a frying pan over a medium heat. Add the garlic and shallots and sauté for 5 minutes, until browned. Stir in the sausagemeat and half the herbs and spices. Season and cook for 15–20 minutes, stirring occasionally, until the pork is browned. Stir in the kale and Gorgonzola, and reduce the heat to low. Preheat the oven to 180°C (350°F/Gas 4).

2. Place the tenderloin between 2 sheets of cling film and pound with a meat tenderizer to a thickness of 5mm (¼in). Lay the tenderloin on a chopping board with 7 pieces of butcher's string placed horizontally under it at equal distance from each other. Spread the stuffing all over and gently roll the meat into a spiral. Wrap with the Parma ham to seal, and tie with the string to secure.

3. Place the tenderloin in a roasting pan and cover with the stock. Sprinkle with the remaining herbs and spices, and roast for 35–40 minutes, or until browned. Rest for 15 minutes. Cut into thick slices, arrange on a serving platter, and serve warm.

ROAST PORK WITH SAGE AND ONION STUFFING

A classic British Sunday lunch dish, the marriage of sage and onion is a perfect foil for the sweetness of pork.

THE CUT Pork loin

SERVES 10–12
PREP 30 mins   **COOK** 2½ hrs

45g (1½oz) butter

1 small onion, finely chopped

100g (3½oz) fresh white breadcrumbs

1 tbsp chopped sage

salt and freshly ground black pepper

2.25kg (5lb) boneless pork loin

1 tsp sea salt

1 tsp plain flour

2 tbsp white wine

500ml (16fl oz) pork or chicken stock

1 bay leaf

1 For the stuffing, heat the butter in a frying pan over a medium heat and fry the onions for 5 minutes, or until soft but not browned. Stir in the breadcrumbs and sage, and season lightly. Remove from the heat and set aside to cool.

2 Preheat the oven to 190°C (375°F/Gas 5). Lay the pork on a chopping board and use a kinfe to make 2cm (¾in) deep slashes at 2.5cm (1in) intervals from top to bottom in the skin. Rub in the sea salt. Turn the meat over, skin-side down, and cut a pocket about 2cm (¾in) deep along the length, season with salt and pepper, and spread the sage and onion stuffing into the pocket. Roll up tightly and tie with butcher's string.

3 Place the pork on a trivet in a roasting tin and bake for 2 hours, basting with the fat every 45 minutes. Then transfer the pork to another roasting tin and reserve the fat. Increase the temperature to 230°C (450°F/Gas 8), return the pork to the oven, and cook for 10 more minutes to crisp up the crackling.

4 Meanwhile, to make the sauce, discard all but 1 tablespoon of the fat from the first roasting tin. Place over a low heat, stir in the flour, scrape up the juices, and cook for 2–3 minutes. Then add the wine and stock, and stir to combine. Bring to the boil, add the bay leaf, and simmer until the sauce begins to thicken. Season and strain. To serve, remove the crackling and carve the meat in thick slices. Serve the gravy separately.

PORK CHOPS COOKED IN FOIL

Cooking the pork chops slowly in foil tenderizes the meat and helps retain moisture.

 **Pork chops**

SERVES 4
PREP 15 mins   **COOK** 1 hr

4 tsp olive oil

4 pork chops

salt and freshly ground black pepper

1 large dessert apple

4 tsp honey

4 sprigs of marjoram or oregano

100ml (3½fl oz) dry cider

mashed potatoes, to serve

green vegetables, to serve

1 Preheat the oven to 180°C (350°F/Gas 4). Cut 4 sheets of baking foil large enough to enclose the chops. Pour a teaspoon of oil on each one and spread over the middle. Dry the chops on kitchen paper, place in the centre of each foil sheet, and season.

2 Cut the apple into quarters, take out the core, slice each piece into 4, and spread over the chops. Top each chop with a teaspoon of honey, a sprig of marjoram, and a splash of cider.

3 Fold the foil over to create a little enclosed parcel. Place on a baking tray and cook in the oven for about 1 hour. Serve hot with mashed potatoes and green vegetables added to the foil parcels.

VARIATION

Slow-cooked pork belly Use pork belly instead of pork chops and prepare as above. Preheat the oven to 140°C (284°F/Gas 1) and slow cook the pork for up to 6 hours.

TONKATSU

This Japanese deep-fried breaded pork with a hot sauce is traditionally served with finely shredded white cabbage.

THE CUT Pork chops

SERVES 4
PREP 30 mins   **COOK** 15 mins

4 boneless pork chops

2 tbsp plain flour

salt and freshly ground black pepper

2 eggs, beaten

50g (1¾oz) panko breadcrumbs

sunflower oil, for frying

1 small white cabbage, finely shredded

FOR THE SAUCE

60ml (2fl oz) Worcestershire sauce

1 tbsp tomato ketchup

1 tsp shoyu sauce

1 Use a knife to score the chops in vertical lines down to the fat. Place the flour in a small bowl and season with salt and pepper. Toss the pork chops in the flour and shake off the excess. Dip them in the beaten egg, and then coat evenly with breadcrumbs.

2 Heat the oil in a deep-fat fryer to 180°C (350°F). Deep-fry the pork chops for 8 minutes, or until golden brown. Remove the meat with a slotted spoon and drain on a plate lined with kitchen paper.

3 For the sauce, mix all the ingredients in a small bowl. Cut the pork in slices and serve on mounds of shredded cabbage, along with the sauce.

CHOUCROUTE GARNIE

Traditionally served with steamed potatoes, this classic dish from the Alsace region of France also has a distinct German influence from the pickled cabbage.

THE CUT Pork chops

SERVES 4
PREP 30 mins   **COOK** 2½ hrs

900g jar of sauerkraut

25g (scant 1oz) lard

400g (14oz) mixed sausages, garlic or cured, cut into bite-sized pieces

4 pork chops

1 large onion, thinly sliced

1 green dessert apple, peeled, cored, and sliced

2 garlic cloves, crushed

2 bay leaves

10 juniper berries

1 tbsp caraway seeds

500ml (16fl oz) dry white Alsace wine

finely chopped flat-leaf parsley, to garnish

1 Preheat the oven to 150°C (300°F/Gas 2). Rinse the sauerkraut in cold water and squeeze dry. Heat the lard in a large casserole over a medium heat. Add the sausages and the chops and cook until well-browned all over. Do this in batches to retain the heat in the casserole. Remove the sausages and chops with a slotted spoon and set aside.

2 Reduce the heat. Add the onion and apple, and cook, stirring occasionally, until softened. Then add the sauerkraut and mix well. Add the garlic, bay leaves, juniper berries, and caraway seeds. Pour in the wine and 240ml (8fl oz) water and mix well.

3 Bring to the boil. Add the pork chops and reduce the heat. Allow to simmer for 10 minutes, then cover and place in the oven for 1 hour. Add the sausages and return to the oven for 1 more hour.

4 Remove from the oven and discard the bay leaf and juniper berries. To serve, place the sauerkraut in the centre of a large platter. Arrange the pork chops around it and garnish with parsley.

VARIETY MIX

You can vary the sausage types from bratwurst, to frankfurters, or even Polish kielbasa. You can even add smoked ham for a different flavour.

BURMESE GOLDEN PORK

Chunky bits of pork mingle with spicy garlic, ginger, and chilli flavours in this wholesome dish.

THECUT Pork loin or leg

SERVES 4–6
PREP 30 mins   **COOK** 2 hrs

1 large onion, chopped

1 whole garlic bulb

100g (3½oz) fresh root ginger, peeled

1kg (2¼lb) lean pork, cut into cubes

1 tsp salt

1 tbsp white wine vinegar

1 tsp chilli powder

100ml (3½fl oz) groundnut oil

2 tsp toasted sesame oil

1 tsp ground turmeric

handful of coriander leaves or 1 red chilli, cut into strips to garnish

1 Place the onion, garlic, and ginger in a food processor and whizz, or crush them using a mortar and pestle. Press the resulting mixture through a fine sieve, or squeeze them using a muslin cloth, to extract the liquid. Set the residue aside.

2 Place a saucepan over a low heat, pour in the extracted liquid, and add the pork, salt, vinegar, chilli, and half the groundnut oil. Bring to a gentle simmer and cook over a low heat for 1½ hours.

3 Place a small saucepan over a low heat and add the remaining groundnut oil and the sesame oil. Add the onion, garlic, and ginger residue and fry gently. Stir in the turmeric and cook over a low heat for 5 minutes.

4 Mince half the cooked pork in a food processor, then stir it into the cooked onion mixture and combine well. Add a little water if it seems dry. Add this mixture to the remaining pork and stir well. Cook over a low heat for a further 20 minutes, until golden brown. Garnish with coriander leaves or strips of red chilli. Serve hot.

COOL COMFORT

Chill this dish in the fridge for a day or two to help the spices intensify and allow the flavours to really develop.

PORK SATAY WITH PEANUT DIPPING SAUCE

Satay is the national dish of Indonesia and a favourite during festivals.

THECUT Pork fillet or tenderloin

SERVES 4
PREP 20 mins, plus marinating
COOK 30 mins

300g (10oz) white onion, chopped

2.5cm (1in) piece of fresh root ginger, peeled and chopped

3 garlic cloves, finely chopped

juice of 1 lime

2 tbsp soy sauce

2 tbsp brown sugar

2 tsp chilli flakes

700g (1lb 8oz) pork fillet or tenderloin, cut into large chunks

1 tbsp vegetable oil

FOR THE SAUCE

4 tbsp peanut butter

2 tbsp soy sauce

4 garlic cloves

1 tbsp ground ginger

juice of 2 limes

4 tbsp vegetable oil

1 Place the onion, ginger, garlic, lime juice, soy sauce, sugar, and chilli flakes in a food processor and pulse to form a smooth paste. Mix the pork with the paste in a bowl or plastic bag and chill in the fridge for 2 hours. Soak 4 bamboo skewers in water for at least 30 minutes.

2 Heat the oil in a large frying pan. Remove the pork from the marinade and thread onto the skewers. Cook over a medium heat for 5–7 minutes, or until well-browned on all sides and cooked through.

3 For the sauce, place the peanut butter, soy sauce, garlic, ginger, and lime juice in a food processor and pulse until combined. Turn the processor on high and add the vegetable oil in a steady stream. Serve the pork hot with the peanut dipping sauce on the side.

CHINESE-SPICED PORK BELLY

A wonderful treatment turns an inexpensive cut of meat into an oriental feast, with the best crackling ever.

THE CUT Pork belly

SERVES 4
PREP 10 mins, plus marinating
COOK 1½ hrs

750g (1lb 10oz) skin-on boneless pork belly

2 tbsp soy sauce

1 tbsp soft light brown sugar

1 tbsp five-spice powder

2 tsp salt

1 tsp sunflower oil

1 With a sharp knife, make criss-cross slits all over the skin of the pork, being careful not to cut through to the meat. Pat the skin dry with kitchen paper.

2 Mix the soy sauce, sugar, five-spice powder, and 1 teaspoon of salt into a thick paste and rub it over the meat side of the pork, keeping the skin dry. Chill in the fridge, skin-side up and uncovered, for at least 8 hours, or overnight.

3 Preheat the oven to 220°C (425°F/Gas 7). Line a roasting tray with foil and position a rack over it. Place the meat, skin-side up, on the rack and rub the skin with the oil and the remaining salt. Heat water in a kettle and half-fill the roasting tray with it.

4 Roast the pork at the top of the oven for 30 minutes, then reduce the temperature to 200°C (400°F/Gas 6) and roast for a further 45 minutes–1 hour, until the skin turns crispy. Remove from the oven, carve into slices, and serve.

DIP IT

Mix soy sauce, grated ginger, Thai sweet chilli sauce, and finely chopped spring onion together with a little water and use as a dip for the sliced pork belly.

CHIPOTLE CINNAMON BACON

This sweet and savoury bacon brings unexpected flair and flavours to the breakfast table.

THE CUT Pork belly

MAKES 450g (1lb) bacon
PREP 15 mins, plus 1 week marinating
COOK 1½ hrs, plus resting

200g (7oz) brown sugar

1 tbsp molasses

2 tbsp sea salt

2 tsp Prague Powder No. 2 curing salt

1 tbsp cinnamon

1 tbsp chipotle powder or smoked paprika

2kg (4½lb) pork belly

YOU WILL ALSO NEED

500g packet of hickory chips

charcoal, for the barbecue

1 Mix together the sugar, molasses, sea salt, curing salt, and spices. Rub the pork belly evenly with the mixture. Place in a plastic bag and refrigerate for at least 1 week.

2 Rinse the bacon under running cold water thoroughly. It should be firm to the touch. Soak the hickory chips in water for 1 hour, then wrap in foil.

3 Remove the rack from the barbecue and spread some charcoal in a ring around the edge. Place the foil-wrapped hickory chips in the centre of the barbecue.

4 Light the charcoal and return the rack to the barbecue. Place the bacon, fat-side up, on the grill. Cover and cook for 1–1½ hours, until the internal temperature of the meat measures 65°C (150°F). If not, transfer it to an oven preheated to 150°C (300°F/Gas 2) and cook until the temperature reaches the required level.

5 Remove from the heat and allow to rest for 30 minutes. Slice and fry the bacon immediately, or store for up to 1 week in an airtight container in the fridge.

PORK BELLY PORCHETTA

This simple version of a classic Italian dish is made using pork belly infused with fresh herbs and fennel.

 **Pork belly**

SERVES 10–12
PREP 30 mins   **COOK** 3½ hrs

5kg (10lb) rectangular piece of skin-on boneless pork belly

freshly ground black pepper

30g (1oz) coarse salt

2 sprigs of thyme, shredded

2 tbsp roughly chopped rosemary

1 tbsp fennel seeds

10 garlic cloves, finely chopped

2 tbsp olive oil, plus extra for greasing

6 tbsp honey

juice of 2 limes

1 Preheat the oven to 250°C (480°F/Gas 9). Lay the pork belly skin-side down on a clean work surface. Sprinkle with pepper and half of the salt, rub well into the meat, and leave for 5 minutes.

2 Sprinkle the thyme, rosemary, and fennel seeds over the meat and then rub in with the garlic. Roll up the pork gently and tie crossways with pieces of butcher's string at 1cm (½in) intervals through the length of the piece. Try to keep as much of the herb mix inside as possible.

3 Grease a roasting tin with a little oil and place the pork in it. Spread the remaining salt along with the oil all over the pork. Roast in the oven for 15 minutes skin-side down, then turn over and roast for a further 15 minutes. Reduce the oven temperature to 150°F (300°C/Gas 2) and cook for 3 hours.

4 Remove the pork from the oven and coat with the honey and lime juice. Roll in the juices for a few minutes, then transfer the meat to a carving board. Stir up the remaining juices and pour into a warmed jug. Cut the meat into thick slices, pour over the sauce, and serve with mashed potato and green peas.

PETIT SALE AUX LENTILLES

Simple to prepare, this classic French home-cured pork is traditionally boiled with lentils, but can also be used in cassoulet and as a base for soups.

THE CUT Pork belly

SERVES 8
PREP 45 mins, plus curing   **COOK** 1½–2 hrs

½ tsp black peppercorns

½ tsp juniper berries

2 sprigs of thyme

7 bay leaves

500g (1lb 2oz) coarse sea salt

15g (½oz) Prague Powder No. 2 curing salt (optional)

2kg (4½lb) skin-on bone-in pork belly

350g (12oz) Puy lentils

10 small carrots (preferably Chantenay)

24 button onions, chopped

10 celery sticks, cut in 2.5cm (1in) lengths

50g (1¾oz) butter

salt and freshly ground black pepper

2 tbsp chopped flat-leaf parsley, to garnish

1 Crush the peppercorns, juniper berries, 1 sprig of thyme, and 5 bay leaves together using a mortar and pestle. Then add the sea salt and the curing salt (if using) and mix to combine.

2 Rub one-third of the salt mixture over the skin-side of the meat, then turn it over and rub the mixture into the other side.

3 Sprinkle half of the remaining salt mixture on a plastic tray and place the meat on it. Sprinkle the remaining half on and around the meat. Cover with cling film, place a clean plastic tray on top, and weigh it down with a 1kg (2¼lb) weight. Leave for 8 hours in a cool place, turning every few hours.

4 Rinse the meat and place it in a large stock pot. Cover with cold water and bring to the boil. Drain and return the pork to the pan. Add 1.7 litres (3 pints) water and bring to the boil. Then reduce the heat and simmer for 30 minutes.

5 Rinse the lentils under cold water and add to the pork along with the carrots, onions, and celery. Add the remaining thyme and bay leaves, and simmer for 1 hour, until the lentils are tender.

6 Remove from the heat and take the pork out of the liquid. Remove the bay leaves, stir in the butter, and season to taste. Cut the pork into thick slices and place in a large dish. Sprinkle with parsley, and serve with the sauce.

HASLET

A traditional British meatloaf made with breadcrumbs, this dish is best eaten the day after you have made it to allow the flavours to develop fully.

THE CUT Pork belly and back bacon

SERVES 6–8
PREP 30 mins   **COOK** 2 hrs, plus cooling

melted pork lard, for greasing

350g (12oz) back bacon, coarsely minced

350g (12oz) pork belly, coarsely minced

1 onion, chopped

175g (6oz) fresh breadcrumbs

1 egg, beaten

1 tsp mustard powder

2 tsp finely chopped sage

120ml (4fl oz) dry cider

salt and freshly ground black pepper

1 Preheat the oven to 180°C (350°F/Gas 4) and grease and line a 900g (2lb) loaf tin with greaseproof paper. Place a large bowl under the blade of a mincer. Using the fine blade, mince the meats together with the onion into the bowl. Add the remaining ingredients to the bowl and mix until well combined.

2 Place the mixture in the prepared loaf tin and press it down firmly with the back of a tablespoon, ensuring there are no gaps in the corners. Cover with foil, place the tin on a baking sheet, and bake in the oven for 2 hours, or until the internal temperature of the meat is 75°C (165°F).

3 Remove the haslet from the oven and set aside to cool. Once cooled, transfer it to a serving platter. Cut into slices and serve with crusty bread and traditional pickles such as piccalilli. It will keep in the fridge, wrapped in foil, for up to 3 days.

BACON JAM

This versatile savoury jam can be used on anything, from breakfast sandwiches to roasted vegetables.

 CUT Streaky bacon

MAKES 600ml (1 pint) jar
PREP 10 mins   **COOK** 1 hr

1 tbsp butter

2 garlic cloves, crushed

500g (1lb 2oz) white onion, chopped

500g (1lb 2oz) thick-cut streaky bacon, chopped

sea salt

1 tbsp chipotle paste

80g (2³⁄₄oz) brown sugar

120ml (4fl oz) white wine

1 tbsp cider vinegar

1 tbsp pectin

1 Melt the butter in a heavy-based frying pan over a medium-low heat. Add the garlic, onion, and bacon to the pan. Season with sea salt and cook for about 20 minutes, stirring frequently, until the bacon caramelizes and becomes crisp.

2 Stir in the chipotle, brown sugar, wine, and vinegar, reduce the heat to a simmer, and cook for 30 minutes. Then stir in the pectin and simmer for 10 more minutes.

3 Remove the pan from the heat. Transfer the hot jam to a 600ml (1 pint) jar or heatproof container. It will store for up to 2 weeks in the fridge.

JAM IT UP

For a delicious side dish, halve some Brussels sprouts and toss them into the hot jam. Roast for 45 minutes, or until they turn crisp.

ZWEIBELKUCHEN

Literally meaning "onion cake", this delicious onion and sour cream German tart is traditionally served during the grape harvest season.

CUT Streaky bacon

SERVES 8
PREP 30 mins, plus rising and proving
COOK 1 hr–1 hr 5 mins

4 tsp dried yeast

3 tbsp olive oil, plus extra for greasing

400g (14oz) strong, white bread flour, plus extra for dusting

1 tsp salt

FOR THE FILLING

50g (1³⁄₄oz) unsalted butter

2 tbsp olive oil

600g (1lb 5oz) onions, finely sliced

½ tsp caraway seeds

sea salt and freshly ground black pepper

150ml (5fl oz) soured cream

150ml (5fl oz) crème fraîche

3 eggs

1 tbsp plain flour

75g (2½oz) smoked streaky bacon rashers, chopped

1 For the crust, dissolve the yeast in 225ml (7½fl oz) warm water. Add the oil and set aside. Sift the flour and salt into a large bowl and make a well in the centre. Pour in the liquid mix, stirring constantly. Use your hands to bring the mixture together to form a soft dough.

2 On a well-floured surface, knead the dough for 10 minutes until soft, smooth, and elastic. Place in a greased bowl, cover with cling film, and leave to rise in a warm place for 1–2 hours, until it doubles.

3 For the filling, heat the butter and oil in a large, heavy-based saucepan. Add the onions and caraway seeds, and season well. Cook gently for 20 minutes, covered, until the onions are soft, but not browned. Remove the lid and cook for 5 more minutes until any excess water evaporates.

4 In a separate bowl, whisk together the soured cream, crème fraîche, eggs, and plain flour, and season well. Add the onion mixture, mix well, and set aside to cool. When the dough has risen, turn it out onto a floured work surface and gently knock it back. Lightly grease the baking tray.

5 Roll the dough out to roughly the size of the tray and use to line the base of the tray, making sure the pie has an upturned edge. Cover with lightly greased cling film and leave to prove in a warm place for 30 minutes until puffy in places.

6 Preheat the oven to 200°C (400°F/Gas 6). Gently push down the dough if it has risen too much around the edges. Spread the filling over, sprinkle over the chopped bacon, and bake in the top shelf of the oven for 35–40 minutes, until golden brown. Remove from the oven and leave to cool for at least 5 minutes before serving. Serve warm or cold.

PASTA CARBONARA

Some say this rich and salty pasta dish was created to feed the hard-working charcoal miners of Italy, hence the name carbonara, derived from *carbonaio*, the Italian word for charcoal burner.

THE CUT Streaky bacon

SERVES 4
PREP 20 mins **COOK** 45 mins

2 tbsp olive oil

4 garlic cloves, crushed

500g (1lb 2oz) white onion, sliced

500g (1lb 2oz) thick-cut streaky bacon, cut into cubes

200g (7oz) fresh or frozen peas

450g (1lb) dried spaghetti

2 eggs

100g (3½oz) freshly grated Parmesan cheese

salt and freshly ground black pepper

1 Heat the oil in a frying pan. Add the garlic and onion, and sauté for 5–10 minutes over a medium heat. Stir in the bacon and reduce the heat slightly. Allow the bacon to crisp, then add the peas and cook for a further 5 minutes.

2 Meanwhile, cook the pasta according to packet instructions until al dente. Strain and reserve some of the cooking liquid.

3 For the sauce, place the egg and grated Parmesan in a large bowl and whisk well to combine. Add a little pasta water to help loosen it if it looks too sticky.

4 Stir the pasta into the pan and cook for 5–10 minutes, making sure it is well coated in the bacon drippings. Remove the pan from the heat and stir in the egg and cheese sauce. Toss well to coat the pasta evenly. Season and serve immediately.

BRANDY BUZZ

Try adding a splash of brandy to the bacon once it has crisped up, then continue cooking until the brandy has evaporated.

BARBECUED RIBS

Time spent cooking meat on the barbecue guarantees a wonderfully succulent appetizer that will be the hit of any party.

THE CUT Pork ribs

SERVES 4
PREP 10 mins
COOK 1 hr 10 mins, plus resting

250g (9oz) brown sugar

3 tbsp cayenne pepper

1½ tbsp mustard powder

3 tbsp salt

1½ tbsp freshly ground white pepper

2 racks of ribs, 750g–1kg (1lb 10oz–2¼lb) each

VARIATION

Oven-roasted pork ribs Try cooking the ribs in the oven instead of on the barbecue. Preheat the oven to 180°C (350°F/Gas 4) at the beginning of step 1. Place the ribs on a baking tray and cook in the oven for 1½ hours. Then remove from the heat, take off the foil, and spoon over the cooking juices from the baking sheet. Then return the ribs to the oven for a further 10 minutes to glaze. Serve hot.

1 Set the barbecue or charcoal grill to its highest setting. Combine the sugar, spices, and seasoning in a small bowl. Place the ribs, meat-side up, on a clean work surface and thoroughly rub over half the spice mix.

2 Place the ribs, meat-side down, on a large sheet of foil. Rub the remaining spice mix over the other side. Cover the ribs with foil and cook over the barbecue for 45 minutes to 1 hour.

3 Remove the ribs from the heat and take off the foil. Leave them to rest for 1–2 minutes. Spoon over the cooking juices from the foil and return the ribs to the barbecue.

4 Cook the ribs on both sides for about 5–9 minutes to glaze and crisp up, and until the internal temperature reaches 65°C (150°F). Remove from the heat and serve hot.

PORK SCHNITZEL WITH CREAMY MUSTARD SAUCE

This quick-to-make, tender pork cutlet with a light sauce is perfect for a mid-week dinner.

 Pork leg steaks

SERVES 4
PREP 10 mins, plus chilling **COOK** 10 mins

FOR THE SCHNITZEL

4 x 100g (3½oz) boneless pork leg steaks

salt and freshly ground black pepper

1 tbsp plain flour

1 egg, beaten

75g (2½oz) day-old white breadcrumbs

1 tbsp olive oil

1 tbsp butter

FOR THE SAUCE

1 tbsp olive oil

½ onion, finely chopped

1 garlic clove, crushed

100ml (3½fl oz) white wine

200ml (7fl oz) double cream

1 tbsp Dijon mustard

pinch of caster sugar

1 If the pork is a little thick, pound it gently with a meat tenderizer, until it is about 2cm (¾in) thick all over.

2 Season the flour and place it on a plate. Place the egg and breadcrumbs in 2 separate shallow bowls. Dust the pork in the flour, shake off the excess, then dip it in the egg. Finally, coat it in the breadcrumbs. Cover and chill for at least 30 minutes to help the coating stick to the meat.

3 Preheat the oven to 180°C (350°F/Gas 4). Heat the oil and butter in a large frying pan over a medium-high heat. Add the pork and cook for 2–3 minutes on each side, until golden brown. Transfer to a baking tray and place in the preheated oven to keep warm.

4 For the sauce, wipe the pan with kitchen paper, heat the oil, and cook the onion gently for 5 minutes. Add the garlic and cook for 1 minute. Then add the wine and allow it to reduce to almost nothing. Add the cream, mustard, and sugar, and simmer until the sauce thickens. Season to taste and serve poured over the pork.

MARINATED LEG OF PORK

A braised leg of pork dish from Germany, the unique marinade gives it the tasty flavour of wild boar.

 Pork leg

SERVES 12
PREP 40 mins, plus 3 days marinating
COOK 4 hrs, plus resting

4kg (9lb) skin-on bone-in pork leg

4 tbsp olive oil

4 tbsp plain flour

500ml (16fl oz) chicken or pork stock

FOR THE MARINADE

1.2 litres (2 pints) red wine

200ml (7fl oz) red wine vinegar

4 carrots, sliced

2 onions, thinly sliced

4 garlic cloves, crushed

6 bay leaves

bunch of flat-leaf parsley

sprig of thyme

sprig of marjoram

1 tbsp black peppercorns

14 juniper berries, crushed

2 tsp coarse salt

FOR THE CABBAGE

1 tbsp olive oil

2 garlic cloves, crushed

1 small white onion, diced

1 head of green cabbage, shredded

500ml (16fl oz) cider vinegar

2 tbsp salt

1 tbsp caraway seeds

1 For the marinade, place all the ingredients in a large saucepan and bring to the boil. Simmer for 5 minutes, remove from the heat, and allow to cool.

2 Score the skin of the pork and place in a large stock pot. Pour the marinade over the meat. Cover with a cloth and leave in a cool place for 3 days, turning occasionally, to ensure it is evenly covered with the marinade.

3 Preheat the oven to 160°C (325°F/Gas 3). Remove the pork from the marinade and pat dry with kitchen paper. Set the marinade aside. Heat the oil in a large casserole, add the pork, and cook until well-browned on all sides.

4 Meanwhile, heat the marinade, including the vegetables, in a separate pan. Remove the pork from the casserole with a slotted spoon, add the flour, and strain the hot marinade into the casserole. Stir to combine. Then pour in just enough stock to make a smooth, thick sauce.

5 Add the pork to the casserole and bring to the boil. Remove from the heat, cover, and transfer to the preheated oven. Cook the pork for 3–4 hours, until the meat is falling off the bone.

6 Meanwhile, for the cabbage, heat the oil in a deep, straight-sided frying pan or Dutch oven. Add the garlic and fry over a medium heat until golden. Stir in the onion and fry for 10 minutes, or until translucent.

7 Add the cabbage to the pan along with 120ml (4fl oz) water, and the vinegar, salt, and caraway seeds. Bring to the boil, reduce to a simmer, cover, and cook over a low heat for 1½ hours. Remove from the heat.

8 Remove the meat from the casserole and keep warm on a serving dish. Skim the excess fat from the casserole and strain the sauce into a pan. Bring to the boil and adjust the seasoning. Add more stock if the sauce is too thick, or boil for 1–2 minutes and reduce if too thin. Carve the meat into slices and serve with the sauce and cabbage.

MUSTARD TWIST

Serve this dish with a mild, German-style, coarsely ground mustard to add a sweet, nutty flavour to the pork.

ASTURIAN BEAN STEW

A Spanish stew with a combination of beans and pork enriched with spices and smoked bacon.

 Gammon or back bacon

SERVES 6
PREP 30 mins, plus 12 hrs soaking of beans and meat
COOK 2 hrs

500g (1lb 2oz) gammon or unsmoked bacon

400g (14oz) dried Fabes beans or other large white beans

2 tbsp olive oil

150g (5½oz) smoked streaky bacon, cut into lardons

1 onion, finely chopped

1 garlic clove, crushed

1 bay leaf

pinch of saffron threads

½ tsp smoked paprika

freshly ground black pepper

2 Morcilla sausages or black pudding

2 chorizo sausages

1 Place the gammon in a large bowl and cover with water. Place in the fridge to soak for 12 hours, changing the water once. Rinse and soak the beans in cold water for 12 hours.

2 Heat the oil in a large, flameproof casserole. Add the streaky bacon and cook, stirring occasionally, for 2 minutes. Then add the onion, reduce the heat, and cook for about 3 minutes, until soft. Stir in the garlic.

3 Drain the gammon and beans, add them to the casserole, and pour in just enough water to cover the meat. Add the bay leaf, saffron threads, smoked paprika, and pepper. Bring to the boil, then reduce the heat. Simmer over a low heat for 1½ hours, stirring occasionally. Add water, if necessary. Add the Morcilla and chorizo sausages, stir to ensure they are evenly distributed, and cook for a further 30 minutes.

4 Remove from the heat and take out the bay leaf. Transfer the gammon and the sausages to a separate bowl and set aside to cool. Once cooled, cut the meat into chunks of about 2½cm (1in) and return to the casserole. Serve in shallow bowls with crusty bread. It is traditionally eaten with a wooden spoon.

PEA, HAM, AND POTATO SOUP

This simple, hearty, comforting soup can be made with leftover ham and tastes even better the next day.

 Ham

SERVES 4–6
PREP 15 mins   **COOK** 2 hrs

1.1kg (2½lb) unsmoked ham

1 bay leaf

1 tbsp olive oil

1 onion, finely chopped

salt and freshly ground black pepper

1 tbsp Dijon mustard

3 garlic cloves, finely chopped

2 sprigs of rosemary

handful of thyme leaves, plus extra to garnish

1.2 litres (2 pints) hot beef stock

450g (1lb) frozen peas

3 potatoes, peeled and chopped into bite-sized pieces

1 Place the ham and bay leaf in a large saucepan, cover with 1.2 litres (2 pints) of water, and bring to the boil. Cover partially, reduce the heat to a simmer, and cook for 1 hour, or until the ham is cooked. Skim away any scum that forms at the surface. Remove the ham from the pan and set aside. Discard the liquid.

2 Heat the oil in a large heavy-based pan over a medium heat. Add the onion and cook for 3–4 minutes, until softened. Season, stir in the mustard, garlic, and herbs, and add a little stock. Bring to the boil, then add the peas and remaining stock. Bring to the boil, reduce the heat to a simmer, and cook for 45 minutes. Top up the soup with hot water as needed.

3 Meanwhile, bring a separate pan of water to the boil. Add the potatoes, bring to the boil, then reduce the heat to a simmer. Cook for 12–15 minutes, until softened. Drain and set aside. Remove the rosemary from the soup and use a stick blender to purée the peas gently.

4 Stir in the potatoes. Remove any fat from the ham, chop into bite-sized pieces, and stir into the soup. Taste and adjust the seasoning, if needed. Garnish with the thyme leaves and serve with wholemeal bread.

FEIJOADA

An authentic Brazilian worker's stew, this dish is made from a variety of fresh and cured pork cuts.

THE CUT Ham hock and pork ribs

SERVES 8
PREP 30 mins, plus 12 hrs
soaking of beans and meat
COOK 3 hrs

1 smoked ham hock, about 450g (1lb)

6 salted pork ribs

500g (1lb 2oz) dried black beans

1 pig's trotter, split

2 garlic cloves, finely chopped

4 bay leaves

400g (14oz) garlic pork sausages, cut into small chunks

4 small oranges, peeled and cut into wedges

1 Place the ham hock and salted ribs in a large bowl and cover with water. Soak them for 12 hours in the fridge, changing the water once. Rinse and soak the beans in cold water for 12 hours.

2 Drain the ham hock, ribs and beans, and place in a large, flameproof casserole. Add the pig's trotter, garlic, and bay leaves. Cover with water and bring to the boil. Reduce to a simmer, skim off any scum, then cover and cook for 2½ hours.

3 Transfer a ladleful of the beans to a bowl and mash them with a fork. Return the mashed beans to the casserole and add the garlic sausages. Simmer for another 30 minutes, or until the meat starts to fall off the bone. Remove from the heat.

4 Pick the meat from the hock and trotter and discard the bones. Cut the meat into chunks and place on a warmed platter. Remove the bay leaves from the casserole. Ladle the beans and sausage stew over the meat and place the orange wedges around the sides. Serve with steamed long-grain rice and spring greens.

PIGGING OUT

You can use any part of the pig for this recipe, such as ears, tails, or nose. Salted ribs are authentic, but if not available, fresh ones will suffice.

HAM HOCK WITH RED CABBAGE

Slow-cooked sweet cabbage is the perfect complement to ham and, with the addition of spices and dried fruit, transforms this humble piece of meat.

THE CUT Ham hock

SERVES 4–6
PREP 20 mins   **COOK** 3 hrs

2 ham hocks, about 1.35kg (3lb) each

1 small red cabbage, cored and finely shredded

2 onions, sliced

4 garlic cloves, finely chopped

a few sprigs of thyme

60g (2oz) raisins

pinch of grated nutmeg

pinch of ground cinnamon

300ml (10fl oz) white wine vinegar

600ml (1 pint) hot vegetable stock (optional)

salt and freshly ground black pepper

1 Preheat the oven to 160°C (325°F/Gas 3). Place the ham hocks in a large, heavy-based saucepan and cover with water. Bring to the boil, then reduce to a simmer. Partially cover, and cook gently for 1 hour. Remove the hams and reserve the cooking liquid, if you wish to use it instead of the vegetable stock (it can be salty).

2 When the hams are cool enough to handle, remove the skin and discard, then place in a large, flameproof casserole. Add the remaining ingredients to the casserole, along with either the stock or the cooking liquid, and tuck the hams in neatly. Season to taste, cover, and place in the oven for 2 hours.

3 Check occasionally to ensure it does not dry out, adding a little hot water, if necessary. Remove the hams, shred the meat, and stir it into the casserole. Serve with baked or roast potatoes.

VARIATION

Ham hock with white cabbage and celery Use 1 small, shredded white cabbage instead of the red cabbage, and add 2 chopped celery sticks along with the other ingredients in step 2. Omit the raisins, nutmeg, and cinnamon and add 1 tablespoon caraway seeds, and cook as above. Serve with plain boiled potatoes.

POT ROAST SMOKED HAM

Ham hock is amazing value and tasty, too. The Jerusalem artichokes add a nutty, creamy texture, but if they're not available you can use parsnips instead.

THE CUT Ham hock

SERVES 4–6
PREP 25 mins   **COOK** 3¼ hrs

2 smoked ham hocks, about 1.35kg (3lb) each

1 bay leaf

1 tbsp olive oil

1 onion, finely chopped

salt and freshly ground black pepper

3 garlic cloves, finely chopped

a few sprigs of thyme

3 carrots, chopped

225g (8oz) Jerusalem artichokes, peeled and sliced

125g (4½oz) yellow split peas

100ml (3½fl oz) dry cider

900ml (1½ pints) hot vegetable stock (optional)

1 Place the ham hocks and bay leaf in a large, heavy-based saucepan. Cover with water and cook for about 2 hours, skimming away any scum that comes to the top of the pan. Remove the hams and, when cool enough to handle, peel away the skins and discard. Set the hams aside. Remove the bay leaf and reserve the cooking liquid, if you wish to use it instead of the vegetable stock (it can be salty).

2 Preheat the oven to 180°C (350°F/Gas 4). Heat the oil in a large, flameproof casserole over a medium heat. Add the onion and cook for 3–4 minutes, until soft. Season to taste, stir through the garlic, thyme, carrots, and artichokes, and cook for 1–2 minutes. Add the split peas and stir to coat. Increase the heat, pour in the cider, and let it bubble for 1 minute. Then add the stock, or the cooking liquid, and bring to the boil. Reduce to a simmer and add the hams to the casserole, tucking them down as much as possible.

3 Cover and place the casserole in the oven for about 1 hour, or until the peas are soft. Check occasionally to make sure it does not dry out too much, adding hot water, if needed. Remove the casserole from the oven and, using a fork, slide the ham meat off the bones and stir it into the casserole. Discard the bones. Taste the casserole and season, if necessary. Serve with fresh crusty bread.

COUNTRY HAM AND EGGS WITH RED EYE GRAVY AND GRITS

A traditional breakfast of the American South, the gravy combines the drippings from pan-fried ham and black coffee.

THE CUT Cured ham

SERVES 4
PREP 15 mins   **COOK** 30 mins

4 tbsp butter

8 slices of thick-cut salt-cured ham

4 large eggs

120ml (4fl oz) black coffee

FOR THE GRITS

750ml (1⅓ pints) chicken stock

200 (7oz) coarse polenta

1 tbsp butter

1 tsp chilli flakes

salt and freshly ground black pepper

250ml (9fl oz) double cream

1 For the grits, heat the chicken stock in a large saucepan. Stir in the polenta, butter, and chilli flakes, and season. Cook for 10 minutes, or until it thickens. Stir in the cream and simmer for 5–10 minutes, stirring occasionally, until thickened.

2 In a frying pan, melt 1 tablespoon of the butter. Fry the ham slices for 2–3 minutes on each side, adding more butter if necessary. Remove the ham using a slotted spoon and place in a warm oven.

3 Meanwhile, melt a little butter in another pan. Fry the eggs, sunny-side up, for 3–6 minutes, or until the yolks have become firm.

4 To make the red eye gravy, pour the coffee and any remaining butter into the pan in which the ham was fried. Increase the heat to medium-high and stir well to mix the ham drippings, butter, and coffee.

5 Place a generous helping of the grits, 2 slices of ham, and an egg on each plate, and serve drizzled with the red eye gravy.

CUBANO

A Latin variation of a grilled ham and cheese sandwich, the Cubano is one of the most popular street foods in Miami.

THE CUT Cooked ham and roast pork

SERVES 4
PREP 15 mins   **COOK** 20 mins

1 Cuban or French bread loaf

yellow mustard

4 slices of leftover roast pork

4 slices of ham

4 slices of Swiss cheese

4 pickled gherkins, sliced lengthways

butter, softened

1 Cut the loaf into 4 x 15–20cm (6–8in) lengths, then slice each in half lengthways. Lightly coat 4 slices of the bread with mustard and layer each with 1 slice of the roast pork, ham, and cheese. Add a gherkin on top and cover with the remaining slices of bread. Brush the top of each sandwich with butter.

2 Place the sandwiches in a plancha grill, or sandwich press, and press down until the cheese has melted and the outside of the bread is crisp. Remove from the grill, cut each sandwich diagonally across, and serve hot.

CROQUE MONSIEUR

This classic Parisian café sandwich has been a favourite – for good reason – since the days of Proust.

CUT Cooked ham

SERVES 6
PREP 10 mins   **COOK** 25 mins

12 slices of French or Italian bread loaf

Dijon mustard

24 slices of ham

1 tbsp butter, for frying

FOR THE BÉCHAMEL

2 tbsp butter

3 tbsp flour

300ml (10fl oz) whole milk

½ tsp sea salt

1 tsp freshly ground black pepper

1 tsp nutmeg

200g (7oz) grated Gruyère cheese

25g (scant 1oz) freshly grated Parmesan cheese

1 Preheat the oven to 200°C (400°F/Gas 6). For the béchamel, melt the butter in a saucepan until it begins to bubble. Then whisk in the flour and cook, stirring constantly, for 2–3 minutes, or until smooth. Whisk in the milk, a little at a time, until it is the consistency of a sauce. Remove from the heat and season, then add the nutmeg, half the Gruyère, and the Parmesan.

2 Lightly coat each slice of the bread with the mustard. Top 6 slices of the bread with 4 slices of ham each. Sandwich together with the remaining 6 slices of bread.

3 Melt the butter in a frying pan, then add the sandwiches and fry for 2 minutes on each side. Transfer to an ovenproof pan and top with the béchamel sauce and remaining Gruyère.

4 Bake in the oven for 5 minutes. Heat the grill on high and grill the sandwiches for 3 minutes, or until bubbling. Serve hot.

VARIATION

Croque madame Prepare the sandwich as above. Then heat 1 tablespoon of oil in a frying pan and fry 6 eggs, 1 at a time. To serve, place 1 fried egg on each sandwich, topped with 1 tablespoon of béchamel sauce.

TOAD IN THE HOLE WITH ONION GRAVY

These sausages encased in crispy batter are a classic comfort food. You can also serve the gravy with grilled chops or mashed potatoes.

CUT Pork sausages

SERVES 4
PREP 25 mins   **COOK** 40–45 mins

FOR THE TOAD IN THE HOLE

130g (4¾oz) plain flour

salt and freshly ground black pepper

4 eggs

300ml (10fl oz) whole milk

½ tsp dried sage

½ tsp English mustard

2 tbsp beef dripping

8 pork and herb sausages

FOR THE ONION GRAVY

2 tbsp olive oil

3 red onions, finely sliced

2 tbsp plain flour

300ml (10fl oz) vegetable stock

splash of red wine (optional)

1 Preheat the oven to 200°C (400°F/Gas 6). Place the flour in a large jug or mixing bowl and season well. Break the eggs, 1 at a time, into the flour, and stir with a fork to incorporate. Gradually add the milk, whisking vigorously after each addition. Stir in the sage and mustard. Set the batter aside.

2 For the gravy, heat the oil in a small, non-stick pan over a medium heat. Add the onions and cook for 5 minutes. Reduce the heat, cover, and cook gently for 30 minutes, stirring occasionally.

3 Meanwhile, place the dripping in a non-stick, heavy-based roasting tin and heat for 5 minutes. Add the sausages and bake for 15 minutes. Space the sausages out evenly in the tin, then carefully pour the batter over. Return to the oven for 25–30 minutes, or until well risen and golden brown.

4 Meanwhile, stir the flour into the onions and cook over a medium heat for 2 minutes, stirring. Gradually pour in the stock, stirring constantly. Season to taste and add the wine (if using). Serve the gravy with slices of toad in the hole.

CHORIZO WITH PATATAS BRAVAS

A fiery tomato sauce meets a creamy aïoli, crisp chorizo, and hot fried potatoes in this Spanish tapas dish.

 THE CUT Chorizo sausage

SERVES 4
PREP 15 mins   **COOK** 40 mins

6 tbsp olive oil

500g (1lb 2oz) onion, finely chopped

4 garlic cloves, crushed

3 tsp smoked paprika

1 tsp chilli flakes

2 x 400g can chopped tomatoes

juice of 1 lemon

salt and freshly ground black pepper

200g (7oz) chorizo sausage

500g (1lb 2oz) waxy potatoes, such as Charlotte or Maris Peer, unpeeled and cut into cubes

1 tsp cayenne pepper

FOR THE AÏOLI

1 garlic clove, crushed

1 egg yolk

200ml (7fl oz) olive oil

1 tbsp lemon juice

1 For the sauce, heat 2 tablespoons of oil in a lidded saucepan and add the onions and garlic. Cook over a medium heat, until softened. Then stir in the smoked paprika, chilli flakes, tomatoes, and lemon juice, and season well. Reduce the heat, cover, and simmer for 10 minutes. Remove from the heat and keep warm.

2 Place the chorizo in a large, non-stick frying pan. Cook for 7–10 minutes, until firm and well-browned, then remove with a slotted spoon and set aside. Add the potatoes, cayenne pepper, and the remaining oil to the pan. Stir to coat and cook over a medium heat, stirring frequently, for 15 minutes. Slice the chorizo into chunks, add to the pan, and cook for 5 more minutes.

3 Meanwhile, make the aïoli. Place the garlic and egg yolk in a food processor along with a pinch of salt, and pulse to combine. With the processor on high, pour in the oil, a little at a time, until it forms a creamy sauce. Stir in the lemon juice.

4 Remove the potatoes and chorizo and place on a serving dish. Pour the sauce over and toss lightly to coat. Top with the garlic aïoli and serve hot.

CAJUN ANDOUILLE GUMBO

Rustic Cajun-style cooking is often a one-pot affair, and this hearty gumbo is a perfect example.

THE CUT Andouille sausage

SERVES 4
PREP 15 mins   **COOK** 1 hr

2 tbsp olive oil

1 large onion, finely chopped

1 green pepper, deseeded and cut into 2cm (¾in) cubes

2 garlic cloves, crushed

25g (scant 1oz) unsalted butter

3 tbsp plain flour

2 x 400g can chopped tomatoes

500ml (16fl oz) hot fish or chicken stock

2 dried red chillies, finely chopped

1 tsp smoked paprika or ancho chilli powder

200g (7oz) okra, trimmed and cut into 2cm (¾in) chunks

250g (9oz) American andouille smoked sausage, peeled and cut into 2cm (¾in) chunks

salt and freshly ground black pepper

1 tbsp thyme leaves

500g (1lb 2oz) raw king prawns, shelled and deveined

2 tbsp finely chopped flat-leaf parsley

1 Heat the oil in a large, heavy-based saucepan. Add the onion and green pepper, and fry gently for 5 minutes, until soft, but not browned. Add the garlic and cook for a further 2 minutes.

2 Add the butter and allow it to melt. Then stir in the flour and reduce the heat to low. Cook, stirring, for 5 minutes, until browned. Add the tomatoes, stock, chillies, smoked paprika, okra, and sausage, and bring to the boil. Taste and season with pepper, and salt if necessary.

3 Reduce the heat to a low simmer and add the thyme. Cook, uncovered, for 30 minutes, stirring occasionally, until the okra is soft and the gumbo is well thickened.

4 Increase the heat and add the prawns. Cook the gumbo, uncovered, for a further 5 minutes, until the prawns are opaque and cooked through. Stir through the parsley. Serve with boiled rice.

BEEF AND VEAL

BEEF AND VEAL

SUCH LARGE CREATURES AS CATTLE ARE BOUND TO IMPRESS; THEY HAVE ALWAYS BEEN A SYMBOL OF RICHES AND POWER. FOR THOUSANDS OF YEARS, CATTLE HAS BEEN USED FOR DOWRIES AND GIFTS, AND ABOVE ALL FOR FEASTING.

CATTLE ARE GRAZING ANIMALS and cannot be raised as intensively as pigs or poultry (although feedlot systems, see below, are fairly intensive), which makes beef expensive. Ideally suited to moist, grass-producing areas, beef cattle fatten very well in cool climates, although British settlers in drier places such as North America, Argentina, and Australia, fostered beef industries that are now significant producers.

A cool climate also makes it possible to age beef to further enhance its flavour. This tradition moved to America with European immigrants, and many famous American suppliers now specialize in dry-ageing their beef for many weeks.

The dairy industry produces huge numbers of surplus male calves that are raised for beef and veal. However, because dairy cattle are selected to put their energy into producing milk, the beef they produce can be lean and of lower quality than the meat from beef breeds. Veal calves produce a particularly delicate and tender white meat.

Older breeding or milking cattle are all eventually used for meat, but this goes into the processing industry and usually only appears for retail sale as processed products.

PRODUCTION METHODS
The following are the main commercial cow production methods:

• **Extensive or grass-fed beef** Some calves begin life indoors before going out to grass; others are born outside and stay on grass all their lives, although they may be housed during severe weather. They are rotated around grass paddocks that are usually fertilized to increase grass growth. Most grass-fed cattle are fed a grain supplement for a few weeks before slaughter to produce a better carcass. However, most beef labelled as "grass-fed" does not advertise this fact.
Diet: grass, with concentrates near the end of their lives.

• **Intensive or housed beef** Cattle are sometimes started off on grass but may then spend the rest of their lives indoors. They are kept in open-sided or ventilated sheds bedded with straw and fed ad lib on a mixed diet of cereals as well as hay, grass, or straw. They have adequate room to move about and lie down. Most will be cross-breeds.
Diet: concentrates, hay, straw, roots.

• **Intensive feedlot beef** The US term for this production method – "concentrated animal feeding operations" – describes it well. Cattle begin life grazing, then for the last 3–4 months of their lives are moved to units, or feedlots, containing thousands of cattle where they are fed on high-energy diets. Antibiotics are used to control disease and to encourage rapid growth. Growth hormones are permitted in the US, but are banned in the EU.
Diet: concentrates.

- **Organic beef** Cattle can be raised in any system, from extensive grass to intensive feedlots, but the feed must all be certified as organic and drug use is likely to be less than in the conventional equivalents. However, some organic marks allow drug use "when necessary", which is open to interpretation, although drug withdrawal periods must be adhered to.

BUYING BEEF
Good beef that has been well aged will be a dark ruby red with creamy white fat. Bright or pale red meat has usually not been aged. Grass-fed beef has slightly yellower fat than grain-fed beef. A lot of marbling (see p15) means that the beef will taste good and stay moist. Very lean beef has less flavour and is prone to drying out when not served pink.

BEEF BREEDS AND CATEGORIES
Beef is more often sold under the name of its breed than any other meat. The most famous is the Scottish Angus, now produced all over the world. But there are many other beef heroes: the Gelbvieh, Hereford, Limousin, Simmental, and Fleckvieh all produce outstanding beef, not to mention the Wagyu breeds used to make well-marbled Japanese beef. Other famous breeds are used for crossing: both the Piedmontese and Belgian Blue produce a double leg muscle and are very lean, while Friesian and Holstein cattle account for a large proportion of dairy beef.

Zebu, or Brahman, cattle have a hump on their neck, which helps them survive in hot countries. Originally from Asia, they are now also found in Africa and South America, notably Brazil, where they were crossed with Charolais to produce the Chanchim.

- **Beef** Most beef comes from steers (castrated males) or heifers (young females). For faster growth, some steers are not castrated, a method that some people consider produces inferior beef. Beef from the dairy industry tends to be leaner but is not usually identified as such. Cross-bred beef is the norm, but if a particular breed is mentioned, it usually means the beef is of better quality.

- **Kobe beef** A Japanese speciality made from Wagyu cattle that are fed only on local grains and grasses to produce extraordinarily well-marbled meat that is very expensive. This style of beef is produced in other areas of Japan too, and in other countries, but should not be confused with the authentic version.

- **Veal** Bob, or bobby, veal comes from calves under one month old, and usually just a few days old. To produce traditional white veal, calves are removed from their mother shortly after birth and fed on a milk formula. They are usually slaughtered at around 20 weeks. Some are confined in crates or stalls, while others are reared in groups in larger pens. Calf crates are banned in the EU and some states of the US.

Calves that stay with their mothers, or that are fed a more varied grain diet, or that eat grass as well as milk, have a variety of names depending on their production: rose veal, grain veal, and pasture or free-range veal. Red or ruby veal and calf meat is a little older with darker meat.

BUFFALO AND BISON
In the prairies of North America, vast herds of native bison roamed the country, but were nearly annihilated in the 19th century by hunting; about two million remain. Some early settlers called bison "buffalo", and the names are interchangeable in the US and the UK. However, bison are a completely different species from buffalo; their horns are distinctively different.

- **Buffalo** The most common species, the water buffalo, comes from Asia. They are primarily used for milk and for traction, although obviously produce meat, too. A few producers raise them exclusively for meat. Water buffalo milk is used to make Mozzarella in Italy. African buffalo are very distant relatives and are not domesticated.

- **Bison** A few enterprising entrepreneurs now raise bison for meat, although this is sometimes sold as "buffalo". It is usually extensively raised on grass and tends to be very lean.

BEEF CUTS

GOOD BEEF SHOULD BE DEEP DARK RED from being dry-aged (hung), and well marbled with fat, although excess fat should have been trimmed off already. If a beef breed is specified, this is a good indicator of quality. Bright red beef has not been aged and will have less flavour.

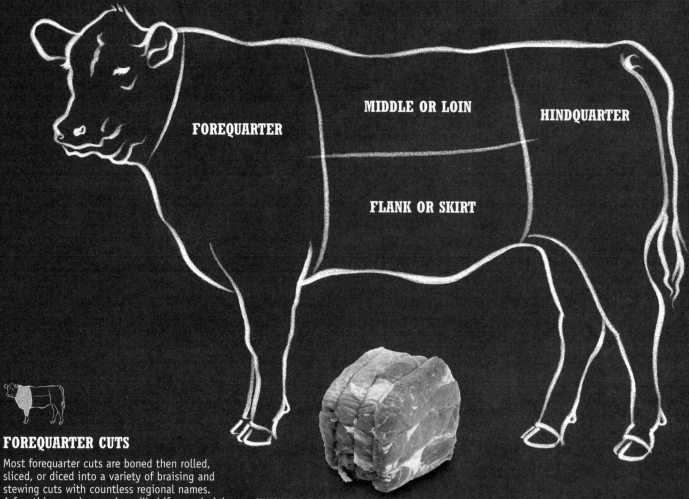

FOREQUARTER

MIDDLE OR LOIN

HINDQUARTER

FLANK OR SKIRT

FOREQUARTER CUTS

Most forequarter cuts are boned then rolled, sliced, or diced into a variety of braising and stewing cuts with countless regional names. A few thin muscles can be grilled if served pink.

CHUCK AND BLADE JOINT Also known as shoulder as it comes from the upper part of the forequarter, this boneless, rolled cut makes a rich braising joint. Otherwise it is sliced or diced for stewing.

FEATHERBLADE OR SPALE BONE STEAK A well-marbled shoulder steak, cut from next to the bladebone, it has a seam of thick gristle running down the middle. With the gristle removed, it is called flatiron and can be grilled or stir-fried.

BRISKET This can be trimmed of excess fat then rolled (above) and braised, but is often brined and made into salt beef. A whole unrolled brisket is a popular cut for long, slow, hot-smoking.

Additional forequarter cuts

• **BONELESS ROLLED BACK RIB ROAST** From behind the neck, this slow-cooking cut has plenty of fat and connective tissue.

• **STEWING STEAK, DICED** Most parts of the shoulder can be diced or sliced for slow cooking.

• **MINCE** Forequarter mince has more fat while leaner mince comes from the shin and hind leg.

• **LEG OF MUTTON CUT** From the top of the leg and leaner than brisket, this cut can be fried if served pink, but is usually braised.

• **SALMON CUT OR GLASGOW FILLET** A neat fish-shaped muscle from the blade bone, which is used for braising.

MIDDLE OR LOIN CUTS

It is difficult to find enough adjectives to describe the superb cuts that come from the beef loin. Whether bone-in or boneless, joint or steak, all are tender and flavoursome.

RIB-EYE STEAK Cut from the forerib joint, this well-marbled steak is deservedly popular. Top cap or deckle, a thin muscle lying over the forerib, is sometimes sold separately for quick-frying.

FILLET OR FILET MIGNON Leaner than loin, this is the most tender cut. When fully trimmed, it makes a luxurious roast, although some prefer more marbled beef. It is also sliced into steaks.

STANDING RIB ROAST, ON THE BONE A superb bone-in roasting joint, this is similar to sirloin, but without the fillet and with more muscle and fat on the outside. It should be well marbled.

Additional middle or loin cuts

- **SIRLOIN ROAST, ON THE BONE** Similar to the standing rib roast but also includes the fillet muscle. T-bone steaks are slices of this joint.

- **BONELESS RIB-EYE ROAST** A well-marbled, tender cut that is easy to carve.

- **SIRLOIN STEAK** A slice of a boned sirloin joint, with marbling and outer fat; a premium steak.

- **LOIN-EYE STEAK** A lean steak from the eye muscle but with all the outer fat removed.

- **PORTERHOUSE STEAK** Cut from the rump end of the sirloin, this is a thick-cut bone-in steak.

FLANK OR SKIRT CUTS

Most cuts from this part of the carcass are used for processing as it is fatty with connective tissue. But there are several thin muscles that can be grilled or fried if served pink.

SHORT RIBS OR BOILING BEEF These chunky pieces of rib have a thick layer of meat and fat. They make good soup, but increasingly are also cooked long and slow in a rich reduction sauce.

HANGER STEAK OR ONGLET A dark muscle from the diaphragm, hanger does little work in the animal so is fairly tender. Other flank muscles are skirt and flank, both thin and fibrous. All can be cooked pink.

TRI-TIP A small triangular muscle from the end of the sirloin that makes good roasts and steaks or cubes for grilling. Another section of tri-tip forms part of the thick flank.

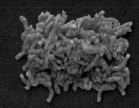

MINCE Fatty flank mince is used for sausages, while leaner mince comes from the shin and hind leg.

HINDQUARTER CUTS

Beef from the hind leg is leaner than loin and forequarter cuts. It yields many fine but slightly cheaper steaks and roasts as well as braising cuts.

BONELESS RUMP Bridging the sirloin and leg, the rump is well marbled and makes excellent steaks and roasts. The thin muscle lying over the top is sold as minute steak or picanha.

TOPSIDE STEAK Not as tender or well-marbled as loin cuts, nevertheless topside makes good roasts and steaks. The thin muscle lying over the whole topside is sometimes sold separately as topside cap or top cap.

SLICED SHIN This lean, boned out shin makes a hearty stew when diced, and has a lovely silky texture.

Additional hindquarter cuts

- **POINT STEAK** The pointed end of the rump muscle next to the sirloin makes good steaks.

- **MINUTE STEAK** Cut from the rump cap, it is sliced thinly and cooked quickly to avoid toughness.

- **TOPSIDE ROLLED ROAST** The most tender leg muscle, topside makes economical steaks and rolled roasts.

- **SILVERSIDE ROLLED ROAST** The larger of the two silverside muscles is generally braised, but can be roasted.

- **SALMON CUT OR EYE OF ROUND** A slim muscle from the silverside, this makes a neat log-shaped joint.

- **TOP RUMP OR THICK FLANK** Made up of several muscles including tri-tip, but is usually sliced for braising.

VEAL, BUFFALO, AND BISON CUTS

Veal, being young, is extremely tender and very pale. Bison and buffalo are slightly darker than beef, with proportionately more forequarter meat. Although in theory all the beef cuts (see pp144–5) could be produced, in reality far fewer cuts are offered. All of these meats are very lean, so roasts need larding (see p232) if cooked beyond pink.

VEAL

Veal cuts are simply smaller versions of beef cuts, although more are used for roasts and steaks since the meat is so much more tender. The sinews in veal – especially white veal – are finer and less obtrusive than in beef. Rose veal and ruby veal comes from older animals, so the sinews in these meats will be slightly thicker.

FOREQUARTER CUTS

The forequarter of veal is almost exclusively used for braising and stewing, the most famous dish being *blanquette de veau* (see p182). The shin when sliced is used for osso buco.

DICED SHOULDER More tender than beef shoulder, this cut still benefits from gentle simmering. It suits delicately flavoured dishes.

MIDDLE OR LOIN CUTS

These are the finest cuts of veal. As it is smaller than beef, some cuts are called by lamb or pork terms: the forerib is sometimes called rack, for example, and the bone-in steaks chops.

RIB ROAST The rib has more marbling than most veal cuts. Its creamy white fat adds flavour and succulence, and the meat, whether roast or chops, is superbly tender.

LOIN CHOP Loin chops are similar to T-bone steaks when they include the bone. When boneless, they are sometimes opened out into lean butterfly chops. Loin is leaner than rib.

HINDQUARTER CUTS

The hindquarter produces some of the largest muscles, so this is traditionally where escalopes are cut from. All hindquarter muscles tend to be leaner than loin.

RUMP STEAK – WHITE VEAL Milk-fed veal is the whitest and usually the youngest veal. A rump steak is a delicious cut and can cope with being sliced thickly. The rump can also be roasted.

RUMP STEAK – ROSE VEAL Rose veal has had access to grass, which makes the meat darker and the fat slightly more yellow. The calves may be older, but the meat is still very tender.

ESCALOPE OF VEAL A very thin, completely trimmed slice of a single muscle. Thicker slices can be flattened out to produce a thin escalope, ready for coating in egg and breadcrumbs.

TOPSIDE (ROLLED JOINT) Sometimes called cushion, this forequarter cut is more tender than beef topside, so makes an excellent but quite lean joint. Can also be cut into steaks or diced for kebabs and fondues.

SHANK, SLICED ON THE BONE (OSSO BUCO) Although osso buco is cut from several different meats, veal shank is the original and authentic cut to use. Slowly braised, the bone marrow gives a rich finish to the dish.

Additional veal cuts

• **SHOULDER ROAST (FOREQUARTER)** Far leaner than beef shoulder, this needs larding before being gently braised.

• **MINCE (FOREQUARTER)** Leaner and milder than beef, veal mince is good for pasta sauces.

• **BRAISING STEAK (FOREQUARTER OR HINDQUARTER)** Comes from the leg or from the shoulder; the leg is more lean and tender.

• **CUTLET (MIDDLE OR LOIN)** A restaurant favourite, these trimmed chops are from the forerib or best end.

• **FILLET (MIDDLE OR LOIN)** A very tender and lean cut, especially once exterior fat is removed.

• **SIRLOIN ROAST (MIDDLE OR LOIN)** Also called fillet or chump end, this is a prime boneless roasting joint.

• **FRENCH RACK (MIDDLE OR LOIN)** A luxury joint from the forerib – a six-rib rack weighs about 1.5kg (3lb 3oz).

• **VEAL BREAST (FLANK)** From the flank, breast is a good cut for stuffing. It has layers of fat.

• **SILVERSIDE (HINDQUARTER)** From lower down the leg than topside, this joint can be roasted or braised.

BUFFALO AND BISON

In the United States, bison meat is often (but not always) called buffalo so it is worth checking which species is being sold, although the meats are similar. Italy and the US are the major exporters of both bison and buffalo. The best buffalo comes from animals grown for meat rather than ex-milking cows. In Asia, buffalo could come from older working animals and the meat could therefore be tougher.

FOREQUARTER CUTS

The forequarter of both buffalo and bison is proportionately larger than the forequarter of beef. However, like beef, most is used for making rich stews and braises, or for mince.

SHOULDER ROAST The best part comes from behind the neck. Not the most tender cut, it is well endowed with fat and connective tissue to keep it succulent as a slow-roast.

MIDDLE OR LOIN CUTS

The middle or loin section of bison and buffalo contains the same tender cuts as beef, although you are less likely to encounter excess exterior fat.

RIB-EYE ROAST, BONELESS From the fore end of the loin, this joint is likely to have a little more fat than most cuts. Even so, it is more successfully cooked rare or pink.

HINDQUARTER CUTS

The hindquarter cuts of bison and buffalo tend to be even leaner than beef, so it is advisable to cook them like venison and serve steaks pink.

RUMP STEAK Despite a covering of fat on the outside of the steak, the meat itself is very lean so should be cooked like venison and served pink to avoid it toughening.

Additional buffalo and bison cuts

• **DICED SHOULDER (FOREQUARTER)** With their large shoulders, there is a wide choice of diced meat for stewing.

• **BRISKET (FOREQUARTER)** There is some fat on a whole brisket, which keeps it moist if left on.

• **FILLET (MIDDLE OR LOIN)** The most tender cut for roasts and steaks. Often sold as tenderloin.

• **LOIN EYE (MIDDLE OR LOIN)** Sometimes called striploin, this is the loin or eye muscle, fully trimmed of fat.

• **TOPSIDE (HINDQUARTER)** A lean cut that is best served either pink or larded and slow-cooked.

PRESERVED BEEF

MANY OF THESE PRESERVED BEEF PRODUCTS are unsmoked to emphasize the flavour of the beef. They are often more expensive than their pork counterparts. Beef sausages often contain pork fat to add juiciness and reduce cost, but some are made without pork to satisfy the kosher and halal markets.

SALT BEEF This was originally made to preserve beef for long sea voyages. The meat is soaked in a strong, spiced brine for some weeks and its bright red colour comes from adding sodium nitrite to the brine.

PASTRAMI An American sandwich meat made from salt-cured beef brisket that is covered in a spice mix and then smoked and cooked. It can be eaten hot or cold.

CARNE DE SOL Also called *jabá*, this speciality of northeastern Brazil is made from beef that is salted and then left to dry in the sun. The name means "meat of the sun".

BRESAOLA From the Italian Alps, bresaola is made from beef from the hind leg that is salted and flavoured with juniper berries for a few days before being dried.

BÜNDNERFLEISCH Also called *viande de Grisons*, this dried beef comes from Switzerland. Boneless beef is marinated in a spiced wine brine and then air-dried. It is not usually smoked.

JERKY This is a variation of South American *charqui* – salted and wind-dried strips of meat. Jerky is marinated in a hot, spicy mixture and is sometimes smoked as well.

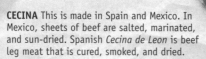

CECINA This is made in Spain and Mexico. In Mexico, sheets of beef are salted, marinated, and sun-dried. Spanish *Cecina de Leon* is beef leg meat that is cured, smoked, and dried.

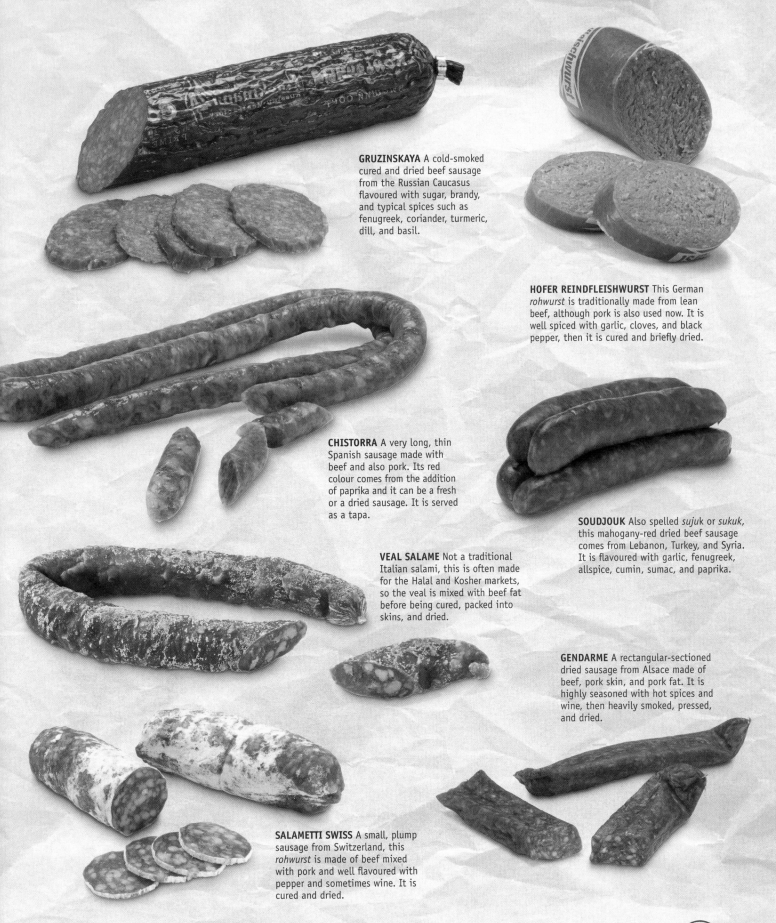

GRUZINSKAYA A cold-smoked cured and dried beef sausage from the Russian Caucasus flavoured with sugar, brandy, and typical spices such as fenugreek, coriander, turmeric, dill, and basil.

HOFER REINDFLEISHWURST This German *rohwurst* is traditionally made from lean beef, although pork is also used now. It is well spiced with garlic, cloves, and black pepper, then it is cured and briefly dried.

CHISTORRA A very long, thin Spanish sausage made with beef and also pork. Its red colour comes from the addition of paprika and it can be a fresh or a dried sausage. It is served as a tapa.

SOUDJOUK Also spelled *sujuk* or *sukuk*, this mahogany-red dried beef sausage comes from Lebanon, Turkey, and Syria. It is flavoured with garlic, fenugreek, allspice, cumin, sumac, and paprika.

VEAL SALAME Not a traditional Italian salami, this is often made for the Halal and Kosher markets, so the veal is mixed with beef fat before being cured, packed into skins, and dried.

GENDARME A rectangular-sectioned dried sausage from Alsace made of beef, pork skin, and pork fat. It is highly seasoned with hot spices and wine, then heavily smoked, pressed, and dried.

SALAMETTI SWISS A small, plump sausage from Switzerland, this *rohwurst* is made of beef mixed with pork and well flavoured with pepper and sometimes wine. It is cured and dried.

MAKING SALT BEEF

Salt beef is easy to make. See page 21 for useful tips on salting and brining. Prague powder (curing salt) can be bought online – it is not essential but gives salted meat its characteristic red colour.

1 For 2.25kg (5lb) rolled brisket, dissolve 600g (1lb 5oz) salt and 30g (1oz) Prague Powder No.1 in 5 litres (8¾ pints) of hot water. Add 2 tbsp ground black peppercorns and allspice, 1 tbsp ground ginger, 2 bay leaves, and 1 sprig of thyme and let it cool.

2 Immerse the brisket completely in the cold brine. Use a weight to keep it submerged. Store in the fridge for a week, turning it each day to distribute the salt, then drain and rinse in clean water.

3 Place the beef in a pan of fresh water, bring slowly to the boil, and simmer gently for between 2 and 4 hours depending on size. When tender, remove the beef to a warm dish. Cover and keep warm.

4 Serve hot, or leave to cool before slicing. Traditional accompaniments include carrots and mashed potatoes (if served hot), or gherkins, pickles, and sauerkraut (if cold).

MAKING PASTRAMI

Brisket needs long, slow smoking. If your smoker cannot cook slowly enough, then transfer the meat to a conventional oven to complete the cooking after 1–2 hours smoking.

1 Unroll the brisket. Follow steps 1 and 2 for Salt Beef (opposite), but add 2 tbsp ground coriander seeds and 250g (9oz) brown sugar as well. Remove the brisket after 4 days and rinse in clean water.

2 Mix together 1 tbsp each of ground black peppercorns and ground coriander seeds. Rub this mixture into the surface of the meat and especially into the fat. Leave overnight in the fridge.

3 Smoke the spiced brisket as slowly as possible for 1–2 hours, until the internal temperature reads 70°C (160°F). See pp22–3 for information on hot-smoking meat. There are various types of smoker you can use, such as this oven-top version.

4 Transfer the brisket to a rack and place this over a roasting tin. Tip 1cm (½in) water into the roasting tin. This will create steam while it is in the oven.

5 Preheat the oven to 120°C (230°F/Gas ½) Envelop the whole tin in foil to make a sealed tent that allows plenty of air around the meat. Place the brisket in the oven.

6 Steam gently for 2–3 hours, or until the internal temperature of the thickest part is 70°C (160°F) and the meat is meltingly tender. Eat hot or cold.

SPICY BEEF AND PEA PATTIES

These patties can be eaten both hot or cold and make a great picnic snack.

THE CUT Minced beef

SERVES 4
PREP 15 mins   **COOK** 15–20 mins

3 tbsp olive oil

1 tbsp grated fresh root ginger

1 onion, chopped

2 garlic cloves, crushed

1 tsp ground cumin

2 tsp ground coriander

200g (7oz) frozen peas, defrosted

500g (1lb 2oz) minced beef

1 egg, beaten

100g (3½oz) fine breadcrumbs

sea salt and freshly ground black pepper

1 red chilli, deseeded and finely chopped

small handful of coriander leaves

2 tbsp chopped mint leaves

1 Heat 1 tablespoon of oil in a large frying pan. Add the ginger, onion, garlic, cumin, and coriander. Cook for about 3 minutes, stirring frequently, until the onions are soft, but not brown. Tip the mixture into a large bowl and leave to cool.

2 Once the mixture has cooled, add the peas, beef, egg, and breadcrumbs to the bowl. Season with salt and pepper and mix well. Then add the chilli, coriander, and mint and mix to combine.

3 Shape the meat mixture into small patties. Heat the remaining oil in a frying pan and fry the patties for 3 minutes on each side, until browned and cooked through. Do this in batches to avoid overcrowding the pan. Remove with a slotted spoon and drain on a plate lined with kitchen paper. Serve hot with mustard or piccalilli.

CHILLI CON CARNE

A Mexican classic, this spicy recipe transforms kidney beans and beef into a firm favourite.

THE CUT Minced beef

SERVES 4
PREP 25 mins   **COOK** 1 hr 45 mins

2 tbsp olive oil

1 onion, finely chopped

1 celery stick, finely chopped

1 green pepper, finely chopped

2 garlic cloves, crushed

500g (1lb 2oz) minced beef

1 tsp dried oregano

2 tsp smoked paprika

½ tsp cayenne pepper

1 tsp ground cumin

1 tsp brown sugar

salt and freshly ground black pepper

400g can chopped tomatoes

250ml (9fl oz) beef stock

1 tbsp tomato purée

400g can kidney beans, drained and rinsed

1 Heat the oil in a large, flameproof casserole or Dutch oven over a medium heat. Add the onion, celery, and green pepper and fry for 10 minutes, until they start to colour at the edges. Then add the garlic and cook for 1 more minute.

2 Increase the heat to high and add the beef. Cook for 5–8 minutes, or until well-browned, breaking up any clumps with a wooden spoon. Then add the oregano, spices, sugar, and season. Cook until the spices are fragrant.

3 Add the tomatoes, stock, and tomato purée. Bring to the boil, then reduce the heat to low. Cover and cook for 1 hour. Then add the kidney beans and cook, uncovered, for a further 30 minutes, until the sauce has thickened slightly. Remove from the heat and serve hot with rice, soured cream, and grated Cheddar cheese if desired.

CLASSIC BURGERS

Using very lean meat can make a burger dry. Mixing in a little fat with the mince keeps the meat juicy, basting it from within while it cooks.

THECUT Minced beef

SERVES 4
PREP 20 mins, plus chilling   **COOK** 10 mins

400g (14oz) minced beef

50g (1¾oz) fresh white breadcrumbs

1 egg yolk

½ red onion, finely chopped

½ tsp dried mustard powder

½ tsp celery salt

1 tsp Worcestershire sauce

sea salt and freshly ground black pepper

4 burger buns, halved

1 round lettuce, shredded, to serve

2 tomatoes, thickly sliced, to serve

1 small red onion, finely sliced, to serve

1 gherkin, finely sliced, to serve

4 tbsp spicy tomato relish, to serve

1 Place the minced beef, breadcrumbs, egg yolk, onion, mustard powder, celery salt, and Worcestershire sauce in a large bowl. Season with pepper and mix until well combined.

2 Use damp hands to divide the mixture into 4 evenly sized balls. Roll each between your palms until smooth, then flatten them to a thickness of 3cm (1¼in) to form large, fat discs.

3 Pat in the edges of the burgers to tidy them up and place on a plate. Cover with cling film and chill in the fridge for 30 minutes. Prepare the charcoal barbecue.

4 Generously season both sides of the burgers with sea salt. Cook the burgers over a hot barbecue for 6–8 minutes, flipping them as needed, until the meat is springy to the touch and the edges charred. The internal temperature of the burgers should be 75°C (165°F).

5 Grill the buns for 1–2 minutes, on the insides only, until lightly toasted. Serve the burgers and buns with the lettuce, tomatoes, sliced onions, gherkins, and relish.

FEATHERBLADE STEAK WITH BLACK OLIVE BUTTER

This lesser-known steak cut is small, sweet to taste, and best when cooked rare.

THECUT Beef featherblade

SERVES 4
PREP 10 mins, plus marinating and chilling
COOK 10 mins, plus resting

2 tbsp rapeseed oil

3 tbsp red wine

2 tbsp chopped rosemary

1 garlic clove, crushed

4 featherblade steaks, about 60g (2oz) each, thinly sliced

sea salt and freshly ground black pepper

FOR THE BUTTER

150g (5½oz) unsalted butter, softened

2 tbsp chopped flat-leaf parsley

50g (1¾oz) pitted black olives, drained and roughly chopped

1 garlic clove, crushed

freshly cracked black peppercorns, to taste

1 Place the oil, red wine, rosemary, and garlic in a shallow dish and whisk together. Add the steaks and mix to coat. Cover and chill in the fridge for 2–3 hours.

2 Meanwhile, for the butter, place all the ingredients, except the cracked peppercorns, in a large bowl. Mash the ingredients well using a fork and season lightly with the cracked peppercorns. Mix to combine.

3 Form the mixture into a sausage shape, and place on a piece of greaseproof paper. Roll the paper up into a tube and twist each end to seal. Chill the butter in the fridge for 30 minutes.

4 Preheat a griddle pan to its highest setting. Remove the steaks from the marinade and place on a lined plate until they reach room temperature. Season the steaks then place them on the griddle pan and cook for 2–3 minutes, on each side, for a rare steak.

5 Remove from the heat and leave to rest on a plate for 3–5 minutes. Remove the butter from the fridge and cut into 8 thick slices. Serve the steaks topped with 2 slices of the black olive butter.

CARBONADE OF BEEF WITH ALE

This hearty dish of Flemish origin uses the deep flavour of dark ale to give a wonderfully sweet and sour sauce.

THE CUT Beef braising steak

SERVES 4–6
PREP 40 mins
COOK 2 hrs 50 mins–3 hrs 25 mins

3 tbsp plain flour, seasoned

1kg (2¼lb) beef braising steak, trimmed and cut into 4cm (1½in) pieces

2–3 tbsp olive oil

2 onions, finely sliced

2 carrots, peeled and sliced

1 tbsp tomato purée

2 garlic cloves, crushed

290ml (10fl oz) brown ale

350ml (12fl oz) beef stock

2 tsp soft brown sugar

1 tbsp red wine vinegar

2 bay leaves

sprig of thyme

handful of flat-leaf parsley, roughly chopped

sea salt and freshly ground black pepper

FOR THE CROUTONS

6 slices of French bread

1 garlic clove, halved

1 tbsp olive oil

2–3 tsp Dijon mustard

1 Preheat the oven to 180°C (350°F/Gas 4). For the croutons, place the bread slices on a clean work surface and rub both sides with the garlic thoroughly. Drizzle the oil over a large baking sheet and place the bread slices on it.

2 Turn the slices over to coat evenly with the oil. Bake the bread in the oven for 15–20 minutes, until crisp and crunchy. Remove from the oven and set aside. Reduce the oven temperature to 150°C (300°F/Gas 2).

3 Place the flour in a large shallow dish. Add the beef pieces, toss to coat evenly, and shake off any excess. Heat 2 tablespoons of oil in a large, flameproof casserole over a medium heat.

4 Add the beef to the casserole and cook, stirring frequently, for about 8 minutes, or until golden brown all over. Do this in batches to avoid overcrowding the pot. Add more oil between batches if needed. Remove the beef with a slotted spoon and place on a plate. Set aside and keep warm.

5 Reduce the heat to low. Add the onions and carrots, and cook for 6–8 minutes, stirring occasionally, until lightly coloured. Then add the tomato purée and garlic and cook, stirring constantly, for about 1 minute.

6 Then add the beef, ale, stock, brown sugar, vinegar, bay leaves, thyme, and half the parsley. Season and bring to the boil. Cover and transfer to the oven. Cook the beef in the oven for 2–2½ hours, stirring occasionally, until tender and cooked through.

7 Remove from the heat. Taste and adjust the seasoning, if necessary. Spread the Dijon mustard over each crouton and arrange them on top of the meat. Return the casserole to the oven for a further 10 minutes to crisp up the croutons. Serve garnished with the remaining parsley.

FILIPINO BEEF STEW

This traditional dish uses a wonderful combination of Asian flavours to enhance the flavour of beef.

THE CUT Beef braising steak

SERVES 4
PREP 20 mins   **COOK** 2½ hrs

4 tbsp sunflower oil

1 tbsp annatto seeds

1kg (2¼lb) beef braising steak, cut into 2.5cm (1in) pieces

2 large onions, sliced

6 garlic cloves, crushed

2 tbsp white wine vinegar

600ml (1 pint) beef stock

2 bay leaves

1 tbsp palm sugar, grated

2 x 400g can coconut milk

2 tsp sea salt

½ tbsp freshly ground black pepper

2 tbsp Thai fish sauce

2 tbsp soy sauce

2 tbsp ground rice, dry roasted until golden brown

4 tbsp crushed roasted peanuts

250g (9oz) aubergine, cut into chunks

250g (9oz) celeriac, peeled and cut into chunks

150g (5½oz) green beans, topped and tailed

6 spring onions, trimmed and shredded, to garnish

1 Heat the oil in a large, lidded saucepan. Add the annatto seeds and fry, covered, until the oil is red. Drain the oil through a sieve and discard the seeds. Return the oil to the pan. Add the meat to the pan and cook for 6–8 minutes until well-browned. Do this in batches to avoid overcrowding the pan. Remove the meat with a slotted spoon and drain on a plate lined with kitchen paper.

2 Add the onions and garlic, reduce the heat to low, and cook for 5 minutes, until the onions are soft and lightly coloured. Return the meat to the casserole and stir to mix. Add the vinegar, stock, bay leaves, sugar, coconut milk, and season. Bring to the boil, and add the fish sauce and soy sauce. Reduce the heat to a simmer, cover, and cook for 1¾–2 hours, until the meat is tender.

3 Add the rice and peanuts to the stew and stir well to mix. Then add all the vegetables and cook, stirring constantly, until they are tender. Remove the bay leaves. Taste and adjust the seasoning, garnish with spring onions, and serve hot.

DAUBE OF BEEF WITH PRUNES

Slow cooking produces a wonderfully sweet sauce and melt-in-your-mouth beef in this classic French dish.

THE CUT Beef braising steak

SERVES 4
PREP 25 mins
COOK 2 hrs 15 mins–2 hrs 45 mins

2 tbsp plain flour, seasoned with salt and pepper

1 tsp dried mixed herbs

900g (2lb) beef braising steak, trimmed and diced

2–4 tbsp olive oil

2 onions, thinly sliced

2 garlic cloves, crushed

2 carrots, sliced into matchsticks

2 bay leaves

zest of 1 orange, cut into pieces

sprig of rosemary

100g (3½oz) ready-to-eat pitted prunes

sea salt and freshly ground black pepper

600ml (1 pint) beef stock

150ml (5fl oz) red wine

1 tbsp tomato purée

1 tsp white wine vinegar

handful of coriander leaves, roughly chopped, to garnish

1 Preheat the oven to 140°C (275°F/Gas 1). Place the flour and dried herbs in a shallow dish. Add the beef pieces, toss to coat, and shake off any excess. Heat 2 tablespoons of oil in a large, non-stick frying pan. Add the onions and fry for 6–8 minutes, until soft and golden brown. Remove with a slotted spoon and place in a large, flameproof casserole or Dutch oven.

2 Add the beef to the pan and cook, stirring, for 5 minutes, or until golden brown. Do this in batches to avoid overcrowding the pan, adding more oil if necessary. Remove with a slotted spoon and add to the casserole. Then add the garlic, carrots, bay leaves, orange zest, rosemary, and prunes to the casserole. Season and mix well.

3 Stir the stock, wine, tomato purée, and vinegar into the casserole. Place the casserole over a high heat and bring to the boil. Then cover and transfer to the oven. Cook in the oven for 2–2½ hours, or until tender. Remove from the oven and season to taste. Garnish with the coriander and serve hot with creamy mashed potatoes.

POTTED BEEF

The beef in this traditional dish has the texture of a coarse pâté and a delicious buttery taste.

THE CUT Beef braising steak

MAKES 600ml (1 pint)
PREP 10 mins **COOK** 5 hrs

450g (1lb) stewing beef steak, trimmed of excess fat, sinew removed, and cut into chunks

sea salt and freshly ground black pepper

1 tsp grated nutmeg

1 bay leaf

pinch cayenne pepper

1 blade of mace

½ tbsp anchovy essence

120g (4¼oz) butter, plus 50g (1¾oz) extra for the topping

1 Preheat the oven to 130°C (250°F/Gas ½). Place the meat in an ovenproof dish. Sprinkle over the black pepper, nutmeg, bay leaf, cayenne pepper, and mace. Drizzle over the anchovy essence and lay the butter on top. Cover tightly with foil and cook for 2–3 hours. Then remove from the oven and stir to mix. Return to the oven for a further 2 hours, or until the meat is tender, and beginning to flake.

2 Remove from the oven and leave to rest for 30 minutes. Transfer the meat to a food processor, pulse until smooth, and season to taste. Remove the bay leaf and mace from the cooking juices and stir the juices into the beef. Divide the mixture between a few ramekins and lightly press it down with the back of a spoon to pack it in firmly. Cover with cling film and place in the fridge to solidify.

3 Heat the extra butter in a small saucepan over a low heat until melted. Add a layer of the melted butter to each ramekin and chill in the fridge for 12 hours. Serve with bread, pickled walnuts, and chutney. The beef will keep in the fridge in airtight containers for 5–7 days.

BEEF GOULASH

This traditional Hungarian stew makes the most of green peppers and tomatoes to enrich the flavour of the dish.

THE CUT Beef braising steak

SERVES 4
PREP 25–30 mins **COOK** 2 hrs 50 mins

1 tbsp vegetable oil

60g (2oz) smoked bacon, diced

6 onions, about 750g (1lb 10oz) in total, chopped

2 tbsp paprika

750g (1lb 10oz) beef braising steak, cut into 4cm (1½in) cubes

2 garlic cloves, finely chopped

½ tsp caraway seeds

2 tomatoes, deseeded and chopped

2 green peppers, sliced

salt and freshly ground black pepper

45g (1½oz) plain flour

1 egg, beaten

120ml (4fl oz) soured cream (optional)

1 Heat the oil in a large flameproof casserole. Add the bacon and cook for 3–5 minutes, stirring, until it is lightly browned and the fat has rendered. Then stir in the onions. Cover the mixture with a piece of foil and then with the lid. Cook over a low heat, stirring occasionally, for 20–25 minutes until the onions are soft and translucent.

2 Preheat the oven to 180°C (350°F/Gas 4). Add the paprika to the casserole, and cook for 2 minutes, stirring to make sure it does not burn. Then add the meat pieces, garlic, caraway seeds, and 500ml (16fl oz) water, and stir to mix. Bring to the boil, stirring, then cover and transfer to the oven. Cook in the oven for 1–1½ hours until the beef is almost tender.

3 Remove from the oven, stir in the tomatoes and peppers, and season. Cover and return to the oven for a further 30–45 minutes until the meat is very soft and the stew rich and thick. Remove from the heat. Taste and adjust the seasoning.

4 Place the flour and a little salt in a bowl. Stir in the egg and mix to combine. Place the casserole over a high heat and bring to the boil. Drop teaspoons of the flour mix into the goulash to form dumplings, reduce the heat to a simmer, and cook for 5–7 minutes until the dumplings are cooked through. Ladle the goulash and dumplings into warmed soup bowls and top with a spoon of soured cream, if using. Serve hot.

KERALA BEEF

This fabulous curry from the southern Indian state of Kerala uses popular local ingredients such as coconut, turmeric, and curry leaves to produce a distinctively hot, spicy, and aromatic dish.

THE CUT Beef braising steak

SERVES 4–6
PREP 20 mins, plus marinating
COOK 1 hr 45 mins – 2 hrs 15 mins

5cm (2in) cinnamon stick

12 black peppercorns

6 cloves

1 tbsp fennel seeds

1½ tbsp coriander seeds

6 cardamom seeds from pods

1 tsp ground turmeric

1 tsp fine salt

1kg (2¼lb) beef braising steak, trimmed and cut into 2.5cm (1in) chunks

2.5cm (1in) piece of fresh root ginger, peeled and finely grated

4 garlic cloves, finely sliced

2 green chillies, deseeded and finely chopped

2 onions, thinly sliced

20 fresh curry leaves, or 16 dried curry leaves

50g (1¾oz) shredded coconut

4 tbsp sunflower, rapeseed, or coconut oil

½ tbsp mustard seeds

handful of coriander leaves, to garnish

handful of thinly sliced dried coconut, to garnish

1 Heat a small frying pan over a medium heat. Add the cinnamon, peppercorns, cloves, fennel, coriander, and cardamom seeds to the pan. Roast the spices, stirring frequently, until lightly coloured and fragrant. Remove from the heat and leave to cool for 2–3 minutes.

2 Use a mortar and pestle to grind the roasted spices to a fine powder and transfer to a large bowl. Add the turmeric and salt, and mix well. Then add the meat, ginger, garlic, chillies, and half the onion and curry leaves. Mix to coat the meat. Cover and leave to chill in the fridge for 1 hour. Preheat the oven to 160°C (325°F/Gas 3).

3 Transfer the meat and marinade to a large, flameproof casserole. Add 375ml (13fl oz) cold water and bring to the boil. Then cover and transfer to the oven. Cook in the oven for 1½–2 hours until the beef is tender. Remove the casserole from the oven and place it, uncovered, over a high heat. Bring to the boil and cook until all the liquid has evaporated, stirring constantly to prevent the curry from sticking to the bottom. Remove and set aside.

4 Heat a large non-stick frying pan. Add the coconut and toast for 2–3 minutes, stirring constantly, making sure it does not burn. Add the oil, mustard seeds, and remaining onion to the pan. Cook for 3–4 minutes, or until the onion is golden brown. Then add the beef mixture and remaining curry leaves. Stir fry until the beef is well-browned and looks dry, but glossy. Serve garnished with coriander and dried coconut.

BOILED BRISKET OF BEEF WITH HERB DUMPLINGS

This traditional British dish is an excellent way of using a cheaper cut of beef. The vegetables and well-spiced dumplings serve as a delicious accompaniment to the brisket.

THE CUT Beef brisket

SERVES 4–6
PREP 20 mins   **COOK** 2 hrs 50 mins

2kg (4½lb) rolled beef brisket

1.5–2 litres (2¾–3½ pints) beef stock

sea salt and freshly ground black pepper

1 large onion, studded with 4 cloves

3 carrots, peeled and chopped into 4cm (1½in) chunks

1 bouquet garni

10 black peppercorns

1 celery stick, chopped into 4cm (1½in) lengths

½ cinnamon stick

2 star anise (optional)

3 leeks, rinsed, trimmed, and chopped into 4cm (1½in) lengths

FOR THE DUMPLINGS

125g (4½oz) self-raising flour

50g (1¾oz) shredded beef suet

1 tsp mixed dried herbs

handful of flat-leaf parsley, chopped

1 tsp horseradish

1 Place the beef in a large, lidded saucepan. Pour in just enough stock to cover the meat and season with 1 teaspoon salt. Place over a medium heat and bring slowly to the boil, skimming off any scum that rises to the surface.

2 Reduce the heat to a simmer. Then add the onion, carrots, bouquet garni, peppercorns, celery, cinnamon, and star anise, if using. Cover and cook for 1¾ hours, skimming the surface occasionally. Then add the leeks and stir lightly to mix. Cover and cook for a further 45 minutes.

3 Meanwhile, for the dumplings, place all the ingredients in a large bowl. Season with salt and pepper and add 5–6 tablespoons water. Mix all the ingredients to form an elastic dough. Divide the dough into 8 small evenly sized pieces and roll them into balls.

4 Remove the meat from the pan and leave to rest in a warm place. Remove and discard the bouquet garni, peppercorns, cinnamon stick, and star anise. Taste and adjust the seasoning, if needed.

5 Add the dumplings, cover, and cook for 15–20 minutes, or until the dumplings expand and rise to the top of the pan. Remove them with a slotted spoon and place on a plate. Strain the stock and reserve the vegetables. Slice the beef, arrange it on warm plates, and serve warm with the vegetables, dumplings, and some of the stock poured over.

SPICED SKIRT OF BEEF WITH BEETROOT, CRÈME FRAÎCHE, AND HORSERADISH

The addition of the beetroot in this recipe adds an earthy flavour and the horseradish adds a lovely piquancy to the dish.

THE CUT Beef skirt

SERVES 4–6
PREP 20 mins   **COOK** 3 hrs, plus resting

2 tbsp plain flour, seasoned with salt and pepper

1kg (2¼lb) beef skirt, cut into 4cm (1½in) pieces

2 tbsp rapeseed oil

knob of butter

1 large onion, diced

2 garlic cloves, crushed

½ red chilli, deseeded and finely diced (optional)

3 tbsp red wine vinegar

200ml (7fl oz) red wine

500ml (16fl oz) beef stock

1 tbsp balsamic vinegar

8 juniper berries, crushed

6 allspice berries, crushed

1 bay leaf

1 tsp chopped thyme leaves

3 tsp brown sugar

8 small beetroots, peeled and halved

sea salt and freshly ground black pepper

1 tbsp cornflour, mixed with a little warm water (optional)

2 tbsp crème fraîche

2 tbsp dry mustard

3 tbsp creamed horseradish

1 Preheat the oven to 150°C (300°F/Gas 3). Place the flour in a large shallow dish. Add the beef pieces, toss to coat evenly, and shake off any excess.

2 Heat the oil and butter in a large flameproof casserole over a high heat. Add the beef and cook for 5–8 minutes, or until well-browned. Do this in batches to avoid overcrowding the pot. Remove with a slotted spoon, place on a plate, and set aside.

3 Reduce the heat to medium. Add the onions, garlic, and chilli (if using) to the casserole. Cook for 5–10 minutes, stirring occasionally, until the onions are softened. Then increase the heat and pour in the red wine vinegar, wine, stock, and balsamic vinegar. Stir to mix and bring to the boil.

4 Then stir in the juniper berries, allspice berries, bay leaf, thyme, and sugar. Return the meat to the casserole along with the beetroot, season with salt and pepper, and stir lightly to mix. Cover and transfer to the oven. Cook the beef in the oven for 2–2½ hours.

5 Remove from the oven and leave to rest for 10 minutes. Remove the bay leaf and skim the surface of any extra fat. If the sauce seems thin, thicken with the cornflour. Combine the crème fraîche, mustard, and horseradish in a bowl and stir into the casserole. Serve with mashed potatoes and celeriac.

DRY-RUBBED STEAK WITH CHIMICHURRI SAUCE

Crusty on the outside and juicy on the inside, this sweet and spicy steak is wonderfully paired with a fresh and tart green sauce of Argentinean origin.

THE CUT Beef skirt or featherblade

SERVES 4
PREP 15 mins, plus chilling
COOK 8–20 mins, plus resting

1 tbsp soft light brown sugar

1 tbsp chopped thyme leaves

½ tsp mustard powder

¼ tsp garlic salt

¼ tsp smoked paprika or ancho chilli powder

salt and freshly ground black pepper

1 beef skirt or feather steak, about 675g (1½lb)

FOR THE CHIMICHURRI SAUCE

6 tbsp olive oil, plus extra for brushing

1½ tbsp red wine vinegar

1 tbsp lemon juice

15g (½oz) flat-leaf parsley, roughly chopped

2 tbsp roughly chopped coriander leaves

1 tbsp roughly chopped oregano leaves

2 garlic cloves, chopped

1 tsp dried red chilli flakes

1 Place the sugar, thyme, mustard, garlic salt, and smoked paprika in a food processor. Season with pepper and grind to form a fine powder. Place the steak on a large piece of cling film and rub the mixture all over. Wrap tightly in the cling film and chill for at least 1 hour.

2 For the sauce, place all the ingredients in a large serving bowl and mix well to combine. Cover with cling film, and chill for at least 1 hour, to allow the flavours to develop.

3 Remove the steak and the sauce from the fridge and bring to room temperature. Set the barbecue to its highest setting. Brush the steak with a little oil and barbecue on both

sides until cooked to your liking – 4–6 minutes on each side for rare, 6–8 minutes on each side for medium, and 8–10 minutes on each side for well-done.

4 Remove the steak from the heat, cover loosely with foil, and leave to rest for at least 10 minutes. Cut the steak into thick slices and serve with the chimichurri sauce.

MAPLE AND MUSTARD CRUSTED RIB OF BEEF

Cooking the meat on the bone adds flavour and keeps the joint moist in this impressive dish, and the mustard crust complements it well.

THE CUT Beef fore rib

SERVES 4–6
PREP 30 mins   **COOK** 2 hrs, plus resting

2-rib fore rib of beef, about 2kg (4½lb)

3 tbsp rapeseed oil, plus extra for greasing

sea salt and freshly ground black pepper

75g (2½oz) fine breadcrumbs

1 tbsp finely chopped rosemary

2 tbsp finely chopped flat-leaf parsley

small bunch of thyme leaves, finely chopped

3 large carrots, roughly chopped into small rounds

500g (1lb 2oz) shallots

2 celery sticks, roughly chopped

4 garlic cloves

400ml (14fl oz) red wine

2 tbsp maple syrup

3 tbsp Dijon mustard, plus 1 tsp extra

100ml (3½fl oz) port wine

500ml (16fl oz) beef stock

4 tsp cornflour, mixed with a little warm water

2 tsp redcurrant jelly

1 Preheat the oven to 200°C (400°F/Gas 6). Rub the beef with 2 tablespoons of oil and season well. Fry the beef in a large frying pan until just brown all over. Remove from the heat. Place the breadcrumbs, rosemary, parsley, and half the thyme in a large bowl. Season, mix well, and press the mixture over the fat on the beef until evenly coated.

2 Place the carrots, shallots, celery, garlic, and remaining thyme and oil in a large roasting tin and mix well. Place the beef on top of the vegetables and cover with an oiled sheet of foil. Roast in the oven for 30 minutes. Then remove the tin from the oven and add half the red wine and a splash of water. Reduce the oven temperature to 180°C (350°F/Gas 4) and roast for a further 40 minutes, adding more water if necessary.

3 Meanwhile, mix the maple syrup and mustard in a small bowl. Remove the tin from the oven and take off the foil. Coat the crust with the maple and mustard mixture, and press down lightly. Return the tin to the oven for a further 30 minutes, until the internal temperature of the meat reaches 60°C (140°F). Remove from the oven. Place the beef on a serving dish and leave to rest for at least 30 minutes.

4 Remove and discard any excess fat from the tin. Add the port wine, stock, and remaining red wine. Place the tin over a high heat and bring to the boil. Then strain and discard the vegetables. Reduce the heat, add the cornflour mixture, and cook the sauce until thickened. Then add the jelly and remaining mustard, season, and serve with the beef.

ROTISSERIE OF RIB-EYE BEEF

If you don't have a rotisserie, you can cook this dish in the oven rotisserie or on a barbecue.

 **THE CUT** Beef rib-eye

SERVES 8
PREP 20 mins, plus marinating
COOK 45 mins–1 hr, plus resting

1.5kg (3lb 3oz) beef rib-eye

FOR THE MARINADE

1 tbsp coarse freshly ground black pepper

1 tbsp chopped rosemary leaves

3 garlic cloves, ground into a smooth paste

2 tsp celery seeds

3 tbsp rapeseed oil

2 tsp brown sugar

zest and juice of 1 lemon

sea salt

FOR THE SAUCE

3 tbsp soured cream or crème fraîche

5 tbsp horseradish sauce

1 tbsp double cream

1 tsp caster sugar

squeeze of lemon

sea salt and freshly ground black pepper

1 Roll the beef into a neat round shape and tie at intervals with a butcher's string. For the marinade, mix all the ingredients in a bowl. Rub into the meat, covering the whole joint, and leave to marinate for 1–2 hours. Set the rotisserie at its medium setting.

2 Thread the beef onto the rotisserie skewer and place on the rotisserie. Season and cook for about 1 hour for a rare piece of beef. Reduce the heat if the meat browns too quickly. Leave to rest in a warm place for 20 minutes.

3 For the sauce, mix all the ingredients in a bowl and season well. Cut the beef into thin slices and serve along with the sauce.

VARIATION

Roasted rib-eye beef Preheat the oven to 190°C (375°F/Gas 5). Cook the beef in the oven to your liking – 1 hour for rare, 1 hour 40 minutes for medium, and 2 hours for well-done. Remove, cover with foil, and rest for 20 minutes. Serve as above.

CORNISH PASTIES

These tasty meat and potato pies were originally made as a portable meal for field workers to carry with them.

 **Beef skirt**

MAKES 4
PREP 20 mins, plus chilling **COOK** 40–45 mins

FOR THE SHORTCRUST PASTRY

100g (3½oz) lard, chilled and diced

50g (1¾oz) unsalted butter, chilled and diced

300g (10oz) plain flour, plus extra for dusting

½ tsp salt

1 egg, beaten, to glaze

FOR THE FILLING

250g (9oz) beef skirt steak, trimmed and cut into 1cm (½in) cubes

80g (2¾oz) swede, peeled and cut into 5mm (¼in) cubes

100g (3½oz) waxy potatoes, such as Charlotte or Maris Peer, peeled and cut into 5mm (¼in) cubes

1 large onion, finely chopped

splash of Worcestershire sauce

1 tsp plain flour

sea salt and freshly ground black pepper

1 For the pastry, rub the lard and butter into the flour until the mixture resembles fine breadcrumbs. Add the salt and enough cold water to bring the mixture together into a soft dough. On a lightly floured surface, knead the dough briefly, then wrap in cling film and chill in the fridge for 30 minutes.

2 Preheat the oven to 190°C (375°F/Gas 5). Mix the filling ingredients together and season well. Roll out the pastry on a well-floured surface to 5mm (¼in) thick. Then fold it in half and flatten it out to 5mm (¼in) thick again. Using a side plate, or saucer, cut 4 circles from the dough. Pile one-quarter of the filling into each circle, leaving a 2cm (¾in) border all around.

3 Brush the border of the pastry with a little beaten egg. Pull both edges up over the filling and press together to seal. Crimp the sealed edge with your fingers to form a decorative ridge along the top. Brush a little beaten egg all over the finished pasties.

4 Bake in the middle of the oven for 40–45 minutes, until golden brown. Cool for at least 15 minutes before serving warm or cold.

CARIBBEAN JERK BEEF

Native to Jamaica, jerk refers to the way a piece of meat is seasoned with spices and then cooked slowly over pimento wood.

 **Beef rib-eye or sirloin**

SERVES 4
PREP 20 mins, plus marinating and resting
COOK 10–15 mins, plus resting

4 x 225g (8oz) rib-eye steak or sirloin steak

sea salt

FOR THE MARINADE

4 tbsp rapeseed oil

1 tbsp white wine vinegar

3 garlic cloves, chopped

1–2 Scotch bonnet chillies, deseeded and roughly chopped

2 tbsp ground allspice

1 tbsp smoked paprika

1 tbsp chopped fresh root ginger

1 tsp ground cinnamon

2 tsp brown sugar

1 tsp dried thyme

FOR THE RELISH

250g (9oz) pineapple, peeled and finely chopped

1 red chilli, deseeded and finely chopped

small handful of coriander leaves, chopped

juice of 1 lime

1 small red onion, finely chopped

1 For the marinade, place all the ingredients in a food processor and pulse until they form a thick paste. Add more oil if it looks too dry. Rub both sides of each steak with the marinade. Leave to marinate in the fridge for 2 hours, or overnight.

2 Prepare the charcoal barbecue or set the gas barbecue to its highest setting. Remove the steaks from the fridge and rest them for at least 25 minutes at room temperature. Season with salt on each side. Cook the steaks on the barbecue for 3 minutes on each side, allowing a crust to form. Then move them to a cool part of the barbecue and cook for a further 2 minutes.

3 Remove from the heat and leave to rest for about 5 minutes. For the relish, mix all the ingredients in a large bowl and leave to rest for at least 20 minutes or for up to 3 hours. Serve the steaks hot with the relish.

BEEF CARPACCIO

In this recipe, lean beef fillet is semi-frozen so it is easy to cut into paper-thin slices, so thin, it's said, that light will shine through them.

 **Beef fillet**

SERVES 4
PREP 20–25 mins, plus freezing

500g (1lb 2oz) beef fillet

8 canned anchovy fillets

45g (1½oz) drained capers

125g (4½oz) rocket

125g (4½oz) Parmesan cheese

1 small onion, very finely diced

juice of 2 lemons

120ml (4fl oz) extra virgin olive oil, or to taste

freshly ground black pepper

1 Wrap the fillet tightly in foil, twisting the ends to seal and forming a cracker shape. Freeze for 2½–3 hours, until firm but not solid.

2 Meanwhile, drain the anchovies and spread out on kitchen paper. If the capers are large, chop them coarsely. Wash and dry the rocket, then strip out and discard any tough stalks. Set aside.

3 Remove the beef from the freezer and discard the foil. If the meat is too hard to cut, let it thaw slightly at room temperature. Using a very sharp knife, cut paper-thin slices of meat from the fillet, slicing as much of the meat as you can. There will be a little left at the end.

4 Arrange the beef slices, overlapping, on 4 plates. Shave over the Parmesan using a vegetable peeler. Divide the anchovies, onion, and capers between the plates. Drizzle the lemon juice over, sprinkle with the olive oil, and top with the rocket. Serve at room temperature with a sprinkling of pepper.

FILLET STEAK WITH BLUE CHEESE SAUCE

This traditional recipe uses Roquefort cheese to make a classic French sauce. However, you can use any other blue-veined cheese instead.

 **Beef fillet**

SERVES 4
PREP 10 mins, plus resting   **COOK** 15 mins

4 x 200g (7oz) beef fillet steak

1 tbsp rapeseed oil

sea salt and freshly ground black pepper

FOR THE SAUCE

50g (1¾oz) unsalted butter

2 shallots, finely diced

4 tbsp dry white wine

1 tbsp brandy

2 tbsp rich beef stock

200ml (7fl oz) double cream

100g (3½oz) Roquefort cheese, crumbled

1 Rub the steaks with oil and season well. Heat a heavy-based frying pan and fry the steaks on each side, 2–3 minutes for rare, 4–5 minutes for medium, and 5–6 minutes for well done. Remove from the heat and leave to rest in a warm place for 3–5 minutes.

2 For the sauce, heat half the butter in a small frying pan over a low heat. Add the shallots, and cook for about 5 minutes, until softened. Then add the wine and brandy, and bring to the boil.

3 Add the stock to the pan and cook the sauce until reduced by half. Then add the cream, mix well, and reduce the heat to a simmer. Cook for about 5 minutes, then whisk in the remaining butter and the cheese. Remove from the heat and strain through a sieve. Season to taste and serve along with the fillet steak.

GRIDDLED BALSAMIC STEAK WITH BEETROOT

This recipe uses balsamic vinegar to highlight the flavour of the beef. The addition of a fresh salad of beetroot, cherry tomatoes, and spring onions adds colour and crunch to the dish.

THE CUT Beef fillet

SERVES 4
PREP 20 mins, plus marinating
COOK 5–10 mins, plus resting

2 tbsp olive oil

1 tbsp red wine

2 garlic cloves, cut into slivers

2 tbsp balsamic vinegar

2 red onions, cut into rings

1 sprig of thyme

1 tsp cracked black peppercorns

4 x 225g (8oz) beef fillet steaks

rapeseed oil, for brushing

sea salt

FOR THE CRÈME FRAÎCHE

2 tbsp crème fraîche

2 tbsp creamed horseradish

1 small beetroot, cooked and finely diced

sea salt and freshly ground black pepper

FOR THE SALAD

4 cooked beetroots, sliced into fine strips

handful of coriander leaves, chopped

12 cherry tomatoes, cut in half

1 bunch of spring onions, trimmed and cut into diagonal slices

1 tsp finely sliced red chilli (optional)

2 large handfuls of baby ruby chard leaves

3 tbsp olive oil

juice of 1 lemon

2 tsp honey

1 Place the olive oil, wine, garlic, balsamic vinegar, red onions, thyme, and peppercorns in a large bowl and mix well. Add the steaks, toss to coat, and leave to marinate for 2 hours.

2 Remove the steaks from the marinade and pat dry with kitchen paper. Reserve the marinade. Heat a griddle pan at its highest setting. Brush the steaks with a little rapeseed oil and season with salt. Fry the steaks for 2¹⁄₂ minutes, on each side, for rare. Reduce the heat if they are cooking too quickly. Cook the steaks for longer if you prefer them medium or well done. Then remove from the heat and leave to rest for 5 minutes.

3 Pour the marinade into the griddle pan and cook for 1–2 minutes over a low heat, until the onions have softened. Then remove from the heat and set aside.

4 For the crème fraîche, mix all the ingredients in a bowl until well combined and season with salt and pepper. Set aside.

5 For the salad, mix the beetroot, coriander, cherry tomatoes, spring onions, chilli (if using), and chard leaves in a bowl. Place the olive oil, lemon juice, honey, and the seasoning in a separate bowl and whisk to make the dressing.

6 Toss the dressing through the salad. Place the salad on 4 plates, top with the steaks and the red onions, and drizzle any remaining beef juices over the steaks. Serve with the horseradish sauce.

PAN-FRIED FILLET OF BEEF

Using the light and low-fat fillet cut of beef, this dish perfectly pairs a tender steak with sweet caramelized garlic and crisp potato and parsnip rösti.

THE CUT Beef fillet

SERVES 4
PREP 30 mins   **COOK** 20–30 mins, plus resting

25g (scant 1oz) unsalted butter

50g (1³⁄₄oz) light brown sugar

2 sprigs of thyme

1 tbsp white wine

1 tbsp white wine vinegar

2 garlic bulbs, blanched and dried

4 x 225g (8oz) beef fillet steaks

1 tbsp olive oil, for brushing

sea salt and freshly ground black pepper

FOR THE RÖSTI

2 large potatoes, peeled and grated

2 large parsnips, peeled, cored, and grated

75g (2¹⁄₂oz) unsalted butter, melted, plus 30g (1oz) extra for frying

pinch of cayenne pepper

1–2 tbsp olive oil

1 Melt the butter in a small, heavy-based saucepan over a medium heat. Add the sugar, thyme, wine, and vinegar. Cook the mixture until it starts to thicken and caramelize, swirling the pan so it colours evenly.

2 Add 1 tablespoon of water to the pan. Then add the garlic, stir to coat in the mixture, and cook for 3–5 minutes, until softened, but still retaining its shape. Remove from the heat and set aside to cool, adding a little more water if it looks too sticky.

3 For the rösti, squeeze out any excess liquid from the potatoes and parsnips and place them in a clean bowl. Add the butter and cayenne pepper, season well, and mix. Heat the remaining butter and the oil in a non-stick frying pan. Divide the potato mixture into 4 portions. Add 1 portion to the pan, press down well, and fry for 2–3 minutes on each side, until golden brown. Remove and keep warm. Repeat with the remaining portions.

4 Lightly brush the steaks with oil and season well. Heat a heavy-based pan over a high heat. Fry the steaks on each side until cooked to your liking – 2–3 minutes on each side for rare, 3–4 minutes on each side for medium, and 5–6 minutes on each side for well done. Remove from the heat and leave to rest in a warm place for 3–5 minutes.

5 Place a rösti on each plate and top with a steak and some caramelized garlic. Drizzle over the cooking juices from the steak and garlic. Serve hot with horseradish or mustard.

FIERY BEEF FILLET WITH ROASTED VEGETABLES

This colourful dish is a fusion of seasonal vegetables with the tender beef fillet.

THE CUT Beef fillet

SERVES 4–6
PREP 20 mins   **COOK** 40 mins, plus resting

1kg (2¼lb) beef fillet, trimmed

3 tbsp rapeseed oil

sea salt and freshly ground black pepper

2 tbsp Madras curry paste

2 tbsp Greek-style yogurt

handful of coriander leaves, chopped

1 tbsp black peppercorns

2 tbsp cumin seeds

1 tbsp coriander seeds

FOR THE VEGETABLES

1 aubergine, sliced lengthways

2 courgettes, sliced

2 red peppers, deseeded and cut into pieces

1 small butternut squash, deseeded and sliced lengthways

2 tbsp Madras curry paste

4 tbsp rapeseed oil

FOR THE YOGURT

350g (12oz) Greek-style yogurt

½ cucumber, peeled, deseeded and finely chopped

1 garlic clove, crushed

2 tbsp shredded mint leaves

1 Preheat the oven to 200°C (400°F/Gas 6). Heat a large frying pan over a high heat. Brush the beef with 1 tablespoon of oil. Add the beef to the pan and brown on all sides. Season, remove from the heat, and leave to cool.

2 Mix the curry paste, yogurt, and coriander in a bowl. Rub the mixture over the meat. Using a mortar and pestle, roughly crush the peppercorns, cumin, and coriander seeds. Sprinkle the spices over the meat evenly, place it in a roasting tin, and drizzle with the remaining oil. Cook in the oven for 35–40 minutes.

3 Meanwhile, place all the vegetables in a separate roasting tin. Mix the curry paste with the oil. Add the spice mix to the vegetables, toss to coat, and place the roasting tin below the beef in the oven. Roast in the oven for 20–25 minutes.

4 Remove the beef and vegetables from the oven. Leave the beef to rest in a warm place for 15 minutes and keep the vegetables warm. For the yogurt, place all the ingredients in a bowl and mix well. Slice the beef into thick steaks, pour over any cooking juices, and serve over the vegetables with the yogurt.

BOEUF EN CROÛTE

Also known as Beef Wellington, this rich and luxurious dish is easy to make and perfect for entertaining. Steps 1–4 can be carried out a day in advance.

THE CUT **Beef fillet**

SERVES 6
PREP 45 mins
COOK 45–60 mins, plus resting

1kg (2¼lb) beef fillet, cut from the thick end, trimmed

salt and freshly ground black pepper

2 tbsp sunflower oil

plain flour, for dusting

500g (1lb 2oz) puff pastry

45g (1½oz) butter

2 shallots, finely chopped

1 garlic clove, crushed

250g (9oz) mixed wild mushrooms, finely chopped

1 tbsp brandy or Madeira

1 egg beaten, to glaze

1 Preheat the oven to 220°C (425°F/Gas 7). Season the meat with salt and pepper. Heat the oil in a large frying pan. Add the beef and fry until browned all over.

2 Transfer the beef to a roasting tin and roast in the oven for 10 minutes. Remove from the oven and set aside to cool. Weighting the meat as it cools will help to make a better shape. Leave the oven on.

3 On a lightly floured surface, roll out one-third of the pastry to a rectangle about 5cm (2in) larger than the base of the beef. Place it on a large baking sheet and prick with a fork. Transfer to the oven and bake for 12–15 minutes until crisp. Leave to cool.

4 Melt the butter in a saucepan. Add the shallots and garlic and fry for 2–3 minutes, stirring until softened. Add the mushrooms and keep stirring for 4–5 minutes until the juices evaporate. Add the brandy. Bring to the boil and boil for 30 seconds. Remove from the heat and set aside to cool.

5 Spread one-third of the mushroom mixture over the cooked pastry. Place the beef on top and spread the remaining mushroom mixture over the meat. Lightly brush the edges of the pastry with a little of the beaten egg. Roll out the remaining pastry and use it to cover the beef, tucking the uncooked pastry underneath the edges of the cooked pastry, pressing it to seal it.

6 Brush the uncooked pastry with the remaining beaten egg. Slit the top for the steam to escape. Bake until cooked to your liking – 30 minutes for rare and 45 minutes for well-done. Cover the pastry loosely with foil if it starts to brown too quickly. Remove from the oven and let it stand for 10 minutes. Use a sharp knife to slice it.

SPICED CHILLI BEEF FILLET WITH RED WINE AND MUSHROOM SAUCE

Serve this hearty roast with buttered spinach, soured cream, and a tangy tomato salsa.

THE CUT Beef fillet

SERVES 4
PREP 5 mins, plus marinating   **COOK** 1 hr

1 tbsp Mexican chilli powder or hot chilli powder

1 tbsp cumin seeds, toasted

2 tbsp extra virgin olive oil

handful of coriander leaves, chopped

sea salt and freshly ground black pepper

1kg (2¼lb) beef fillet

3 tbsp olive oil

1 large red chilli, deseeded and chopped

1 onion, finely chopped

2 garlic cloves, crushed

500ml (16fl oz) red wine

500g (1lb 2oz) flat mushrooms, cleaned and sliced

1 tbsp tomato purée

1 tbsp honey

250ml (9fl oz) beef or chicken stock

1 tbsp coriander leaves, chopped

vegetable oil, for greasing

handful of flat-leaf parsley, to garnish

1 Combine the chilli powder, cumin, extra virgin olive oil, coriander, and a little black pepper in a bowl, rub the mixture over the fillet, and leave to marinate for at least 2 hours, or overnight.

2 Preheat the oven to 200°C (400°F/Gas 6). Heat 2 tablespoons of the olive oil in a saucepan over a low heat. Add the chilli, onion, and garlic, and cook for 5 minutes until soft. Add the wine, increase the heat, and cook until reduced by half.

3 Heat the remaining oil in a separate pan and cook the mushrooms until soft. Add the tomato purée and honey, and cook for 1 minute, then add the stock and stir in the coriander leaves. Then add to the wine mixture and simmer for 10–15 minutes, until the sauce is thick and glossy.

4 Heat a large frying pan. Brush the fillet with the vegetable oil, seal on all sides, and season. Remove from the heat and place in a roasting tin. Cook in the oven for 30–40 minutes. Remove and leave to rest. Garnish with the parsley and serve hot with the sauce and mashed potatoes.

VIETNAMESE BEEF SOUP

Slow-cooked beef stock flavoured with gentle spices makes this dish special. You can add extra spring onions, chillies, or julienned carrots and bean sprouts.

THE CUT Beef fillet steak

SERVES 4–6
PREP 15 mins   **COOK** 1 hr 25 mins

675g (1½lb) meaty beef bones

1 tbsp dark soy sauce

1 tbsp olive oil

1 star anise

1 tsp black peppercorns

1 cinnamon stick

½ tbsp Thai fish sauce

1 onion, finely chopped

3 garlic cloves, finely chopped

1 chilli, deseeded and finely chopped

1 lemongrass stalk, trimmed, tough outer leaves removed, and finely chopped

2.5cm (1in) piece of fresh root ginger, peeled and finely sliced

salt and freshly ground black pepper

350g (12oz) fillet steak, finely sliced across the grain

60g (2oz) vermicelli noodles, soaked in hot water for 5 minutes (or as per the packet's instructions) and drained

bunch of green spring onions, trimmed and finely sliced

1 Place the beef bones in a large bowl, pour over the soy sauce, and toss lightly to coat. Heat a little oil in a large, heavy-based saucepan over a medium-high heat. Add the bones and cook for about 15 minutes, stirring occasionally, until the meat is no longer pink.

2 Transfer the bones to a large, lidded stock pan, pour over 1.4 litres (2½ pints) water, and add the star anise, peppercorns, cinnamon, and fish sauce. Bring to the boil, then reduce the heat to a simmer. Cover partially and cook for 1 hour. Strain the stock, through a sieve, into a pan, topping up with water to 900ml (1½ pints), if necessary, and set aside.

3 Heat the remaining oil in a large, heavy-based pan. Add the onion to the pan and cook for 3–4 minutes, until softened but not browned. Then stir in the garlic, chilli, and lemongrass and cook for a further 1 minute.

4 Pour in the beef stock, add the ginger, and adjust the seasoning, if needed. Gently simmer for 2–3 minutes, then add the sliced steak and cook for 2–3 minutes. Add the noodles and spring onions, stir to mix, and remove from the heat. Ladle the soup into warmed bowls and serve hot.

BEEF STROGANOFF

A popular dish of sautéed pieces of beef served with a sour cream sauce, it dates back to mid 19th-century Russia.

 **Beef fillet**

SERVES 4–6
PREP 10 mins   **COOK** 15–20 mins

60g (2oz) butter

2 tbsp olive oil

1 large onion, finely diced

sea salt and freshly ground black pepper

225g (8oz) chestnut mushrooms, sliced

pinch of grated nutmeg

750g (1lb 10oz) beef fillet, cut into thin strips

1 tbsp brandy

2 tsp Dijon mustard

pinch of hot paprika

200ml (7fl oz) soured cream

100ml (3½fl oz) double cream

dash of beef stock

1 Melt half the butter and 1 tablespoon of the oil in a large frying pan over a medium heat. Add the onion and season with salt and pepper. Cook for 5 minutes, or until the onion is softened, but not coloured.

2 Pour the remaining oil into the pan. Add the mushrooms and nutmeg, season well, and cook for about 5 minutes. Remove the onion and mushrooms with a slotted spoon, place on a plate lined with kitchen paper, and set aside.

3 Melt the remaining butter in the pan over a high heat. Add the strips of beef when the butter starts to foam up, then cook for 2–3 minutes, until brown on the outside, but still pink inside. Then add the brandy and set it alight to burn off the alcohol.

4 Return the onion and mushrooms to the pan, and cook for 2–3 minutes. Then add the mustard, paprika, soured cream, double cream, and stock. Stir to mix and cook until it bubbles slightly. Taste and adjust the seasoning if needed, and serve immediately with buttered rice.

BEEF TARTARE

Made from chopped beef and served with a raw egg on top, this dish was popular in early 20th-century France. You can also use sirloin of beef and loin of venison.

 **Beef fillet**

SERVES 2
PREP 15 mins

400g (14oz) aged beef fillet, chilled

6 cornichons, finely chopped

1 tbsp capers, rinsed and finely chopped

1 tbsp finely chopped flat-leaf parsley

2 shallots, finely chopped

1 tsp Dijon mustard

2 anchovy fillets, rinsed and finely chopped (optional)

tabasco sauce, to taste

sea salt and freshly ground black pepper

2 eggs

1 Finely trim off the exterior of the beef fillet, then cut it into thin slices across the grain using a very sharp knife (see p18). Dice the beef into very small pieces and place in a large bowl.

2 Add the cornichons, capers, parsley, shallots, mustard, anchovies (is using), and tabasco sauce to the bowl. Season and mix gently with a fork. Taste and adjust the seasoning, if needed.

3 Divide the beef mixture into 2 equal portions and place each on a square of greaseproof paper or saucers. Crack the eggs and separate the whites from the yolks. Place one yolk on top of each portion of the beef tartare. Serve with sourdough toast or duck fat chips and a lamb's lettuce salad.

WASABI BEEF AND PAK CHOI

Japanese wasabi paste, a type of hot mustard, is extremely strong, so you need only a little of it to lift the flavour of the grilled beef steaks.

THE CUT Beef sirloin steak

SERVES 4
PREP 10 mins   **COOK** 10 mins, plus resting

3 tbsp olive oil

2 tsp wasabi paste

4 x 200g (7oz) beef sirloin steaks

200g (7oz) pak choi, cut lengthways into 8 pieces

5 garlic cloves, grated or finely chopped

1 tbsp dark soy sauce

salt and freshly ground black pepper

1 Place 1 tablespoon of oil and the wasabi paste in a shallow bowl and mix to combine. Add the steaks and mix to coat evenly. Heat 1 tablespoon of oil in a large frying pan over a medium-high heat and fry the steaks to your liking – 2–3 minutes on each side for medium-rare or 5 minutes on each side for well done. Remove and leave to rest in a warm place for 5 minutes.

2 Add the remaining oil to the pan, reduce the heat to low, and add the pak choi. Fry for 1–2 minutes, turning once or twice, then add the garlic and soy sauce. Fry for 1 more minute, or until the pak choi has just wilted. Cut the steak into 1cm (½in) slices, season, and place on a plate. Serve hot with the pak choi.

COUNTRY FRIED STEAK WITH PEPPER GRAVY

Also known as "chicken fried steak" for its similarity to fried chicken, this dish is American home cooking at its best.

THE CUT Beef sirloin steak

SERVES 4
PREP 15 mins, plus overnight marinating
COOK 35 mins

250ml (9fl oz) whole milk

salt and freshly ground black pepper

1 tsp cayenne pepper

4 x 150g (5½oz) tenderized rump or sirloin steaks

1 egg

200g (7oz) plain flour, seasoned with salt and pepper

150ml (5fl oz) peanut or sunflower oil, for frying

FOR THE GRAVY

30g (1oz) plain flour

500ml (16fl oz) whole milk

FOR THE FRIES

1kg (2¼lb) waxy potatoes, such as Désirée, cut into wedges

4 smoked streaky bacon rashers

1 onion, chopped

2 garlic cloves, crushed

pinch of chilli flakes

1 Place the milk in a large bowl. Season with salt and pepper, add a pinch of the cayenne pepper, and mix well. Add the steaks, toss lightly to coat, and leave to marinate in the fridge overnight.

2 Remove the steaks from the marinade. Beat the egg with a little of the milk marinade in a small bowl. Combine the flour and the remaining cayenne pepper in a bowl. Heat the oil in a frying pan over a high heat. Toss the steaks in the flour, then dip into the milk mixture, and again in the flour. Fry for 3–5 minutes on each side, or until golden brown and cooked through. Remove and set aside. Drain two-thirds of the oil from the pan. Add the flour and whisk to form a thick paste. Then slowly add the milk, 250ml (9fl oz) at a time, stirring constantly, until it forms a thick gravy. Remove and season generously with pepper.

3 For the fries, cook the potatoes in a pan of boiling water for 20 minutes. Then drain and set aside to cool. When cool enough to handle, cut them into 2cm (¾in) strips, leaving the skins on. Fry the bacon in a large, non-stick frying pan until crisp. Remove from the pan and crumble the bacon. Add the potatoes, onion, garlic, chilli flakes, and bacon to the pan. Season and cook over a medium heat, until the potatoes are crisp. Serve the steaks with a generous portion of the gravy and fries on the side.

THAI BEEF SALAD

This colourful salad is healthy, easy to cook, and has a wonderful tangy flavour.

THE CUT Beef sirloin steak

SERVES 4
PREP 15 mins   **COOK** 10 mins, plus resting

2 x 225g (8oz) beef sirloin steaks, thick cut

vegetable oil, for brushing

sea salt and freshly ground black pepper

lime wedges, to serve

FOR THE DRESSING

2 tbsp Thai fish sauce

3 tbsp lime juice

1 large garlic clove, thinly sliced

1 tbsp soy sauce

2 tsp brown sugar or palm sugar

2 tsp peanuts, toasted and chopped

1 tbsp groundnut oil

2 bird's eye chillies, deseeded and finely chopped

FOR THE SALAD

1 heart of romaine lettuce, rinsed, dried, and finely sliced

10 cherry tomatoes, cut in half

3 shallots, finely sliced

4 spring onions, trimmed and sliced diagonally

handful of coriander leaves, chopped

small handful of Thai basil leaves or mint leaves

½ cucumber, halved, deseeded, and sliced diagonally

1 For the dressing, mix the fish sauce, lime juice, garlic, soy sauce, sugar, peanuts, oil, and chillies in a bowl and stir until the sugar has dissolved. For the salad, place all the ingredients in a bowl and toss to mix. Set aside.

2 Heat a griddle pan to its highest setting. Brush the steaks with oil and season with salt and pepper. Cook the steaks on the griddle pan for 3–4 minutes on each side, depending on how you like your steak.

3 Remove from the heat and leave to rest for about 5 minutes. Cut the steaks into thin slices and add to the salad. Then add the dressing, toss to coat, and transfer to a large serving platter. Serve the salad with lime wedges.

GINGER, HONEY, AND SOY-GLAZED SIRLOIN OF BEEF

A spicy marinade with a fresh, juicy mango and chilli salsa that perfectly complements the succulent steak.

THE CUT Beef sirloin

SERVES 4
PREP 30 mins, plus marinating
COOK 10–15 mins, plus resting

3 tbsp soy sauce

5 tbsp honey

½ tsp five-spice powder

2cm (¾in) piece of fresh root ginger, peeled and finely grated

1 garlic clove, cut in half

sea salt and freshly ground black pepper

4 x 225g (8oz) beef sirloin steaks

2 tbsp rapeseed oil

FOR THE SALSA

1 large ripe mango, peeled and diced

1 red chilli, deseeded and finely sliced

1 red onion, finely diced

juice of 1 lime

small bunch of coriander leaves, roughly chopped

1 Place the soy sauce, honey, five-spice powder, ginger, and garlic in a bowl and mix well. Season with pepper and add the steaks. Rub the mixture into both sides of the steak and leave to marinate in the fridge for 20–30 minutes. Preheat the oven to 200°C (400°F/Gas 6).

2 Heat the oil in a griddle pan over a medium heat. Season the steaks with salt and cook on the griddle pan for 1 minute on each side. Transfer to the oven and cook to your liking – 1 minute for rare, 3–4 minutes for medium, and 5 minutes for well done.

3 Remove from the pan and rest for 3–5 minutes in a warm place. For the salsa, mix all the ingredients in a bowl, season, and leave for 1–2 minutes. Serve the steaks hot with the salsa on the side. The salsa can be made up to 3 hours in advance.

STEAK AND WILD MUSHROOM PIE

This delicious and hearty steak pie is both homely and extravagant. Slow cooking the beef and mushrooms together gives the dish a wonderful earthy flavour.

THE CUT Beef braising steak

SERVES 4–6
PREP 50–55 mins, plus chilling
COOK 2½–3 hrs

500g (1lb 2oz) mixed wild mushrooms, fresh, or 75g (2½oz) dried wild mushrooms, soaked for 30 minutes and drained

30g (1oz) plain flour, seasoned with salt and pepper

1kg (2¼lb) beef braising steak, cut into 2.5cm (1in) cubes

4 shallots, finely chopped

900ml (1½ pints) beef stock or water

6 parsley sprigs, leaves finely chopped

salt and freshly ground black pepper

FOR THE PASTRY

250g (9oz) plain flour, plus extra for dusting

½ tsp fine salt

175g (6oz) unsalted butter, diced

1 egg, beaten, to glaze

1 Preheat the oven to 180°C (350°F/Gas 4). Slice the mushrooms. Place the flour in a shallow dish, add the meat, and toss to coat. Place the meat, mushrooms, and shallots in a large flameproof casserole. Add the stock and bring to the boil, stirring constantly. Cover and cook in the oven for 2–2¼ hours, until tender.

2 Meanwhile, for the pastry, sift the flour and salt into a bowl. Rub in one-third of the butter until the mixture resembles breadcrumbs. Add 100ml (3½fl oz) water and bring the mixture together to form a dough. Chill for 15 minutes.

3 On a lightly floured surface, roll out the dough to a 15 x 38cm (6 x 15in) rectangle. Dot the rest of the butter over two-thirds of the pastry. Fold the unbuttered side over half the buttered side. Then fold the remaining buttered side over to enclose the butter between layers of dough. Turn the dough over and use a rolling pin to seal the edges. Wrap in cling film and chill for 15 minutes. Then roll it out to 15 x 46cm (6 x 18in) and fold it again as above. Seal and chill for 15 minutes. Repeat this process 3 more times, chilling for 15 minutes between each turn.

4 Add the parsley to the meat, season, and pour into a 2 litre (3½ pint) pie dish. Increase the oven temperature to 220°C (425°F/Gas 7). Roll out the pastry on a floured surface to a size larger than the pie dish. Cut a strip from the edge, dampen the rim of the dish, and press the strip onto it. Place the rolled out pastry over the pie, seal, and brush with the beaten egg. Make a hole in the centre of the pie and add a pie funnel to allow steam to escape. Chill for 15 minutes, then bake for 25–35 minutes until golden brown. Cover the pastry with foil if it starts to brown too quickly. Remove from the heat and serve hot.

BEEF FAJITAS WITH GUACAMOLE AND TOMATO SALSA

A popular Tex-Mex recipe, this dish pairs the flavoursome rump steak with cajun spices and fresh, tangy sauces.

THE CUT Beef rump

SERVES 4
PREP 25 mins   **COOK** 10–15 mins, plus resting

1 tbsp olive oil

4 tsp Cajun spice

4 x 175g (6oz) beef rump steaks, 2cm (¾in) thick

8 flour tortillas

4 tbsp soured cream, to serve

FOR THE SALSA

450g (1lb) tomatoes, skinned

handful of coriander leaves, chopped

½ red onion, finely chopped

1 green chilli, deseeded and finely chopped

3 tbsp lime juice

sea salt and freshly ground black pepper

FOR THE GUACAMOLE

2 ripe avocados, halved and stones removed

2 tbsp lime juice

1 tbsp olive oil

1 red onion, finely chopped

1 garlic clove, crushed with sea salt

1 small green chilli, deseeded and finely chopped

1 For the salsa, roughly chop the tomatoes, removing the core from around the stem, but not the seeds. Place the tomatoes in a bowl and add the coriander, onion, chilli, and lime juice. Season and mix well.

2 For the guacamole, scoop the avocado flesh into a bowl and mash gently with a fork. Add the lime juice, oil, onion, garlic, and chilli and mix well. Taste and season, if needed. Cover with cling film and place in the fridge to avoid it going brown.

3 Heat a griddle pan at its highest setting. Place the oil and Cajun spice in a small bowl and mix well. Rub the steaks with the oil mix evenly. Fry the steaks until cooked to your liking – 2–2½ minutes on each side for rare, 3–3½ minutes on each side for medium-rare, about 4 minutes on each side for medium, and about 5 minutes on each side for well-done. Remove from the heat and leave to rest for 3–5 minutes in a warm place.

4 Warm the tortillas in a dry frying pan. Cut the steaks into strips and divide the meat between the tortillas. Top with the guacamole and salsa, and roll-up the tortillas. Serve hot with soured cream.

STEAK AU POIVRE

A classic French Bistro dish, this pepper steak recipe dates back to the 19th century.

THE CUT Beef fillet or sirloin

SERVES 4
PREP 10 mins   **COOK** 15 mins, plus resting

3 tbsp black peppercorns

4 x 200g (7oz) beef fillet or sirloin steaks, 4–5cm (1½–2in) thick

sea salt

1 tbsp olive oil

75g (2½oz) unsalted butter, chilled and cut into cubes, plus a knob extra

3 shallots, finely chopped

100ml (3½fl oz) brandy or Cognac

150ml (5fl oz) rich beef stock

150ml (5fl oz) double cream

1 Crush the peppercorns using a mortar and pestle and place in a shallow dish. Add the steaks, toss to coat, then season with salt. Heat the oil in a large, heavy-based frying pan over a medium heat.

2 Cook the steaks in the frying pan until cooked to your liking – 2½–3 minutes on each side for rare, 3–4 minutes on each side for medium-rare, and 5–6 minutes on each side for medium to well-done. Make sure you don't burn the pepper when cooking the steak for more than 4 minutes. Remove from the heat and leave to rest for about 5 minutes in a warm place.

3 Reduce the heat to low and add a knob of butter to the pan. Add the shallots and cook for about 5 minutes. Then add the brandy and increase the heat to help ignite it, and allow the alcohol to burn off.

4 Add the stock and cream. Bring to the boil rapidly and cook until the liquid is reduced by half and has thickened enough to coat the back of a spoon. Whisk in the butter and season to taste. Pour the sauce over the steaks, and serve with duck fat chips and a green salad.

THE ULTIMATE STEAK

Good-quality steak needs very little embellishment. Frying is a simple method of cooking it that produces great results. The thickness of the steak will affect the cooking time.

THE CUT Beef rib-eye steaks

SERVES 1
PREP 30 mins   **COOK** 8–14 mins, plus resting

2 x 3cm (1½in) thick beef rib-eye steaks

1–2 tbsp butter, softened

salt and freshly ground black pepper

COOKING STEAK TO PERFECTION

BLUE Cook for 2–3 minutes in total, until just seared and the steak feels very soft when pressed. The interior of the steak should be reddish purple. The meat inside is cool and no blood runs out.

RARE Cook for 6–8 minutes in total, until drops of blood appear on the surface and the steak feels spongy. The interior of the steak should be red and it will be warm. If rested, the blood will disperse evenly.

MEDIUM Cook for 10–12 minutes in total, including resting, which makes it evenly pink. Stop frying when drops of juice become visible on the surface. The steak offers resistance and the interior is pink.

WELL DONE Cook for 12–14 minutes in total. If resting time is included in the 14 minutes, the steak will stay moist. When done, it is well browned, feels firm, and the juices are clearly visible on the surface.

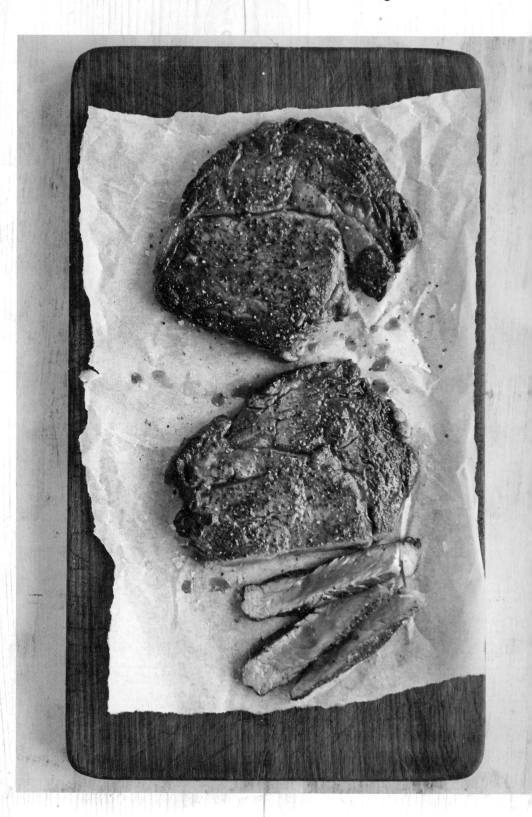

1 Heat a heavy-based frying pan over high heat. Heat 1–2 tbsp of butter in the pan until it simmers. Use tongs to carefully lay the steaks in the pan, taking care in case the fat splashes. Press down the steaks with a slotted spatula to ensure that they are in contact with the pan. Then reduce the heat slightly, to avoid the fat burning, and sear untouched for 1–2 minutes.

2 Use the tongs to lift the steaks and check the underside. If well browned, turn them over and brown the other side, seasoning the browned side with salt and pepper. If the steak is not yet well browned, turn the heat up slightly and make sure they are browned before turning them over to brown the other side. Blue steaks need no further cooking.

3 Continue to fry the steaks, turning them every 1–2 minutes, until cooked to your liking (see left for cooking times). Reduce the heat if the butter starts to burn. Remember that thinner steaks cook more quickly. Lightly press the steaks with your finger to check for doneness (see right) and remove from the pan. Leave to rest on a warmed plate for 3–5 minutes before serving.

TESTING FOR DONENESS

With experience, the cook can simply prod a steak or roast with a fork to know how well cooked it is. Here is a guide to how it should feel. If you are still unsure, you can always slice into a steak and take a look.

RARE Hold your hand with the fingers extended gently forwards. Prod the muscle between the thumb and forefinger to feel how soft it is. This is how a rare steak should feel. If the fingers are held limp, this is how a blue steak will feel.

MEDIUM Stretch out your fingers as far as they will go. Now prod between the thumb and first finger where shown. This is how a medium steak feels. It will become firmer while resting, so can be taken out of the pan when softer than this.

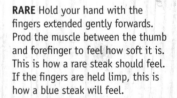

WELL DONE Clench your fist tightly and prod between the thumb and forefinger. The muscle feels much firmer; this is well-done meat. Resting is important for well-done meat as it removes any pinkness but retains some moisture.

ROAST BEEF

Roast beef, Yorkshire puddings, and gravy make this a quintessential British Sunday lunch.

THE CUT Beef rump

SERVES 4–6
PREP 10 mins
COOK 1 hr 45 mins, plus resting

1.5kg (3lb 3oz) rump of beef

salt and freshly ground black pepper

1 tbsp olive oil

2 tbsp beef dripping (optional)

2 tbsp plain flour

300ml (10fl oz) beef or vegetable stock

1 Preheat the oven to 200°C (400°F/Gas 6). Season the beef with salt and pepper. Heat the oil in a medium, heavy-based frying pan. Add the beef and cook until seared on all sides.

2 Place the beef in a roasting tin, transfer to the oven, and roast for 20 minutes. Reduce the oven temperature to 160°C (325°F/Gas 3) and cook the beef for 1 hour 10 minutes for rare, or 1 hour 25 minutes for medium-rare.

3 Remove the joint from the tin, place on a warmed plate, and cover with foil. Set aside for at least 20 minutes to allow the meat to rest, making it moist and easy to carve.

4 Meanwhile, place the roasting tin on the hob and warm the cooking juices through (if you don't have any juices, add the dripping). Stir in the flour and cook for 2–3 minutes, stirring to form a smooth paste. Gradually add the stock, stirring, to make a rich gravy. Pour in any juices from the rested beef and stir well. Carve the meat, and serve with Yorkshire puddings and the gravy.

CLEVER LEFTOVERS

Leftover roast beef and roast potatoes can make the basis of a delicious hash. Try serving it with a beetroot, orange, and watercress salad and some horseradish crème fraîche.

CHINESE SPICED BEEF AND NOODLE SOUP

This well-spiced, aromatic, and cleansing soup makes for a great snack or a light main course.

THE CUT Beef shin

SERVES 4
PREP 30 mins
COOK 2 hrs 50 mins – 3 hrs 50 mins

100g (3½oz) dried egg Chinese noodles

3 tsp brown sugar

2 tbsp light soy sauce

½ tbsp dark soy sauce

2 tbsp shaoxing rice wine

3 tsp chilli bean sauce

a handful of bean sprouts

4 Chinese cabbage leaves, shredded

2 spring onions, finely sliced

a small handful of coriander leaves

FOR THE BEEF STOCK

2 beef shin bones, about 20cm (8in) long

2 banana shallots, halved lengthways

3 whole carrots, halved

8 black peppercorns

FOR THE SOUP

2 tbsp groundnut oil

1 onion, chopped

2cm (¾in) piece of fresh root ginger, grated

2 garlic cloves, crushed

1–2 red bird's eye chilli

500g (1lb 2oz) shin of beef, cut into 3cm (1¼in) cubes

1 star anise

1 tsp Chinese five-spice powder

½ cinnamon stick

sea salt and freshly ground black pepper

1 Preheat the oven to 200°C (400°F/Gas 6). For the beef stock, place the shin bones in a roasting tin. Add the shallots and carrots, transfer to the oven, and roast the bones and vegetables for 35–40 minutes, until the bones are browned but not burnt.

2 Remove from the oven and transfer the bones and vegetables to a large saucepan. Pour over 2.5 litres (4½ pints) of water, add the peppercorns, and bring to the boil. Then reduce the heat to a simmer and cook for 1 hour. Skim away any froth that rises to the surface. Strain the stock, discard the bones, and reserve the carrots and stock.

3 Meanwhile, for the soup, heat the oil in a large saucepan over a medium heat. Add the onion and cook until soft. Then add the ginger, garlic, and chillies and cook for a further 1 minute.

4 Add the beef to the pan and fry until well-browned. Do this in batches to avoid overcrowding the pan. Then add all the remaining soup ingredients along with the stock and season with salt and pepper. Bring to a gentle simmer. Cook for 1–2 hours, until the meat is tender, topping up with more stock if needed. Then strain the liquid into a clean pan. Transfer the meat to a platter and set aside. Discard the star anise and cinnamon stick.

5 Bring a large pot of water to the boil and cook the noodles according to packet instructions. Drain and rinse under cold water. Set aside.

6 Add the carrots to the stock, reserved earlier, and cook for about 5 minutes. Mix the brown sugar, light and dark soy sauce, rice wine, and chilli bean sauce in a small bowl and stir this into the soup.

7 Then return the meat to the pan and bring to a gentle simmer for 1 minute. Remove from the heat. Just before serving, divide the noodles and bean sprouts between 4 deep bowls. Stir the Chinese cabbage into the soup and ladle the hot soup over each bowl. Garnish with chopped spring onions and coriander and serve immediately.

BRAISED SHIN OF BEEF IN RED WINE

In this rich and luxurious stew, beef shin is slow cooked to a melt-in-your-mouth, flavourful tenderness. Simple and delicious, it makes for real comfort food.

THE CUT Beef shin

SERVES 6–8
PREP 45 mins   **COOK** 2½ hrs

4 tbsp rapeseed oil, plus extra if needed

200g (7oz) streaky bacon lardons

18 small shallots

200g (7oz) chestnut mushrooms, quartered

1 onion, finely chopped

3 garlic cloves, chopped

200g (7oz) flat mushrooms, chopped

1.5kg (3lb 3oz) beef shin, trimmed and cut into 5cm (2in) chunks

3 tbsp plain flour, seasoned with salt and pepper

750ml (1¼ pints) red wine

400g can of chopped tomatoes

sprig of thyme

1 large bay leaf

2 tbsp chopped flat-leaf parsley

400ml (14fl oz) beef stock

sea salt and freshly ground black pepper

1 Preheat the oven to 150°C (300°F/Gas 2). Heat 2 tablespoons of the oil in a heavy-based frying pan. Add the bacon and cook gently until browned, then transfer to a large casserole or Dutch oven. Add the shallots to the pan and fry until golden. Transfer to the casserole. Then fry the chestnut mushrooms until golden and add to the casserole. Fry the onion and garlic in the pan until golden, then add the flat mushrooms and cook until softened. Add more oil if needed. Transfer to the casserole.

2 Heat the remaining oil in a saucepan. Toss the beef in the flour, fry in the pan until browned, and transfer to the casserole. Discard the fat from the pan, add one-quarter of the wine, and bring to the boil, scraping any residue from the bottom. Add the tomatoes, return to the boil, then transfer to the casserole along with the thyme, bay leaf, 1 tablespoon of parsley, the remaining wine, and the stock. Mix well and season.

3 Cover and cook in the oven for about 2–2½ hours, stirring occasionally and adding more stock if necessary. Remove from the oven, taste and adjust the seasoning, and take out the thyme and bay leaf. Thicken the sauce, if preferred, and serve garnished with the remaining parsley.

BOEUF BOURGUIGNON

A simplified version of a French classic, the beef here is meltingly rich and tender.

THE CUT Beef shin

SERVES 4–6
PREP 30 mins   **COOK** 2 hrs 45 mins

4 tbsp olive oil

100g (3½oz) bacon lardons

2 onions, finely chopped

4 thin carrots, cut into 2cm (¾in) slices

1 celery stick, finely chopped

150g (5½oz) button mushrooms, halved if large

1kg (2¼lb) stewing beef, such as shin, cut into 3cm (1in) cubes

2 tbsp plain flour, seasoned with salt and pepper

350ml (12fl oz) red wine

250ml (9fl oz) beef stock

salt and freshly ground black pepper

1 bouquet garni

1 Preheat the oven to 150°C (300°F/Gas 2). Heat 2 tablespoons of the oil in a large casserole. Fry the bacon for 1–2 minutes until lightly browned. Add the onions, carrots, celery, and mushrooms and cook for 5 minutes. Set aside.

2 Pat the beef with kitchen paper to remove excess blood. Mix with the flour until well coated and shake off any excess. Heat the remaining oil in the pan and fry the beef until well-browned. Do this in batches to avoid overcrowding the pan. Set aside.

3 Pour the wine and stock into the pan, stirring to dislodge any meaty residue. Season well, add the bouquet garni, and return the meat and vegetables. Cover and cook in the oven for 2½ hours, until very tender. Remove the bouquet garni and serve with buttered noodles.

WINE ICE CUBES

Freeze leftover wine in ice-cube trays for use in cooking. Once frozen, transfer to a freezer bag. Add a cube or two to a casserole or stew for added flavour.

BRAISED BRISKET OF BUFFALO

Onions and beer provide the texture and flavour for the sauce in this slow-cooked dish.

CUT **Buffalo brisket**

SERVES 6–8
PREP 15 mins   **COOK** 3–4 hrs, plus resting

1.5kg (3lb 3oz) buffalo brisket

1 tsp salt

½ tsp freshly ground black pepper

2 tbsp olive oil

4 onions, sliced

1 bay leaf

350ml (12fl oz) light beer

1 tbsp balsamic vinegar

1 Preheat the oven to 160°C (325°F/Gas 3). Pat the meat dry with kitchen paper to remove any excess blood. Season with the salt and pepper. Heat the oil in a large, deep casserole, add the meat, and cook for about 10 minutes until browned all over. Remove with a slotted spoon, place on a plate lined with kitchen paper, and set aside.

2 Add the onions to the casserole and cook until browned. Then return the meat to the casserole and add the bay leaf, beer, and vinegar. Pour in just enough water to cover the meat and bring to the boil. Then cover and transfer to the oven for 3½ hours.

3 Remove from the oven and leave to rest, uncovered, for 15 minutes. Then transfer the meat to a carving board and cut into thick slices. Arrange the meat on a large platter, remove the bay leaf, and pour the cooking juices over. Serve with roast vegetables and mashed potatoes.

MOIST MEAT

Buffalo meat is leaner than beef, so cook it whole in a liquid. This helps keep the moisture in.

ROAST RACK OF VEAL WITH PESTO

Make this dish visually appealing by criss-crossing two ribs of veal to make a Guard of Honour before roasting. It is lovely served with sautéd potatoes.

CUT **Rib of veal**

SERVES 4
PREP 10 mins
COOK 1 hr 15 mins, plus resting

50g (1¾oz) butter, plus a knob extra

3 tbsp olive oil

6-rib roast of veal, about 1.5kg (3lb 3oz) in total, trimmed

sea salt and freshly ground black pepper

2 onions, halved

4 garlic cloves, crushed

a few sprigs of rosemary

1 bay leaf

250ml (9fl oz) white wine

1 Preheat the oven to 180°C (350°F/Gas 4). Heat the butter and oil in a roasting tin over a high heat. Add the veal to the tin and fry until browned all over. Season with salt and pepper.

2 Add the onions, garlic, rosemary, and bay leaf. Pour over the wine and roast in the oven for 45 minutes to 1 hour, basting regularly with the juices. Remove from the oven, place the rib on a serving dish, and leave to rest for 10 minutes.

3 Meanwhile, place the roasting tin over a low heat to reduce the cooking juices. Add the knob of butter and whisk well to combine. Taste and adjust the seasoning, if needed. Carve the veal and serve along with the cooking juices.

RED BISON CURRY

A fresh-tasting Thai curry, this dish uses the prime cut of meat. Cooked quickly, the meat retains its flavour and texture.

CUT **Bison sirloin**

SERVES 4
PREP 20 mins   **COOK** 25 mins

1 tbsp vegetable oil

450g (1lb) bison sirloin steak, cut into strips

400ml can coconut milk

100ml (3½fl oz) beef stock

1 tbsp Thai fish sauce such as Nam Pla

1 tbsp brown sugar

3 tbsp red curry paste

1 bell pepper, deseeded and sliced

1 carrot, sliced

115g (4oz) chestnut mushrooms, sliced

1 tbsp chopped basil leaves

1 Heat the oil in a large frying pan over a medium heat. Add the meat and fry for about 5 minutes, until well-browned. Remove with a slotted spoon, place on a plate, and set aside.

2 Add the coconut milk, stock, fish sauce, sugar, and curry paste to the pan. Whisk to combine all the ingredients, reduce the heat to a simmer, and cook for about 5 minutes.

3 Then add all the vegetables and cook, stirring occasionally, for a further 10 minutes, until the vegetables are soft and the sauce has thickened slightly. Return the meat to the pan and add the basil. Serve hot with jasmine rice.

VARIATION

Red beef curry Use beef sirloin steak in place of the bison, and 100g (3½oz) sliced mangetout peas or okra in place of the carrots. Cook as above and serve hot.

VEAL SCALOPPINE WITH SALSA VERDE

A typical Italian dish, it is traditionally served with salsa verde or a tomato or wine sauce.

THE CUT Veal sirloin

SERVES 4
PREP 15–20 mins   **COOK** 5 mins, plus resting

4 x 180g (6¼oz) veal sirloin medallions

8 slices Parma ham

12 sage leaves

freshly ground black pepper

2 tbsp unsalted butter

a dash of olive oil (optional)

FOR THE SALSA

3 tbsp finely chopped flat-leaf parsley

grated zest and juice of 1 small lemon

2 tbsp capers, drained and rinsed, if in salt, and finely chopped

2 garlic cloves, crushed

150ml (5fl oz) olive oil

½ tsp Dijon mustard

sea salt

1 Place the veal between 2 sheets of cling film and flatten slightly using a rolling pin or mallet. Remove from the cling film and set aside. Spread out 2 slices of ham on a plate and top with 3 sage leaves. Place the veal on top of the sage leaves and season with pepper. Wrap the ham around the veal and repeat with each medallion.

2 Meanwhile, for the salsa, place the parsley, lemon zest, capers, and garlic in a bowl. Add the lemon juice, oil, and mustard. Toss well to coat, and taste and adjust the seasoning, if needed.

3 Heat the butter in a large frying pan. Add the veal, when the butter starts to foam, and fry until golden on both sides. Add the oil, if required. Leave the veal to rest for 2 minutes and serve with the salsa verde.

VEAL ESCALOPES WITH PEPPERS

This dish is a northern Italian classic. Give the escalopes enough room in the pan, or they will steam instead of developing a crisp crust.

CUT Veal escalope

SERVES 6
PREP 20–25 mins, plus chilling
COOK 9–12 mins

6 veal escalopes, about 375g (13oz) in total

30g (1oz) plain flour, seasoned with salt and pepper

2 eggs, lightly beaten

60g (2oz) dried breadcrumbs

60g (2oz) freshly grated Parmesan cheese

4 tbsp olive oil, plus extra if needed

1 garlic clove, finely chopped

2 small green peppers, deseeded and cut into strips

2 small red peppers, deseeded and cut into strips

salt and freshly ground black pepper

7–10 sprigs of oregano, leaves picked and finely chopped, plus extra to serve

30g (1oz) butter

1 lemon, sliced, to serve

1 Place the veal pieces between two sheets of cling film and flatten using a rolling pin or mallet until they are 3mm (⅛in) thick. Remove from the cling film and set aside.

2 Sift the flour onto a large plate. Place the beaten eggs in a shallow dish. Mix the breadcrumbs and Parmesan in a small bowl and spread on another sheet of baking parchment. Coat the escalopes in the flour and shake off any excess. Then dip them in the egg, and finally coat with the breadcrumbs and cheese mixture. Chill in the fridge for 30 minutes.

3 Heat 2 tablespoons of the oil in a frying pan. Add the garlic and peppers, season, and sauté until soft, stirring occasionally. Remove from the heat, add the oregano, and keep warm.

4 Heat the butter and remaining oil in a large frying pan over a medium-high heat. Fry the escalopes for 1–2 minutes on both sides until golden brown and no longer pink in the centre. Reduce the heat if the crumbs start to burn. Do this in batches to avoid overcrowding the pan, adding more oil between batches if necessary. Transfer to a plate lined with kitchen paper and keep warm. Serve with the peppers, lemon slices, and a sprig of oregano.

VEAL SCHNITZEL WITH FRIED EGG, CAPERS, AND PARSLEY

The national dish of Austria, it is usually served with a green salad, lemon, and parsley.

CUT Veal sirloin

SERVES 4
PREP 20 mins, plus chilling **COOK** 15 mins

4 veal sirloin steaks, 200g (7oz) each

2 tbsp plain flour, seasoned with salt and pepper

2 large eggs, lightly beaten

150g (5½oz) breadcrumbs

50g (1¾oz) butter

2 tbsp clarified butter

2 tbsp olive oil

4 eggs, to serve

1 tbsp capers, rinsed

1 tbsp chopped flat-leaf parsley

1 Place the steaks between two sheets of cling film and flatten using a rolling pin or mallet until 3mm (⅛in) thick. Remove from the cling film and set aside.

2 Place the flour in a large bowl. Place the beaten eggs in a separate bowl and put the breadcrumbs on a plate. Coat each piece of veal in the flour and shake off any excess. Then dip them in the egg, and finally coat with the breadcrumbs. Chill in the fridge for 30 minutes.

3 Remove the veal pieces from the fridge. Heat the butter and half the oil in a deep-sided frying pan. Add the veal pieces and fry for 2–3 minutes on each side, until crisp and golden brown. Remove with a slotted spoon and place on a plate. Set aside and keep warm.

4 Heat the remaining oil in a separate frying pan and fry the eggs. To serve, place each piece of veal on a warm plate, then top with the capers, parsley, and a fried egg. Serve with a green salad, a little clarified warm butter, and a lemon wedge.

ROAST VEAL WITH LEMON, OLIVES, AND CHERRY TOMATOES

Perfect for the summer months, this delicious roast has a unique balance of sweet, salty, and sharp flavours.

 **THE CUT** Veal fillet

SERVES 6
PREP 20 mins   **COOK** 1½ hrs, plus resting

zest of 1 lemon

1kg (2¼lb) veal fillet

2 tbsp olive oil

sea salt and freshly ground black pepper

2 onions, chopped

200ml (7fl oz) white wine

4 garlic cloves, thinly sliced

1 preserved lemon, rinsed and cut into 4 wedges

250g (9oz) cherry tomatoes on the vine

50g (1¾oz) black olives

50g (1¾oz) green olives

2 sprigs of lemon thyme

2 sprigs of rosemary

a knob of butter

handful of flat-leaf parsley, roughly chopped, to garnish

1 Preheat the oven to 150°C (300°F/Gas 2). Rub lemon zest all over the meat. Heat the oil in a roasting tin over a high heat. Add the meat and fry on both sides, until well-browned. Season with salt and pepper.

2 Add the onions and 2–3 tablespoons of the wine to the tin. Baste the meat with the cooking juices. Pour in the rest of the wine and transfer the roasting tin to the oven. Roast the veal for 50–60 minutes, basting every 15–20 minutes with the cooking juices.

3 Remove from the oven and transfer the meat to a serving dish and leave to rest in a warm place. Add the garlic, lemon wedges, tomatoes, black and green olives, thyme, and rosemary to the tin. Return to the oven for a further 15 minutes.

4 Remove the roasting tin from the oven, add the butter, and stir gently into the mixture. Taste to adjust the seasoning. Carve the veal into slices and place them on a plate with the olives, lemon, and tomatoes. Pour over the buttery juices, garnish with some parsley, and serve hot.

BLANQUETTE DE VEAU

This classic French dish has a rich, creamy sauce that is thickened with the careful addition of egg yolks.

 **THE CUT** Veal shoulder

SERVES 4
PREP 15 mins   **COOK** 1 hr 40 mins

600g (1lb 5oz) veal, cut into 4cm (1½in) pieces

1 bouquet garni

1 celery stick, roughly chopped

1 carrot, roughly chopped

salt and freshly ground black pepper

100ml (3½fl oz) white wine

12 button onions

300g (10oz) button mushrooms

2 egg yolks

4 tbsp double cream

handful of flat-leaf parsley leaves, chopped, to garnish

1 Place the meat, bouquet garni, celery, and carrot in a 2-litre (3½-pint) heavy-based, flameproof casserole. Season well and add the wine. Then pour in 500ml (16fl oz) water, bring to the boil, and skim off any scum that rises to the surface.

2 Then reduce the heat, cover, and simmer for 1 hour, stirring occasionally. Add the onions and mushrooms and bring to the boil. Cover and simmer for 30 minutes. Remove the bouquet garni.

3 Whisk together the egg yolks and cream in a jug, and whisk in a little of the cooking juices. Then slowly pour the egg and cream mixture into the casserole, stirring constantly. Cook gently until the sauce thickens. Remove from the heat, scatter the parsley over the meat, and serve with steamed green vegetables and mixed basmati and wild rice.

GOAN VEAL KEBABS

Inspired by Portuguese cuisine, Goan dishes usually contain coconut, rice, intense spices, and, of course, chilli.

 **Veal topside**

SERVES 4–6
PREP 15 mins, plus marinating and soaking
COOK 15 mins, plus resting

1kg (2¼lb) veal topside, cut into 4cm (1½in) strips

sea salt and freshly ground black pepper

FOR THE MARINADE

5cm (2in) cinnamon stick

10 cloves

2 large dried red chillies, torn into small pieces

5cm (2in) piece of fresh root ginger, roughly grated

1 large onion, chopped

1 tsp turmeric powder

2 tbsp tamarind paste

2 tsp brown sugar

100ml (3½fl oz) cider vinegar

2 tbsp rapeseed oil

4 garlic cloves, crushed

1 tsp salt

½ tsp freshly ground black pepper

1 For the marinade, crush the cinnamon and cloves in a mortar and pestle. Toast the mixture in a dry frying pan over a low heat until fragrant. Then add the red chilli. Remove from the heat and set aside to cool. Place the rest of the ingredients in a food processor along with the spice mix, then pulse to form a smooth paste.

2 Transfer the mixture to a large bowl, add the meat, and mix well. Cover and chill in the fridge for 2 hours. Meanwhile, soak 6 wooden skewers in cold water for 30 minutes. Set the barbecue to its highest setting, or heat a ridged griddle pan at its highest setting.

3 Remove the meat from the fridge and thread it onto the skewers. Cook the kebabs over a barbecue or ridged griddle pan, turning regularly, for 6–8 minutes, or until cooked through. Season the meat from time to time.

4 Remove from the heat and rest the kebabs for 2–3 minutes. Serve hot with toasted fresh coconut naan breads and mint yogurt.

SPINACH-STUFFED VEAL

These stuffed rolls can be cooked up to two days ahead, covered, and refrigerated. Their flavour will mellow over time.

 **Veal escalope**

SERVES 4
PREP 45–50 mins　　**COOK** 30–40 mins

500g (1lb 2oz) spinach leaves, trimmed

4 tbsp olive oil, plus extra if needed

45g (1½oz) walnuts, chopped

30g (1oz) freshly grated Parmesan cheese

grated nutmeg

8 garlic cloves, finely chopped

salt and freshly ground black pepper

8 veal escalopes, about 625g (1lb 6oz) in total

1 onion, thinly sliced

1 carrot, thinly sliced

2 celery sticks, thinly sliced

250ml (9fl oz) dry white wine

250ml (9fl oz) chicken stock

1 Bring a saucepan of water to the boil, add the spinach, and simmer for 1–2 minutes, then drain. Squeeze to remove excess water, then chop. Heat 2 tablespoons of the oil in a frying pan and add the spinach. Stir until all the moisture has evaporated. Remove from the heat and add the walnuts, Parmesan, nutmeg, and half the garlic. Stir well. Taste and adjust the seasoning.

2 Place the veal pieces between two sheets of cling film and flatten using a rolling pin or mallet until 3mm (⅛in) thick. Remove from the cling film and set aside. Place the escalopes on a clean work surface and season with salt and pepper. Divide the spinach stuffing evenly between the veal escalopes. Roll up the meat, tucking in the ends, and tie the rolls with pieces of butcher's string.

3 Heat the remaining oil in a frying pan over a high heat. Add the veal rolls and cook for 2–3 minutes, turning occasionally, until well-browned all over. Remove with a slotted spoon, transfer to a plate, and set aside.

4 Stir the onion and remaining garlic into the pan and cook until softened. Then add the carrot and celery, reduce the heat, and cook for 8–10 minutes, until tender. Pour in the wine, bring to the boil, and simmer to reduce by half.

5 Return the meat to the pan and add the stock. Cover and simmer for 30–40 minutes, until tender. Strain the liquid into a saucepan, reserving the vegetables, and boil until reduced to 180ml (6fl oz). Slice the veal rolls and serve with the sauce.

LAMB AND GOAT

LAMB AND GOAT

WE HAVE VISIONS OF SHEEP GRAZING SALT-WASHED MARSHES NEAR THE SEA, OR SURVIVING ON THE ROCKY SHORELINES OF NORTHERN ISLANDS. WE ALSO THINK OF GOATS CLIMBING UP TREES TO FORAGE FOR SCARCE LEAVES IN DRY, INHOSPITABLE SCRUBLAND.

BOTH SHEEP AND GOATS are remarkably efficient at living off some of the poorest pastures in the world. As they are small animals, they are easy to keep and were domesticated before cattle or pigs, providing us with wool, milk, and delicious meat.

Until recently, however, most sheep were kept primarily for milk and wool. Meat was a by-product that generally came from animals that were older than the ones we eat today. Lamb was a luxury item, used – and still used – for feasting: at Muslim weddings, births, and on religious holidays;

for Jewish Passover; and at the Easter meal for Christians. In many countries, though, lamb is not a common meat.

Goats have been a major source of meat, as well as milk, throughout the arid regions of Africa and, especially, Asia. These regions contain about 60 per cent of the world's goat population. Elsewhere, some goats are reared specifically for meat, but most are kept in dairy units where surplus young males are sold for meat. Mature goat meat is widely available where there is a thriving milk industry.

BROWSERS AND GRAZERS

Sheep and goats are both ruminants, mammals with four-chambered stomachs that they can store food in prior to digestion. Goats are browsers rather than grazers and prefer leaves and shrubs, whereas sheep prefer short vegetation. When raised for milk production, both sheep and goats will have a higher energy diet and are more likely to be reared indoors, with food such as hay and alfalfa, along with concentrates, as feed. But in many hot countries they are still herded and grazed on whatever vegetation is available.

PRODUCTION AND FEED

Sheep and goats raised specifically for meat are largely grazed outside. Some sheep are raised in the hills, sometimes on salt marshes or on seashores. The vegetation in these special environments gives a distinctive and much prized flavour to the meat. Large flocks of sheep are reared on ranches in South America, Australia, and New Zealand, which has the highest density of sheep in the world. Sheep and meat goats are also raised fairly intensively in fertilized, grass paddocks as part of arable rotations. Root crops, such as swedes or turnips and fodder beet, are fed in the winter, and concentrates may also be given, either during lambing or kidding, or to finish the fattening process before slaughter. However, the chances of lamb and young goat being intensively reared are far fewer than with other species.

UNTIL RECENTLY, MOST SHEEP WERE KEPT FOR MILK AND WOOL. MEAT WAS A BY-PRODUCT, SO IT GENERALLY CAME FROM ANIMALS OLDER THAN THOSE WE NOW EAT.

DIPS AND DOSES

Where sheep and goats are free-ranging there are few serious health issues, but during periods or systems of more intensive management, sheep and goats are usually dosed to prevent or treat parasites, flies, and foot rot. Controversial sheep dips, such as those using organophosphates, can be harmful to the environment and, most people think, to farmers as well. They need careful handling and many would like to see them banned.

ORGANIC LAMB

Like other livestock, organic lamb can be raised in a number of ways, although feed must be organic. Some very extensively raised lamb may not carry an organic mark, but may well be just as "organic" as some certified lamb. Organophosphates have been permitted on organic farms in some countries where other suitable treatments are absent.

LAMB AND GOAT BREEDS

• **Sheep** Of the hundreds of sheep breeds, many – like the famous Spanish Merino – are wool breeds. Others are bred for milk production. In most lamb-producing countries, meat breeds are crosses between hardy breeds and productive ones.

Britain has more breeds of sheep than any other country and many breeds, such as Romney, Suffolk, and Cheviot, are seen in flocks across the world. The Dorset Horn crossed with the Blackhead Persian sheep created the popular Dorper breed. Similarly, the Texel, a large breed from the Netherlands, has been adopted in many countries as a fast-growing meat-producing sheep. Each country has its special heritage breeds, such as the Herdwick, the Welsh Mountain sheep, and the Scottish Blackface.

Fat-tailed sheep: This is a special group of breeds from Asia, the Middle East, and Africa where they thrive in arid conditions. They are reared for meat, but their main speciality is their very long tails that have been selected to produce especially

delicious fat which is highly prized.
• **Goat meat breeds** Outside Asia and Africa, specialized meat production is comparatively new and most goats are dairy breeds. The South African Boer is one of the most common meat breeds (it is a cross between native and imported breeds), followed by the Spanish and Anglo Nubian, a multi-purpose breed developed by crossing Indian and Middle Eastern goats.

LAMB AND GOAT CATEGORIES

• **Milk-fed lamb or baby lamb** This is 4–10 weeks old and has a very delicate flavour.
• **Spring lamb** This is 3–6 months old, although since so much lamb is sold very young anyway, the term is not often used.
• **Lamb** Lamb meat can be up to one year old and has a mild, but distinctive, flavour.
• **Hogget or yearling mutton** At 1–2 years old, the meat from a hogget is still tender, but it has a more pronounced flavour than lamb, with a little more fat.
• **Mutton** This comes from sheep of two years of age and upwards, so is more

variable. The fat and meat has a much stronger "sheep" taste. Mutton can be tough if very old.
• **Kid (young goat)** Up to 14 months old, goat meat has a delicate flavour similar to young lamb. It has several names. Milk-fed goat, or baby goat, is usually well under three months old and often eaten before it starts grazing. Capretto and cabrito are used to describe the meat from young goats in the 2–12 month age range, and chevon is about 6–14 months old.
• **Goat** An adult goat is more than 14 months old. When older than about three years, its meat can have a powerful flavour, especially if it comes from a male. Old goat meat is sometimes called mutton.

BUYING LAMB AND GOAT

Young lamb does not have a great deal of fat, but well-finished lamb can contain a lot, particularly in the forequarter cuts. The back legs are always the leanest part. Hogget is likely to be fatter than lamb. Mutton fat is harder than lamb fat and has a stronger taste. Most goat meat is fairly lean.

LAMB AND GOAT CUTS

The meat from these extensively reared animals tastes sweet and their versatile meat is perhaps not as common as it should be. Although goat and old mutton can be cut exactly like lamb, they are generally cut more simply. Hogget and younger mutton is cut as lamb.

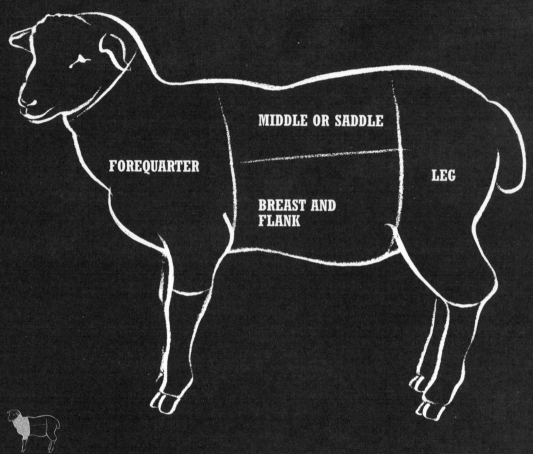

MIDDLE OR SADDLE

FOREQUARTER

BREAST AND FLANK

LEG

GOAT AND KID

Goat is much leaner than lamb and mutton. Young goat meat is sometimes called chevon or cabrita to distinguish it from older, stronger, goat meat. Kid is 4–14 months old.

- **WHOLE LEG** A prime joint, the leg can be roasted or braised whole or boned and rolled. Whole legs weigh around 2kg (4½lb).

- **WHOLE SADDLE, BONE-IN WITHOUT RIBS** The most tender cut, the saddle can be roasted whole, divided into a rack or chops for grilling and barbecuing, or boned out and trimmed for a neat premium roast.

- **WHOLE SHOULDER** A whole shoulder is at its best slowly cooked in foil until the meat falls off the bone. The shank can be removed, but cooked slowly it becomes tender too.

- **DICED GOAT** Perfect for curries and stews, diced goat meat is usually boneless. Some recipes ask for diced goat meat with the bone in but this may need to be ordered.

- **KID** Milk-fed kid has a delicate, pale meat and is particularly tender, but older kid meat is also tender and mild-flavoured. Sold whole and in primals (leg, shoulder, and saddle).

FOREQUARTER CUTS

Many traditional dishes use slow-cooked forequarter cuts as their flavour is superb. Sliced neck, shoulder, and shin all have different textures. Most cuts can be grilled and fried as well.

DICED FOREQUARTER There are many uses for diced lamb, from kebabs to stews. The fat content means the meat is kept moist, whether quickly or slowly cooked. Diced leg is far leaner.

SHOULDER CHOPS These are also sold without the bone. Good for the barbecue, but also delicious when slow-cooked as the meat stays succulent. Bandsaw-cut chops may have bone splinters.

WHOLE SHOULDER, BONE-IN WITH SHANK This joint is quite thin so cooks quickly, but the high fat content means it is better cooked to well-done. Try slashing the meat and rubbing in flavourings.

Additional forequarter cuts

- **SHOULDER, BONED AND ROLLED** This cut is good roasted or braised, although it has more fat than the leg.

- **NECK FILLET** A neat little cut that can be quickly roasted. Perfect for two.

- **SLICED NECK OR SCRAG** The perfect cut for Irish stew; the bones keep the meat sweet.

MIDDLE OR SADDLE CUTS

These tender cuts are the best part of the lamb. Boneless loin steaks may be called noisettes or medallions, and small log-shaped loin roasts may be called a pavé.

BEST END OR RACK This cut can be cooked as a whole piece and sliced into chops at the table if it has been chined. French trimming the ends (see p193) gives a neat appearance.

DOUBLE LOIN CHOPS Cut from the rump end of the loin and with the backbone chined, these chops have both loin and fillet meat and are the most succulent of all the chops.

LOIN OF LAMB, LARDER TRIMMED Also called cannon, this perfectly trimmed tender muscle is lamb at its most elegant. Best cooked to rosy pink and especially good with a herb crust.

Additional middle or saddle cuts

• **SADDLE** A premium joint from the best part of the back (from the chump to the start of the ribs), cut just like venison.

• **BARNSLEY CHOPS** This slice of saddle makes a generous portion; it has both loin and fillet meat.

• **BUTTERFLY STEAKS** These steaks must be completely trimmed or they curl up when cooking.

BREAST AND FLANK CUTS

Breast and flank fat is harder than pork fat, so flavours and cooking methods need to take this into account.

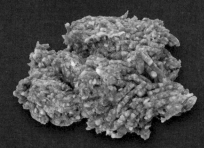

MINCE Lamb mince is poplular for inexpensive dishes such as shepherd's pie, meatballs, and koftes. Flank mince is very fatty, shoulder mince is less so, but leg mince is the leanest.

BREAST AND FLANK This fatty cut has thick connective tissue so needs slow cooking. It can also be cooked on the barbecue. The breast can be stuffed and rolled for a cheap dish.

LEG CUTS

Leg meat is leaner than loin and shoulder meat, but has just enough fat to keep it moist whether cooked pink or well-done. Diced leg makes excellent kebabs and tagine.

WHOLE LEG, ON THE BONE A whole leg is the perfect size for a family. The chump half is easier to carve without the pelvic bone. The other half may have the shank removed.

CHUMP CHOPS Despite their name, chump chops are usually boneless. From the top of the leg, they are very tender with a good flavour. They can be fried, grilled or braised.

SHANK, BONE-IN A popular pub cut, this little joint needs slow cooking. With caramelized root vegetables and some red wine, it produces a wonderfully rich dish. One shank makes a generous serving.

Additional leg cuts

• **ROLLED LEG OF LAMB** A whole rolled leg sometimes includes the shank but smaller roasts are always boneless.

• **BUTTERFLIED LEG** Legs are slashed deeply and opened out so they can be rubbed with flavourings (see p192).

• **BONELESS LEG STEAK** Perfect for grilling or frying, this is a fairly lean cut of lamb.

PRESERVED LAMB AND GOAT

PRESERVED LAMB PRODUCTS are found where lamb is most common: in northern European countries and around the Mediterranean fringe. Goat products tend to come from southern Europe, Asia, and Africa, where goats are herded in large numbers. Many of these tasty preparations are dark in colour and have an intense flavour.

REESTIT MUTTON From the Shetland Islands, reestit mutton is brined and then hung to dry in the rafters where the peaty smoke imparts a special flavour. A Norwegian version called *Fenalår* is made from whole lamb legs.

PASTIRMA From the Middle East, Balkans and Turkey, pastirma is prepared from salted lamb and goat, washed, dried and pressed, covered in a paste of hot spices and further dried.

MERGUEZ OR MIRQAZ A spicy cured or dried sausage common throughout North Africa. Lamb and goat are flavoured with lemon, harissa, and hot chillies, which make it bright red.

FÅREPØLS This Norwegian dried sausage is made of mutton and pork and sometimes includes the blood. Flavourings include ginger or juniper and, typically, syrup.

RYYNIMAKKARA Made with cooked oats or barley groats and flavoured with ginger, cloves, and pepper, this Finnish sausage originally contained no meat. Nowadays, however, it contains lamb among other meats.

SPEKEPØLSE A common cured, smoked, and dried Danish sausage; many forms exist. As well as lamb, pork and even vegetables such as cabbage or potatoes are also added.

MARANHO OR BURLHÕES This Portuguese sausage is cooked in the goat's stomach. It is flavoured with rice, ham, paprika, and mint.

LOUKANIKO A Greek lamb sausage often containing pork as well. Flavourings include pepper, cumin, sometimes orange peel, and either leeks or oregano.

BILTONG This is made in South Africa from many meats, including goat and mutton. The meat is sprinkled with vinegar, lightly spiced, and then dried in the sun.

BUTTERFLYING A LEG

A leg is boned to spread the meat out more evenly and thinly so is ideal for grilling and barbecuing. The pelvic bone is at the widest, meatiest end, the shank at the narrowest.

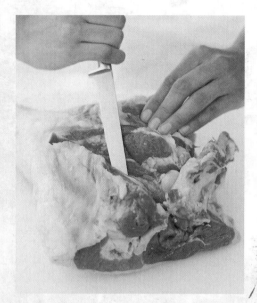

1 Place the lamb fleshiest side down. Grip the end of the pelvic bone in one hand and work around it with the tip of a boning knife to expose the bones. Now make an incision at the pelvic bone and cut through the skin and meat along the entire length of the thighbone.

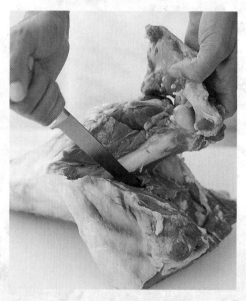

2 Pare the meat away from the thighbone, using short strokes and keeping the knife tilted towards the bone. Use the tip of the blade to avoid slashing the meat. As the meat falls away, pull the bone upwards.

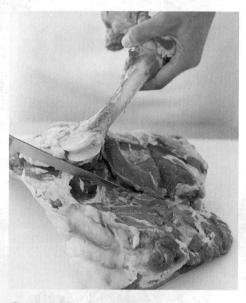

3 Once the whole thighbone is exposed, pull it right up from the shank bone and pare away all the meat from the bone and cartilage around the knuckle joint. If any cartilage comes off with the meat, cut it off and discard it.

4 Pare the meat away from the shank bone (it is easy to see the edge of the bone) and cut through any remaining meat, and tendons. All 3 leg bones can now be lifted out in one piece.

5 Open out the meat and lay it flat. Using a stroking movement, cut into the thickest part of the largest muscles to make everything as uniform a thickness as possible.

6 Open out the slashed "wings" to make a roughly square shape. If it is to be rolled, then slivers can be cut from over-thick areas and tucked into the thinnest parts to make an even shape.

FRENCH TRIMMING A RACK

A rack, or "carré", is an elegant joint that makes the most of the single lean eye muscle and is easy to carve into portions. It can be cooked unadorned or have a crust applied to the outside.

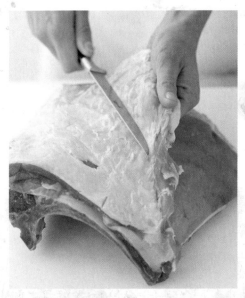

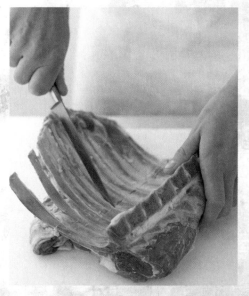

1 On one side of the joint there may be a soft, cartilaginous piece of shoulderblade under the skin. If so, lift the flap and cut it out with a flexible boning knife, holding the knife blade flat to avoid cutting into the muscle.

2 Slip the boning knife beneath the membrane of skin and outer fat, and rip it off with your other hand. Shave off excess fat, or remove all the fat and sinew until only the eye muscle remains.

3 With a small, very sharp knife, cut between the ribs with the blade right next to the bones to cut out the strips of meat, fat, and papery sinew that holds them together.

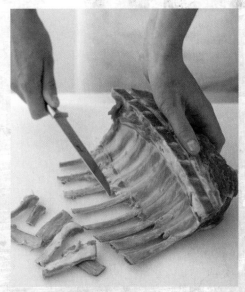

4 Holding the knife blade about 4cm (1½in) away from the main eye muscle, slice off the fatty flap. If you prefer really lean meat, cut closer to the muscle. Reserve the flap and trimmings to make stock.

5 Lay the rib bones on the chopping board. Take a cleaver and, with one stroke, chop off the ends of the bones so that they all come off in a straight line. With a utility or chef's knife, carefully strip off the fine skin that surrounds the bones for an attractive presentation.

6 Hold the joint upright. With a saw or cleaver, cut off the backbone (or "chine") from the rack. Try to do this with just 1 or 2 clean and accurate strokes. If you leave any traces of backbone on the joint, it will prevent you from slicing the cutlets apart after cooking.

GRILLED LAMB KOFTAS

These easy-to-make, authentic Greek lamb koftas are fresh, spicy, and bursting with flavour.

THE CUT Minced lamb

SERVES 8
PREP 30 mins, plus resting
COOK 8–12 mins

1 large onion, grated

1 tbsp coarse salt

900g (2lb) finely minced lamb

2 eggs, lightly beaten

2 tbsp chopped coriander leaves

2 tsp ground cumin

1 tsp dried thyme

½ tsp ground allspice

freshly ground black pepper

olive oil, for greasing

1 Place the onion and salt in a bowl, mix well, and leave for 15 minutes. Then use a fine sieve to squeeze the juice from the salted onions into a separate bowl.

2 Add the lamb, eggs, coriander, cumin, thyme, allspice, and pepper to the bowl. Combine all the ingredients, kneading the mixture lightly for 2–3 minutes. Cover and leave to rest for 30 minutes at room temperature.

3 Heat a griddle pan over a medium heat. Oil 8 metal skewers. Divide the lamb mixture into 8 equal portions and shape each into a sausage shape. Slide the koftas onto the skewers, smoothing the ends down so they do not slip off while cooking. Brush a little oil on each kofta.

4 Cook the koftas on the griddle pan for about 8 minutes, turning occasionally, until browned and evenly cooked on the outside, but still a little pink on the inside. These koftas will be cooked to medium-rare. If you prefer them well-done, cook for 2–3 minutes more. Slide the koftas off the skewers and leave to cool slightly for 2–3 minutes. Serve hot with pitta bread and sliced tomatoes.

VARIATION

Barbecued goat koftas Use minced goat meat instead of lamb and prepare as above. Barbecue the koftas instead of cooking over a griddle pan and serve with spiced flatbreads and Greek-style yogurt.

MOUSSAKA

This delicious Greek recipe may take a while to prepare, but the layers of sauces, grilled vegetables, and mince really make it well worth the time spent.

THE CUT Minced lamb

SERVES 4
PREP 1 hr   **COOK** 2 hrs 25 mins, plus resting

350g (12oz) waxy potatoes, such as Charlotte or Maris Peer, peeled

1 large aubergine, cut lengthways into 1cm (½in) thick slices

FOR THE SAUCE

2 tbsp olive oil, plus extra for brushing

1 onion, finely chopped

2 garlic cloves, finely chopped

450g (1lb) minced lamb

400g can chopped tomatoes

200ml (7fl oz) beef, lamb, or chicken stock

1 small glass of red wine (optional)

2 tbsp finely chopped flat-leaf parsley

½ tsp dried thyme

½ tsp dried oregano

½ tsp ground cinnamon

salt and freshly ground black pepper

FOR THE BÉCHAMEL

50g (1¾oz) butter

50g (1¾oz) plain flour

400ml (14fl oz) whole milk

pinch of grated nutmeg

25g (scant 1oz) freshly grated Parmesan cheese

1 egg, beaten

1 For the sauce, heat the oil in a large, heavy-based saucepan over a medium heat. Add the onion and cook for about 5 minutes, until softened. Then add the garlic and cook for 1 more minute. Increase the heat, add the lamb, and cook until well-browned. Then add the tomatoes, stock, wine (if using), herbs, and cinnamon. Season and bring to the boil. Then reduce the heat to a simmer, and cook for 1–1 hour 15 minutes, until the liquid evaporates.

2 Meanwhile, boil the potatoes in a large pan of salted water, until cooked through. Drain, slice lengthways, and set aside. Set the grill to its highest setting. Spread the aubergine slices on a baking sheet, brush with the oil, and grill until browned. Turn, brush the other side with oil, and grill until browned. Set aside.

3 Preheat the oven to 180°C (350°F/Gas 4). For the béchamel, melt the butter in a small pan over a medium heat. Whisk in the flour and cook for 2 minutes. Then remove from the heat and gradually whisk in the milk. Return to the heat and cook, stirring, until thickened. Add the nutmeg and Parmesan, season well, and cook over a low heat for 10 minutes. Remove from the heat and whisk in the beaten egg.

4 Spread half the meat in a 20cm (8in) square ovenproof dish. Cover with half the aubergine, then half the béchamel. Arrange the potatoes in an overlapping layer, then add the rest of the meat, aubergine, and béchamel. Bake for 1 hour until golden brown. Leave to rest and serve hot.

LAMB BURGERS WITH ROASTED TOMATO RELISH

The addition of cream and fresh herbs to the mince makes for burgers that are very succulent and full of flavour.

THE CUT Minced lamb

SERVES 4
PREP 20 mins, plus chilling
COOK 8–10 mins, plus resting

500g (1lb 2oz) lean minced lamb

handful of coriander leaves, finely chopped

2 shallots, finely chopped

1 tsp ground cumin

1 red chilli, deseeded and finely chopped

2 garlic cloves, crushed and finely chopped

1 tsp ground cinnamon

1 tbsp chopped flat-leaf parsley

1 tbsp chopped mint

pinch of ground allspice

1 tbsp double cream

2 tbsp fine breadcrumbs

grated zest of 1 lemon

sea salt and freshly ground black pepper

rapeseed oil, for brushing

FOR THE RELISH

450g (1lb) cherry tomatoes

1 red onion, finely diced

1 garlic clove, finely chopped

3 tbsp olive oil

1 tsp of sugar

handful of coriander leaves, chopped

1 Place all the burger ingredients in a large bowl and mix lightly to combine. Make 4 round, 3cm (1in) thick patties without compressing the meat too much. Chill the patties for 30 minutes.

2 Heat a heavy-based non-stick frying pan over a medium heat. Brush the patties lightly with oil and fry them until cooked to your liking – 4 minutes on each side for medium and 5 minutes on each side for well-done. Leave to rest for about 2 minutes.

3 For the relish, place all the ingredients, except the coriander, in a frying pan and cook for 8–10 minutes, until soft. Cool the mixture slightly, then squeeze the tomato flesh out of the skins and transfer to a bowl. Add the onions and garlic to the bowl and stir in the coriander. Serve the patties in burger buns along with the relish.

FORFAR BRIDIES

A traditional Scottish pie, ideal for eating when out and about on the hills, at a football match, or on a picnic.

 THE CUT Minced lamb

SERVES 4
PREP 20 mins, plus chilling and resting
COOK 40 mins

FOR THE PASTRY

250g (9oz) strong white flour

75g (2½oz) plain flour, plus extra for dusting

½ tsp salt

175g (6oz) butter, chilled and diced

FOR THE FILLING

500g (1lb 2oz) minced lamb

75g (2½oz) beef suet, grated

1 onion, finely chopped

1 tbsp chopped flat-leaf parsley

salt and freshly ground black pepper

1 For the pastry, place all the ingredients in a food processor and pulse until the mixture resembles fine breadcrumbs. Transfer the mixture to a large bowl, add 3–4 tablespoons of iced water, and mix to form a dough. Bring together to form a ball, wrap in cling film, and chill for 2 hours.

2 Preheat the oven to 200°C (400°F/Gas 6). For the filling, place all the ingredients in a large bowl and mix well to combine. Remove the pastry from the fridge and divide it into 4 equal portions. On a lightly floured surface, roll each portion out into an oval shape. Place one-quarter of the meat mixture onto one side of each pastry oval, leaving a border around the edges.

3 Moisten the edges of the pastry ovals with water. Fold the pastry over to enclose the filling and crimp the edges with a fork to neaten and seal. Make a small hole on the top of each pie to allow steam to escape, and leave to rest for 1 hour. Place on a baking tin and bake for 40 minutes. These pies can be served warm or cold.

VARIATION

Beef bridies Use minced beef in place of lamb, and marjoram in place of parsley. Add 1 teaspoon mustard to the filling and cook the pies as above.

GREEK LAMB STEW

A complete meal in itself, this rich and hearty stew only needs some crusty bread to soak up the delicious juices.

 Lamb shoulder

SERVES 4
PREP 30 mins   **COOK** 2 hrs 10 mins

2 tbsp olive oil

700g (1lb 9oz) boneless shoulder or neck fillet of lamb, trimmed and cut into bite-sized pieces

1 red onion, finely chopped

2 garlic cloves, finely chopped

200ml (7fl oz) dry white wine

2 x 400g can chopped tomatoes

100g (3½oz) pitted Kalamata olives

3 sprigs of thyme

100g (3½oz) kritharáki or orzo pasta

salt and freshly ground black pepper

100g (3½oz) feta cheese, crumbled

small bunch of mint leaves, finely chopped

1 Preheat the oven to 150°C (300°F/Gas 2). Heat 1 tablespoon of oil in a large, heavy-based, flameproof casserole or Dutch oven over a medium heat. Cook the meat until well-browned. Do this in batches to avoid overcrowding the pan. Remove with a slotted spoon and set aside on a plate lined with kitchen paper.

2 Add the remaining oil to the casserole. Then add the onion and cook for 5 minutes, stirring occasionally, until softened. Add the garlic and cook for 2 more minutes.

3 Add the wine and tomatoes to the casserole and stir to mix. Return the lamb to the pan, add the olives and thyme, and bring to the boil. Season well, cover, and cook in the oven for 1½ hours.

4 Remove from the oven, discard the thyme, then add in the pasta, and stir. Adjust the seasoning and return to the oven for a further 15 minutes. Mix the feta and mint in a small dish. Serve the stew hot with the cheese mixture sprinkled over.

LAMB KEBABS WITH YOGURT AND POMEGRANATE

These Greek-inspired kebabs are easy to make and are traditionally served with a refreshing yogurt dressing.

 Lamb shoulder

SERVES 4
PREP 30 mins, plus marinating
COOK 10 mins

350g (12oz) lean lamb shoulder, cut into cubes

½ tsp ground cumin

½ tsp ground coriander

½ tsp garam masala

¼ tsp ground cinnamon

olive oil, for brushing

seeds from 1 pomegranate, to serve

FOR THE DRESSING

1 shallot, finely chopped

1 garlic clove, chopped

1 tbsp chopped mint

½ cucumber, peeled, deseeded, and chopped

300g (10oz) Greek-style yogurt

pinch of salt

1 Place the lamb in a large bowl. Add the cumin, coriander, garam masala, and cinnamon to the bowl and mix to coat the meat in the spices. Leave to marinate for 30 minutes.

2 For the dressing, place the shallots, garlic, mint, cucumber, and yogurt in a large serving bowl. Add the salt, mix well to combine, and set aside.

3 Heat a large, heavy-based frying pan or a griddle pan. Divide the lamb cubes into 4 equal portions and thread them onto 4 skewers. Brush the pan with a little oil and grill the meat for 8 minutes, turning regularly, until well-browned.

4 Remove from the heat. Sprinkle over the pomegranate seeds, remove the kebabs fom the skewers, and transfer to a serving plater. Serve with a dollop of the yogurt dressing, couscous, and pitta bread.

LAMB AND BARLEY STEW

A richly satisfying dish, its flavour intensifies greatly after keeping for a day or two.

CUT Leg of lamb

SERVES 4
PREP 30 mins   **COOK** 2 hrs

3 tbsp oil or lamb fat

salt and freshly ground black pepper

450g (1lb) leg of lamb, diced

1 onion, finely sliced

2 carrots, sliced

2 celery sticks, finely sliced

2 garlic cloves, crushed

1 tbsp plain flour

300ml (10fl oz) white wine

1 tbsp tomato purée

2 strips lemon peel

1 bay leaf

sprig of thyme

30g (1oz) pearl barley

1 tbsp chopped flat-leaf parsley

1 Preheat the oven to 160°C (325°F/Gas 3). Heat 2 tablespoons of oil in a large, flameproof casserole. Season the lamb and cook for 4–5 minutes, until well-browned. Do this in batches to avoid overcrowding the pan. Remove with a slotted spoon and set aside on a plate lined with kitchen paper.

2 Reduce the heat and add the remaining oil to the casserole. Add the onions, carrots, and celery and cook, stirring constantly, until softened. Stir in the garlic and cook for 1 more minute.

3 Return the meat to the casserole, stir in the flour, and mix through. Then add the wine, tomato purée, lemon peel, bay leaf, and thyme. Pour in just enough water to cover and bring to the boil. Then add the barley, stirring to combine. Cover and cook in the oven for 1½ hours until the lamb is tender.

4 Remove from the oven and take out the bay leaf, thyme, and lemon peel. Taste and adjust the seasoning, if needed. Stir in the parsley and serve with mashed potatoes and greens.

VARIATION

Goat and barley stew Use goat in place of the lamb, medium oatmeal in place of the flour, and cider in place of the wine. Cook as above and serve hot.

LAMB FILLET BASTED WITH ANCHOVY PASTE

Anchovies give the lamb a punchy flavour in this dish. You can use ready-made anchovy paste, or make your own as shown here.

CUT Lamb neck

SERVES 4
PREP 15 mins, plus marinating
COOK 20 mins, plus resting

1 whole lamb neck fillet, about 675g (1½lb)

2 spring onions, trimmed and roughly chopped

150g jar salted anchovies in oil, drained

2 tbsp capers in vinegar, drained

3 tbsp olive oil

1 Set the grill at its medium setting. Score the lamb fillet in a criss-cross pattern, about 1cm (½in) deep. Place the onions, anchovies, capers, and olive oil in a food processor and pulse to a fine paste.

2 Place the lamb in a large shallow dish and coat with the anchovy paste, making sure it gets into the scores. Leave to marinate in the fridge for about 30 minutes.

3 Cook the lamb fillet in the lower part of the grill for 15–20 minutes, turning occasionally, until browned and cooked to your liking.

4 Remove from the heat, transfer to a plate, and leave to rest in a warm place for at least 10 minutes. Cut the meat into 1cm (½in) slices and serve with warm pitta bread, hummus, and seasonal salad leaves.

LANCASHIRE HOTPOT

A traditional dish from northwest England, it uses the rich-tasting neck of lamb and kidneys.

THE CUT Neck of lamb and kidneys

SERVES 4
PREP 15 mins **COOK** 2 hrs 40 mins

4 lamb kidneys, about 200g (7oz) in total

1kg (2¼lb) neck end of lamb

salt and freshly ground black pepper

1 tbsp vegetable oil

3 tsp butter, plus 1 tsp extra for greasing

1kg (2¼lb) floury potatoes, such as Maris Piper or Red Duke of York, thinly sliced

3 onions, finely sliced

2 sprigs of thyme

2 bay leaves

1 tsp caster sugar

450ml (15fl oz) lamb stock

1 Preheat the oven to 160°C (325°F/Gas 3). Slice the kidneys in half horizontally. Then remove the skins and cut out the cores. Season the kidneys and lamb with salt and pepper.

2 Heat the oil in a frying pan over a high heat, add all the meat, and cook for about 10 minutes, until browned. Remove with a slotted spoon and set aside on a plate lined with kitchen paper.

3 Grease the bottom of a large casserole dish. Use half the potatoes to arrange an overlapping layer at the bottom and season lightly. Then layer with the meats, onions, thyme, and bay leaves. Sprinkle over the sugar.

4 Top with the remaining potatoes, overlapping, to cover the meats fully. Pour in just enough stock to cover the meat, leaving the top layer of the potatoes dry. Season lightly.

5 Melt the butter in a saucepan and brush over the top of the potatoes. Cover and cook in the oven for 2 hours. Then remove the lid, increase the temperature to 200°C (400°F/Gas 6), and cook for a further 30 minutes to brown the edges of the potatoes. Remove from the heat and take out the thyme and bay leaves. Serve hot with cabbage or greens.

IRISH STEW

An economical dish that uses inexpensive cuts, it has a long cooking time, which ensures a rich and intense flavour.

THE CUT Neck or shoulder of lamb

SERVES 4
PREP 25 mins **COOK** 3 hrs

900g (2lb) stewing lamb from the neck or shoulder, trimmed and cut into 3cm (1in) pieces

130g (4¾oz) pearl barley

1 large onion, roughly chopped

3 carrots, roughly sliced

200g (7oz) swede, roughly chopped

4 potatoes, roughly chopped

4 sprigs of thyme

salt and freshly ground black pepper

1 litre (1¾ pints) hot lamb stock

1 Place half the meat in a large, heavy-based casserole. Top with half the barley, half the vegetables, 2 sprigs of thyme, and season well. Repeat the layers using up the remaining meat, barley, vegetables, and thyme. Season well.

2 Pour over the stock, place the casserole over a high heat, and bring to the boil. Skim off any scum that rises to the surface.

3 Reduce the heat to a simmer, cover, and cook for 3 hours, stirring occasionally. Taste and adjust the seasoning, if needed. Remove from the heat and serve hot in bowls with crusty bread.

TAJINE BIL MISHMISH

This tajine "with apricots" is a take on a traditional Moroccan dish.
The dried apricots and orange juice help produce its distinct flavour.

THE CUT **Lamb shoulder**

SERVES 4
PREP 10 mins, plus marinating
COOK 1½ hrs

1 onion, thinly sliced

1 tsp ground coriander

1 tsp ground cumin

1 tsp ground ginger

1 tsp dried thyme

2 tbsp sunflower oil or groundnut oil

900g (2lb) boneless lamb shoulder,
cut into 2.5cm (1in) cubes

2 tbsp plain flour

300ml (10fl oz) orange juice

600ml (1 pint) hot chicken stock

115g (4oz) ready-to-eat dried apricots

salt and freshly ground black pepper

handful of mint leaves, roughly chopped,
to garnish (optional)

1 Place the onion, coriander, cumin, ginger, thyme, and 1 tablespoon of the oil in a large non-metallic bowl. Mix to combine. Then add the lamb and mix to coat in the marinade. Cover and leave to marinate in the fridge for at least 3 hours, or overnight.

2 Preheat the oven to 160°C (325°F/Gas 3). Place the flour in a small bowl and stir in the orange juice until smooth. Set aside. Heat the remaining oil in a large frying pan over a high heat. Add the lamb mixture and fry, stirring frequently, for about 5 minutes, or until well-browned.

3 Transfer the lamb to a large flameproof tajine. Add the flour mixture and stir. Pour in the stock, return to the heat, and bring to the boil, stirring constantly. Remove from the heat, cover, and cook in the oven for 1 hour.

4 Remove from the oven and stir in the apricots. Cover and cook in the oven for a further 20 minutes, or until the lamb is tender. Remove and adjust the seasoning, if needed. Sprinkle over the mint leaves (if using) and serve hot.

ROAST LAMB LOIN WITH GOAT'S CHEESE

The lavender in this dish provides a light aromatic touch to the robust flavour of the lamb, resulting in a beautifully balanced dish.

THE CUT Lamb loin

SERVES 4–6
PREP 25 mins, plus marinating
COOK 25 mins, plus resting

4 boneless lamb loins, about 150g (5½oz) each, trimmed

3 tsp wholegrain mustard

2 sprigs lavender leaves, roughly chopped

2 tbsp chives, roughly chopped

100g (3½oz) soft rindless goat's cheese

1 tbsp double cream, plus extra if needed

1 tsp black peppercorns, cracked

2 tbsp rapeseed oil, for frying

20g (¾oz) rocket leaves

12 asparagus spears, trimmed, blanched, and halved

1 tbsp flat-leaf parsley, chopped

1 tbsp oregano leaves, chopped

FOR THE CROUTONS

2 slices of 1cm (½in) thick wholemeal bread, crusts removed

1 tbsp butter, softened

½ garlic clove, crushed

FOR THE VINAIGRETTE

50ml (1½fl oz) wholegrain mustard

50ml (1½fl oz) rapeseed oil

50ml (1½fl oz) cider vinegar

juice of 1 lemon

2 tsp runny honey

sea salt and freshly ground black pepper

1 Fry the lamb loins in a dry, hot frying pan until well-browned. Remove from the heat and leave to cool. When cool enough to handle, coat the lamb in the mustard, and sprinkle with the lavender and 1 tablespoon chives. Wrap tightly in cling film and chill in the fridge for 30 minutes. Preheat the oven to 190°C (375°F/Gas 5)

2 For the croutons, cut the bread into 1cm (½in) cubes. Melt the butter in a small pan with the garlic, add the bread, and stir until thoroughly coated. Transfer to a small baking sheet and bake for about 8 minutes.

3 For the vinaigrette, place all the ingredients in a small bowl, whisk to combine, and set aside. Place the goat's cheese and cream in another bowl and lightly beat the mixture with a fork until soft peaks form. Add more cream, if needed, to help loosen the mixture. Add the peppercorns and remaining chives, mix well, and set aside.

4 Heat the oil in a frying pan and fry the lamb for 1–2 minutes on each side, until an even crust forms. Bake on a baking sheet for 8–10 minutes. Remove and leave to rest for 10–15 minutes.

5 Mix the rocket, asparagus, parsley, oregano, and croutons in a bowl. Place the salad in the centre of a plate and add 3 spoonfuls of the creamed goat's cheese around it. Cut each lamb loin in half diagonally and place over the salad. Drizzle over the vinaigrette and serve hot.

LAMB FILLET WITH TOMATO AND BASIL SALAD

Garlic, chilli, rosemary, and parsley combine to add piquancy to this flash-grilled marinated lamb. The colourful salad adds a refreshing punch to the dish.

THE CUT Lamb fillet

SERVES 4
PREP 15 mins, plus marinating
COOK 20 mins, plus resting

3 tbsp olive oil

1 large garlic clove, crushed

1½ tbsp finely chopped flat-leaf parsley, plus extra to garnish

sprig of rosemary, leaves picked

small pinch of dried chilli flakes

salt and freshly ground black pepper

165g (5¾oz) lamb fillet, trimmed

drizzle of extra virgin olive oil, to serve

FOR THE SALAD

2 ripe plum tomatoes, cut into quarters lengthways

250g (9oz) cherry tomatoes on the vine, separated but still with their stems

125g (4½oz) yellow bell or cherry tomatoes, halved

small handful of basil leaves

1 small garlic clove, crushed

½ small red onion, thinly sliced into rings

1½ tbsp extra virgin olive oil

1 Place the olive oil, garlic, parsley, rosemary, and chilli flakes in a large bowl. Season and mix well. Add the lamb and mix to coat the meat in the marinade. Chill in the fridge for at least 1 hour.

2 Heat the barbecue or charcoal grill. Grill the lamb over a medium heat for 8–10 minutes on each side for medium-rare, or until cooked to your liking. Transfer to a plate, cover with foil, and leave to rest in a warm place for 20 minutes.

3 For the salad, place all the ingredients in a bowl, season, and toss gently. Slice the lamb diagonally and arrange on a platter, scatter with the parsley and a drizzle of extra virgin olive oil. Serve hot with the salad.

LAMB CHOPS IN PAPER WITH FENNEL

These chops are enclosed in paper parcels while cooking. This lets them steam in their own juices, using minimum fat for maximum flavour.

THE CUT Lamb loin chops

SERVES 4
PREP 25–30 mins   **COOK** 35–40 mins

1kg (2¼lb) fennel bulbs, stalks and roots trimmed and any tough outer layers removed

4 tbsp olive oil

2 garlic cloves, finely chopped

400g can chopped tomatoes

3 tbsp pastis

salt and freshly ground black pepper

4 lamb loin chops, each 2.5cm (1in) thick, tails cut and reserved, about 625g (1lb 6oz) in total

melted butter, for brushing

1 egg, beaten with ½ tsp salt, to glaze

1 Thinly slice each fennel bulb, reserving some green fronds for the garnish. Heat 2 tablespoons of oil in a frying pan over a medium heat. Add the fennel and garlic and fry for 6–8 minutes, until the fennel begins to soften.

2 Add three-quarters of the tomatoes and the pastis to the pan. Season well and cook, stirring occasionally, for 20–25 minutes until the mixture is thick and most of the moisture has evaporated.

3 Meanwhile, season the lamb chops and tails with salt and pepper. Heat the remaining oil in

a separate frying pan over a high heat. Cook the meat for 1–2 minutes on each side, until well-browned. Remove with a slotted spoon, place on a plate lined with kitchen paper, and set aside.

4 Fold a large sheet of baking parchment measuring about 30 x 37.5cm (12 x 15in) in half, and draw a curve to make a heart shape when unfolded, large enough to leave a 7.5cm (3in) border around a chop. Cut out the heart shape with scissors. Repeat to make 4 paper hearts.

5 Preheat the oven to 190°C (375°F/Gas 5). Open out and brush each paper heart with the butter, leaving a border of about 2.5cm (1in) unbuttered. Brush the unbuttered border of each paper heart with the beaten egg.

6 Divide the fennel mixture between the 4 paper hearts, placing it over 1 half. Top with a lamb chop and tail, spoon a little of the reserved tomato over, and top with a fennel frond. Fold the other half of the paper over the filling and stick the 2 sides of the hearts together. Make small pleats to seal the edges of the paper cases and twist the ends to finish.

7 Place the parcels on a baking sheet and bake for 10–14 minutes until puffed up and brown. Serve the parcels hot with steamed asparagus on the side, allowing each diner to open their own parcel.

LAMB LOIN WITH RED PEPPERS

A colourful dish, this tender prime cut of meat provides a sweet counterpoint to the flavour of the pepper.

THE CUT Lamb loin

SERVES 4–6
PREP 30 mins   **COOK** 15 mins

4 red peppers

4 lamb loins, about 200g (7oz) each, trimmed and sinew removed

salt and freshly ground black pepper

3 tbsp olive oil

120ml (4fl oz) white wine

250ml (9fl oz) lamb or chicken stock

115g (4oz) butter, chilled and diced

handful of basil leaves, to garnish

1 Set a griddle pan over a medium heat. Wash the peppers and pat dry with kitchen paper. Roast the peppers, turning occasionally, for about 15 minutes, or until the skin is blackened and loose in places. Leave to cool, then rub the skin off. Cut the peppers in quarters and discard the seeds. Chop the flesh into 2.5cm (1in) pieces and set aside.

2 Pat the lamb dry with kitchen paper to remove any excess blood and season well. Heat the oil in a large, heavy-based frying pan over a high heat. Add the lamb and cook for 5 minutes until well-browned. Then reduce the heat and cook for a further 3–4 minutes, turning over once. Remove with a slotted spoon and drain on a plate lined with kitchen paper. Cover and set aside in a warm place.

3 Increase the heat and pour the wine into the pan. Bring to the boil and cook until reduced by half. Add the stock and boil again until reduced by half. Then add the pepper, heat through, and remove the pan from the heat. Stir in the butter to form a light sauce. Taste and adjust the seasoning, if needed.

4 Slice the lamb loins at an angle into 3 or 4 pieces each. Arrange on hot plates and top with the peppers and sauce. Garnish with a few torn basil leaves and serve hot.

RACK OF LAMB WITH PARSLEY CRUMB

Medium is considered the best way to cook a rack of lamb, with the meat at its most succulent. The breadcrumbs mixed with parsley give a crisp finish to this dish.

THE CUT Rack of lamb

SERVES 6
PREP 35–40 mins   **COOK** 25–30 mins, plus resting

2 racks of lamb, chine bones removed, about 750g–1kg (1lb 10oz–2¼lb) each

2 garlic cloves, cut into slivers

2 tbsp olive oil

salt and freshly ground black pepper

4 slices of white bread, crusts removed

45g (1½oz) butter

small bunch of flat-leaf parsley, leaves only, finely chopped

FOR THE GRAVY

125ml (4¼fl oz) white wine

250ml (9fl oz) lamb, beef, or chicken stock

1–2 tbsp cornflour, mixed with a little warm water (optional)

1 Preheat the oven to 230°C (450°F/Gas 8). French trim both the racks of lamb (see p193). Then make several incisions in the meat using the sharp point of a knife and push the garlic slivers into the slits. Transfer the racks to a large roasting tin and place them with the ribs facing down. Wrap the bones in foil to prevent them from burning. Spoon the oil over the meat and sprinkle with salt and pepper.

2 Roast the rack in the oven for 25–30 minutes, basting with the cooking juices at least twice, until the meat shrinks away from the bones and the internal temperature of the meat reaches 60°C (140°F).

3 For the parsley crumb, place the bread in a food processor and pulse to form crumbs. Melt the butter in a frying pan, add the breadcrumbs, and cook for 2–3 minutes, stirring, until just golden. Stir in the parsley and season.

4 Transfer the racks to a chopping board. Discard the foil covering the bones, then cover the racks with more foil and set aside to rest. Set the grill at its highest setting.

5 For the gravy, discard the fat from the roasting tin. Add the wine to the tin and boil until reduced by half, stirring to dissolve the roasting juices from the bottom of the tin. Add the stock and boil for 5–7 minutes, until the gravy is well flavoured. Season to taste, strain, and keep warm. For a thicker gravy, add the conflour to the sauce and mix well.

6 Press the breadcrumb mixture onto the top of the racks and baste with the roasting juices. Grill the racks, breadcrumb-side up, for 1–2 minutes until lightly browned, making sure the breadcrumb coating does not burn. Carve and serve on warmed plates with the gravy on the side.

RACK OF LAMB WITH CELERIAC GALETTES

This dish makes for easy entertaining and involves no carving. Celeriac is a worthy accompaniment for lamb.

THE CUT Rack of lamb

SERVES 4
PREP 30 mins   **COOK** 45–55 mins

60g (2oz) butter, plus an extra knob of butter

1 small onion, chopped

1 carrot, finely chopped

2 streaky bacon rashers, chopped

1 garlic clove, crushed

300ml (10fl oz) red wine

1 tbsp tomato purée

1 tbsp chopped flat-leaf parsley

300ml (10fl oz) lamb stock

1 tbsp redcurrant or quince jelly

sea salt and freshly ground black pepper

1 tbsp rapeseed oil

4 x 3-rib mini racks of lamb, trimmed

FOR THE GALETTES

300g (10oz) waxy potatoes, such as Charlotte, thinly sliced

1 celeriac, peeled and thinly sliced

50g (1¾oz) butter, melted

½ tsp celery salt

freshly ground white pepper

1 tbsp chopped rosemary leaves

1 Preheat the oven to 180°C (350°F/Gas 4) and line a baking sheet with baking parchment. For the galettes, place the potato and celeriac in a large bowl. Pour the melted butter over, season with the celery salt and white pepper, and sprinkle over the rosemary.

2 Place the celeriac on the baking sheet in 4 overlapping disc-like shapes, roughly 12cm (5in) in diameter. Place the potato in neat overlapping circles over each disc. Make sure the galettes are spaced out evenly to avoid sticking to each other during cooking. Bake for 40–45 minutes until tender.

3 Heat half the butter in a heavy-based saucepan. Sauté the onion, carrot, bacon, and garlic for 2 minutes, until soft. Add the wine, tomato purée, and parsley and cook for 5–10 minutes to reduce by half. Add the stock and jelly, and cook for 5 minutes to reduce by a third. Strain, return to the pan, beat in the remaining butter, and season.

4 Increase the temperature to 200°C (400°F/Gas 6). Heat the oil and the knob of butter in a frying pan. Add the racks and fry for about 5 minutes, until well-browned. Season and cook in the oven for 10–15 minutes. To serve, place the lamb on the galettes and drizzle over the cooking juices.

CHARGRILLED LAMB CUTLETS AND AUBERGINE WITH RED CABBAGE SLAW

Red cabbage coleslaw gives this grilled lamb and aubergine dish a refreshingly different twist.

THE CUT Lamb cutlet

SERVES 4
PREP 25 mins **COOK** 12–16 mins, plus resting

12 lamb cutlets, about 100g (3½oz) each, trimmed

2 tbsp olive oil

salt and freshly ground black pepper

1 aubergine, about 300g (10oz), thinly sliced lengthways

½ small red cabbage

100g (3½oz) fine green beans, trimmed, blanched, and thinly sliced diagonally

1 small cucumber, thinly sliced or shaved lengthways

1 small red onion, thinly sliced in rounds

2 celery sticks, peeled and thinly sliced diagonally

60g (2oz) hazelnuts, chopped

small handful of chives, snipped

2 tbsp extra virgin olive oil

1 tsp balsamic vinegar

1 Set the grill at its medium setting. Brush the lamb cutlets with oil and season with salt and pepper. Grill the cutlets for 3–5 minutes on each side, or until cooked to your liking. Remove from the heat, transfer to a plate, and set aside to rest in a warm place.

2 Increase the grill to high. Brush the aubergine slices with a little oil and season with pepper. Grill the aubergine for about 3 minutes on each side until golden. Remove from the heat and transfer to the plate along with the lamb.

3 Finely slice or shred the red cabbage and place in a large bowl. Add all the remaining ingredients, season with salt and pepper, and toss gently. Serve the lamb cutlets and the aubergine slices with the cabbage coleslaw on the side.

SLOW-COOKED LAMB RIBS WITH FATTOUSH SALAD

The spices in the marinade cut through the meaty richness of the ribs from the lamb breasts.

THE CUT Lamb breast ribs

SERVES 4–6
PREP 30 mins, plus marinating
COOK 3½–4 hrs

FOR THE RIBS

2kg (4½lb) lamb ribs from the breast

250ml (9fl oz) white wine

2 garlic cloves, crushed

3 cinnamon sticks

1 tsp salt

2 star anise

6 black peppercorns

FOR THE MARINADE

1 tsp cumin seeds

2 tsp coriander seeds

3 cardamom seeds from pods

1 tsp ground cinnamon

½ tsp ground allspice

1 red chilli, deseeded and chopped

2 garlic cloves, crushed

grated zest and juice of 1 lemon

100ml (3½fl oz) olive oil

2 tbsp runny honey

handful of coriander leaves, chopped

FOR THE SALAD

1 cucumber, peeled, halved lengthways, deseeded, and diced

bunch of radishes, trimmed and thinly sliced

1 red onion, finely chopped

200g (7oz) cherry tomatoes, quartered

seeds from 1 small pomegranate

bunch of flat-leaf parsley, leaves only, roughly chopped

juice of 1 lemon, plus extra if needed

1 tbsp sumac powder, plus extra if needed

sea salt and freshly ground black pepper

2 pitta breads

1 tbsp olive oil

1 Preheat the oven to 200°C (400°F/Gas 6). For the lamb, place all the ingredients in a large saucepan, add just enough water to cover, and bring to the boil. Cover tightly and bake in the oven for 2 hours, or until tender. Drain and cool. Discard the cooking liquid.

2 Heat a frying pan over a medium heat. Add the cumin, coriander, and cardamom seeds and roast, stirring constantly, until fragrant. Remove from the heat, cool slightly, and crush in a mortar and pestle.

3 Transfer the crushed spices to a large non-metallic bowl. Add all the remaining marinade ingredients and mix well. Cut the lamb into single ribs and add to the bowl. Mix to coat the ribs in the marinade. Chill in the fridge for at least 2 hours, or overnight.

4 Preheat the oven to 140°C (275°F/Gas 1). Place the lamb ribs in a large roasting tin, cover with foil, and roast in the oven for 1 hour. Then remove from the oven, take off the foil, and turn the ribs over. Return the tin to the oven for a further 30 minutes. Then remove from the heat.

5 For the salad, place all the ingredients, except the pitta bread and oil, in a large bowl. Heat a frying pan over a medium heat and warm the pitta breads on both sides. Remove from the pan, cut it into small cubes, and add to the salad. Then add the oil and toss to coat. Taste and add more lemon juice or sumac powder, if desired. Place the ribs on a plate and serve hot with the salad.

THAI-SPICED LAMB SALAD WITH LIME DRESSING

The bright, vibrant colours of this spicy lamb salad really sing out, making it perfect for a summer lunch.

THE CUT Lamb chump or leg

SERVES 4
PREP 10 mins   **COOK** 7–10 mins, plus resting

grated zest and juice of 5 limes

3 tsp palm sugar or Demerara sugar

1 red chilli, deseeded and finely chopped

½ tsp Thai fish sauce

1 tsp tamarind

3 tbsp groundnut oil

500g (1lb 2oz) boneless lamb chump or leg

100g (3½oz) Thai glass noodles, cooked

3 shallots, finely sliced

handful of coriander leaves

12 Thai basil leaves

small handful of mint leaves

50g (1¾oz) roasted peanuts, coarsely ground

1 For the dressing, place the lime zest and juice, sugar, chilli, fish sauce, tamarind, and 1 tablespoon of oil in a small bowl. Mix to combine all the ingredients and dissolve the sugar. Set aside.

2 Cut the lamb into 6 equal strips. Heat a griddle pan and add the remaining oil. Sear the lamb for about 2 minutes on each side. Do not overcook the lamb – it should be rare. Leave to rest for 3 minutes.

3 Slice the lamb thinly and place in a large bowl. Add the glass noodles, dressing, shallots, herbs, and peanuts, and toss to combine. Divide the salad between 4 plates and serve immediately.

HAY-ROASTED LEG OF LAMB WITH ANCHOVIES AND CAPER SAUCE

Cooking with hay imparts a wonderful grassy and smoky flavour to the meat. It also keeps the meat succulent.

 **Lamb leg**

SERVES 8–10
PREP 30 mins, plus chilling and resting
COOK 2 hrs 15 mins, plus resting

25g (scant 1oz) butter, melted, plus extra for greasing

2 handfuls of clean hay

2kg (4½lb) white bread flour

3kg (6½lb) leg of lamb, bone left whole

10 good quality anchovies in salt, rinsed

8 garlic cloves, cut into slivers

grated zest of 1 lemon and juice of half a lemon

sea salt and freshly ground black pepper

bunch of thyme

bunch of rosemary

1 egg, beaten

FOR THE SAUCE

500ml (16fl oz) chicken stock

2–3 tbsp small capers in vinegar, drained and roughly chopped

splash of red wine or sherry vinegar

2 large handfuls of mint leaves, finely chopped

large knob of butter, diced and chilled

2 tsp redcurrant jelly

1–2 tsp arrowroot, mixed with a little water (optional)

1 Preheat the oven to 180°C (350°F/Gas 4) and grease a large baking tray. Soak the hay in cold water for 15 minutes. Place the flour in a mixer, add 1 litre (1¾ pints) water, and pulse for about 5 minutes to form a dough. Chill the dough in the fridge for 30 minutes.

2 Make small slits all over the leg of lamb. Slice the anchovies in half and use to wrap the garlic slivers. Insert them into the slits on the lamb.

3 Divide the dough into 2 portions and roll each out to a size large enough to cover the lamb and about 1cm (½in) thick. Lay 1 pastry piece over the baking tray. Squeeze out the water from the hay, and spread it over the pastry, leaving a border of at least 5cm (2in) around the edges.

4 Place the lamb on the hay and brush with the melted butter. Sprinkle the lemon zest and juice over the lamb. Season and place the herbs on top. Lift the hay up and wrap evenly around the lamb. Brush the edges of the dough with cold water. Place the second piece of pastry on top of the lamb, making sure the bone protrudes out to allow heat to penetrate into the centre of the joint. Pinch, roll, and crimp the edge of the dough together. Brush with the beaten egg and leave to rest for about 20 minutes.

5 Place the lamb in the oven and bake for about 2 hours. Then remove from the oven and check for doneness. The internal temperature of the meat should be 60°C (140°F) for medium and 65°C (150°F) for well-done. Cook for a further 10–15 minutes, if needed, then remove from the heat. Leave to rest for 30 minutes, then crack open the crust, remove the hay, and pour out any juice or fat into a small saucepan.

6 For the sauce, heat the saucepan containing the fat and juice over a medium heat. Add the stock, and stir to deglaze. Cook the sauce until reduced by half. Then remove from the heat and strain into a bowl. Return the sauce to the pan and cook over a medium heat for 3–4 minutes.

7 Add the capers, vinegar, mint, butter, and redcurrant jelly. Stir well and season to taste with salt and pepper. If the sauce tastes a little bitter, add a bit more of the redcurrant jelly. If the sauce seems too thin, thicken it with a little arrowroot. Place the lamb on a large platter, pour over the caper sauce, and serve hot.

ON THE SIDE

This dish can be served with mashed cannellini beans with rosemary, boulangerie potatoes, or dauphinoise gratin. Buttered kale or spinach are also great accompaniments.

LAMB CUTLETS WITH BUTTERNUT SQUASH, BEANS, AND MINT

The sweet, dense orange flesh of butternut squash marries well with the tender lamb in this autumnal dish.

 **Lamb cutlets**

SERVES 4
PREP 15 mins   **COOK** 30 mins

2 tbsp olive oil

pinch of five-spice powder

pinch of cayenne pepper

salt and freshly ground black pepper

8 lamb cutlets, about 100g (3½oz) each

1 butternut squash, halved, deseeded, peeled, and roughly chopped

10 cherry tomatoes

125g (4½oz) fine green beans, trimmed

handful of mint leaves, roughly chopped

1 Preheat the oven to 200°C (400°F/Gas 6). Pour half the oil in a small bowl and add the five-spice powder and cayenne pepper. Season with salt and pepper and mix well.

2 Brush the cutlets with half the spice mix and place in a roasting tin. Add the squash to the remaining spice mix and toss lightly to coat. Add the squash to the tin. Cook in the oven for 20–30 minutes, or until the lamb is cooked to your liking and the squash is golden.

3 Meanwhile, place the tomatoes and beans in a bowl and toss with the remaining oil. Add to the roasting tin for the last 10 minutes of cooking so they are just lightly charred in places. Remove from the heat, sprinkle with mint, and serve hot.

VARIATION

Pork chops with sweet potatoes, beans, and thyme
Use 4 lean pork chops instead of the lamb cutlets, and 1 teaspoon of Cajun spice instead of the five-spice powder and cayenne pepper. Substitute 1 large sweet potato, peeled and cut into chunks, instead of the butternut squash. Cook for 30–40 minutes until tender, adding the cherry tomatoes and beans for the last 10 minutes of cooking, as in step 3. Sprinkle with a handful of thyme leaves instead of mint and serve hot.

BARBECUED LAMB WITH MINT HOLLANDAISE

In this recipe, a herby hollandaise sauce adds a lovely, buttery contrast to the crispy meat.

THE CUT Lamb leg steak

SERVES 4
PREP 30 mins   **COOK** 45 mins, plus resting

250g (9oz) asparagus, cleaned and trimmed

200g (7oz) courgettes, cut on the diagonal

1 large red pepper, deseeded and cut into 8 pieces

1 red onion, cut into 8 wedges

4 tbsp olive oil

sea salt and freshly ground black pepper

4 lamb leg steaks, about 200g (7oz) each

2 large garlic cloves, cut in half

FOR THE HOLLANDAISE

6 black peppercorns, coarsely crushed

1 shallot, finely chopped

150ml (5fl oz) white wine

100ml (3½fl oz) white wine vinegar

4 egg yolks

250g (9oz) unsalted butter, chilled and diced

2 tbsp chopped mint leaves

1 Preheat the barbecue to its highest setting. Place the vegetables in a bowl, add 3 tablespoons of the oil, and toss to coat. Season and grill them until charred and just soft. Adjust the seasoning if needed, set aside, and keep warm.

2 Rub the lamb steaks with the garlic and the remaining oil. Cook the steaks on the barbecue for 4–5 minutes on each side, until pink. Allow to rest for 3–5 minutes in a warm place.

3 For the hollandaise, place the peppercorns, shallot, wine, and vinegar in a large saucepan over a medium heat. Bring to the boil and boil rapidly, until reduced to 1 tablespoon of liquid.

4 Meanwhile, place a stainless steel or glass bowl over a saucepan of simmering water. Strain the reduced vinegar mixture into the bowl, discarding the peppercorns and shallots. Whisk in the egg yolks, until thick and just warm. Do not overheat the yolks or they will scramble.

5 Add the butter slowly, whisking to make a thick, smooth sauce. Season, add the mint, and spoon the sauce into bowls. Slice the steaks, and serve with the vegetables and mint hollandaise.

LAMB WITH LEMON AND OLIVES

Using whole lemons adds a sharpness of flavour to this dish and the olives give it a nice Mediterranean touch.

 **Leg of lamb**

SERVES 4
PREP 10 mins   **COOK** 35 mins, plus resting

3 tbsp olive oil

bunch of spring onions, trimmed and finely chopped

500g (1lb 2oz) boneless lean leg of lamb, cut into bite-sized pieces

6 garlic cloves, finely sliced

1 lemon, cut into eighths

1 tsp chopped rosemary leaves

handful of flat-leaf parsley, chopped

1 tsp paprika

3 tbsp green olives, pitted

salt and freshly ground black pepper

1 Preheat the oven to 200°C (400°F/Gas 6). Heat the oil in a frying pan over a medium heat. Add the spring onions and cook for 5 minutes, or until softened. Then add the lamb and cook, stirring occasionally, for 5 minutes, or until no longer pink.

2 Add the garlic and lemon and cook for 1 minute. Then add the remaining ingredients and cook for about 2 minutes, stirring well. Transfer the mixture to a small baking dish, packing it in tightly. Add 2 tablespoons of water, mix well, and then bake for 20 minutes.

3 Remove from the oven and allow to rest for about 10 minutes. Serve with fresh crusty bread and a crisp green salad.

BARBECUED MOROCCAN LEG OF LAMB

A favourite barbecue food, leg of lamb makes a perfect roast joint. Butterfly it for extra flavour (see p192).

 **Leg of lamb**

SERVES 4
PREP 20 mins, plus marinating and chilling
COOK 40 mins, plus sealing

2 tsp ground cinnamon

3 tsp ground coriander

3 tsp ground cumin

4 tbsp harissa paste

1 tbsp ground turmeric

4 garlic cloves, crushed

100ml (3½fl oz) olive oil, plus 2 tbsp extra for frying

4 tbsp finely chopped flat-leaf parsley

2 large handfuls of coriander leaves, finely chopped

4 tbsp lemon juice and zest of 1 lemon

1.5–2kg (3lb 3oz–4½lb) boneless leg of lamb

500ml (16fl oz) full-fat yogurt

FOR THE COUSCOUS

250ml (9fl oz) orange juice

4 tbsp lemon juice

2 tsp ground cinnamon

500g (1lb 2oz) instant couscous

75g (2½oz) butter

3 tbsp olive oil

200g (7oz) frozen peas, blanched for 2 minutes

400g can chickpeas, rinsed and drained

100g (3½oz) pistachios, chopped

50g (1¾oz) currants

6 spring onions, trimmed and finely sliced

3 tbsp chopped flat-leaf parsley

3 tbsp chopped coriander leaves

3 tbsp chopped mint leaves

sea salt and freshly ground black pepper

1 In a small bowl, mix all the spices, half the turmeric, and half the garlic. Pour the oil into a large bowl and add half the spice mix. Then add the parsley, coriander, lemon juice, and zest. Mix well, then add the lamb, coating it in the spice mix. Chill for 1 hour.

2 Preheat the oven to 190°C (375°F/Gas 5). Place the yogurt in a large bowl, add the remaining spice mix, and stir to combine. Cover and chill in the fridge for about 1 hour. Remove the lamb from the marinade. Heat the oil in a frying pan. Add the lamb and cook for 3–4 minutes on both sides, until well-browned.

3 Transfer the lamb to a large, ovenproof dish and cook in the oven for about 40 minutes. Set the barbecue to 190°C (375°F/Gas 5). Remove the lamb from the oven and cook on the barbecue for a further 15–20 minutes, depending on your taste. Then remove from the heat, cover with foil, and leave to rest for 15 minutes.

4 For the couscous, pour the orange and lemon juice into a measuring jug and add enough water to increase the total quantity to 600ml (1 pint). Pour into a saucepan, add the cinnamon, and bring to the boil. Remove from the heat. Add the couscous and stir to mix. Cover and leave for 5 minutes. Then add the butter and olive oil, and use a fork to fluff up the couscous.

5 Add the peas, chickpeas, pistachios, currants, spring onions, parsley, coriander, and mint to the couscous. Mix well and season with salt and pepper. Slice the meat across the grain and arrange on a serving dish. Serve hot with the couscous, the spicy yogurt, and rocket leaves.

VARIATION

Barbecued Moroccan goat Use a leg of goat in place of the lamb and pine nuts in place of the pistachios. Cook as above and serve warm with the spicy yogurt and couscous.

LEG OF LAMB COOKED IN RED WINE

The mushrooms and tomatoes make a great base for the luscious sauce in this perfect family dish.

 **Leg of lamb**

SERVES 6–8
PREP 20 mins   **COOK** 2 hrs, plus resting

2.25kg (5lb) boneless leg of lamb

2 garlic cloves, cut into thin slivers

salt and freshly ground black pepper

1 large onion, thinly sliced

2 tbsp olive oil

400g can chopped tomatoes

½ tsp dried oregano

½ tsp dried thyme

2 bay leaves

bottle of red burgundy wine

2 tsp butter

225g (8oz) button mushrooms, sliced

1 Preheat the oven to 230°C (450°F/Gas 8). Score the lamb and slide in the slivers of garlic and the salt and pepper. Scatter the onion over the base of a roasting tin, place the lamb on top, and pour the oil over. Roast in the oven for 20 minutes.

2 Remove the tin from the oven, and reduce the heat to 180°C (350°F/Gas 4). Arrange the tomatoes around the lamb, add the herbs, and pour in half the wine. Return the tin to the oven and cook for a further 1 hour.

3 Heat the butter in a frying pan, add the mushrooms, and sauté for 2–3 minutes until lightly browned. Add to the tin and pour in the remaining wine. Return the tin to the oven and cook for 30 minutes.

4 Remove the lamb from the roasting tin, cover with foil, and leave to rest for 15 minutes. Place the roasting tin over a medium heat and cook the sauce for 10 minutes, stirring, to reduce. Remove from the heat and strain into a saucepan, pushing the vegetables through with the back of a ladle.

5 Discard any leftover vegetables and return the pan to the heat. Reduce the heat to a simmer and cook, stirring occasionally, until the sauce has thickened. Season with salt and pepper and remove from the heat. Carve the lamb and arrange on a serving dish. Serve hot with the sauce, roasted carrots, and boiled potatoes.

BUTTERFLIED LEG OF LAMB

A fruity herb-based marinade and boneless meat makes for very quick cooking and easy serving.

THE CUT **Leg of lamb**

SERVES 6–8
PREP 30 mins, plus marinating
COOK 40 mins, plus resting

200ml (7fl oz) red wine

3 tbsp marmalade

2 tbsp red wine vinegar

1 small onion, finely chopped

2 tsp dried marjoram

2 tsp dried rosemary

1 large bay leaf

1 tsp sea salt

¼ tsp ground ginger

2 garlic cloves, crushed

3kg (6½lb) boneless leg of lamb, butterflied (see p192)

1 For the marinade, place all the ingredients, except the meat, in a saucepan and simmer for 15 minutes over a low heat. Remove from the heat and leave to cool slightly. Place the lamb skin-side down in a large, lidded plastic container and pour the marinade over it. Cover and leave to marinate in a cool place for 8 hours, turning occasionally.

2 Set a large griddle pan or barbecue at its medium setting. Pat the meat dry with kitchen paper and place it, fat-side down, on the pan. Cook the lamb for 10 minutes, then turn over and brush with a little marinade. Cook for a further 10 minutes, then turn and brush with the marinade once more. Cook for another 20 minutes, turning and basting with the marinade.

3 Remove from the heat and leave to rest for at least 15 minutes. Carve the meat into slices and serve with hot pepper jelly and a crisp salad.

VARIATION

Butterflied leg of roe deer Use a butterflied leg of roe deer in place of the lamb, redcurrant jelly in place of marmalade, and 4 crushed juniper berries in place of the marjoram. Cook as above and serve hot.

ROAST LEG OF LAMB

In this aromatic roast dish, the juices from the lamb provide the basis for the simple yet flavoursome gravy that accompanies it. See p192 for how to bone a leg.

THE CUT Leg of lamb

SERVES 6–8
PREP 40 mins
COOK 1½ hrs, plus resting

2.25kg (5lb) leg of lamb, bones removed, and reserved

1 onion, roughly chopped

1 large carrot, roughly chopped

2 garlic cloves, unpeeled and crushed

3 sprigs of thyme

3 tbsp olive oil

salt and freshly ground black pepper

2 tsp chopped rosemary

1 tsp chopped marjoram

1 tsp tomato purée

1 Preheat the oven to 200°C (400°F/Gas 6). Place the bones, onions, carrots, garlic, and thyme in a large roasting tin. Drizzle over 2 tablespoons of oil and toss to coat the bones and vegetables. Transfer the roasting tin to the oven and roast for 10 minutes, or until browned.

2 Meanwhile, season the lamb and rub with the remaining oil. Remove the roasting tin from the oven and place the lamb on the roasted bone and vegetable mixture. Return the tin to the oven to roast for 40 minutes, occasionally basting the meat with the cooking juices.

3 Remove from the oven and pour out one-third of the fat. Add 500ml (16fl oz) water and sprinkle over the herbs. Reduce the temperature to 180°C (350°F/Gas 4), return the tin to the oven, and cook for 40 minutes, occasionally basting with the cooking juices. Remove and transfer the lamb to a serving dish. Cover with foil and set aside to rest in a warm place.

4 Place the roasting tin over a medium heat, add the tomato purée, and scrape up the pan juices. Reduce the heat and simmer for 5 minutes, until reduced to a light gravy. Strain, discarding the bones and pushing the vegetables through the sieve to add texture to the sauce. Taste and adjust the seasoning if needed. Carve the meat and serve along with the gravy.

TURKISH LAMB AND POMEGRANATE PILAF

Fragrant and full of colour, this pilaf has layers of flavour. Add in different fruits and nuts for variety – dates and almonds are often used in Turkish cuisine.

THE CUT Lamb leg

SERVES 4–6
PREP 15 mins   **COOK** 1 hr

2 tbsp olive oil, plus extra for drizzling

675g (1½lb) leg of lamb, cut into bite-sized pieces

1 onion, finely chopped

salt and freshly ground black pepper

3 garlic cloves, finely chopped

1 green chilli, deseeded and finely sliced

1 tsp dried mint

1 tsp ground cinnamon

60g (2oz) golden sultanas or regular sultanas

350g (12oz) easy-cook basmati rice

900ml (1½ pints) hot lamb stock

60g (2oz) hazelnuts, toasted and roughly chopped

small handful of dill, finely chopped

seeds from 1 pomegranate

75g (2½oz) feta cheese, crumbled (optional)

1 Heat the oil in a large, flameproof casserole over a medium-high heat, add the lamb, and cook for 6–8 minutes until browned on all sides. Do this in batches to avoid overcrowding the pan. Remove with a slotted spoon and set aside.

2 Add the onion to the casserole and cook over a medium heat for 3–4 minutes until soft. Season with salt and pepper, stir in the garlic, chilli, mint, and cinnamon, and cook for another 2 minutes. Stir in the sultanas.

3 Add the rice and stir through, so all the grains are coated and the juices soaked up. Return the lamb to the casserole, pour over the stock, and reduce to a simmer. Partially cover and cook for 30–40 minutes, topping up with a little more hot stock if it begins to dry out. Taste and adjust the seasoning, then stir through the hazelnuts and dill, and scatter with the pomegranate seeds. Top with crumbled feta (if using) and serve hot.

LAMB SHANKS WITH BUTTER BEANS AND CELERY

Pot-roasting keeps the meat moist, and the creamy beans add a deep contrast of flavour.

THE CUT Lamb shanks

SERVES 4
PREP 20 mins, plus overnight soaking
COOK 1½ hrs

2 tbsp olive oil

salt and freshly ground black pepper

4 bone-in lamb shanks, about 200g (7oz) each

1 onion, cut in 4 circles

240ml (8fl oz) lamb or chicken stock

225g (8oz) dried butter beans, soaked overnight

1 garlic clove

600ml (1 pint) full-fat milk

grated nutmeg

2 tbsp double cream

9 celery stalks, diced

1 tbsp chopped flat-leaf parsley

1 Heat 1 tablespoon of the oil in a large, flameproof casserole. Season the lamb shanks, add to the casserole, and cook for 6–8 minutes, until well-browned. Remove with a slotted spoon. Pour out and reserve 1 tablespoon of fat from the pan.

2 Preheat the oven to 180°C (350°F/Gas 4). Spread the onion circles over the bottom of the casserole and place a lamb shank on each onion. Pour in the stock and bring to the boil. Cover and place in the oven for 1¼hrs, turning the shanks frequently, until the meat is tender.

3 Meanwhile, pinch the beans out of their skins. Discard the skins, rinse the beans, and drain. Place in a large, lidded saucepan. Add the garlic and milk and bring to a simmering point, but do not boil. Continue to simmer, adding the nutmeg, and seasoning. Cover partially and cook for about 1 hour, stirring occasionally, until the beans are tender and the milk has reduced. Pour in the cream.

4 In a large frying pan, heat the remaining oil and the reserved lamb fat. Add the celery and fry for 4–5 minutes, until lightly browned. Stir into the bean mixture with the parsley. Spread the bean mixture at the bottom of 4 hot bowls. Place a shank over the beans and pour over some of the cooking juices from the casserole. Serve hot.

MOROCCAN MUTTON WITH PRUNES AND APRICOTS

The unusual combination of meat with honey and dried fruits, and the addition of the nutty flavoured Argan oil lends exotic flavours to this traditional Berber dish.

THE CUT Mutton shoulder

SERVES 4
PREP 15 mins, plus soaking **COOK** 3½ hrs

85g (3oz) dried prunes, pitted

85g (3oz) dried apricots, pitted and halved

150ml (5fl oz) black tea

2 tbsp argan oil or vegetable oil

1kg (2¼lb) boneless mutton shoulder, cut into cubes

2 onions, finely chopped

½ tsp ground turmeric

½ tsp ground ginger

1½ tsp ground cinnamon

½ tsp ground cumin

½ tsp Ras el hanout powder

2 tbsp honey

200ml (7fl oz) lamb or chicken stock

4 tbsp Greek-style yogurt

1 tbsp chopped mint

60g (2oz) flaked almonds, toasted

1 Preheat the oven to 160°C (325°F/Gas 3). Place the prunes and apricots in a small bowl, and pour the black tea over. Cover and leave to soak for 30 minutes.

2 Heat 1 tablespoon of oil in a large, flameproof casserole over a medium heat. Add the meat and cook for 7–8 minutes until well-browned. Remove with a slotted spoon and set aside.

3 Pour the remaining oil into the pan. Add the onions and cook, stirring occasionally, for 4–5 minutes until lightly coloured and softened. Stir in the spices and cook for a further 2 minutes.

4 Return the meat to the casserole. Add the honey, stock, and the dried fruits with their soaking liquid. Stir until well-combined and bring to a simmer, but do not boil. Cover and cook in the oven for 3 hours, or until the meat is tender.

5 Remove from the oven. Place the yogurt and mint in a small bowl and mix well to combine. To serve, sprinkle the almonds over the meat and serve with a dollop of the yogurt and couscous.

MUTTON HAM

An unusual alternative to ham from a pig, this leaner, tender ham is a great winter filler.

THE CUT Mutton leg

SERVES 10
PREP 30 mins, plus 7 days curing
COOK 3–4 hrs, plus overnight resting and cooling

225g (8oz) sea salt

115g (4oz) dark brown sugar

2 tsp Prague powder No.2 curing salt

1 tbsp coriander seeds

1 tbsp allspice berries

5 juniper berries

12–13 black peppercorns

1 bone-in leg of mutton, about 2.5kg (5½lb)

1 leek, roughly chopped

1 large onion, unpeeled and cut in 2 pieces lengthways

4 carrots, roughly chopped

6 cloves, stuck into the onion pieces

2 celery sticks, roughly chopped

bunch of parsley

sprig of thyme

200g (7oz) black treacle

1 In a bowl, mix the salt, sugar, and curing salt. Use a mortar and pestle to grind the coriander seeds, allspice berries, juniper berries, and 10 peppercorns to a coarse paste. Add to the salt and sugar mixture.

2 Place the mutton leg in a large ceramic dish and thoroughly rub the spice mix all over. Cover with a kitchen towel, and put in a cool place. Leave to cure for 7 days, turning the leg daily and rubbing in any liquid it yields. Use vinyl gloves to handle the meat to prevent it from spoiling.

3 Rinse the mutton in cold water to remove excess salt. Place the vegetables, herbs, and remaining peppercorns in a large stock pot. Add the ham and treacle and pour in just enough water to cover the meat. Bring to the boil, then reduce the heat, and simmer for 3–4 hours.

4 Remove from the heat and leave to cool in the liquid for 1 hour, or until completely cold. Remove the ham from the pot and discard the rest. Wrap the ham tightly with a kitchen towel, and place on a plastic tray. Cover with another plastic tray and weigh it down with 1kg (2¼lb) weights. Leave overnight. Slice and serve with a salad, pickle, and baked potatoes.

MUTTON CURRY WITH COCONUT AND GINGER

The combination of coconut and cashew nuts in this vibrantly flavoured dish gives it contrasting textures.

THE CUT Mutton shoulder

SERVES 6
PREP 15–20 mins   **COOK** 1½–2 hrs

115g (4oz) desiccated coconut

2 tsp chopped fresh root ginger

1 onion, chopped

1 garlic clove

4 red chillies, deseeded and roughly chopped

1 tbsp chopped coriander leaves

1 tsp ground turmeric

2 tbsp plain yogurt

1 tbsp coriander seeds

1 tbsp sesame seeds

2 tbsp vegetable oil

900g (2lb) mutton shoulder, cut into cubes

¼ tsp grated ginger

115g (4oz) cashew nuts, finely chopped

1 Use a mortar and pestle to grind the coconut, chopped ginger, onion, garlic, chillies, coriander, and turmeric to form a paste. Place in a bowl, add the yogurt, and mix to combine. Set aside.

2 Heat a lidded, heavy-based saucepan over a medium-low heat. Place the coriander and sesame seeds on a chopping board and crush them with the back of a spoon. Add to the pan and roast for 2–3 minutes, stirring lightly, until browned. Remove from the heat and set aside.

3 Clean the pan with kitchen paper. Add the oil and place over a medium heat. Add the meat to the pan, sprinkle over the grated ginger, and mix. Cook for 3–4 minutes until well-browned. Then add the yogurt and spice paste, stir to coat, and cook for 2–3 minutes.

4 Add the roasted spices and just enough water to cover the meat. Reduce the heat, cover, and simmer for 1½ hours, or until the mutton is tender. Serve over rice, sprinkled with cashew nuts.

KASHMIRI MUTTON WITH TURNIPS

Slow cooking the meat results in a succulent and flavourful dish. Keep the meat and turnips the same size for added appeal.

THE CUT Mutton leg

SERVES 6
PREP 15 mins   **COOK** 2 hrs

900g (2lb) lean leg of mutton, cut into cubes

2 tbsp vegetable oil

1 tsp grated ginger

200ml (7fl oz) full-fat yogurt

4 small turnips, quartered

¼ tsp salt

1 tsp garam masala

1 tsp ground turmeric

½ tsp chilli powder

2 tsp ground coriander

1 tsp sugar

2 tbsp chopped coriander leaves

1 Pat the meat dry with kitchen paper to remove any excess blood. Heat the oil in a large casserole over a high heat. Add the mutton, sprinkle over the ginger, and cook for about 5 minutes, until well-browned. Do this in batches to avoid overcrowding the pan.

2 Add the yogurt and stir to coat the meat. Allow to scorch a little for added flavour in the curry. Add a little water, then stir in the turnips, salt, and spices. Then add just enough water to cover and bring to the boil.

3 Reduce the heat to a simmer, cover, and cook for about 1½ hours, until tender. Stir in the sugar and half the coriander. Garnish with the remaining coriander, and serve with chapattis to soak up the sauce.

GIGOT OF MUTTON COOKED IN MILK WITH CAPERS

The luscious sauce enriched with savoury cooking juices and herbs is a real winter warmer. This dish is great served with mashed potatoes and peas.

THE CUT Mutton leg

SERVES 8
PREP 30 mins   **COOK** 2–3 hrs, plus resting

2.5kg (5½lb) boneless leg of mutton, trimmed

1 litre (1¾ pints) full-fat milk

2 large onions, studded with 2 cloves each

2 carrots, roughly chopped

sprig of rosemary

1 bay leaf

sprig of thyme

6 black peppercorns

FOR THE SAUCE

2 tbsp butter

2 tbsp plain flour

3 tbsp capers in vinegar, plus a little of the vinegar juice

2 tbsp chopped flat-leaf parsley

salt and freshly ground black pepper

1 Place the leg of mutton in a large stockpot and pour the milk over. Add the vegetables, herbs, and peppercorns to the pan, cover, and bring to

the boil. Reduce the heat to a simmer and cook for 2–3 hours, until the meat is cooked through and the juices run clear when the meat is pierced at its thickest point. Remove the meat from the pot and set aside to rest in a warm place.

2 For the sauce, strain the cooking stock. Pour half the milky stock back into the pot, place it over a low heat, and simmer for 10 minutes. Melt the butter in a separate saucepan and stir in the flour. Cook gently for 1–2 minutes. Add the hot, milky stock, a little at a time, and stir slowly until it forms a smooth sauce. Then add the capers and parsley, and adjust the seasoning. To serve, cut thick slices from the mutton leg and arrange on a platter with the sauce poured over.

NO WASTE!

Freeze the remaining cooking stock from the sauce. Use ¾ of the milky stock along with 125ml (4fl oz) water to prepare the caper sauce as above. Pour this sauce over leftover roast lamb and serve hot.

SCANDINAVIAN LEG OF MUTTON WITH HONEY MUSTARD AND ROOTS

A grand dish, this is simple to prepare as all the vegetables are cooked with the meat.

THE CUT Mutton leg

SERVES 6–8
PREP 30 mins
COOK 1 hr 50 mins, plus resting

2.7 kg (6lb) leg of mutton

450g (1lb) parsnips, cut into even-sized chunks

450g (1lb) kohlrabi, cut into even-sized chunks

500g (1lb 2oz) red-skinned potatoes, quartered

450g (1lb) carrots, cut into even-sized chunks

4 onions, quartered

1 whole garlic bulb, unpeeled and crushed with the back of a knife

240ml (8fl oz) dark beer

250ml (9fl oz) lamb or beef stock

1 tbsp olive oil

sea salt

2 tsp chopped rosemary

3 tbsp Swedish honey mustard

1 Preheat the oven to 200°C (400°F/Gas 6). Remove the leg of mutton from the fridge at least 2 hours before cooking, to bring it up to room temperature.

2 Place all the vegetables and garlic in a large, deep roasting tin. Pour in the beer, stock, and oil. Sprinkle over the salt and rosemary.

3 Pat the leg dry with kitchen paper and rub with some salt and the honey mustard. Place it on a rack above the vegetables so that the fat and juices run into the roasting tin.

4 Transfer the tin to the oven and roast for 20 minutes, then reduce the heat to 180°C (350°F/Gas 4) and cook for a further 1½ hours, or until the internal temperature of the meat reaches 60°C (140°F).

5 Remove from the oven and leave the meat to rest for at least 20 minutes in a warm place. Arrange the vegetables in a large serving tray. Carve the meat into slices and serve on top of the vegetables. Squeeze the garlic out from the skins and spread over the meat.

GOAT STEW WITH CABBAGE

The meat and cabbage, flavoured with caraway, are cooked separately and combined just before serving.

 **Goat leg**

SERVES 4

PREP 30 mins   **COOK** 2 hrs

3 tbsp vegetable oil

3 tsp butter

1kg (2¼lb) leg of goat, cut into cubes

1 large onion, roughly chopped

2 garlic cloves, chopped

2 tsp tomato purée

¼ tsp ground cloves

¼ tsp grated ginger

pinch of cayenne pepper

4 carrots, thickly sliced

juice of 1 lemon

450ml (15fl oz) lamb or beef stock

2 sprigs of thyme

1 bay leaf

1 cabbage

salt

2 tsp caraway seeds

1 Heat the oil and 1 teaspoon of the butter in a large, flameproof casserole. Add the meat, and fry until well-browned. Then add the onion and garlic, and fry until the onions have softened.

2 Stir in the tomato purée, cloves, ginger, and cayenne pepper, and cook for 1 more minute. Then add the carrots, lemon juice, stock, thyme, and bay leaf, and bring to the boil. Reduce the heat, cover, and simmer for 1½–2 hours.

3 Meanwhile, cut the cabbage into quarters, remove the core, and shred very finely. Place in a large bowl of salted water for half an hour. Then drain all but a few tablespoons of the cabbage soaking water.

4 Melt 2 teaspoons of butter in a large saucepan over a medium heat. Add the cabbage and stir to coat in the butter. Cover and steam for 4 minutes. Then stir in the caraway seeds and cook, uncovered, until all the water has evaporated.

5 Remove from the heat and discard the thyme and bay leaf. Mix the goat stew and cabbage together, and serve hot in bowls.

HONEYED GOAT SHOULDER WITH FLAGEOLET BEANS

The creamy texture of the beans perfectly complements the sweetness of the meat, which has a subtle, herby flavour.

THE CUT Goat shoulder

SERVES 4

PREP 5 mins   **COOK** 2hrs, plus resting

juice and zest of 1 lemon

2 tbsp honey

1 tsp olive oil

½ garlic bulb

1kg (2¼lb) goat shoulder

sea salt and freshly ground black pepper

150ml (5fl oz) chicken or vegetable stock, plus extra if needed

4 sprigs each of thyme, rosemary, and oregano

FOR THE FLAGEOLET BEANS

30g (1oz) butter

1 onion, finely chopped

1 garlic clove, finely chopped

2 x 410g can flageolet beans, drained

1 tsp rosemary leaves, finely chopped

100ml (3½fl oz) chicken or vegetable stock

3 tbsp double cream

1 Preheat the oven to 180°C (350°F/Gas 4). Line a roasting tin with greaseproof paper. Mix the lemon juice and zest, honey, and oil in a bowl and set aside. Place the garlic bulb in the centre of the tin, then place the meat on top and rub over the lemon and honey mix. Season, pour in the stock, and place the herbs over the top.

2 Cook in the oven for 1½ hours. Check the meat after 1 hour. If it is browning too much, turn down the oven temperature. If the stock has evaporated, add in more. Remove from the oven and allow to rest for 20 minutes.

3 For the flageolet beans, melt the butter in a frying pan, add the onions and garlic, and sweat for 5–10 minutes, until soft, but not coloured. Add the flageolet beans and rosemary, and stir well to coat in the onion mixture.

4 Add the stock, bring to the boil, and simmer for 3 minutes, until thick. Add the cream, boil for 1 more minute, and season. Carve the meat and arrange on a serving dish. Serve with the flageolet beans and the cooking juices.

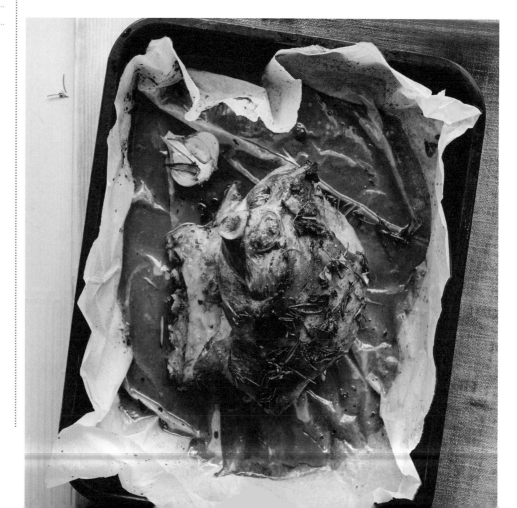

WEST INDIAN CURRIED GOAT

Lime juice helps to tenderize the meat before cooking, and Jamaican rum and butter enrich the spicy sauce.

 **Goat leg**

SERVES 4
PREP 10 mins, plus marinating
COOK 1 hr

1kg (2¼lb) leg of goat, cut into cubes

juice of 2 limes

3 large onions, finely chopped

2 tsp chopped chives

2 tsp chopped flat-leaf parsley

1 whole red chilli

½ tsp ground ginger

1 tsp ground allspice

2 tbsp vegetable oil

1 tsp cumin seeds

5 garlic cloves, chopped

2 tbsp curry powder

2 tbsp tomato purée

2 x 400ml can coconut milk

2 sprigs of thyme

1 bay leaf

1 tbsp dark rum

2 tsp butter, chilled and diced

1 Place the meat in a large bowl, pour over the lime juice, and leave to marinate for 15 minutes. Meanwhile, place the onions, chives, parsley, chilli, and ground spices in a bowl, and mix to combine.

2 Heat the oil in a large, heavy-based saucepan, add the cumin, and toast to release the flavours. Reduce the heat, stir in the garlic and curry powder, and cook for 1–2 minutes. Add the tomato purée and the coconut milk and bring to the boil.

3 Add the meat and lime juice to the pan. Then stir in the onion and herb mix. Add the thyme and bay leaf, stir thoroughly, and bring to the boil.

4 Reduce the heat to a simmer and cook, uncovered for 40 minutes or until the meat is cooked through. Check and top up with water if the liquid evaporates too quickly. Remove from the heat, remove the bay leaf, and stir in the rum and butter. Serve with red beans and rice.

GOAT, ALE, AND MUSHROOM POT PIE

Slow-cooking the goat meat with ale, rosemary, and bay leaf intensifies its flavour in this delicious pie dish.

 **Goat shoulder**

SERVES 4–6
PREP 30 mins   **COOK** 1 hr 45 mins

2 tbsp plain flour, seasoned with salt and pepper

1kg (2¼lb) goat shoulder, cut into bite-sized pieces

2 tbsp rapeseed oil, plus extra if needed

12 baby onions

2 carrots, peeled and diced

250g (9oz) chestnut mushrooms, quartered

2 garlic cloves, finely chopped

2 tbsp tomato purée

¼ tsp ground allspice

150ml (5fl oz) ale

500ml (16fl oz) meat stock

1 sprig of rosemary

1 bay leaf

sea salt and freshly ground black pepper

2 tsp brown sugar

1 large sheet ready-rolled puff pastry

1 egg, lightly beaten

1 Preheat the oven to 150°C (300°F/Gas 2). Place the flour in a large bowl, add the meat, and toss to coat lightly. Heat the oil in a large pan and fry the meat until golden brown on all sides. Transfer the meat to a large, flameproof casserole and set aside.

2 Add more oil to the pan, if needed, and fry the onions, carrots, and mushrooms, stirring occasionally until lightly browned. Add the garlic, tomato purée, and allspice. Mix well and add to the casserole. Add the ale, stock, rosemary, and bay leaf. Bring to the boil, season, and add the sugar. Cook for a further 5–10 minutes to reduce the gravy, then transfer to the oven.

3 Cook in the oven for 1 hour 20 minutes, or until the meat is just cooked. Season with salt and pepper. Increase the temperature to 220°C (425°F/Gas 7). Place the meat and the vegetables in a 2.2 litre (3½ pints) pie dish with a pie funnel in the centre and leave to cool.

4 Cut a 2.5cm (1in) wide strip of pastry. Brush the rim of the pie dish with the beaten egg, press the strip on the rim, and brush again with egg. Cover the dish with the pastry, making a hole for the funnel. Press the edges together, trim the pastry, and flute all round. Brush the top with egg, place on a baking tray, and bake in the centre of the oven for 20–25 minutes until golden brown and crisp.

GAME

GAME

IN THIS BOOK, "GAME" INCLUDES ANIMALS AND BIRDS THAT ARE HUNTED FOR FOOD. HOWEVER, SOME GAME SPECIES ARE NOW ALSO REARED, BOTH ON A DOMESTIC SCALE AND QUITE INTENSIVELY. ALSO INCLUDED ARE SOME SPECIES THAT ARE NOT WILD BUT WHOSE FLESH IS VERY LEAN AND COOKS LIKE WILD GAME.

GAME IS BROADLY DIVIDED into furred game (animals) and feathered game (birds), and the latter are further divided into land birds and waterfowl.

Wild game is likely to vary in age and condition; it could be young and tender or old and tough, too thin or over fat, or anywhere in between. Therefore assessment and preparation are crucial. Farmed game is more consistent and comes from younger animals. Often (but not always) milder in flavour, it can be made more intense by careful hanging.

A HEALTHY MEAT

Game meats are what human beings evolved to eat; they are the best possible meat for our health. Since they have not been selectively bred, and because their diet consists largely of wild food, the profile of their meat is perfect. It is very low in fat, and what fat there is has a favourable saturated-to-unsaturated ratio. Also, any fat tends to be on the outside of the meat, so can be trimmed easily. Darker game meats contain more iron than any domestic meat and valuable vitamins, such as B6 and B12, as well as potassium, phosphorus, riboflavin, niacin, and zinc. However,

although their diet is mostly wild, as with any wild animal that lives close to intensive farmland, there is always a possibility that wild game could have eaten recently sprayed crops.

FURRED GAME

• **Venison** There are 40 species of deer, some smaller than a lamb, others larger than cattle. With careful butchery and good cooking, even old venison can be turned into a gourmet meal.

• **Wild boar** Found in many countries, wild boar is also farmed for meat and crossed with domestic pigs. The meat from feral pigs may be sold as wild boar.

• **Kangaroo** Great numbers of kangaroo were culled in Australia as pests. Nowadays, culling is carried out more carefully under licence and the meat is exported worldwide.

• **Rabbit** Wild rabbits exist in many parts of the world and are also widely reared commercially and privately. Domestic rabbits are much larger than wild ones. There is no "close season" (see opposite for more about game seasons).

• **Hare** Some hares live in open grassland, others in the mountains, and in some countries they are farmed. They are not usually sold when rearing young.

• **Guinea pig** Most commonly reared in Peru, guinea pigs are regarded there as a delicacy. They are also eaten in parts of Asia and served in ethnic restaurants.

• **Horse** Most comes from ex-riding or working animals that are usually quite old, although some meat from wild horses comes from younger animals.

• **Squirrel** Squirrels live in temperate woodland. Reds are a protected species in most countries. Greys are larger and more commonly eaten; they are trapped or shot. There is no close season.

FEATHERED GAME

• **Pheasant** A popular game bird, wild pheasant exist in most continents, eating seeds and insects. Pheasants are also reared and released for sport; while captive their food consists of commercial rations.

• **Grouse** Grouse species include willow, hazel, red-legged grouse, the larger black grouse, and capercaillie. They inhabit forests and mountains of the Northern hemisphere.

• **Partridge** Partridges exist in most parts of the Northern hemisphere on agricultural margins where they eat seeds and insects. They are also widely reared for release into the wild for shooting.

• **Pigeon** Found the world over, there are around 300 species of pigeon. They eat seeds, plants, and fruit. They are also commercially reared; these young birds are called squabs.

• **Guinea Fowl** Originally from Africa, guinea fowl were domesticated for centuries

in Europe and are now sold around the world. Although considered game, most guinea fowl are now intensively reared.

• **Quail** The common quail is native to the Middle East and Mediterranean but most countries have native species that migrate in huge numbers. They are also farmed intensively in large numbers.

• **Ostrich** Native to Africa, the ostrich's diet is mainly vegetarian with a few insects. They are now farmed in many countries where they eat commercial rations as well as grass.

• **Wild goose** Wild geese probably fly further in their migrations than any other bird, so unless you have one hatched that year, the meat could be tough. There are many different species.

• **Mallard (large wild duck)** Of all the waterfowl, mallard is the best known and widespread, migrating to all continents of the world. Their diet consists mainly of vegetation, seeds, and grain crops with some crustaceans.

• **Snipe** One of the smallest of the game birds, snipe live on marshy uplands and fields; they are very difficult to shoot. They are often eaten with their entrails intact.

• **Teal** One of the smallest duck species, teal are renowned for their flavour. Any duck shot by the seashore may have a fishy flavour; those shot inland taste the best.

• **Woodcock** Living in deciduous or mixed coniferous woodland, large numbers migrate out of Northern Scandinavia and Russia to Europe and North America. They are notoriously difficult to shoot.

GAME SEASONS

In most countries, game animals and birds have a "close season": a period during which the animal may not be killed or

its meat sold. There are also some species that can never be bought and sold. In some countries, such as the United States, it is illegal to sell any indigenous wild game, nevertheless it is eaten in large quantities.

Close seasons are designed to protect animals while they breed and rear their young. However, some species that have become pests due to over population have no close seasons. Farmed game is often exempt from close seasons; when in doubt, check online or with the local authority. Each country has its own laws, although the spring and summer are typically the periods during which close seasons apply.

Wild game is usually regarded as a winter treat, and traditional recipes tend to reflect this. But species that have no season, or are exempt, may be bought and cooked all year round. So bear in mind that because game meat is so lean, it makes superb and refreshing summer eating when people prefer to eat less fatty food. New recipes reflect this lighter approach to these meats.

BUYING GAME

Where protected wild game can be sold, it can only be bought in season. Often, game has to be bought from a licensed game dealer, who may be the hunter, a game farmer, or a butcher. Some supermarkets sell a limited selection, as do farmers' markets, and it can usually be obtained online. Wild game that has no season is usually at its best in the late summer and autumn.

Small game animals, such as hare and rabbit, are usually sold whole and skinned, although occasionally they are jointed into

pieces. Large game animals, such as deer and boar, are butchered like domestic meats, although usually there is a smaller variety of cuts.

Game birds were traditionally sold with their feathers on and undrawn (not gutted); today most are sold oven-ready. Male birds are bigger than females and so, regardless of sex, it is better to cook two or more of the same age and size so that they cook evenly. In the case of larger game birds, increasingly it is the deboned breasts that are sold. Occasionally, the skinned crown of a bird is sold to be roasted on its own; these need to be barded with bacon or fat. Small game birds are sometimes sold spatchcocked (see p61), that is, split down the middle and opened out so that they will cook evenly when grilled or barbecued.

Unfortunately, some dealers handle game badly, so avoid any that is badly bruised, has too much torn skin, or broken legs.

FURRED GAME CUTS

GAME MEAT IS VERY LEAN AND CAN TOUGHEN if incorrectly cooked. Farmed game is more tender. Cook roasts and steaks pink or rare and cook stews gently (see the venison cooking chart on p45). Recipes for game can usually be interchanged successfully, especially where the meat is of the same colour.

MIDDLE OR SADDLE CUTS

Venison saddle (the whole back) provides the finest textured and most tender meat of all, either as a bone-in joint, or as boneless, de-sinewed loin eye and fillet.

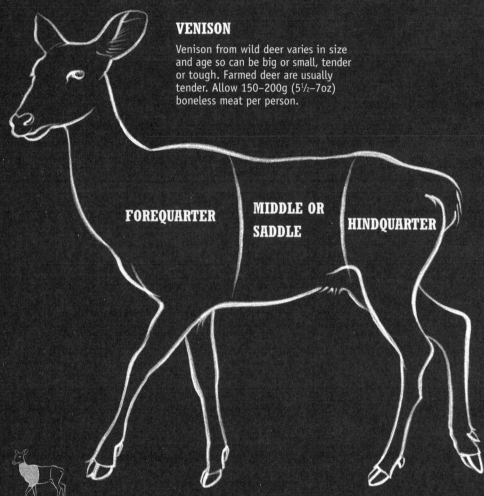

VENISON

Venison from wild deer varies in size and age so can be big or small, tender or tough. Farmed deer are usually tender. Allow 150–200g (5½–7oz) boneless meat per person.

FOREQUARTER

MIDDLE OR SADDLE

HINDQUARTER

WHOLE SADDLE JOINT The finest roasting joint. When from older deer, the outer skin and silvery sinews are often removed before cooking.

LOIN EYE, LARDER TRIMMED Easy to cook and reliably tender, though best if not overcooked. Medallion steaks are cut from this joint.

FOREQUARTER CUTS

Most of the forequarter is used for stewing and mince, although the shoulder of young deer makes good roasts and frying steaks. Venison shoulder is extemely lean.

FILLET OR TENDERLOIN Even more tender than loin, this small muscle is only cut from larger deer. The chain steak should be removed.

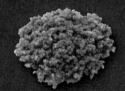

MINCE Venison mince is tasty but lean, so add fat or vegetables for succulence. Good for meatballs, burgers, and all minced dishes.

DICED VENISON Diced shoulder venison is used for stews and pies. Diced haunch can be stewed, or stir-fried if from young deer.

HINDQUARTER CUTS

The back leg (haunch) is very lean. Young deer can be roasted on the bone but older deer have thick sinews and benefit from being separated into individual de-sinewed muscles.

WHOLE HAUNCH, BONE-IN. Roasting the whole leg is a good way to cook a small deer.

HAUNCH, ROLLED JOINT Large deer haunches are often boned and trimmed to make a lean, flavoursome roasting joint. Best cooked medium or rare.

TOPSIDE STEAK From young deer this makes a tender grilling steak, cooked pink, otherwise it is best fried or braised.

Additional venison cuts

- **SHOULDER ROAST, BONED AND ROLLED** Braise slowly for a rich dish. Being lean it needs larding and basting.

- **FRENCH RACK** The eye muscle ensures this cut will be tender. Cook quickly to pink.

- **CUTLETS** Grill or fry if young, braise if old.

- **LOIN EYE STEAKS** Cut from the saddle and trimmed; the most tender steak of all.

- **HAUNCH CHOPS AND STEAKS** Small deer hanches can be sliced with or without bone. Grill or fry.

- **WHOLE SALMON CUT PAVÉ** A useful small muscle from the silverside. Roast, or slice into medallions.

- **THICK FLANK, JOINT AND STEAKS** Remove the outer cap then roast, or slice into frying or braising steak.

- **SHANK, ON-BONE AND TRIMMED** Takes longer to cook than lamb shank but is delicious and succulent.

- **OSSO BUCO** Takes longer to cook than veal but makes a very rich dish.

RABBIT

Wild rabbit can be tough unless young. Farmed rabbits are much bigger and more tender. Allow 250–350g (8–12oz) per person; the back legs and saddle have the most meat.

On wild rabbit, the forequarter .... has very little meat on it; farmed rabbit shoulders are more meaty and tender.

HARE

The back legs and saddle are the most meaty cuts. A whole adult feeds 6–8 people, a leveret (young hare) 4–5. Ask for the blood if making a civet. Lowland hares have the best flavour.

.... It is advisable to remove the thin outer skin, especially from the saddle.

WILD BOAR

The meat of wild boar and feral pigs is dark and lean. Young wild boar, called marcassin, make the best eating; older boar can be very tough.

KANGAROO

Kangaroo is not unlike venison in both taste and texture, and, like venison, can vary in age. Steaks and stew are the most common cuts. Allow 150–200g (5½–7oz) boneless meat per person.

HORSE

A slightly sweet, rich meat, horse is a very good source of iron. Steaks, stewing meat, and tasty mince are the most common cuts.

SQUIRREL

Grey is the most commonly eaten species. They are difficult animals to skin. The flavour is best when they are fat from eating nuts and berries. Allow one squirrel per person.

GUINEA PIG

Most commonly seen in Peru and some Asian countries. The flavour is not unlike rabbit or dark chicken meat, although it is fattier. One feeds 1–2 people.

FEATHERED GAME CUTS

Game birds that migrate long distances can be tough unless they are hatched during the year. They should be either cooked quite pink or else braised or simmered gently. The meat also makes very tasty mince dishes. Young birds are more versatile and can also be roasted, or grilled if spatchcocked (see p61).

PARTRIDGE

Red partridge are the most common, although grey and chukar partridge have better flavour. Young birds have paler flesh and are more tender than old ones. Allow one per person.

PHEASANT

Pheasant meat is paler than most game birds. When not hung, it tastes similar to free-range chicken. Yellow fat means they have been feeding on maize. A hen pheasant feeds 2–3, a cock 3–4.

QUAIL

Most quail available for sale are intensively farmed and so are young and tender. Best spatchcocked (see p61), or stuffed and roasted. Allow one per person.

PHEASANT BREAST
Remove the silver sinew to prevent the meat from curling in the pan.

GROUSE

Grouse are never farmed and their diet gives the dark flesh a unique flavour that is particularly renowned. It is often served with the feet still attached. Allow one per person.

PIGEON

Wild pigeon has lean, dark red meat that needs careful cooking. Domestic squabs are much younger, fatter, and more tender. Allow one pigeon or 2–3 breasts per person.

PIGEON BREAST This is delicious cooked pink and sliced thinly.

MALLARD

Mallard (large wild ducks) have dark flesh and are far smaller and leaner than domestic ducks, so need careful cooking or the meat can become dry. A mallard feeds 1–2 people.

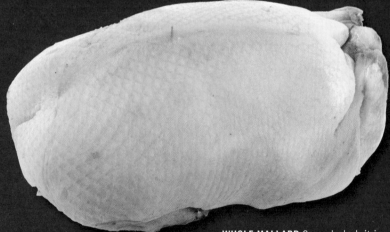

WHOLE MALLARD Once plucked, it is not easy to know how old a wild bird may be and therefore whether it should be roasted or braised. If the skin tears easily, it is young; if not, it is old.

MALLARD BREAST Wild duck breasts are thin and cook extremely quickly, especially when there is no fat on them.

TEAL (SMALL DUCK)

These tiny birds are renowned for their flavour. Like all wild duck, they are lean and need careful cooking so they don't dry out. Allow one per person.

WOODCOCK

Woodcock are considered one of the most delicious game birds, especially when cooked with the entrails (or "trail") intact and the head on. May need ordering in advance. Allow one per person.

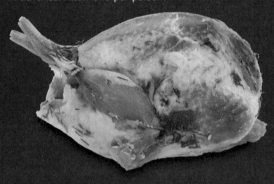

GUINEA FOWL

Guinea fowl has a flavour halfway between chicken and pheasant. Although tender, the meat is quite lean and inclined to be dry if not cooked carefully. One feeds four people.

OSTRICH

Ostrich meat is dark and lean. Young farmed ostrich tastes like mild venison and is tender. However, they are long-lived birds so wild ones can be tough.

SNIPE

Often cooked with their entrails (or "trail") intact, so mention this when ordering otherwise they will be plucked and drawn. May need ordering in advance. Allow 1–2 per person.

WILD GOOSE

Wild goose can be quite tough. However, its meat is dark and flavoursome, and full of iron; it makes good mince and stew. One goose breast will feed 2–3 people.

PRESERVED GAME

THE RANGE OF PRESERVED GAME MEATS must be among the oldest in the world, dating from before domesticated animals. Today, countries with populations of large game animals are the ones with the greatest variety of preserved game products, with venison and wild boar being the most common.

ALHEIRA DE CACA A delicate pale smoked sausage from Portugal made from game meats bound with breadcrumbs sometimes flavoured with paprika and garlic.

SLINZEGA Made in Valtellina in the Italian Alps, Slinzega is similar to bresaola (see p148) but uses smaller strips of meat. Traditionally it was made with horse meat but is also made with venison or pork.

SMOKED VENISON Venison is dry cured and smoked for eating raw in Scandinavia, Austria, Switzerland, and Scotland.

PEMMICAN A traditional native American preparation, pemmican is made by pounding dried game meats with melted fat and wild berries. It was widely eaten by early explorers and is still marketed.

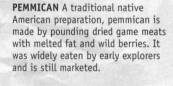

CHARQUI This South American jerky is made from thin slices of salted and wind-dried meat usually llama or horse and sometimes beef. North American jerky is usually marinated in spicy dressings before being dried and sometimes smoked.

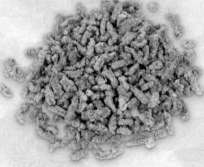

KUIVALIHA Also known as *kapaliha*, this is made from strips of meat, often reindeer venison, that are dried over a few weeks in Finland when the spring weather is appropriate.

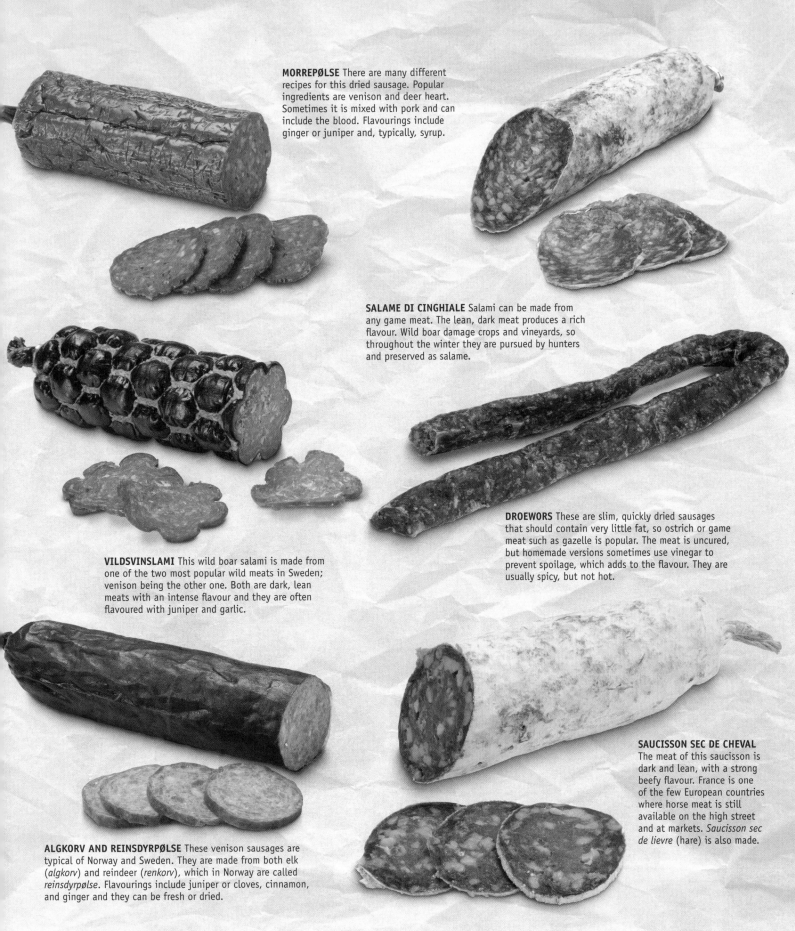

MORREPØLSE There are many different recipes for this dried sausage. Popular ingredients are venison and deer heart. Sometimes it is mixed with pork and can include the blood. Flavourings include ginger or juniper and, typically, syrup.

SALAME DI CINGHIALE Salami can be made from any game meat. The lean, dark meat produces a rich flavour. Wild boar damage crops and vineyards, so throughout the winter they are pursued by hunters and preserved as salame.

VILDSVINSLAMI This wild boar salami is made from one of the two most popular wild meats in Sweden; venison being the other one. Both are dark, lean meats with an intense flavour and they are often flavoured with juniper and garlic.

DROEWORS These are slim, quickly dried sausages that should contain very little fat, so ostrich or game meat such as gazelle is popular. The meat is uncured, but homemade versions sometimes use vinegar to prevent spoilage, which adds to the flavour. They are usually spicy, but not hot.

ALGKORV AND REINSDYRPØLSE These venison sausages are typical of Norway and Sweden. They are made from both elk (*algkorv*) and reindeer (*renkorv*), which in Norway are called *reinsdyrpølse*. Flavourings include juniper or cloves, cinnamon, and ginger and they can be fresh or dried.

SAUCISSON SEC DE CHEVAL The meat of this saucisson is dark and lean, with a strong beefy flavour. France is one of the few European countries where horse meat is still available on the high street and at markets. *Saucisson sec de lievre* (hare) is also made.

KEEPING GAME MEAT MOIST

Game meat is usually very lean and therefore it is less forgiving of being cooked incorrectly. Below are some ways of making sure that the meat stays moist.

KEEP THE MEAT PINK

When grilling, frying, or roasting lean meat, the easiest way to keep it moist is to make sure there are still pink juices in the meat. Lean meat has no marbling of fat, so it can turn from moist to dry very quickly, but pink meat cannot be dry. The secret is to part-cook the meat then rest it until rare or medium rare: roast, grill, or fry the meat at a high heat to brown it. Then finish the cooking by resting the meat at a low temperature that evenly distributes the juices. Use a meat thermometer to check how the meat has cooked (see p29).

SPATCHCOCK BIRDS

Poultry or feathered game can be spatchcocked – split in half and opened out – to allow the different thicknesses of meat to cook more quickly and evenly (see p61).

COOK IN A LIQUID

Cooking lean meat gently in a liquid will ensure it stays moist. Stew small pieces of meat in a liquid to keep the meat moist and add extra flavour. Poach whole birds or a joint in liquid, and make sure that the hot meat stays in the liquid while it cools so that it absorbs moisture. Then drain off the liquid, slice the meat or remove it from the bone, and gently warm it up in the liquid or a sauce to serve.

ADD SUCCULENT TEXTURES

Serve the meat with vegetables with a slippery texture – such as cooked onions, mushrooms, peppers, prunes, aubergine, and apricots – either as side dishes or cooked with the meat. These not only add flavours, but can make eating game even more sumptuous.

USE CREAMY SAUCES

Creamy sauces are ideal for any meat that is inclined to be dry as they can make the meat feel more succulent. See pp30–31 for suggestions. Small pieces of meat have proportionately more surface covered with sauce than large pieces, so they feel moister in the mouth.

LARDING MEAT

It is not necessary to lard meat that is to be served pink. Larding meat – inserting fat into it – makes it succulent; it is most effective when meat is cooked to well done, for example when braising and pot-roasting.

USE A LARDING NEEDLE TO "SEW" LONG STRIPS OF PORK back fat into the meat. Push it right into the centre, so all the meat gets lubricated. Alternatively, make deep holes in the meat with a small sharp knife and slide frozen strips of fat into them.

BARDING MEAT

Barding protects the outer surface of meat from drying out while being roasted. It is quite unnecessary to bard any meat when cooking it pink or rare – unless it is spit-roasted, or a really large joint that needs protection.

USE BUTCHER'S STRING TO TIE SHEETS OF PORK FAT, bacon, or vegetable leaves over the meat before cooking. Remove them towards the end of cooking to brown the surface of the meat. Avoid using strong flavours on delicate game.

JOINTING A RABBIT

Rabbit is best skinned (see pp306–7) as soon as it is shot. If sold in fur, wash the carcass after skinning. Young wild rabbit and farmed rabbit has tender flesh that can be roasted. Stew or simmer old rabbit.

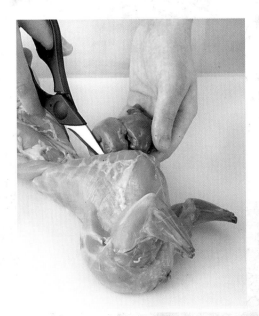

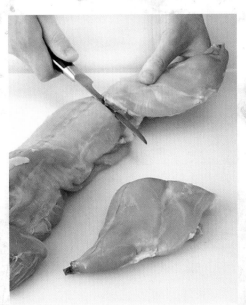

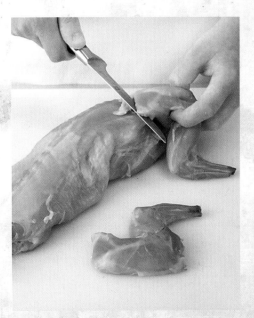

1 Place the rabbit on its back on the work surface. Using kitchen scissors, cut away the liver from the cavity and set aside.

2 Next, remove the leg by cutting through the ball and socket joint in the direction of the backbone, with a very sharp boning knife.

3 Repeat this with the other leg and set it aside. Turn the rabbit over and cut off each foreleg as close to the ribcage as possible.

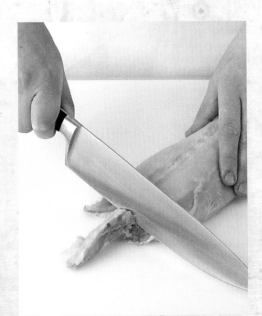

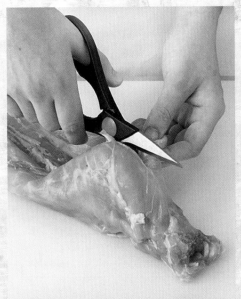

4 Once all the legs have been removed, use a sharp chef's knife to cut away the backbone that is now visible. Press hard on the knife in order to make a clean cut through the bone.

5 Flip the rabbit over onto its back again, and cut right up through the breastbone using sharp kitchen scissors. The breast meat should separate into two even sections.

6 Turn the rabbit over once more, tucking the breast sections neatly underneath. Make a clean cut with a chef's knife so that there are just 4 ribs attached to the loin.

CIVET OF VENISON

The delicious flavours of bacon in the sauce balance wonderfully with the venison in this dish. Preparing all the garnish is well worth the trouble.

CUT Venison shoulder

SERVES 8
PREP 1 hr, plus overnight marinating
COOK 2 hrs

350ml (12fl oz) red wine

1 onion, thinly sliced

3 tbsp brandy

3 tbsp olive oil

salt and freshly ground black pepper

1.5kg (3lb 3oz) stewing venison, diced

FOR THE SAUCE

60g (2oz) butter

225g (8oz) bacon lardons

2 large onions, chopped

1 large carrot, peeled and diced

2 garlic cloves, crushed

2 tbsp plain flour

1 bay leaf

sprig of thyme

200g (7oz) button mushrooms, sliced

500ml (16fl oz) game or chicken stock

FOR THE GARNISH

225g (8oz) butter

2 tsp caster sugar

24 small onions or shallots

150ml (5fl oz) game or chicken stock

24 small button mushrooms

8 slices white bread, cut into triangles and crusts removed

chopped flat-leaf parsley, to garnish

1 Place the red wine, onion, brandy, and oil in a large bowl. Season with salt and pepper and mix to combine all the ingredients. Add the venison, mix well, and leave in a cool place overnight.

2 Preheat the oven to 180°C (350°F/Gas 4). For the sauce, heat the butter in a large flameproof casserole over a medium heat. Add the bacon and cook for 5 minutes until well-browned. Then add the onions and carrots and stir for about 5 minutes until lightly browned. Drain the meat and reserve the marinade. Pat dry with kitchen paper and add to the casserole. Increase the temperature and stir to mix.

3 Add the garlic and flour to the casserole and stir well for 1–2 minutes to coat. Strain the marinade and add to the casserole along with the herbs and mushrooms. Add just enough stock to cover and bring to the boil. Place in the oven for 1½ hours.

4 Meanwhile, for the garnish, melt 60g (2oz) of the butter and the sugar in a heavy-based saucepan and add the onions. Lightly shake the pan to coat the onions. Add just enough stock to cover and boil rapidly to cook, until the liquid evaporates, leaving the onions coated in caramel. Remove from the heat and set aside.

5 Heat another 60g (2oz) butter in a separate pan. Add the mushrooms and cook until lightly browned. Season with salt and pepper.

6 Fry the bread in the remaining butter until brown and crisp. Place the meat in a large shallow serving dish, top with the mushrooms and caramelized onions, and arrange the fried bread triangles around the edge. Garnish with parsley and serve alongside mashed potatoes and green vegetables.

VENISON, SHALLOT, AND CHESTNUT HOTPOT

Lean venison, sweet chestnuts, dried mushrooms, and shallots come together in this dish to make a rich, robust casserole full of flavour.

CUT Venison shoulder or haunch

SERVES 4
PREP 30 mins   **COOK** 2 hrs 15 mins

2 tbsp plain flour

2 tbsp thyme leaves

salt and freshly ground black pepper

550g (1¼lb) boneless shoulder or haunch of venison, cut into bite-sized pieces

knob of butter

2 tbsp olive oil

125g (4½oz) bacon lardons, sliced, or pancetta lardons, cut into cubes

125g (4½oz) shallots

1 glass of red wine

50g (1¾oz) dried mushrooms, such as shiitake, oyster, or porcini, soaked in 300ml (10fl oz)

warm water for 20 minutes

125g (4½oz) ready-cooked chestnuts

500ml (16fl oz) hot vegetable stock

3 sprigs of rosemary

1 Preheat the oven to 150°C (300°F/Gas 2). Place the flour, thyme, and seasoning in a bowl, add the venison pieces, and toss well to coat. Heat the butter with 1 tablespoon of the oil in a cast-iron pan. Add the venison and cook over a medium heat, stirring frequently, for 6–8 minutes, or until lightly coloured. Do this in batches to avoid overcrowding in the pan. Remove with a slotted spoon and set aside.

2 Add the bacon to the pan and stir for 5 minutes, or until well-browned and crisp. Remove with a slotted spoon and set aside. Then add the

remaining oil to the pan. Add the shallots and cook over a medium-low heat for 8 minutes, or until soft and turning golden. Return the meat to the pan, season with pepper, then add the wine and boil for 2 minutes. Stir to scrape up the crispy bits from the bottom of the pan.

3 Drain the mushrooms, reserving the liquid, and add to the pan. Then strain the reserved liquid and add to the pan. Stir in the chestnuts, pour in the stock, and add the rosemary. Cover and place in the oven for 2 hours, or until the meat is tender, topping up with a little hot water if necessary. Serve hot.

VENISON AND RED WINE STEW

Venison is a good source of low-fat protein, and its treatment in this recipe gives it a rich, satisfying flavour.

THE CUT Venison shoulder

SERVES 4
PREP 15 mins
COOK 2 hrs 30 mins – 2 hrs 45 mins

3 tbsp olive oil

4 shallots, halved

2 celery sticks, finely chopped

1 carrot, finely chopped

2 garlic cloves, finely chopped

2 tbsp plain flour

½ tsp grated nutmeg

½ tsp ground allspice

salt and freshly ground black pepper

675g (1½lb) boneless shoulder or other stewing venison, cut into bite-sized chunks

4 tbsp redcurrant jelly

finely grated zest and juice of 1 orange

300ml (10fl oz) red wine

150ml (5fl oz) beef stock

1 bay leaf

1 Preheat the oven to 150°C (300°F/Gas 2). Heat 1 tablespoon of the oil in a flameproof casserole and fry the shallots, celery, and carrot for 3 minutes. Add the garlic and cook for 2–3 minutes more. Remove with a slotted spoon and set aside.

2 Place the flour, nutmeg, and allspice in a large plastic bag, season well, and add the meat. Shake the bag lightly to coat the meat. Tip it into a sieve and shake to remove excess flour.

3 Add the remaining 2 tablespoons of oil to the casserole. Add the meat and cook for 8–10 minutes over a medium heat, until well-browned all over. Do this in batches to avoid overcrowding the pan. Remove with a slotted spoon and set aside. Add the redcurrant jelly, orange zest and juice, wine, stock, and bay leaf to the casserole. Season and stir until the jelly has melted.

4 Return the vegetables and meat to the casserole, stir, and reduce the heat to a simmer. Cover and cook in the oven for 2–2½ hours, or until the meat is tender. Remove the bay leaf and serve hot with potato and celeriac mash.

BRAISED SHOULDER OF VENISON

Thyme is an excellent companion for the meat, and the onions cut across the grain provide a silky sauce.

THE CUT Venison shoulder

SERVES 4–6
PREP 15 mins   **COOK** 2 hrs 50 mins

1.35kg (3lb) bone-in venison shoulder

salt and freshly ground black pepper

2 tbsp vegetable oil

30g (1oz) butter

300g (10oz) onions, sliced across the grain

1 tsp caster sugar

4 sprigs of thyme

1 bay leaf

1 Preheat the oven to 180°C (350°F/Gas 4). Season the shoulder with the salt and pepper. Heat the oil in a large, lidded saucepan. Add the meat and cook for about 10 minutes, until well-browned all over. Remove the meat with a slotted spoon and set aside.

2 Melt the butter in the pan, and add onions, sugar, and a little salt and pepper. Stir to mix and cook for about 8 minutes, until coloured. Make sure the mixture does not burn.

3 Return the meat to the pan and add about 500ml (16fl oz) water. Then add the herbs and season well. Bring to the boil, then transfer to the oven, and cook for 2½ hours. Remove from the oven and keep warm.

4 Strain the sauce, pushing the juices and onions through a sieve with the back of a ladle. Remove the bay leaf, and taste and adjust the seasoning if required. Carve the meat into slices and serve hot with the sauce poured over.

VARIATION

Braised shoulder of lamb Use a bone-in shoulder of lamb in place of the venison and replace the thyme with rosemary. Add 2 teaspoons redcurrant jelly with the water in step 3, and cook as above.

BARBECUED HAUNCH OF VENISON

A lovely dish for a summer evening, the freshness of the marinade lightens the richness of the meat.

◤THECUT Venison haunch

SERVES 10–12
PREP 15 mins   **COOK** 30 mins, plus resting

4 garlic cloves

2 chillies, deseeded

3 sprigs of rosemary, chopped

2 tbsp runny honey

2 tbsp rapeseed oil

1 small piece of fresh root ginger, crushed

juice of 2 limes

4–5kg (8–10lb) whole haunch of venison, butterflied (see p192)

sea salt and freshly ground black pepper

1 Using a mortar and pestle, pound the garlic, chillies, and rosemary until coarsely ground. Transfer to a small bowl and add the honey, oil, and ginger. Place the marinade in a plastic bag large enough to hold the haunch. Pour in the lime juice, then put the haunch in and seal, rubbing the mixture into the skin through the bag. Leave for 1 hour at room temperature.

2 Preheat the barbecue to its medium setting. Remove the haunch from the bag and season with salt and pepper. Cook the haunch on each side for 15 minutes, until well-browned. Remove and leave to rest on a carving platter for at least 10 minutes. Carve into thin slices and serve hot.

CINGHIALE IN DOLCE FORTE

A classic Italian dish for wild boar – the orange and chilli add a real touch of spice.

◤THECUT Wild boar haunch

SERVES 6
PREP 45 mins, plus 2 days marinating
COOK 2½–3 hrs

1.5kg (3lb 3oz) wild boar, cut into 3cm (1in) cubes

3 tbsp olive oil

1 onion, finely chopped

2 tsp ground chilli

75g (2½oz) prunes, stoned

1 tbsp raisins

100ml (3½fl oz) chicken stock

zest of 1 orange

1 tbsp brown sugar

50g (1¾oz) bitter chocolate

salt and freshly ground black pepper

FOR THE MARINADE

500ml (16fl oz) red wine

100ml (3½fl oz) red wine vinegar

1 bay leaf

sprig of thyme

1 carrot, chopped

1 onion, chopped

1 celery stick, chopped

2 tsp ground cinnamon

2 tsp grated nutmeg

2 tsp ground allspice

1 For the marinade, place all the ingredients, except the spices, in a large, heavy-based saucepan. Then add half the spices, bring to the boil, and leave to cool. Place the meat in an airtight plastic container, pour the marinade over, and chill for 2 days.

2 Strain the marinade, remove the meat, and pat dry with kitchen paper. Reserve the liquid and discard the vegetables. Heat the oil in a lidded, heavy-based pan over a medium heat. Add the meat and cook for 4–5 minutes until well-browned. Do this in batches to avoid overcrowding the pan.

3 Add the onion and cook for 3–4 minutes until softened. Stir in the remaining spices, the chilli, prunes, raisins, reserved liquid, and stock. Bring to the boil then reduce the heat to a simmer. Skim off the fat, cover, and cook for 2 hours, or until the meat is cooked through.

4 Stir in the orange zest, sugar, and chocolate. Taste and adjust the seasoning if needed. Serve hot with polenta.

VENISON CUTLETS WITH CHANTERELLES

This truly rich but earthy flavoured dish is given depth with shallots and cream.

◤THECUT Venison cutlet or steak

SERVES 4
PREP 30 mins   **COOK** 25 mins

8 venison cutlets or steaks, about 170g (6oz) each

salt and freshly ground black pepper

1 tbsp sunflower oil

115g (4oz) butter

1 shallot, finely chopped

450g (1lb) chanterelles, trimmed and sliced

100ml (3½fl oz) game stock

100ml (3½fl oz) double cream

1 Pat the cutlets dry with kitchen paper to remove any excess blood. Season well with salt and pepper. Heat the oil and half the butter in a large, heavy-based saucepan. Add the cutlets as the butter foams up and cook for 5–10 minutes, until well-browned on both sides. Do this in batches to avoid overcrowding the pan.

2 Reduce the heat and cook the cutlets for a further 5 minutes. Then remove with a slotted spoon, set aside on a plate, and keep warm. Add the remaining butter to the pan. Stir in the shallots and the chanterelles and cook for 5 minutes, stirring occasionally.

3 Add the stock and cook until reduced by half. Stir in the cream and season. As the sauce thickens, remove from the heat. Stir in any juices that have collected from the resting cutlets. Serve with two cutlets on each plate, with the sauce swirled around.

VENISON SAUSAGES, CELERIAC GRATIN, AND BRAISED RED CABBAGE

This hearty dish is full of flavours and textures and makes for some wonderful comfort food.

THE CUT Venison sausage

SERVES 4
PREP 25 mins **COOK** 2 hrs

50g (1¾oz) unsalted butter

25g (scant 1oz) caster sugar

1 tsp salt

6 tbsp rice wine vinegar, white wine vinegar, or cider vinegar

1 red cabbage, finely shredded, about 1kg (2¼lb)

2 dessert apples, peeled, cored, and grated

2 heaped tbsp redcurrant jelly

FOR THE GRATIN

30g (1oz) unsalted butter, softened

650g (1½lb) celeriac (trimmed weight), peeled and thinly sliced

2 garlic cloves, crushed

salt and freshly ground black pepper

400ml (14fl oz) single cream

8–12 venison sausages

1 Preheat the oven to 160°C (325°F/Gas 3). Place the butter, sugar, salt, vinegar, and 6 tablespoons water in a large, flameproof casserole. Bring to the boil and simmer for 1 minute.

2 Add the cabbage and return to the boil. Cover tightly with 2 layers of foil and the lid, place on the lowest shelf of the oven, and cook for 1½ hours. Then stir in the apples and jelly, adding water if it looks dry. Replace the foil and lid, and return to the oven for 30 more minutes.

3 Meanwhile, for the gratin, lightly grease a large, shallow, ovenproof dish with butter, and layer in half the celeriac. Sprinkle the garlic over, season well, and layer in the remaining celeriac. Pour over the cream and dot with the remaining butter.

4 Cook the gratin in the top shelf of the oven for 1 hour 15 minutes, until soft when pierced with a knife. Grill the sausages for 5–10 minutes, turning, until browned all over. Serve with the gratin and cabbage.

VENISON STEAK WITH BLACKBERRIES

A simple method of cooking this lean meat quickly, the blackberries in the dish provide a tangy accompaniment.

THE CUT Venison haunch steak

SERVES 4
PREP 5 mins **COOK** 15 mins

4 venison haunch steaks, about 200g (7oz) each

1 tbsp sunflower oil

50g (1¾oz) butter, chilled and diced

salt and freshly ground black pepper

4 tbsp blackberry wine or red wine

2 tbsp redcurrant jelly

150g (5½oz) blackberries

1 Pat the steaks dry with kitchen paper to remove any excess blood. Season well. Heat the oil and 1 teaspoon of butter in a heavy-based pan over a medium heat. Place the steaks in the hot pan and cook for 4–5 minutes on each side.

2 Reduce the heat and cook for another 5 minutes, turning once, until well-browned. Remove the meat from the pan, cover with foil, and set aside. Then add the wine, redcurrant jelly, and blackberries to the pan. Bring to the boil, stirring gently to melt the jelly.

3 Once the sauce has thickened, remove from the heat and whisk in the remaining butter. Do not boil the sauce again, or else the butter will separate. Serve the steaks with the sauce poured over.

WILD BOAR CURRY

This dry, spicy curry is a Sri Lankan delicacy. The addition of fennel seeds and ginger gives a lovely aroma.

THE CUT Wild boar haunch

SERVES 6
PREP 20 mins   **COOK** 2–3 hrs

1.35kg (3lb) wild boar, cut into cubes

salt and freshly ground black pepper

2 tbsp sunflower oil

6 small onions, thinly sliced

2 red chillies, deseeded and chopped

1 tsp fennel seeds

6 garlic cloves, sliced

2.5cm (1in) piece of fresh root ginger, peeled and finely chopped

½ tsp turmeric powder

1 tbsp wine vinegar

1 tsp salt

juice of 1 lime

1 Place all the ingredients, except the lime juice, in a large, heavy-based saucepan. Add 300ml (10fl oz) water to just about cover the meat, and bring to the boil.

2 Reduce the heat to a simmer and cook gently for 2–3 hours, or until tender and well cooked, stirring occasionally. Make sure the liquid does not dry out before the meat is cooked through.

3 Remove from the heat and stir in the lime juice. Serve hot with boiled or steamed rice.

KANGAROO TAIL AND CHICKPEA SOUP

A typical Australian outback recipe that is simple but full of flavour and textures. Perfect for chilly winter evenings.

THE CUT Kangaroo tail

SERVES 4
PREP 20 mins   **COOK** 2 hrs

1 tbsp olive oil

1 kangaroo tail, about 1kg (2¼lb) cut into joints

1 onion, diced

5 garlic cloves, crushed

400g can chopped tomatoes

1 tbsp tomato purée

2 star anise

400g can chickpeas, drained

1 carrot, diced

500ml (16fl oz) beef or chicken stock

3 bay leaves

salt and freshly ground black pepper

1 tbsp roughly chopped mint, to garnish

1 Heat the oil in a flameproof casserole. Add the tail pieces and cook over a medium heat for 4–5 minutes, stirring occasionally, until well-browned. Remove and set aside.

2 Reduce the heat, add the onions and cook for 3–4 minutes, stirring, until lightly coloured and softened. Add the garlic and stir for 1 minute. Add the tomatoes, tomato purée, star anise, chickpeas, and carrot.

3 Return the meat to the casserole and add enough stock to cover the meat. Add the bay leaves and stir to mix. Reduce the heat to a simmer, cover, and cook for 1½ hours, or until the meat is tender. Season. Ladle into bowls, sprinkle over the mint, and serve.

VARIATION

Ox tail soup Use ox tail in place of the kangaroo tail, cooked haricot beans in place of the chickpeas, and cook as above.

RABBIT PIE WITH LEMON AND SAGE

A lovely old recipe from South West England, in which a crust is created from breadcrumbs flavoured with lemon and sage.

THE CUT Whole rabbit

SERVES 6
PREP 15 mins   **COOK** 2 hrs

2 rabbits, about 3kg (6½ lb) in total, jointed into 6 pieces each (see p233)

plain flour, seasoned with salt and pepper, for dusting

450g (1lb) fresh breadcrumbs

6 large onions, finely chopped

zest of 1 lemon

2 tbsp finely chopped sage

salt and freshly ground black pepper

2 eggs, beaten

2 tbsp milk

5 rindless streaky bacon rashers

1 Preheat the oven to 200°C (400°F/Gas 6). Dust the rabbit pieces with the flour, and place in a straight-sided casserole.

2 Place the breadcrumbs, onions, lemon zest, and sage in a large bowl. Season with salt and pepper, add the beaten eggs and milk, and mix well to combine and bind.

3 Cover the rabbit pieces with the bacon and spread the stuffing over the top. Cook in the oven for 2 hours. Cover with foil if it starts to brown too early. Serve hot alongside green beans.

VARIATION

Chicken pie with lemon and tarragon Use chicken drumsticks in place of the rabbit and tarragon in place of the sage. Mix 1 teaspoon of English mustard with the milk and add to the casserole along with the other ingredients in step 2. Assemble the pie as above, but cook it in the oven for 1 hour instead of 2 hours.

RABBIT WITH MUSTARD

A French classic with a piquant contrast in flavours, good with both farmed and wild rabbits.

THE CUT Whole rabbit

SERVES 3–4
PREP 15 mins   **COOK** 1–1½ hrs

1 tbsp olive oil

2 tbsp Dijon mustard

salt and freshly ground black pepper

1 rabbit, about 1.5kg (3lb 3oz), jointed into 6 pieces (see p233)

4 tbsp dry white wine

4 tbsp double cream

1 Preheat the oven to 230°C (450°F/Gas 8). In a large bowl, mix the oil, mustard, half a teaspoon salt, and a sprinkle of pepper. Dip the rabbit pieces in the mixture and mix until well coated. Place the pieces in a gratin dish and cook in the oven for 5 minutes.

2 Remove from the oven. Add 100ml (3½fl oz) water, cover with foil, and return to the oven, reducing the heat to 160°C (325°F/Gas 3). Cook for 1 hour, or until the meat is tender. Remove the meat pieces from the dish, cover with foil, and set aside.

3 Pour the wine in the gratin dish and cook over a high heat for 3–5 minutes, stirring to dislodge any bits that may have stuck to the bottom. When the wine has reduced by one-third, stir in the cream, reduce the heat, and season to taste. Cook for 3–5 minutes, or until the sauce is thick enough to coat the back of a spoon. Strain the sauce. Place the rabbit pieces in a serving dish, pour the sauce over, and serve hot.

VARIATION

Braised chicken legs with mustard Use 1.5kg (3lb 3oz) chicken legs instead of the rabbit. Marinate as before, then cook in a large, heavy-based pan for 7–8 minutes, until well-browned on all sides. Make the sauce as before. Arrange the chicken legs on a plate, pour the sauce over, and serve with small boiled potatoes and seasonal vegetables.

RABBIT SALAD

Luscious rabbit meat is a perfect foil for the crunchy, brightly coloured salad of fresh seasonal produce.

CUT **Rabbit saddle**

SERVES 4
PREP 30 mins   **COOK** 25 mins

2 bone-in rabbit saddles, about 225g (8oz) each
salt and freshly ground black pepper
1 tbsp groundnut oil
2 carrots, cut crossways into 5cm (2in) pieces
1 celery stick, peeled
2 white turnips
handful of sorrel leaves
1 tsp butter
2 tsp sunflower seeds

FOR THE DRESSING

2 tbsp extra virgin olive oil
juice of ½ lemon
½ tsp Dijon mustard

1 Remove the skin flaps from the sides of the saddles. Use a sharp knife to remove the fine membrane that covers the flesh of the saddle. Pat the meat dry with kitchen paper to remove any excess blood. Season with salt and pepper.

2 Heat the oil in a lidded saucepan. Place the saddles, skin-side down, and cook for 4 minutes, until well-browned. Flip, reduce the heat, cover, and cook for 15–20 minutes. Remove from the pan, cover with foil, and set aside.

3 Slice the carrot pieces lengthways into 3–4 pieces, depending on the thickness. Then slice them into thin matchsticks. Slice the celery and turnips in the same way.

4 For the dressing, mix all the ingredients in a large bowl. Add the vegetables and sorrel leaves, toss to coat, and set aside. Remove each loin of rabbit, cutting parallel to the bone, and cut the 2 fillets from under the bone. Cut the meat into bite-sized chunks.

5 Melt the butter in a pan, add the sunflower seeds, and stir until the butter starts foaming. To serve, place a small mound of the salad on a plate and top with the rabbit slices. Add a spoonful of sunflower seeds and a drizzle of the foaming butter.

HARE STEW WITH MUSHROOMS

A young hare is marinated in olive oil and garlic and then cooked simply with earthy mushrooms.

CUT **Whole hare**

SERVES 4
PREP 30 mins, plus marinating
COOK 1 hr 5 mins

1 leveret (young hare), about 1.3kg (3lb), jointed into 8 pieces (see p233)
30g (1oz) butter
100g (3½oz) streaky bacon lardons
1 tbsp brandy
200ml (7fl oz) game stock
4 tomatoes, skinned, deseeded, and chopped
115g (4oz) chestnut mushrooms, trimmed and sliced

FOR THE MARINADE

100ml (3½fl oz) olive oil
salt and freshly ground black pepper
3 garlic cloves, unpeeled and crushed
juice of 1 lemon

1 Place all the marinade ingredients in a large bowl and mix to combine. Add the leveret, mix to coat, and leave to marinate for 4 hours at room temperature.

2 Melt the butter in a large, lidded saucepan over a low heat. Add the bacon and cook for 5–10 minutes, until lightly coloured.

3 Remove the meat from the marinade and reserve the liquid. Increase the heat to medium, add the meat, and stir to coat. Cook for 15 minutes, turning occasionally, until well-browned.

4 Pour the brandy into the pan. Remove and discard the garlic from the marinade. Add the marinade to the pan, then add the stock, tomatoes, and mushrooms. Season well and reduce the heat to a simmer. Cover and cook for 40 minutes, until the meat is tender. Remove from the heat and serve hot with spätzle or pappardelle.

SADDLE OF HARE WITH BEETROOT

This simple and colourful dish brings together a creamy beetroot sauce and the rich, earthy flavour of hare.

 THE CUT Hare saddle

SERVES 4
PREP 45 mins, plus overnight marinating
COOK 30 mins, plus resting

2 saddles of hare, about 700g (1½lb) each

2 tsp olive oil

350g (12oz) cooked beetroots, thinly sliced

2 tbsp chopped shallots

2 tbsp red wine vinegar

200ml (7fl oz) double cream

1 tsp Dijon mustard

snipped chives, to garnish

FOR THE MARINADE

500ml (16fl oz) red wine

1 carrot, diced

1 large onion, finely chopped

sprig of rosemary

1 bay leaf

½ tsp salt

8 black peppercorns

8 juniper berries

2 cloves

1 Use a knife to remove the membrane covering the saddles. Combine all the marinade ingredients in a large bowl, add the meat, and mix to coat. Cover and leave overnight, or for about a day.

2 Preheat the oven to 250ºC (480ºF/Gas 9). Remove the meat from the marinade and pat dry with kitchen paper. Strain the marinade, retain the liquid, and discard the rest.

3 Heat the oil in a large, heavy-based pan over a high heat. Add the meat and cook for 3–4 minutes, until well-browned. Remove from the pan and transfer to a large roasting tin.

4 Place the roasting tin in the oven and cook for 10–15 minutes. The meat should still be pink. Cover with foil and leave to rest in a warm place. Remove about three-quarters of the fat from the pan.

5 Place the roasting tin over a medium heat. Add the beetroot and cook for 1–2 minutes. Then add the shallots and cook for 2 minutes, stirring occasionally, until softened. Pour in the vinegar and 4 tablespoons of the marinade, and cook for about 1 minute.

6 Add the cream and mustard to the sauce. Stir to mix, and season well. Cook the sauce, stirring, until reduced to a light coating consistency, but do not cook it for long.

7 Remove from the heat and keep warm. Remove the loins from the top of the saddle and the fillets from the bottom. Carve the meat lengthways and serve with the beetroot sauce.

HARE IN CHOCOLATE SAUCE

This classic Italian dish uses a small amount of chocolate to enhance the flavour of the hare.

 **Whole hare**

SERVES 6

PREP 45 mins   **COOK** 2½ hrs, plus resting

1 hare, about 2kg (4½lb) jointed into 12 pieces (see p233)

4 tbsp plain flour, seasoned with salt and pepper

1 tbsp rapeseed oil

85g (3oz) butter

115g (4oz) bacon lardons

1 large onion, thinly sliced

salt and freshly ground black pepper

sprig of marjoram

1.2 litres (2 pints) chicken stock

115g (4oz) caster sugar

120ml (4fl oz) white wine vinegar

60g (2oz) chocolate, at least 75 per cent cocoa solids

30g (1oz) pine nuts

60g (2oz) raisins

1 Preheat the oven to 160°C (325°F/Gas 3). Pat the hare pieces dry with kitchen paper to remove any excess blood. Place the flour in a shallow bowl. Add the meat, toss to coat, and shake off any excess.

2 Heat the oil and half the butter in a large, flameproof casserole. Add the meat when the butter begins to foam, and cook for about 10 minutes, until well-browned all over. Remove with a slotted spoon and set aside.

3 Reduce the heat and add the remaining butter to the casserole. Add the bacon and onion, and cook, stirring, until softened. Season, then add the marjoram and stock and bring to the boil.

4 Cover and place in the oven for 1½ hours. Remove from the oven, mix the sugar and vinegar in a small bowl, and stir into the casserole. Return the casserole to the oven for 30 minutes.

5 Remove from the oven and grate the chocolate into the casserole. Stir in the pine nuts and raisins, and leave to rest for 15 minutes. Serve warm with polenta and a green salad.

BREAST OF PHEASANT WITH SMOKED PAPRIKA

In this simple Spanish dish, the pheasant is given an alluring smoky taste by the addition of paprika in the sauce.

 Pheasant breast

SERVES 4

PREP 10 mins   **COOK** 30 mins

4 skinless pheasant breasts, about 100g (3½oz) each

30g (1oz) butter

2 shallots, finely chopped

2 garlic cloves, chopped

1 tsp smoked paprika

120ml (4fl oz) dry vermouth

150ml (5fl oz) double cream

pinch of salt

juice of ½ a lemon

1 Pat the pheasant breasts dry with kitchen paper to remove any excess blood. Heat the butter in a lidded heavy-based saucepan over a medium heat.

Add the pheasant breasts when the butter begins to foam, making sure the side that had the skin is facing down. Cook for about 10 minutes, until lightly coloured. Then reduce the heat to low and turn them over. Cover and cook for a further 5 minutes. Remove from the pan and keep warm.

2 Add the shallots and garlic to the pan, cook for 5 minutes until softened, and add the paprika. Scrape up the juices from the bottom of the pan and stir well. Pour in the wine and bring to the boil.

3 Pour in the double cream, reduce the heat to a simmer, and cook gently until the sauce coats the back of a spoon. Taste and adjust the seasoning and add the lemon juice. Remove from the heat and strain the sauce, reserving the liquid. Place the breasts in a serving dish, pour the sauce over, and serve with pilaf rice.

FAISAN NORMANDE

A traditional recipe from northern France, the gamey taste of the bird is balanced by crisp apples and a creamy brandy sauce.

THE CUT Whole pheasant

SERVES 2
PREP 20 mins   **COOK** 1 hr

salt and freshly ground black pepper

1 young pheasant, about 500g (1lb 2oz)

50g (1¾oz) butter, softened

1 tbsp sunflower oil

5 tbsp Calvados

240ml (8fl oz) double cream

2 dessert apples, such as Cox or Braeburn, peeled, cored, and cut into wedges

1 Preheat the oven to 180°C (350°F/Gas 4). Season the meat and spread 20g (¾oz) of the butter over the legs and breast. Heat the oil in an oval casserole over a low heat. Add the pheasant, breast-side down, and cook each breast for 5 minutes, until browned. Then turn the bird onto its back, cover, and cook in the oven for 40–45 minutes.

2 Remove from the oven, transfer the pheasant to a serving dish, and keep warm. Strain off most of the fat from the casserole. Then pour over the Calvados, bring to the boil, and cook for 2 minutes until the alcohol has evaporated. Add the cream and continue to reduce the sauce by boiling, until the sauce coats the back of a spoon. Taste and adjust the seasoning.

3 Heat the remaining butter in a frying pan. Add the apples and fry until lightly browned, but still retaining their shape. Place the pheasant in a serving dish with the apples arranged around it and serve with the sauce.

POT ROAST PHEASANT WITH BACON

Pot roasting helps to retain the moisture and the bacon adds flavour to this very lean bird.

THE CUT Whole pheasant

SERVES 2
PREP 20 mins
COOK 1 hr 20 mins, plus resting

2 slices streaky bacon

1 young pheasant, about 500g (1lb 2oz)

2 tbsp sunflower oil

60g (2oz) butter

sprig of thyme

1 bay leaf

300ml (10fl oz) white wine

salt and freshly ground black pepper

1 Place the bacon over the breasts of the pheasant and tie with a string to hold it in place. Preheat the oven to 180°C (350°F/Gas 4).

2 Heat the oil and butter in a heavy-based flameproof casserole or Dutch oven over a medium heat. Add the pheasant, breast-side down, and cook each breast for 5 minutes, until browned.

3 Then turn the bird onto its back. Add the thyme, bay leaf, and wine, lifting the pheasant slightly to get some liquid under it and season. Cover partially, then transfer the casserole to the oven, and cook for 45 minutes.

4 Remove from the heat and leave to rest, covered, for 15 minutes. Then remove the pheasant and set aside. Place the casserole over a high heat and boil the sauce for 5 minutes, or until thickened. Stir well and strain into a warmed jug.

5 Cut the string from the pheasant and remove the legs. Place the legs on 2 separate plates. Carve the meat from the breast into thick slices and place on the legs. Top with the bacon, pour the sauce over, and serve with braised red cabbage.

PÂTÉ DE GIBIER EN CROÛTE

Made with a hot water crust, this delicious raised game pie provides a magnificent centrepiece for any party or occasion. The stock can be made a day in advance and then gently warmed.

THE CUT Mixed game

SERVES 8–10
PREP 2½ hrs, plus overnight marinating, resting, and cooling
COOK 1½ hrs, plus chilling

FOR THE FILLING

450g (1lb) game livers, such as pheasant, hare, and rabbit, or lamb livers

3 tbsp vermouth

225g (8oz) boneless lean game meat, such as venison, pheasant, or rabbit

115g (4oz) pork fat

1 venison heart, trimmed

3 rindless streaky bacon rashers

1 shallot, finely chopped

1 garlic clove, crushed

1 egg, beaten

¼ tsp ground cloves

¼ tsp ground allspice

salt and freshly ground black pepper

FOR THE PASTRY

450g (1lb) plain flour

¼ tsp salt

175g (6oz) lard, diced

150ml (5fl oz) milk

1 egg yolk, beaten, plus 1 egg beaten to glaze

FOR THE JELLY STOCK

2 large onions

2 pig trotters

900g (2lb) pork bones

1 large carrot

1 celery stick

2 bay leaves

2 tbsp dry sherry

GAME RECIPES

1 For the filling, trim the livers of discolouration and connective threads. Roughly chop them, place in a bowl, and pour over the vermouth. Cover and leave to marinate in a cool place overnight. Place the game pieces, pork fat, venison heart, and bacon in a food processor and pulse until minced.

2 Transfer the minced mixture to a bowl and add the shallots and garlic. Then pour in the egg and add the spices to the bowl. Season the mixture with salt and pepper and mix well. Cover and leave to marinate in a cool place overnight.

3 For the pastry, sift the flour and salt into a bowl, mix, and make a well in the centre. Boil the lard and milk in a pan. Pour the hot liquid into the well and use a wooden spoon to mix to form a smooth dough. Add the beaten yolk as it cools and combine well. When cool enough to handle, roll the dough out to about 1cm (½in) thick. Fold it in three and roll out again. Cover with cling film and leave to rest in a cool place for 30 minutes.

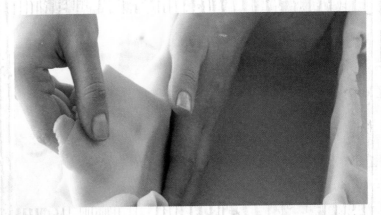

4 For the jelly stock, place all the ingredients in a pan, cover with water, and bring to the boil. Then reduce the heat to a simmer and cook for 2 hours. Strain, season with 1 teaspoon salt and a good grinding of pepper, and cook until reduced to about 750ml (1¼ pints). Remove from the heat, skim off the fat, and leave to cool. Preheat the oven to 180°C (350°F/Gas 4). Meanwhile, line a pie or loaf tin with two-thirds of the pastry.

5 Mix the livers with the game mixture and press into the tin. Roll out the remaining pastry and use to cover the mixture. Brush the edges with a little water and squeeze them together. Brush the top with a little beaten egg, decorate it with pastry trimmings, and brush with the remaining egg. Slit a small hole in the middle of the pastry large enough to hold a funnel. Bake for 1½ hours.

6 Remove the pie from the oven and leave to cool in the tin. When both the pâté and the stock are cool, but not cold, use a funnel to pour the stock slowly into the pâté through the hole. Leave to allow the stock to settle into the mould. Chill in the fridge for at least 12 hours. To remove the pie from the tin, wrap the tin in a hot wet tea towel, then run a knife round the edge of the tin before turning it out. It will keep in the fridge for several days.

GEORGIAN PHEASANT

An unusual dish from the Caucasus region, this recipe uses oranges and sweet wine to create an aromatic sauce.

THE CUT Whole pheasant

SERVES 2–3
PREP 30 mins **COOK** 1 hr 15 mins

900g (2lb) muscat grapes

juice of 4 oranges

120ml (4fl oz) Georgian wine or Hungarian Tokay

1 green tea bag

200g (7oz) walnut halves

1 pheasant, about 800g (1¾oz)

85g (3oz) butter

salt and freshly ground black pepper

30g (1oz) plain flour

handful of chopped flat-leaf parsley, to garnish

1 Preheat the oven to 190°C (375°F/Gas 5). Place the grapes in a food processor and pulse until they reach the consistency of a purée. Strain and place in a large bowl. Add the orange juice and wine and mix to combine.

2 Place the tea bag in a small bowl and pour over 120ml (4fl oz) boiling water. Brew the tea for 5 minutes, then strain and discard the tea bag. Spread the walnuts at the bottom of a large casserole. Place the pheasant on top and pour over the grape mixture.

3 Place the casserole over a medium heat, add half the butter, and pour over the tea. Add just enough water, if needed, to ensure the liquid covers the bird. Season and bring to the boil. Cover and cook in the oven for 1 hour.

4 Remove from the oven, transfer the pheasant to a serving dish, and set aside. Strain the liquid into a wide saucepan and bring to the boil over a high heat. Cook the liquid until reduced by half.

5 Meanwhile, mix the flour and remaining butter in a small bowl to form a paste. Add the flour paste to the pan, a little at a time, whisking constantly to form a sauce. Slice the pheasant breasts and cut the legs in two. To serve, pour the sauce over the meat and garnish with parsley.

ROAST GROUSE

Considered to be the king of game birds, in this dish the rich, coarse meat of the grouse is flavoured with heather and served with liver pâté and toast.

THE CUT Whole grouse

SERVES 4
PREP 30 mins **COOK** 30 mins

4 tsp blueberries

115g (4oz) butter

4 sprigs of heather (optional)

4 young grouse, about 300g (10oz) each, drawn with the livers reserved

salt and freshly ground black pepper

flour, for dusting

2 streaky bacon rashers

4 small slices of toast

150ml (5fl oz) game or chicken stock

1 Preheat the oven to 220°C (425°F/Gas 7). Place the blueberries, half the butter, and heather (if using) in the body cavities of each bird. Sprinkle evenly with salt and pepper and dust with the flour, shaking off any excess.

2 Place the remaining butter with the bacon in a roasting tin and place in the oven, until the fat has melted. Add the grouse to the tin and baste with the drippings. Roast the grouse in the oven for 10 minutes, then remove and baste again. Return to the oven, reduce the heat to 180°C (350°F/Gas 4), and cook for a further 10 minutes.

3 Remove from the oven. Transfer the grouse and bacon to a serving dish and keep warm. Place the roasting tin over a medium heat, add the grouse livers, and fry for 5 minutes. Remove from the tin and crush them with the back of a fork to form a paste. Spread the liver pâté on the toasts.

4 Pour off the excess fat from the pan, add the stock, and simmer to reduce by half. Taste and adjust the seasoning, if needed, and strain into a warmed jug. Place each grouse on a separate plate, along with 1 toast and half a rasher of bacon. Serve warm with the gravy on the side.

VARIATION

Roast squab You can use a young, fairly plump squab in place of the grouse and prepare as above.

CHARTREUSE OF PARTRIDGE

The combination of bird, bacon, and cabbage is simply stunning in this vintage French dish.

THE CUT Whole partridge

SERVES 6
PREP 1 hr   **COOK** 2 hrs, plus resting

6 French partridges, 250g (9oz) each

salt and freshly ground black pepper

1 tbsp vegetable oil

115g (4oz) butter

2 Savoy cabbages

450g (1lb) bacon, skin removed

1 bay leaf

sprig of thyme

4 large carrots

350ml (12fl oz) game or chicken stock

90ml (3fl oz) dry white wine

1 Preheat the oven to 230°C (450°F/Gas 8). Season the partridges with salt and pepper. Heat the oil and 30g (1oz) of the butter in a roasting tin over a medium heat. Add the partridges and fry until well-browned. Then transfer to the oven and roast them, breast-side up, for 15–20 minutes. Remove from the oven, transfer to a serving dish, and leave to rest for 15 minutes. When the partridges are cool enough to handle, remove the legs and breasts, and discard the rest.

2 Boil a large pan of water and add a teaspoon of salt. Remove the outer leaves of the cabbage, discard the discoloured ones, and reserve the hearts. Rinse the leaves in cold water and plunge in the boiling water for about 3 minutes.

Then drain in a colander and run under a cold tap to arrest the cooking. Drain the cold leaves and dry on a clean kitchen towel.

3 Heat another 30g (1oz) of butter in the roasting tin over a medium heat. Add the bacon and cook until well coloured. Cut the cabbage hearts into quarters, making sure you keep the central core intact. Move the bacon to the sides of the tin, add the cabbage hearts, and cook until lightly coloured.

4 Add the bay leaf, thyme, carrots, and just enough water to cover the vegetables and bring to the boil. Cover with foil and place in the oven. Reduce the temperature to 200°C (400°F/Gas 6) and braise for 1 hour. Remove the vegetables and bacon with a slotted spoon and set aside. When cool enough to handle, slice the bacon and carrots and remove the stalks from the braised cabbage.

5 Increase the temperature to 220°C (425°F/Gas 7). Grease a 25 x 12cm (10 x 5in) ovenproof dish with the remaining butter. Trim the stalks of the blanched cabbage leaves. Place the largest and most intact leaf at the bottom of the dish and keep another one for the top. Line the dish with the leaves overhanging at the top to allow for a fold in, making sure they overlap and there are no gaps.

6 Spread two quarters of the braised cabbage over the base of the dish and season lightly with salt and pepper. Layer evenly with the breast meat. Cover with another two quarters of braised cabbage, season lightly with pepper, and top with the bacon slices. Add a third layer of cabbage, season lightly, and top with the carrots and legs. Season and cover with the last of the braised cabbage, pushing it down gently to make sure everything is in place. Top with the last cabbage leaf, bring in the overhanging leaves to seal, and bake for 30 minutes.

7 For the sauce, bring the stock and wine to the boil in a saucepan and cook until reduced by half. Season and pour into a warm jug. Turn the Chartreuse out onto a large plate, and serve with the sauce and plain boiled potatoes.

ROAST PARTRIDGE, WITH LEGS BRAISED IN PUY LENTILS

In this modern method of cooking the bird, the legs are cooked longer, with the crowns served pink. The lentils in the dish help make it hearty and satisfying.

THE CUT Whole partridge

SERVES 4
PREP 30 mins   **COOK** 1½ hrs, plus resting

1 tbsp vegetable oil

4 partridges, about 250g (9oz) each, legs and crowns separated

1 tsp butter

1 celery stick, roughly chopped

1 large carrot, diced

1 onion, chopped

300g (10oz) Puy lentils, rinsed

2 tbsp red wine

1 bay leaf

sprig of thyme

4 streaky bacon rashers

1 Heat the oil in a small, flameproof casserole or Dutch oven, add the partridge legs, and cook for 5–10 minutes over a high heat, until well-browned. Remove from the heat and set aside. Reduce the heat, add the butter, and stir in the celery, carrots, and onions. Cook for 5 minutes, stirring to colour lightly. Preheat the oven to 200°C (400°F/Gas 6).

2 Add the lentils and continue to cook for 5 minutes, stirring to combine. Pour in the red wine and add the herbs, bring to the boil, and return the legs to the casserole. Add just enough water to cover the meat and bring to the boil. Reduce the heat to a simmer, cover, and cook for 1 hour, until the meat falls off the bone.

3 Meanwhile, wrap each crown with 1 rasher of bacon, season well, and roast in the oven for 15–20 minutes. Remove and leave to rest in a warm place for 30 minutes.

4 Remove the legs from the casserole and boil the liquid until reduced by half, leaving the lentils coated in a thin layer of sauce. Taste and adjust the seasoning, and remove from the heat. Lightly shred the meat from the legs with a fork and return to the casserole. Stir to combine. To serve, ladle a large helping of the lentils and leg meat on 4 plates, then slice the breast meat from the bone and place on top.

PIGEON PASTILLA

This traditional and popular street food found in the markets of Marrakech is a blend of sweet, sour, and exotic flavours, all in one dish.

THE CUT Whole pigeon

SERVES 4
PREP 30 mins   **COOK** 2 hrs

140g (5oz) butter, softened

3 pigeons, about 285g (10oz) each

3 red onions, thinly sliced

small bunch of coriander

small bunch of flat-leaf parsley

pinch of saffron threads

1 tbsp clear honey, plus extra to taste

1 cinnamon stick

salt and freshly ground black pepper

150g (5½oz) almonds, toasted and roughly chopped

6 eggs, lightly beaten

1 tsp orange flower water

12 sheets ready-made filo pastry

2 tbsp icing sugar, for dusting

1 tbsp ground cinnamon, for dusting

1 Melt 85g (3oz) of the butter in a wide, lidded saucepan. Tie the herbs with a piece of butcher's string. Add the pigeons, onions, herbs, saffron, honey, and cinnamon stick to the pan. Season, cover with 750ml (1¼ pints) water, and bring to the boil. Reduce the heat to low, cover, and cook for 1 hour.

2 Remove the pigeons. Increase the heat and cook for 10 minutes, uncovered, to reduce the liquid. Meanwhile, use a fork to shred the meat roughly off the bones. Discard the bones. Return the shredded meat to the pan and remove and discard the herbs. Reduce the liquid until it just covers the bottom of the pan.

3 Add the almonds and 4 of the beaten eggs to the pan and stir to mix. Cook lightly, stirring, until curds of cooked egg form. Taste and season with salt, or add honey if it needs sweetening. Then add the orange flower water, remove from the heat, and set aside to cool. Preheat the oven to 150°C (300°F/Gas 2).

4 Melt the remaining butter in a small pan. Lay 4 sheets of the pastry on a clean work surface. Lightly brush each of the sheets with the melted butter, place another sheet on top of the first, and brush with more butter. Repeat the pastry layers until all the sheets are used up.

5 Use a slotted spoon to place a quarter of the meat mixture in the centre of each pastry pile. Fold the corners of the pastry over the mixture to make a five-sided circular sealed parcel. Brush each parcel with the remaining melted butter. Then brush with the beaten egg and place them on a baking sheet. Transfer to the oven and bake for 45 minutes. Remove from the oven and serve hot, dusted with icing sugar and cinnamon.

THAI SWEET AND SOUR PIGEON

The tangy vegetable sauce adds colour and flavour to this simple Thai dish. Chopping the vegetables into similar-sized pieces adds to the visual appeal of this dish.

THE CUT Pigeon breast

SERVES 4
PREP 30 mins   **COOK** 40 mins

2 tbsp white wine vinegar

1 tbsp soy sauce

½ tbsp plain flour

1 tbsp vegetable oil

8 pigeon breasts, about 50g (1³/₄oz) each

4 garlic cloves, crushed

½ tsp salt

1 onion, thinly chopped

2 sweet peppers, deseeded and chopped

400g can chopped tomatoes

1 small cucumber, peeled, deseeded, and chopped

2 tbsp chopped coriander leaves

1 Place the vinegar, soy sauce, and flour in a bowl. Mix to form a thin lumpy paste and set aside. Heat the oil in a lidded, heavy-based saucepan over a medium heat. Add the pigeon breasts and cook for 1–2 minutes on both sides.

2 Add the garlic and the salt, and stir to mix for 1 minute. Then add the onion and peppers and cook for 5 minutes, stirring frequently to coat in the juices.

3 Add the tomatoes and cucumber and stir to combine. Pour in the vinegar paste, mix thoroughly, and bring to the boil. Then reduce the heat to a simmer, cover, and cook for 30 minutes, stirring occasionally, until the sauce takes on a glossy sheen. Remove from the heat, garnish with chopped coriander, and serve hot with rice.

SALAD OF PIGEON BREAST

A selection of herbs and coloured leaves makes this salad a refreshing first course.

 Pigeon breast

SERVES 4
PREP 15 mins   **COOK** 10 mins, plus resting

4 pigeon breasts, about 50g (1¾oz) each

salt and freshly ground black pepper

1 tsp rapeseed oil

1 tsp butter

125g (4½oz) mixed salad leaves, such as mizuna, rocket, baby chard, sorrel, and lollo rosso, washed, dried, and stalks removed

125g (4½oz) mixed herbs, such as chervil, tarragon, and flat-leaf parsley, washed, dried, and stalks removed

FOR THE DRESSING

120ml (4fl oz) olive oil

30ml (1fl oz) white wine vinegar

1 tsp wholegrain mustard

1 Pat the pigeon breasts dry with kitchen paper to remove any excess blood. Season with salt and pepper.

2 Heat the oil and butter in a heavy-based saucepan. When the butter starts to foam, add the pigeon breasts, skin-side down, and cook for about 2 minutes, until well-browned.

3 Reduce the heat and turn over the pigeon breasts. Cover partially and cook for a further 2 minutes. Remove from the heat and leave to rest for 5 minutes.

4 For the dressing, mix all the ingredients in a large bowl. Chop the mixed salad leaves and herbs into bite-sized pieces, add them to the dressing, and toss to coat. Divide the greens equally on 4 plates. Slice the pigeon breasts vertically and place on top of the greens. Serve immediately.

VARIATION

Salad of chicken breast Use 2 skin-on chicken breasts in place of the pigeon breasts. Pan fry the meat for 10–15 minutes, then remove and rest for 5 minutes. Slice them vertically and serve as above with the dressing and greens.

GAME CASSEROLE

This highly flavoured stew with mushrooms, celery, and carrots is best served with creamy mashed potatoes.

 Mixed game

SERVES 4
PREP 30 mins   **COOK** 1 hr 15 mins

675g (1½lb) (boned weight) mixed game, such as pheasant, venison, and duck, cut into bite-sized pieces

plain flour, for dusting

salt and freshly ground black pepper

1 tbsp olive oil

1 tbsp brandy

1 onion, finely chopped

2 garlic cloves, grated or finely chopped

2 celery sticks, finely diced

2 carrots, finely diced

1 bouquet garni

275g (9½oz) chestnut mushrooms, quartered

1 glass of dry white wine

2 tsp redcurrant jelly

750ml (1¼ pints) hot chicken stock

1 Preheat the oven to 180°C (350°F/Gas 4). Dust the meat lightly with a little flour, then season well with salt and pepper. Heat half the oil in a cast-iron pan, add the meat, and cook over a medium heat, stirring occasionally, for 6–8 minutes, or until browned on all sides. Remove with a slotted spoon and place in a casserole.

2 Add the brandy to the pan and stir to deglaze. Then add the rest of the oil, if needed, and the onion. Cook over a low heat for 6 minutes, or until soft. Stir in the garlic, celery, carrots, and bouquet garni and cook over a low heat, stirring occasionally, for 8 minutes, or until tender.

3 Stir in the mushrooms, then increase the heat, add the wine, and boil for 2 minutes while the alcohol evaporates. Pour the mixture into the casserole with the meat, then stir in the redcurrant jelly. Pour in the stock, cover with a lid, and cook in the oven for 1 hour, or until the meat is tender. Add hot water during the cooking, if needed.

BRAISED QUAIL LUCULLUS

Named after a Roman epicure gourmet, this dish uses a light grape and wine sauce to enhance the delicate flavour of quail.

 **Whole quail**

SERVES 4
PREP 30 mins   **COOK** 1 hr

8 quails, about 150g (5½oz) each

16 streaky bacon rashers or pancetta lardons

2 tbsp vegetable oil

2 tbsp butter

1 onion, chopped

200ml (7fl oz) white wine

300ml (10fl oz) chicken stock

2 tbsp brandy

20 seedless green grapes, skinned

salt and freshly ground black pepper

juice of 1 lemon

1 tbsp chopped flat-leaf parsley, to garnish

1 Wrap each quail in 2 rashers of bacon and tie securely with butcher's string. Heat the oil and 1 tablespoon of butter in a large, lidded heavy-based saucepan. Add the birds and cook for 8–10 minutes, until well-browned. Do this in batches to avoid overcrowding the pan. Remove with a slotted spoon and set aside.

2 Add the onion to the pan and stir for about 5 minutes, until softened and evenly browned. Reduce the heat, add the wine, and return the quails to the pan. Cook gently for 10 minutes, occasionally basting with the wine as it reduces. Then pour in the stock, cover, and simmer for about 20 minutes, until just cooked.

3 Remove the quails with a slotted spoon and set aside. Add the brandy and grapes and simmer for 5–10 minutes to reduce the sauce by half. Taste and adjust the seasoning, if needed, and remove from the heat. Stir in the lemon juice and remaining butter to form a light sauce.

4 Cut the strings from the quail, but leave the bacon intact. Divide the quails on 4 plates with the grapes. Pour over the sauce, garnish with the parsley, and serve hot with plain boiled potatoes and green vegetables.

GUINEA FOWL WITH SMOKED BACON

This stunning dish brings together powerfully flavoured ingredients that lift the gamey flavour of the bird.

 **Whole guinea fowl**

SERVES 4
PREP 1 hr, plus overnight marinating
COOK 40 mins

1 guinea fowl, about 1.1 kg (2½lb), jointed into 10 pieces

freshly ground black pepper

10 thin smoked streaky bacon rashers

3 tbsp groundnut oil

30g (1oz) butter

1 tbsp plain flour

1 litre (1¾ pints) chicken stock

160g (5½oz) baby onions

5 tbsp double cream

2 tbsp Crème de cassis

FOR THE MARINADE

1 litre (1¾ pints) full-bodied red wine such as Rioja, Bordeaux, or Merlot wine

sprig of rosemary

1 bay leaf

sprig of thyme

1 garlic clove, unpeeled and crushed

1 Season the meat with pepper. Wrap each piece in a rasher of bacon and fix it in place with a cocktail stick. Mix the marinade ingredients in a large bowl. Add the meat, mix to coat, and chill in the fridge overnight.

2 Remove the meat from the marinade and pat dry with kitchen paper. Strain the garlic and herbs from the marinade, set aside, and reserve the liquid. Heat the oil in a frying pan, add the meat, and fry for 4 minutes on each side, until well-browned, making sure the pieces are still wrapped in the bacon. Remove from the pan.

3 Heat the butter in a flameproof casserole and add the browned meat. Add the strained garlic and herbs and shake the pan gently to mix. Sprinkle over the flour and stir for 1–2 minutes to coat. Then pour in the marinade and stock, and add the onions. Bring to the boil, reduce the heat to a simmer, and cook for about 20 minutes.

4 Remove the meat and onions. Remove the cocktail sticks, making sure the bacon is still wrapped, if possible. Cook the sauce for 10 minutes to reduce a little. Then add the cream and Crème de cassis, bring to the boil, and cook for 10 more minutes, until reduced by half. Strain through a fine sieve. Arrange the meat alongside the onions, pour the sauce over, and serve with mashed potatoes garnished with chopped herbs.

OSTRICH STEAKS

The flavour of the breast steaks, a lean meat, is greatly enhanced with an easy-to-prepare marinade.

THE CUT Ostrich breast steak

SERVES 4
PREP 15 mins, plus marinating
COOK 10 mins, plus resting

4 ostrich breast steaks, about 140g (5oz) each

1 tbsp rapeseed oil, plus extra for brushing

2 tbsp Worcestershire sauce

1 garlic clove, crushed

sprig of rosemary, roughly chopped

salt and freshly ground black pepper

¼ tsp sumac

1 Place all the ingredients, except the steaks, in a large bowl and mix well to combine. Pour the marinade into a plastic bag, add the steaks, and seal the bag. Shake the bag gently to coat the meat. Leave to marinate for 30 minutes at room temperature.

2 Preheat a griddle pan or grill to its highest setting. Remove the steaks from the marinade, pat dry with kitchen paper, and brush lightly with the oil.

3 Grill the steaks for about 4 minutes on each side, until lightly coloured. Then reduce the heat to low and cook for a further 4 minutes on each side, until well done. Then leave the steaks, skin-side up, on the grill for a further 5 minutes. Leave to rest for 5 minutes, then serve hot with some grilled mushrooms and chips.

MATCH UP

A mild mustard sauce, grilled mushrooms, or a crunchy green salad with a light dressing would be the perfect accompaniments to the delicate flavour of the ostrich.

BREAST OF WILD GOOSE

This lean bird is kept moist by being wrapped in foil and cooked with vermouth; the resulting juices make for a fine sauce.

THE CUT Wild goose breast

SERVES 2
PREP 15 mins   **COOK** 2 hrs

2 tsp rapeseed oil

1 onion, finely sliced

2 sprigs of rosemary

2 skinless wild goose breasts, about 175g (6oz) each

salt and freshly ground black pepper

4 tbsp dry vermouth

4 tbsp double cream

1 tsp lemon juice (optional)

1 Preheat the oven to 160°C (325°F/Gas 3). Cut two squares of foil, about 30cm (12in) each, and brush the centre with the oil. Place half a sliced onion, a sprig of rosemary, and then the goose breast on each sheet. Season well and drizzle over the vermouth. Roll up the edges of the foil to enclose, place on a baking tray, and cook in the oven for 2 hours.

2 Open the packages a little at one end. Pour the juices into a small saucepan, bring to the boil, and cook until reduced by half. Reduce the heat to a simmer, add the cream, and cook until the sauce coats the back of a spoon. Taste and adjust the seasoning, and add a little lemon juice if needed. Slice the meat thinly and serve with the sauce poured on top.

VARIATION

Breast of wild duck You can use 2 skinless wild duck breasts in place of the goose breasts, and thyme in place of the rosemary and cook as above.

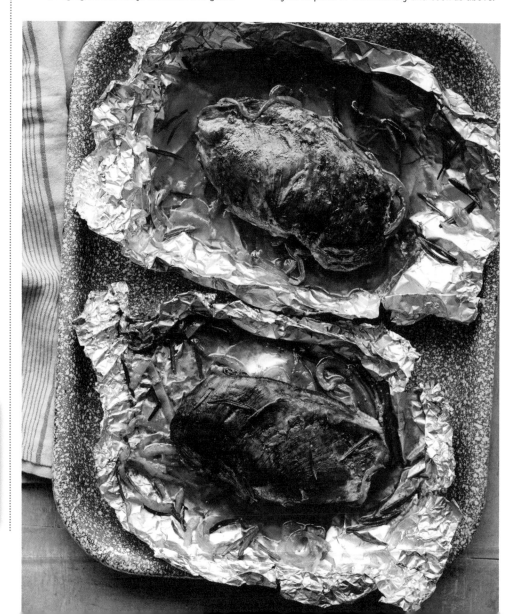

SLOW ROASTED WILD GOOSE

Soft fruit and butter provide the moisture required to cook a wild goose and add a contrasting flavour as well.

THE CUT Whole wild goose

SERVES 4
PREP 30 mins   **COOK** 2 hrs, plus resting

115g (4oz) butter, softened

115g (4oz) blackberries

115g (4oz) raisins

1 orange, cut in half and zest grated

1 garlic clove, crushed

salt and freshly ground black pepper

1 skinless wild goose, about 2.5kg (5½lb)

1 large onion, sliced in rings

1 bay leaf

6 streaky bacon rashers

1 Preheat the oven to 180°C (350°F/Gas 4). Place the butter, fruits, orange zest, and garlic in a large bowl. Season with salt and pepper, mix to combine, and form into a ball. Place the stuffing in the body cavity of the goose. Use one orange half to seal firmly the cavity of the bird.

2 Place 2 large sheets of foil on a clean work surface. Layer the centre of the sheet with the onion and place the bay leaf on top. Then place the goose, breast-side up, on top. Spread 4 rashers of bacon over the breast and 2 over the legs.

3 Wrap the goose in the foil to ensure that it is fully enclosed. Leave just a little space to allow air and heat to escape. Place in a roasting tin and roast in the oven for 1 hour. Then unwrap the foil, turn the bird over, and reseal the parcel. Return to the oven for 1 more hour.

4 Remove from the oven, open the foil parcel a little, and pour off about 300ml (10fl oz) of the liquid into a small saucepan. Turn the bird over so it is breast-side up, and leave to rest for 15 minutes. Boil the cooking juices, taste and adjust the seasoning, and squeeze over the juice from the remaining orange half if necessary. Carve the goose into slices and serve with the gravy on the side.

BREASTS OF WILD DUCK WITH SAUCE BIGARADE

Bigarade is the Provençal word for the Seville or bitter orange, a perfect match for this wild fowl.

THE CUT Wild duck breast

SERVES 4
PREP 15 mins   **COOK** 30–35 mins, plus resting

1 tbsp rapeseed oil

4 wild duck breasts, about 225g (8oz) each

salt and freshly ground black pepper

2 tsp plain flour

240ml (8fl oz) game stock

zest and juice of 2 Seville oranges

1 tbsp Grand Marnier

1 tbsp sherry vinegar

1 tsp caster sugar

1 Heat the oil in a heavy-based saucepan over a high heat. Pat the duck breasts dry with kitchen paper to remove any excess blood. Season all over, place skin-side down in the pan, and sear for 2–3 minutes. Turn the meat over and reduce the heat. Cover and cook for 5 minutes. Remove with a slotted spoon, cover with foil, and leave to rest in a warm place.

2 Stir the flour into the pan and cook for 1–2 minutes to colour lightly. Pour in the stock, orange juice, Grand Marnier, and sherry vinegar. Reduce the heat to a simmer and cook until the sauce just coats the back of a spoon. Taste and adjust the seasoning, add the sugar, and strain into a small pan. Then add the zest, simmer for 1–2 minutes, and remove from the heat. Carve the meat into thin slices and serve with the sauce and wild rice.

GAME TERRINE

Lined with bacon and with lean fillets of game through the middle, this terrine makes an impressive dish. It is best served a day later to allow the flavours to develop fully.

THE CUT Mixed game

SERVES 8–10
PREP 35–40 mins, plus marinating   **COOK** 1 hr

2 boneless pheasant breasts, about 100g (3½oz) each

3 tbsp Benedictine or Drambuie

450g (1lb) minced lean game, such as venison or pheasant

1kg (2¼lb) minced pork belly

2 tsp salt

½ tsp freshly ground black pepper

4 garlic cloves, crushed

2 tsp Worcestershire sauce

30 pistachios, shelled

15–20 streaky bacon rashers

2 bay leaves

1 Slice the pheasant breasts lengthways into strips. Rub the pieces with the Benedictine and leave to marinate in a cool place for 1 hour. Preheat the oven to 190°C (375°F/Gas 5).

2 Place the minced game and pork in a large bowl and mix well. Add the salt, pepper, garlic, and Worcestershire sauce. Pour in the Benedictine from the marinade, add the pistachios, and mix well to combine. Line an earthenware terrine with the bacon, leaving enough of an overhang to allow it to fold over the top when the terrine is filled.

3 Place one-third of the mince mixture over the bacon, pushing it firmly into the corners so that there are no air pockets. Top with half the pheasant strips, and another third of the mince mixture, and press down firmly. Place the remaining pheasant strips over the top and add the remaining mince mixture. Fold the bacon over to cover the mixture completely. Cut extra pieces of bacon to fill in if there are any gaps. Place the bay leaves on top and cover with foil.

4 Place the terrine on a baking sheet and cook in the oven for 1 hour, or until the juices run clear when pierced with a skewer. Leave to cool and refrigerate. To serve, cut into slices and serve with toast.

SALMIS OF TEAL

A traditional method of serving game birds, this dish uses the livers to make a rich sauce.

THE CUT Whole teal

SERVES 4
PREP 45 mins   **COOK** 1 hr, plus resting

4 streaky bacon rashers

2 teal, about 175g (6oz) each, legs removed and livers retained

1 large onion, chopped

6 juniper berries, crushed

1 celery stick, chopped

1 bay leaf

salt and freshly ground black pepper

350ml (12fl oz) red wine

1 tsp butter

2 slices of white bread, soaked in stock and squeezed dry

1 Preheat the oven to 220°C (425°F/Gas 7). Place 2 bacon rashers side by side lengthways on a chopping board. Place one teal on top of the rashers, wrap the rashers around, tying with pieces of butcher's string to secure. Repeat for the other teal. Transfer to a roasting tin and roast in the oven for 15 minutes. Remove and set aside to rest for 15 minutes.

2 Use a sharp knife to remove the breasts from the roasted teals. Slice the meat on one side of the breast bone and following the contour of the bone, cut down to the back of the bird just below the wing. Place the breast meat on a plate, cover with foil to keep warm, and set aside. Roughly chop the rest of the bird and keep aside.

3 Pour the fat and juices from the roasting tin into a large, heavy-based pan. Add the chopped meat, the onion, juniper berries, celery, and bay leaf. Season with salt and pepper and pour in the wine. Bring to the boil, then reduce the heat and simmer for 30 minutes until the sauce reduces by half. Remove from the heat and set aside.

4 Melt the butter in a pan. Add the livers and cook for 4–5 minutes, until well-browned. Transfer the livers to a sieve along with the soaked bread slices, mash with the back of a spoon, and strain into a bowl. Strain the sauce into a pan, skim off any impurities, and whisk in the liver mixture. Heat the sauce gently, but do not boil. Cook for 5–6 minutes, or until it takes on a creamy texture. Slice the teal breasts thinly and arrange on a plate. Pour the sauce over and serve.

FASINJAN

A classic Iranian dish, the addition of pomegranate molasses provides an exotic sweetness.

🔪CUT Whole wild duck

SERVES 4
PREP 15 mins   **COOK** 1 hr 30 mins–2 hrs

3 tbsp vegetable oil

2 wild ducks, about 500g (1lb 2oz) each, jointed into 6 pieces each

1 onion, roughly chopped

250g (9oz) walnuts, roughly chopped

3 tbsp pomegranate molasses, plus extra to garnish

juice of 1 lemon

1 tbsp caster sugar

salt and freshly ground black pepper

chopped flat-leaf parsley, to garnish

pomegranate seeds, to garnish

1 Heat the oil in a large, lidded, heavy-based pan. Add the duck pieces and cook for 5–7 minutes, until they turn brown on all sides. Remove with a slotted spoon and set aside.

2 Add the onion to the same pan and cook, stirring occasionally, for 3–4 minutes until browned. Then stir in the walnuts and cook over a low heat for 2–3 minutes, stirring occasionally. Add the molasses, 450ml (15fl oz) water, lemon juice, and sugar, and bring to the boil.

3 Add the duck pieces to the pan, season with salt and pepper, and reduce the heat to a simmer. Cover and cook for 1½ hours, or until the meat is tender. To serve, ladle a spoonful of the meat over boiled rice. Sprinkle with the chopped parsley and pomegranate seeds, and serve hot.

OSTRICH BURGERS

A lean alternative to the beef burger, served with savoury ingredients that complement the richness of the meat.

🔪CUT Minced ostrich

SERVES 4
PREP 15 mins, plus chilling   **COOK** 10 mins

800g (1¾lb) minced ostrich meat

1 onion, finely chopped

2 tbsp chopped flat-leaf parsley

1 tbsp capers, drained and chopped

4 anchovy fillets, chopped

salt and freshly ground black pepper

1 Place all the ingredients in a large bowl, season well, and mix to combine. Divide the meat mixture into 4 equal-sized balls and gently flatten to make patties. Chill the patties in the fridge for at least 1 hour to help firm them up.

2 Cook the patties on a hot barbecue or a griddle pan for 2 minutes on each side for medium-rare, or reduce the heat and cook for about 5 minutes, on each side, for well done. Do not cook the patties for long over a high heat as they will dry out fast. Serve with burger buns, mustard, and piccalilli.

VARIATION

Pheasant burgers Use minced pheasant meat in place of minced ostrich. Add a teaspoon of chopped dried cranberries and ¼ teaspoon of ground coriander to the meat mixture in step 1 to prevent the patties from becoming too dry. Cook as above.

OFFAL

OFFAL

IN THE RUSH TO EAT EVER MORE EXPENSIVE OR CONVENIENT CUTS OF EASILY PREPARED MEAT, THE SATISFACTION GIVEN BY TEXTURE IS TOO OFTEN IGNORED, YET IT IS THE TEXTURE OF OFFAL AS MUCH AS ITS TASTE THAT IS SO APPEALING. THE VARIETIES OF TEXTURE RUN FROM CRUNCHY TO CREAMY; THE FLAVOURS FROM DELICATE TO POWERFUL. IT IS THESE CONTRASTS THAT DIFFERENTIATE OFFAL FROM ORDINARY MEAT.

OFFAL IS SOMETIMES REFERRED to as "variety meats" or "organ meats", but these delicacies comprise an extraordinarily diverse collection of taste and texture sensations. Some types of offal are indeed organs, such as liver, kidney, and heart; some are extremities, such as head, feet, and tail; others could be described as off-cuts from the main carcass, such as bones, fat, and membranes. This is truly the "nose-to-tail" section of the book.

Although every country has its favourite types of offal and ways of cooking them, the Middle East seems to be the centre of the offal world, with the most delicious and inventive ways of using every scrap of an animal; surely the best and most sustainable approach to meat eating. In fact, immigrant communities often retain a fondness for the offal dishes of their home country, where waste is sacrilege. Equally, many offal dishes have now been rediscovered by modern chefs, who are thrilled by the diversity they offer.

BUYING OFFAL

As a general rule, organ meat should be cooked or frozen within 24 hours. Many items spoil quicker than ordinary meat

and do not improve with hanging. Therefore, most offal is removed before the carcass is hung to mature. Some items may need to be specially ordered in advance. Traditional butchers, whether indigenous or those catering to communities' specialist needs, are usually the best source of the less common types of offal. It is a measure of your butcher whether or not he can get these cuts for you.

THESE DELICACIES COMPRISE AN EXTRAORDINARILY DIVERSE COLLECTION OF TASTE AND TEXTURE SENSATIONS

COOKING OFFAL

With only a few exceptions – some liver being one – most offal tends to be cooked thoroughly, whether it is by lengthy, gentle simmering or by slow stewing. Sometimes, this is followed by slicing and frying, or roasting. In recent years, though, some cuts that were traditionally stewed or baked (such as heart) are now also enjoyed when quickly fried and served pink, as one would cook a piece of steak. Other recipes, however, involve both lengthy preparation and prolonged cooking, but the reward is a dish full of complex flavour and texture

that is very inexpensive to prepare. These are not dishes suited to working people with little time or inclination to cook, but perfect for those for whom food preparation is deeply satisfying and an economical way of feeding a family.

HEALTH BENEFITS

Most offal is rich in nutrients and essential fatty acids, and low in harmful fat. However, where organ meats, such as chicken liver, come from intensively farmed animals, it should be thoroughly cooked to avoid salmonella poisoning. Organs that act as filters, such as kidney and liver, can accumulate drug residues that are most likely to be found in intensively farmed animals, although all producers must adhere to drug withdrawal periods.

OFFAL — ORGAN MEAT

AS WELL AS PROVIDING A VARIETY OF INTERESTING flavours and textures, organ offal is rich in nutrients and essential fatty acids, and most is low in fat. Organ offal should be bought very fresh and cooked or frozen quickly as it spoils easily, particularly any that act as filters.

LIVER

Liver is a good source of iron and probably the most popular of all the offal cuts. Poultry, veal, lamb, and venison liver have a delicate, sweet flavour; ox and pig liver taste stronger.

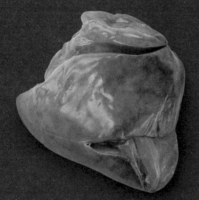

LAMB'S LIVER A sweet-tasting liver, lamb's liver is also at its best quickly fried until pink. Best sliced thinly.

PIG'S LIVER This strongly flavoured liver is popularly used in pork terrines and pâtés. It can also be fried or braised.

HEART

This muscle has a texture like fine-grained meat. Poultry hearts are sold as a delicacy, and in Scandinavia deer hearts are smoked and dried. Trim off excess fat.

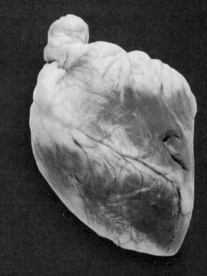

KIDNEYS

As well as being a main ingredient, kidneys are added to slow-cooked dishes to enhance flavour. Ox kidneys are large clusters while other species, such as lamb (below) are single and sold whole.

LAMB'S HEART A meaty muscle that can be sliced and fried or braised, or it can be served whole, stuffed, and baked.

POULTRY LIVER All poultry liver (such as chicken liver, above) has a particularly subtle, sweet flavour, with fattened duck and goose liver being highly prized.

POULTRY HEARTS All poultry hearts are tiny (such as chicken hearts, above), so several are needed for each portion. They are most commonly grilled or quickly fried.

CALF'S LIVER Pale and delicate, calf's liver is the most tender of all. It is best lightly cooked so that it is still a little pink.

SWEETBREADS

An easily digestible delicacy, sweetbreads can be from several organs, most commonly the pancreas and the thymus, but testicles and the parotid gland are also sometimes sold as sweetbreads.

THYMUS SWEETBREADS The thymus is a gland that lies in the throat or neck. Sweetbreads are usually blanched before their final cooking.

PANCREAS SWEETBREADS Pancreas is only present in young animals such as calf and lamb, so it is in short supply and can be expensive.

BRAIN

Brain has a delicate flavour and creamy texture. Both calf's and lamb's brain are esteemed, but there is very little difference other than size between the brains of animals.

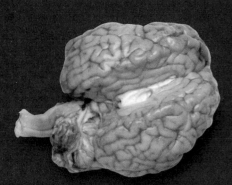

TRIPE

Of a ruminant's four stomachs, tripe is usually made from three: blanket tripe from the omasum, honeycomb tripe (below) from the reticulum, and large pudding casings from the abomasum. Tripe complements both mild and spicy flavours.

INTESTINES

A few recipes exist using the intestines of young milk-fed animals but most are used for sausage casings. Sometimes they are chopped and added to coarse-cut sausages such as andouillette.

LUNGS

An organ traditionally used in peasant dishes. Nowadays, because of its spongy texture, it is generally used only in manufactured products such as sausage, and puddings such as the Scottish haggis.

SPLEEN

Spleen, or melt, usually comes from pig, ox, or calf and tastes like kidney. Normally made into manufactured products, it can also be stuffed and stewed or used for sandwiches.

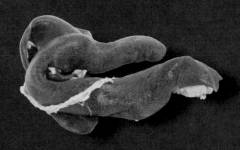

GIZZARD

Used by a bird to grind up its food, this is a tough muscle but its flavour is useful for stocks and soups. When cooked as a confit, gizzards become very tender.

PREPARING ORGAN MEAT

• Many kinds of organ meat can be bought ready prepared but others need a little time spent on them before cooking. See pp266–7 for how to prepare kidneys, liver, sweetbreads, gizzard, and brains – the most common types of offal.

• If any wild game liver still has the bile duct attached (a small sac containing a dark green liquid), this should be carefully removed as the taste is powerfully bitter.

OFFAL – OTHER CUTS

These offal cuts are the external extremities of the animal. Many of them are simply muscles that can be cooked like other cuts, although they may contain more fat or bone than carcass cuts. Others are gelatinous or cartilaginous and their particular textures can be emphasized by simmering or roasting.

ANIMAL FEET AND TENDONS

An excellent source of gelatine, used to make clear jellies and aspic and to give a silky texture to stocks. Calf's feet and pig's trotters are made into dishes.

HEAD

Most commonly simmered, deboned, and moulded in its own jelly as brawn. Boiled calf's head is served along with the feet. A decorated roast boar's head makes a celebratory dish.

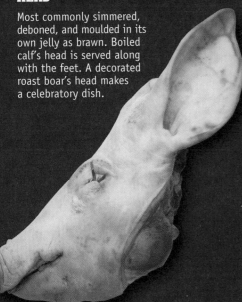

CHEEK OR JOWL

A choice morsel off any animal (although it can be tough) it is included along with the head in brawn, and is also cured, cooked, and rolled in breadcrumbs to make a type of ham.

TONGUE

A nutritious delicacy with a soft melting texture. Tongues of all animals are used, even tiny rabbit and songbird tongues. Beef and reindeer tongues are smoked after being skinned.

POULTRY NECK

Although there is some meat on the neck, it is not easily accessible so it is used for soup and stock. Duck and goose neck skins are stuffed and cooked.

POULTRY FEET

Chicken, duck, and goose feet are not traditionally used in Western cooking, but their crunchy, gelatinous texture makes them much appreciated in Chinese cuisine. They need lengthy simmering to soften the cartilage.

TAIL

Oxtail is strong-flavoured and meaty. Deer tails make broth in Chinese medicine. Fat-tailed sheep is highly prized in the Middle East for its distinctive brown fat. Pig's tails make a snack.

SKIN

Skin adds texture. When boiled it adds gelatinous succulence, when fried or roasted it adds a crisp finish. Pork skin can be left on a roast to make "crackling".

FAT

Hard back fat is used as a sheet to lard or baste roasting joints and the caul fat membrane is used to encase meat patties. Lard cubes are used in salami-style sausages.

BONES

Poultry carcasses are used for soups and stocks. Spinal cord is a prized delicacy in some countries. Knuckle and marrow bones make aspic and jelly, and improve soups and stocks.

EAR

Calf and pig ears are the most common, although lamb's ears are also enjoyed. The cartilage never completely softens and the crunchy texture forms part of their appeal.

MUZZLE

Used to add texture to dishes such as brawn, muzzle is also cooked and served in its own jelly or stewed in a spiced broth with other parts of the head.

BLOOD

Most commonly used for black pudding, which appears in most countries. Duck and goose blood is also mixed with spices and fat and baked into a little patty.

PRESERVED OFFAL

PRESERVED PRODUCTS MADE OF OFFAL are less common than those made with other meats because most offal is very perishable. For this reason, many offal products are either fresh (such as most blood sausages), or only partly preserved to extend their shelf life (such as brawn, haggis, and foie gras).

CHOURIÇO DE SANGUE Most countries make black pudding. Some have pork fat added; others have meat, rice or other grains as well. This Portuguese blood sausage is smoked and dried to preserve it.

FOIE GRAS Geese and ducks are fattened to produce this sumptuous liver, which is cooked and stored in its own fat to preserve it.

HAGGIS The Scots' national dish, haggis is made of sheep's liver, heart, lungs, and fat, as well as oatmeal. The ingredients are stuffed into a sheep's stomach and cooked. It is only lightly preserved.

ZUNGENWURST Large pieces of pork tongue, skin, fat, and meat are bound with blood, oatmeal, and suet to make this attractive German *kochwurst* ("cooked sausage").

COU FARCIE DE CANARD The neck skin of duck is stuffed with shredded cooked meat and chunks of foie gras, then cooked to lightly preserve it.

ANDOUILLE A large French cutting sausage made of brined pig's tripe and intestines that are coiled into skins, then cooked and sometimes smoked.

BATH CHAPS Pork cheeks are cured in a flavoured brine to partly preserve them. These little hams are then cooked, skinned, and rolled in breadcrumbs.

FIGATELLU This hard sausage from Corsica is made with pork liver and blood, studded with fat. It is then dried and smoked.

PORK SCRATCHINGS Thin strips of pork rind (skin) are fried or roasted, which renders any attached fat. Lightly salted, they make a popular crunchy snack.

SALCESON Popular in many countries, brawn is made from boiled pig's head. Like this Polish version, the meat is lightly preserved in its own jelly. Some versions contain other offal.

DRIED CHICKEN FEET Easily preserved by being cleaned and dried, chicken feet (sometimes called Phoenix claws) are popular in Chinese cuisine.

PREPARING ORGAN MEAT

Most organ meat has some kind of a membrane. This needs to be removed before cooking as it will toughen and can make the meat distort. It is usually very easy to peel off.

PREPARING KIDNEYS FOR FRYING

A whole veal kidney is shown here. Beef and veal kidneys, which have multiple lobes, are very different to lamb, pig, and deer kidneys, which have a simple shape and usually very little fat to remove.

PREPARING LIVER

Liver is at its best if it is cooked pink, or else very gently and slowly – otherwise it can taste bitter.

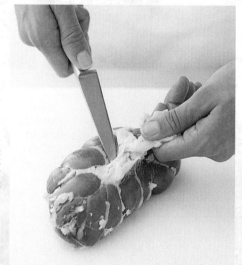

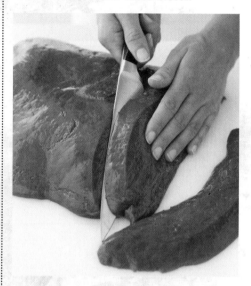

1 Carefully pull away and discard the white fat (suet) that surrounds the whole kidney – it will come away quite easily.

2 Lay the kidney upside down. With the point of a paring knife, cut around the fatty core and pull it away to release the membrane covering the kidney.

CALF'S LIVER This is excellent for frying because it cooks very quickly over a high heat. Cut away any membranes and arteries with a utility or small slicing knife, then slice the liver thickly.

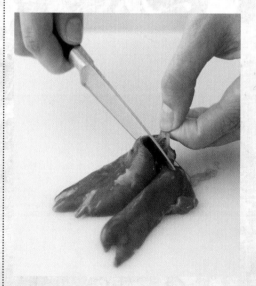

3 Discard the core. Peel the membrane off the whole kidney – it will slip off easily when you tug with your fingers.

4 Cut the kidney into bite-sized pieces following the natural lobes, then cut off the fatty cores from each piece. The kidney is now ready for frying.

CHICKEN LIVER Chicken livers are always good value. To clean chicken livers, use a paring knife to cut away any green patches, membrane, and the fibres around the centre of each.

PREPARING SWEETBREADS

Soaking sweetbreads whitens them and softens the fine filament that covers them.
If they are not to be used within 24 hours, soak them, then blanch them in salt water.

1 Soak the sweetbreads in cold running water for 1–2 hours, then peel off as much of the filament and patches of blood as possible. The filament is firm enough to peel off easily.

2 Soak them again in a solution of 1 tablespoon of vinegar per 1.5 litres (2¾ pints) water for a further 1–2 hours. Then peel off any remaining filament plus any small tubes that are to be found in and around the pieces.

PREPARING GIZZARD

The gizzard is usually already cleaned when bought with domestic poulty giblets, but you will need to clean and prepare the gizzards of game birds.

1 Cut the gizzard almost in half, right through the gritty part in the centre; they are tough muscles to cut. Turn them inside out to remove the grit and gizzard contents, then rinse thoroughly under running water.

2 Trim off any soiled pieces round the cut edges and then trim off all the thick silver skin surrounding it. Finally, slice or peel off the thick inner membrane that was next to the grit, trimming off any soiled parts.

PREPARING BRAINS

Remove excess blood by soaking the brains in strong brine for four hours. Then rinse, or leave in a bowl under a cold running tap. Peel off the membrane. Remove any bone fragments and as much remaining blood as possible. Poach very gently for 5 minutes. Leave to cool. Slice if wished.

MAKING BLACK PUDDING

These French-style black puddings are soft and creamy. Our recipe uses fresh pig's blood, but dried pig's blood can be bought from butchers' suppliers and reconstituted.

1 Mix together 1 tsp mixed spice, 1 tsp brown sugar, 85g (3oz) salt, 4 heaped tbsp finely chopped parsley, and 175g (6oz) breadcrumbs. Stir these into 3 litres (5¼ pints) fresh pig's blood with 750ml (1¼ pints) double cream. Dice 1.5kg (3lb 3oz) pork back fat into 7–10mm (¼–½in) cubes.

2 Fry 1.5kg (3lb 3oz) onions gently in 150g (5½oz) unsalted butter or 100ml (3½fl oz) vegetable oil in a large frying pan until softened but not browned. Cool and then add to the blood mixture. Stir in the diced fat, and mix everything together very thoroughly.

3 Knot one end of a 7m (23ft) length of ox runner. Fit the open end on to a funnel's nozzle, and pull the remaining skin on to the nozzle. Pour the blood mixture into the nozzle and start to fill the skin.

4 When pouring the blood mixture into the ox runner, grip the nozzle tightly to prevent the skin slipping off. Fill the skins quite loosely, as the mixture swells when cooked. Knot the end of the skin firmly.

5 Leave the pudding as a coil, or tie it into rings. To do this, divide the pudding into lengths and tie the ends with string. Then fold the skin over the knot and re-tie, then tie both ends together. This prevents the puddings from bursting at the ends, and makes them easier to handle.

6 Half-fill a large boiling pan with water and place a rack on the bottom. Bring the water to the boil, then remove the pan from the heat. Lower the puddings in carefully, and return the pan to a very low heat. Do not boil, or the puddings may burst.

7 If the puddings float, prick them with a sterilized needle or cocktail stick. Cook them very gently for 15 minutes, then prick them again. If the liquid that emerges is bloody, cook for another 5 minutes, or until the liquid comes out brown.

8 Drain off the water carefully because the hot puddings are fragile, or lift them out using the rack. Fill a clean sink with cold water, and cool the puddings in it for 15 minutes before handling. Refrigerate the puddings to make them firm, then cut them into slices to cook.

FAGGOTS

The mix of pork and pork offal seasoned with sage and onion makes this a flavoursome and highly nutritious dish.

THE CUT Pig liver and heart

SERVES 6
PREP 1 hr **COOK** 1 hr

900g (2lb) skinless boneless pork belly, trimmed and sinew removed

900g (2lb) streaky bacon rashers

250g (9oz) pig's liver

1 pig's heart

¼ tsp grated nutmeg

¼ tsp ground ginger

1 tsp chopped sage

1 tsp chopped marjoram

1 onion, chopped

¼ tsp each salt and freshly ground black pepper

550g (1¼lb) brown breadcrumbs

3 large eggs, lightly beaten

1 pig's caul, about 400g (14oz)

250ml (9fl oz) chicken stock

1 Preheat the oven to 190°C (375°F/Gas 5). Roughly chop all the meats and place them together in a large bowl. Add the spices, herbs, onion, salt, and pepper, and pass through a meat mincer.

2 Transfer the meat mixture to a large bowl. Add the breadcrumbs and eggs, mix to combine, and form into small balls of 60g (2oz) each.

3 Soften the caul in water and spread it out. Cut into squares large enough to cover each faggot. Wrap the caul around the faggots and place them in a roasting tray. Add in a little stock to prevent them from drying out, and cook in the oven for about 1 hour. Remove from the oven and spoon over the pan juices. Serve with mashed potatoes and some green vegetables such as peas.

PORK AND LIVER TERRINE

A classic country-style pâté with layers of ham, it is enriched with both cream and eggs.

 CUT Chicken liver and pork fat

SERVES 8
PREP 1 hr   **COOK** 1½ hrs

1 tbsp butter

1 onion, finely chopped

125g (4½oz) chicken livers, trimmed

250g (9oz) lean pork leg or shoulder

115g (4oz) pork fat

¼ tsp ground allspice

pinch of ground cloves

pinch of grated nutmeg

2 garlic cloves, crushed

2 tbsp brandy

2 eggs, lightly beaten

150ml (5fl oz) double cream

salt and freshly ground black pepper

200g (7oz) streaky bacon rashers, thinly sliced

200g (7oz) ham, thinly sliced

1 bay leaf

1 Preheat the oven to 180°C (350°F/Gas 4). Heat the butter in a frying pan, add the onion, and cook gently until soft and lightly browned. Set aside.

2 Mince the livers, pork, and fat. Place the meat in a large bowl, and add the spices, garlic, and brandy. Then add the eggs, cream, and cooked onions. Season and mix well to combine.

3 Line a 1 litre (1¾ pint) terrine with the bacon, leaving enough of an overhang to cover the added contents. Place one-third of the mixture over the bacon, pushing it firmly into the corners so that there are no air pockets. Cover with half the ham slices, then another third of the meat mixture, and press down firmly. Place the remaining ham slices over the top and add the remaining meat mixture. Fold the bacon over to cover the mixture completely. Cut extra pieces of bacon to fill in if there are any gaps. Place a bay leaf on the top and cover with the lid.

4 Place the terrine in a bain marie and cook in the oven for 1½ hours, or until the juices run clear when pierced in the middle. Leave to cool. Press the terrine down using weights, and leave for at least 3 days. To serve, turn the pâté out of the terrine and cut into slices.

CALF'S LIVER WITH SAGE

The aroma of sage leaves permeates the quickly cooked liver in this classic dish. Replace the lemon juice with balsamic vinegar for a sweet and sour twist.

 **CUT** Calf liver

SERVES 4
PREP 15 mins   **COOK** 5 mins

2 tbsp plain flour, seasoned with salt and pepper

450g (1lb) calf's liver, trimmed and sliced

1 tsp olive oil

1 tbsp butter, plus an extra knob of butter

handful of sage leaves

juice of 1 lemon

1 Place the flour in a shallow dish. Add the liver, toss to coat lightly, and shake off any excess. Heat the oil and 1 tablespoon of butter in a large frying pan over a medium-high heat. As the butter starts to foam, add the liver, making sure the pieces do not touch, and cook for about 2 minutes on each side. Do this in batches to avoid overcrowding the pan. Remove the liver from the pan, place on a serving dish, and keep warm.

2 Reduce the heat and add a knob of butter to the pan. Then add the sage leaves and, as soon as they start to fizzle, add the lemon juice. Place the sage leaves over the liver, pour over the buttery juices, and serve hot.

VARIATION

Calf's liver with bacon Cook a few rashers of bacon in the same pan as the liver, until browned. Place the bacon on the liver and add a knob of butter to the pan. Cook the butter and bacon juices, stirring, until they start to foam. Pour the cooking juices over the liver and bacon. Serve hot.

SAUTÉED LIVER, ONIONS, AND POTATOES

The sweet, caramelized onions are the star of this delicious dish, and can be cooked the night before if you want to get ahead.

THE CUT Calf's liver

SERVES 6
PREP 15–20 mins   **COOK** 1 hr

90ml (3fl oz) olive oil

1kg (2¼lb) large onions, sliced

salt and freshly ground black pepper

750g (1lb 10oz) calf's liver

FOR THE MASHED POTATOES

635g (1lb 6oz) potatoes, peeled and cut into chunks

4 tbsp milk

60g (2oz) butter

1 Heat two-thirds of the oil in a frying pan over a low heat. Add the onions, season lightly, and cover with foil. Cook the onions for 25–30 minutes, stirring occasionally, until softened.

2 Remove the foil from the pan, increase the heat to medium-high, and cook, stirring constantly, for 5–7 minutes until caramelized

and golden, but not browned. Transfer to a bowl with a slotted spoon, leaving any excess oil in the pan.

3 Meanwhile, place the potatoes in a saucepan with salted water, cover, and bring to the boil. Simmer for 15–20 minutes until tender. Drain thoroughly and mash with a fork. Heat the milk in a separate saucepan, add the butter, season, and mix. Gradually add the hot milk to the potatoes, beating until light and fluffy. Taste and adjust the seasoning, and keep warm.

4 Slice the liver about 5mm (¼in) thick and season. Heat the remaining oil in the pan over a high heat. Add the liver and cook for 45–60 seconds on each side, until just browned, but still pink inside. Transfer to a plate and keep warm. Return the onions to the pan and stir quickly over a high heat for 30–60 seconds until very hot. Season and serve at once on warmed plates with the mashed potatoes.

VENISON LIVER WITH ONIONS

A glorious combination of melting liver and sweet, almost caramelized, onions, this classic comfort food takes minutes to prepare.

THE CUT Venison liver

SERVES 4
PREP 15 mins   **COOK** 1 hr

4 tbsp olive oil

60g (2oz) butter

450g (1lb) onions, thinly sliced

½ tsp thyme leaves

splash of lemon juice

salt and freshly ground black pepper

plain flour, seasoned with salt and pepper, for dusting

600g (1lb 5oz) venison liver, trimmed, sinew removed, and cut into 1cm (½in) slices

chopped flat-leaf parsley, to garnish (optional)

1 Heat half the oil and half the butter in a large frying pan over a high heat. Add the onions and stir to coat in the fat until they start to colour. Reduce the heat to low, add the thyme, and cook for 45 minutes, stirring occasionally, until the

onions are soft and lightly browned. Add the lemon juice and season, then set aside in the pan to keep warm.

2 Heat the remaining oil and butter in a frying pan. Place the flour in a shallow dish. Add the liver, toss to coat, and shake off any excess. Fry the liver in the pan for 1 minute on each side, until golden brown on the outside, but still pink inside. Do this in batches to avoid overcrowding the pan.

3 Spoon the onions onto a warm serving platter and arrange the liver on top. Garnish with some parsley, if you like, and serve with mashed potatoes.

VARIATION

Lamb livers with onions Use lamb livers in place of venison liver and add 1 teaspoon balsamic vinegar to the onion mixture. Cook as above and serve hot.

MOROCCAN SKEWERED LIVERS AND HEARTS

This grilled dish of tender meat is the perfect addition to a summer barbecue, and is delicious served rare.

THE CUT Lamb liver and heart

SERVES 4
PREP 15 mins, plus soaking and marinating
COOK 5–6 mins

450g (1lb) lamb livers, trimmed

450g (1lb) lamb hearts, trimmed

2 garlic cloves, crushed

1 tbsp chopped parsley

1 tsp ground cumin

1½ tsp paprika

sea salt

1 tbsp olive oil

1 Soak 12 wooden skewers in cold water for at least 1 hour. Remove the sinew and connective tissue from the livers and hearts. Chop the hearts into cubes suitable for slipping onto a skewer.

2 Place the livers and hearts in a large bowl. Add the remaining ingredients and mix to coat. Leave to marinate for at least 1 hour at room temperature.

3 Set the grill at its medium setting. Thread the livers and hearts onto the skewers, alternating between the two. Grill for 3–4 minutes, turning occasionally as they cook, until browned and evenly cooked on the outside, but still pink on the inside. Serve hot with a green salad and tahini.

DO NOT CHOP!

The livers should be left whole to ensure that they do not fall off the skewer during both the cooking and serving process.

QUICK FRY VENISON HEARTS

The easy-to-prepare marinade adds a depth of flavour to this meltingly tender meat.

▶CUT Venison heart

SERVES 2
PREP 15 mins, plus marinating
COOK 5 mins, plus resting

1 large or 2 small venison hearts, trimmed and gristle removed

115ml (4oz) olive oil

2 tbsp red wine vinegar

sprig of rosemary, bruised

1 tsp juniper berries, crushed

salt and freshly ground black pepper

1 tsp butter

2 tsp olive oil

1 Slice the hearts into 1cm (½in) thick pieces and place in a bowl. In a separate bowl, mix the oil, vinegar, and herbs. Season with a pinch of salt and a few grinds of pepper.

2 Pour the oil and herb mixture over the hearts. Mix well to coat and leave to marinate overnight, or for about 12 hours.

3 Remove the hearts from the marinade and pat dry with kitchen paper. Heat the butter and oil in a heavy-based frying pan over a high heat.

4 Add the hearts to the pan and brown for 1 minute on each side. Remove from the heat. Remove the hearts from the pan, place on a serving dish, and leave to rest for at least 4 minutes. Serve hot with a green salad and chips.

COOK WITH CARE

It is very important to dry the hearts really well before cooking to ensure that they cook quickly and remain tender.

DIRTY RICE

A classic recipe from America's Deep South, this dish gets its name from the colour given by the meat.

▶CUT Chicken liver

SERVES 6
PREP 15 mins   **COOK** 1 hr, plus resting

4 tbsp olive oil

1 onion, finely chopped

½ celery stick, finely chopped

1 green pepper, finely chopped

250g (9oz) minced pork

200g (7oz) chicken livers, trimmed and finely chopped

1 green chilli, deseeded and finely chopped

2 garlic cloves, finely chopped

1 tsp smoked paprika

1 tsp coriander seeds, crushed

300g (10oz) long-grain white rice

salt and freshly ground black pepper

750ml (1¼pints) hot chicken stock

large sprig of thyme

handful of flat-leaf parsley leaves, finely chopped

1 tbsp finely chopped oregano leaves

1 Preheat the oven to 160°C (325°F/Gas 3). Heat 3 tablespoons of oil in a large, flameproof casserole or Dutch oven. Add the onion, celery, and green pepper and cook for about 5 minutes, until soft. Remove from the casserole and set aside.

2 Pour the remaining oil into the casserole and increase the heat to high. Add the pork and the chicken livers, and cook for about 5 minutes, turning occasionally, until the meat is well-browned. Then add the chilli, garlic, smoked paprika, and coriander seeds, and cook for a further 2 minutes.

3 Return the vegetables to the pan, stir in the rice, and season well. Then add the hot stock and thyme, and bring to the boil. Stir the rice well, cover, and transfer to the oven. Cook in the oven for 30–40 minutes, stirring occasionally, until the rice is cooked and the stock absorbed.

4 Remove from the heat and leave to rest for about 5 minutes. Remove and discard the thyme and stir in the parsley and oregano. Taste and adjust the seasoning, if needed. Serve hot.

LAMB HEARTS STEWED WITH PRUNES

The natural sweetness of this warm and flavoursome dish is enhanced by the addition of dried prunes.

THE CUT Lamb heart

SERVES 4
PREP 20 mins **COOK** 1 hr 45 mins

2 tbsp butter

16 baby onions

2 lamb hearts, trimmed and sliced

1 tbsp plain flour

200ml (7fl oz) red wine

sea salt and freshly ground black pepper

1 clove

1 tsp redcurrant jelly

12 dried prunes, pitted

zest of 1 lemon

1 Melt the butter in a large saucepan over a medium heat. Add the onions and cook for about 5 minutes, or until lightly browned. Remove from the pan and set aside.

2 Pat the hearts dry with kitchen paper to remove any excess blood. Place the flour in a shallow dish. Add the hearts, toss lightly to coat, and shake off any excess. Add the hearts to the pan and cook until well-browned.

3 Pour the wine and 200ml (7fl oz) water into the pan. Season well and add the clove and redcurrant jelly. Cover the pan and simmer for 1 hour 15 minutes. Check occasionally, and add more water if it looks like it is drying out.

4 Then add the prunes and lemon zest, return the onions to the pan, and cook for a further 20 minutes, or until the meat is cooked. Taste and adjust the seasoning. If the sauce looks too thin, remove the meat, onions, and prunes, and reduce a little by rapid boiling. Return the ingredients to the pan and stir through. Serve hot with rice or mashed potatoes.

VARIATION

Rabbit stew with prunes Use rabbit in place of the lamb hearts, and brown flour in place of the plain flour. Add 1 teaspoon chopped rosemary and cook as above.

CHICKEN LIVER WITH MARSALA

This delicious dish uses a simple sauce from the Piedmont region of Italy, where wild mushrooms, including truffle, grow in abundance.

THE CUT Chicken liver

SERVES 4
PREP 15 mins, plus soaking
COOK 10 mins

60g (2oz) butter

400g (14oz) chicken livers, trimmed

2 shallots, finely chopped

30g (1oz) dried ceps, soaked in water for 30 minutes and the water reserved

1 tsp tomato purée

4 tbsp Marsala

1 Heat the butter in a large saucepan over a medium heat. Add the livers and fry for about 2 minutes. Remove with a slotted spoon, place on a plate lined with kitchen paper, and set aside.

2 Add the shallots to the pan and cook until soft. Then add the ceps and tomato purée and stir to combine. Stir in the Marsala and shake the pan lightly to mix through.

3 Return the livers to the pan and mix well to coat with the sauce. Taste and adjust seasoning, if needed, and add a little of the reserved soaking water if the sauce seems too thick. Serve hot with tagliatelle mixed with a little truffle oil.

VARIATION

Lamb liver with dry sherry Use lamb livers, cut into small pieces, in place of the chicken livers, 75g (2½oz) button mushrooms in place of the dried ceps, and dry sherry in place of the Marsala. Cook as above and serve hot.

CHICKEN LIVER PÂTÉ

This rich and smooth pâté is flavoured with brandy, sage,
and garlic. Easy to make, it serves as a delicious starter.

THE CUT Chicken liver

SERVES 8–10
PREP 20 mins **COOK** 10 mins

300g (10oz) butter, softened

225g (8oz) chicken livers, trimmed

¼ tsp sage

1 garlic clove

2 tbsp brandy

sea salt and freshly ground black pepper

50g (1¾oz) clarified butter, to seal

VARIATION

Chopped liver with boiled eggs Heat 3 tablespoons
of chicken fat in the saucepan over a medium
heat. Add 1 chopped onion, season with a pinch
of salt, and fry gently for about 6 minutes until
softened. Remove from the pan and set side.
Add 3 more tablespoons of chicken fat to the
pan. Add the chicken liver, when the fat is hot,
and cook until lightly coloured, but still pink
inside. Do not overcook the livers. Transfer the
ingredients to a food processor. Add another 3
tablespoons of chicken fat and 1 roughly chopped
hard-boiled egg. Pulse briefly until the livers are
roughly chopped and still coarse. Season to taste
and transfer the mixture to a large bowl. Top with
another finely chopped hard-boiled egg and some
crispy chicken skin, if you like, and chill. Serve
with slices of challah bread and pickles.

CREAMY CONSISTENCY

For a very smooth pâté, at stage 4 press
the processed mixture through a sieve
using the back of a ladle. Make sure you
do this before the butter begins to cool.

1 Trim the livers of any discolouration and pat dry with kitchen paper to remove any excess blood. Heat 100g (3½oz) of the butter in a saucepan over a medium heat. Add the livers and cook for 8 minutes, stirring, until cooked through. Then add the sage and garlic and cook, stirring, for 1–2 minutes.

2 Pour in the brandy and season with half a teaspoon of sea salt and a good grinding of pepper. Tip the mixture into a food processor, scraping up all the bits with a wooden spatula. Pulse the mixture thoroughly, adding the remaining butter a little at a time, to create a smooth paste.

3 Transfer the paste to a ramekin, pressing it down lightly with the back of a spoon to pack it firmly in. Leave to cool and set.

4 Cover the cooled mixture with a layer of the clarified butter and place in the fridge to chill overnight. Serve cold with toast.

CALF BRAINS
IN BLACK BUTTER

The touch of lemon cuts through the creamy texture in this easy-to-cook, melt-in-the-mouth delicacy.

 **Calf brain**

SERVES 4
PREP 30 mins, plus soaking and chilling
COOK 25 mins

2 calf brains

2 tbsp flour, seasoned with salt and pepper

2 tbsp olive oil

1 tbsp butter

1 tbsp chopped flat-leaf parsley

juice of 1 lemon

FOR THE COURT BOUILLON

1 small onion, sliced

5 black peppercorns

1 bay leaf

6 flat-leaf parsley stalks

sprig of thyme

1 tbsp white wine vinegar

1 Place the brains in a large saucepan, cover with cold water and leave to soak for about 2 hours, changing the water twice to remove the blood.

2 For the court bouillon, place all the ingredients in a large saucepan big enough to hold the brains and add 1.5 litres (2¾ pints) cold water. Bring to the boil and then reduce the heat to a simmer. Add the brains to the pan and poach for 20 minutes. Then drain and leave to cool. Chill the cooled meat in the fridge for at least 3 hours.

3 Peel off the membrane using a pair of scissors and slice the brains. Place the flour in a large shallow dish. Add the brains, toss lightly to coat, and shake off any excess. Heat the oil and 1 tablespoon of butter in a large frying pan over a medium heat. When the butter starts to foam, add the brains and fry for 5 minutes, until lightly browned all over. Remove with a slotted spoon and drain on a plate lined with kitchen paper.

4 Heat the remaining butter in the pan until it begins to turn brown and produces a distinct nutty smell. Pour in the lemon juice and swirl it in the pan. Divide the brains between 4 warm plates, sprinkle over the parsley, and pour the butter and lemon mix over. Serve immediately.

LAMB SWEETBREADS CROSTINI

A delicious first course or light dish, the crunchy toast sets off the creamy texture of the sweetbreads.

 **Lamb sweetbreads**

SERVES 4
PREP 10 mins, plus pressing
COOK 10 mins

750g (1lb 10oz) lamb sweetbreads

75g (2½oz) flour, seasoned with salt and pepper

100g (3½oz) butter

1 tbsp capers

1 tbsp chopped flat-leaf parsley

sea salt and freshly ground black pepper

juice of 1 lemon

round toasts cut from a day-old baguette

1 Thoroughly rinse the sweetbreads with water. Blanch them in hot water for 1–2 minutes, then plunge in cold water to cool.

2 Peel off and discard the outer skin using a pair of scissors. Press the sweetbreads between two plates with a weight on top, for 1 hour. Then slice the sweetbreads into 2.5cm (1in) pieces. Place the flour in a shallow dish. Add the meat, toss to coat, and shake off any excess.

3 Heat the butter in a frying pan over a medium heat. When the butter starts to foam, add the sweetbreads and cook for 5–6 minutes, until lightly browned all over. Then add the capers and parsley, season well, and squeeze over the lemon juice. Remove from the heat and spoon the sweetbreads onto the toasts. Serve hot.

PERFECT SUBSTITUTE

Lamb sweetbreads can be replaced with veal sweetbreads and prepared in the same way.

PIG KIDNEYS TURBIGO

A homely and comforting brunch or supper dish, it is full of spicy, earthy flavours. It is thought to have been named after one of Napoleon III's battle victories.

THE CUT Pig kidney

SERVES 4
PREP 30 mins **COOK** 20 mins

4 pig kidneys

salt and freshly ground black pepper

1 tsp oil

2 tsp butter

4 chipolata sausages, halved

1 small onion, chopped

140g (5oz) button mushrooms, quartered

2 tsp Dijon mustard

1 tbsp red wine (optional)

splash of Worcester sauce

1 Slice the kidneys in half horizontally and slice each half vertically. Remove as much of the white core as you can, cut into even slices, and season.

2 Heat the oil and 1 teaspoon of butter in a frying pan. When the butter begins to foam, add the kidney pieces, spaced well apart. Fry for about 5 minutes, until well-browned. There should be a little blood still showing. Remove from the pan and set aside.

3 Add the chipolatas to the pan and cook over a medium heat for 1–2 minutes, until well-browned. Reduce the heat, add the remaining butter, and stir in the onions. Cook until soft. Then add the mushrooms and fry for 1–2 minutes.

4 Stir in the mustard, add the red wine, if using, and simmer for 1–2 minutes. Return the kidneys to the pan along with any juices they may have exuded. Add the sauce, heat through, and check the seasoning. Serve hot with pilaf rice.

ANDALUCIAN TRIPE

This traditional Spanish stew is flavoured with chorizo and made tender with slow cooking.

THE CUT Ox tripe

SERVES 4
PREP 30 mins, plus soaking **COOK** 3 hrs

4 dried sweet red peppers

2 tbsp extra virgin olive oil

60g (2oz) unsalted butter

1 slice of white or brown bread

1 onion, finely chopped

2 garlic cloves, chopped

75g (2½oz) chorizo, sliced

2 tbsp chopped flat-leaf parsley

½ x 400g can chopped tomatoes

1 walnut, shelled

¼ tsp ground cloves

¼ tsp ground cumin

sea salt and freshly ground black pepper

200ml (7fl oz) white wine

500g (1lb 2oz) cooked ox tripe, cut into 2.5cm (1in) pieces

400g can chickpeas, drained

1 Soak the dried peppers in warm water for 1 hour. Heat the oil and butter in a saucepan over a medium heat. Add the bread and fry until crisp and golden on both sides. Remove with a slotted spoon and set aside.

2 Add the onion to the pan and fry until softened. Stir in the garlic and cook until soft. Then add the chorizo, parsley, and tomatoes. Cook the mixture, stirring, for 1–2 minutes.

3 Meanwhile, place the walnut, bread, cloves, cumin, and a little salt in a mortar and grind with a pestle until quite fine.

4 Drain the peppers, cut them in half, and remove the seeds. Then scrape out the flesh, discarding the skins. Add to the pan along with the wine, tripe, and chickpeas. Season and add just enough water to cover. Reduce the heat to a simmer, cover, and cook for 2–3 hours, until the tripe is tender.

5 Stir in the walnut and spice mixture and cook for 1–2 minutes, until the sauce thickens a little. Serve as a tapas or in earthenware bowls sprinkled with a little paprika and some crusty bread.

TRIPES À LA MODE DE CAEN

A classic French dish using the cider and Calvados of the region to create a satisfying homely dish.

 THE CUT Ox tripe and calf's foot

SERVES 4
PREP 30 mins   **COOK** 3 hrs

1 onion, quartered

1 leek, trimmed

4 garlic cloves

2 cloves

bunch of flat-leaf parsley

300g (10oz) pork fat

1 kg (2¼lb) ox tripe, including all four types, blanched and cut into 5cm (2in) squares

3 large carrots, cut in thin slices

1 calf's foot, blanched and cut in half lengthways

240ml (8fl oz) cider

1 tsp sea salt

freshly ground black pepper

1 tbsp Calvados

1 Wrap the onion, leek, garlic, cloves, and parsley in a muslin cloth and tie with butcher's string. Spread the fat over the bottom of a large, heavy-based saucepan. Place half the tripe over it, cover with half the carrots, and then half the calf's foot. Place the muslin bag over, add another layer of the tripe, followed by the remaining carrots and calf's foot.

2 Pour in the cider and just enough water to cover the tripe well, season, and place over a low heat. Push the tripe under the liquid to prevent it from blackening. Cover the pan with greaseproof paper. Bring to a simmer, but do not boil. Then cover and simmer for 2½ hours, or until the tripe and foot are very tender.

3 Remove from the heat and discard the muslin. Then remove the calf's foot and separate the meat from the bones. Discard the bones. Stir the meat back into the pan with the Calvados, taste and adjust the seasoning. Serve in large, hot soup plates with a crusty baguette.

BLACK PUDDING

This northern English version of the traditional European blood sausage is made with barley and oatmeal.

 THE CUT Pig's blood

SERVES 15
PREP 30 mins, plus soaking and cooling
COOK 1½ hrs

oil, for greasing

500g (1lb 2oz) barley or pearl barley

1.2 litres (2 pints) full-fat milk

250g (9oz) bread, torn into small pieces

1.2 litres (2 pints) fresh pig's blood, or reconstituted dried pig's blood

500g (1lb 2oz) beef suet, grated

250g (9oz) fine oatmeal

2 tsp dried sage

2 tsp each salt and freshly ground black pepper

1–2 tbsp butter, for frying

1 Preheat the oven to 180°C (350°F/Gas 4). Grease 2 large roasting tins. Rinse the barley under cold running water. Transfer to a pot, add enough water to cover, and cook over a low heat for 30 minutes. Drain and set aside.

2 Warm the milk until lukewarm, add the bread, and leave to soak for 10 minutes. Pour the blood into a large bowl and stir in the milk and bread mixture. Add the barley, suet, oatmeal, and sage. Season with salt and pepper and mix thoroughly to combine.

3 Divide the mixture equally between the 2 roasting tins, making sure they are no more than three-quarters full. Press down to get an even finish. Bake for about 1 hour. Remove from the oven and leave to cool. Then cut into squares and fry in a little butter. Serve with fried apples, or alongside mashed potatoes, if you like.

BRAWN

Pig's head has been cooked the world over and this method of extracting all the meat into a firm set mould is classically European.

THECUT Pig's head and trotters

SERVES 10
PREP 1 hr   **COOK** 4½ hrs, plus setting

1 pig's head, about 8.5kg (17lb), split in two

2 pig trotters, about 300g (10oz) each, rinsed

bunch of sage or parsley stalks

2 garlic cloves, crushed

2 tsp black peppercorns

3 bay leaves

2 tsp sea salt

skin of 1 onion

2 green chillies (optional)

salt and freshly ground black pepper

2 tbsp chopped flat-leaf parsley

1 tbsp chopped marjoram

1 Place the meats in a large pan. Add all the other ingredients, except the herbs, and cover with water. Bring to the boil, then reduce the heat to a simmer. Skim off any froth and cook for about 4 hours, or until the meat falls off the bone. Remove from the heat and leave to cool.

2 Strain the cooking liquid and return to the pan. Boil rapidly, skimming off any froth, until reduced by half.

3 Meanwhile, remove the trotters. Remove all the meat from the head and discard the bones. Roughly chop the meat and season.

4 Strain the stock through a fine sieve into a bowl. Wipe the pan clean. Pour about 500ml (16fl oz) of the stock back into the pan. Add the meat and herbs, and simmer for about 5 minutes.

5 Pour into a pudding bowl or terrine mould. Leave to set in a cool place until the jelly is set solid. Dip the base of the terrine in hot water to unmould its contents, and then turn it out onto a serving platter. Serve with a salad, toast, and mustard or baked potatoes.

CHITTERLINGS

Often called Chitlins, this lightly spiced dish from America's Deep South is made by slow-cooking pig intestines.

THECUT Pig intestines

SERVES 4
PREP 15 mins, plus washing and soaking
COOK 3½ hrs

2kg (4½lb) chitterlings (pig intestines)

2 potatoes

2 tbsp malt vinegar

1 onion, sliced

2 sweet red peppers, deseeded and sliced

1 tsp chilli flakes

2 garlic cloves, finely crushed with a little salt

2 tbsp white wine vinegar

250ml (9fl oz) chicken stock

1 Wash the chitterlings thoroughly under cold running water, removing any discoloured membrane. Place them in a large bowl, cover with water, and soak for 2 hours.

2 Remove the chitterlings from the bowl and wash again under cold running water. Place them in a separate bowl, add the potatoes and malt vinegar, and leave to soak for another 2 hours.

3 Drain and rinse the chitterlings and discard the potatoes. Place the chitterlings in a large saucepan. Add the onion, peppers, chilli flakes, garlic, and vinegar. Then add the stock and just enough water to cover.

4 Place the pan over a high heat and bring to the boil. Then reduce the heat to a simmer and cook for 3½ hours, stirring occasionally, until the chitterlings are tender. Remove from the heat and serve hot with greens.

OX TONGUE WITH BEETROOT AND CAPERS

Ox tongue needs to be brined and cooked in advance. This tenderizes it and enhances the flavour.

THE CUT Ox tongue

SERVES 6
PREP 15 mins, plus cooling and curing
COOK 3–4 hrs

1.5–2kg (3lb 3oz– 4½lb) ox tongue

2 beetroots, roasted or lightly boiled, peeled, and sliced into thick matchsticks

2 tbsp small capers

FOR THE BRINE

300g (10oz) sea salt

200g (7oz) brown sugar

3 bay leaves

5 juniper berries

FOR THE COURT BOUILLON

3 celery sticks

2 onions, halved

2 leeks, trimmed

1 carrot

2 tsp black peppercorns

1 whole garlic bulb, cut in half horizontally

1 cinnamon stick

2 bay leaves

sprig of thyme

sprig of rosemary

FOR THE DRESSING

2 tsp Dijon mustard

2 tbsp olive oil

1 tbsp white wine vinegar

juice from ½ lemon

1 tbsp chopped flat-leaf parsley

salt and freshly ground black pepper

1 For the brine, place all the ingredients in a large saucepan. Add 2 litres (3½ pints) cold water and bring to the boil. Remove from the heat and leave to cool completely. Pour the brine into a large non-reactive container and add the ox tongue. Leave to cure for 2–5 days.

2 Remove the ox tongue from the brine, rinse, and pat dry with kitchen paper. Discard the brine. For the court bouillon, place all the ingredients in a large, deep saucepan. Pour in 1.5 litres (2¾ pints) of water and add the ox tongue. Bring to the boil and skim off any grey scum that rises to the surface.

3 Reduce the heat to a simmer, cover partially, and cook for 3–4 hours, until tender. Remove from the heat and leave to cool. When cool enough to handle, remove the tongue, take off the skin, and trim any bone and gristle from around the root. Discard the cooking liquid.

4 For the dressing, place all the ingredients in a small bowl, whisk to combine, and season to taste. Mix the beetroots and the capers in a separate bowl. Slice the tongue thinly and place on 4 plates. Sprinkle over the beetroots and capers and drizzle over the dressing.

LAMB TONGUE WITH GREENS AND SMOKED BACON

This dish has a remarkable combination of colour, flavour, and texture, and makes for a perfect first course.

THE CUT Lamb tongue

SERVES 6
PREP 15 mins, plus soaking and cooling
COOK 1 hr

6 lamb tongues, about 100g (3½oz) in total, soaked in cold water for at least 2 hours

peel of 1 lemon

2 cinnamon sticks

½ tsp sea salt

1 small green cabbage, such as Savoy or Hispi

3 tbsp olive oil

140g (5oz) smoked back bacon, cut into lardons

1 tsp soy sauce

1 Rinse well and drain the lamb tongues. Place them in a large saucepan and cover with about 750ml (1¼ pints) water. Bring to the boil over a high heat, and skim off any froth that rises to the surface. Then add the lemon peel, cinnamon, and salt. Reduce the heat to a simmer and cook for about 45 minutes until the meat is tender.

2 Meanwhile, remove the tough outer leaves of the cabbage. Cut the cabbage into quarters and shred finely. Wash thoroughly in a colander. Set aside with the leaves still wet.

3 Remove the tongues from the pan and leave to cool. When cool enough to handle, remove the skin, pat dry with kitchen paper, and keep warm.

4 Heat the oil in a large frying pan over a high heat. Add the bacon and fry until well-browned. Then add the cabbage and stir thoroughly to coat in the oil and bacon juices. Cook for a few minutes until it wilts.

5 Add the soy sauce and mix thoroughly. Remove from the heat. Place mounds of the cabbage mixture on 4 warmed plates. Slice the lamb tongues, place them on the cabbage and dribble over any cooking juices. Serve hot.

CALF TONGUE

An easy-to-prepare dish, it is usually served with the cooking liquid poured over the tongue, as its delicate flavour goes well with the tender meat.

THE CUT Calf tongue

SERVES 4
PREP 15 mins   **COOK** 3 hrs, plus cooling

1 calf tongue, about 200g (7oz)

1 celery stick, roughly chopped

6 black peppercorns

small onion, studded with 5 cloves

1 whole garlic bulb

1 Place all the ingredients in a large stock pot. Pour in just enough water to cover the meat. Bring to the boil, then reduce the heat to a simmer, and skim off any grey scum that rises to the surface. Cook the tongue for about 3 hours. Remove from the heat and leave the tongue to cool completely in the stock.

2 Remove the tongue from the pot. Peel the skin using a sharp knife. Strain the stock and reserve the liquid. Cut the tongue into thick slices and serve hot with some of the cooking liquid poured over. It can also be served cold, cut into thin slices, along with mustard and piccalilli.

VARIATION

Calf's head and feet with vinaigrette You can use calf's head and feet in place of the tongue, and cook the dish for 4 hours. Remove the meat from the bones, discarding the skin and bones. For the vinaigrette, combine 3 tablespoons of olive oil, 1 tablespoon of lemon juice, and 1 teaspoon wholegrain mustard in a bowl. Season with a pinch of salt, 3 grinds of black pepper, and a pinch of caster sugar. Mix well to combine. Serve the meat cold with the vinaigrette.

PIED DE COCHON À LA STE MENEHOULD

In this classic French method of preparing pig trotters, slow-cooking with vinegar helps to soften the bones so that they can be eaten as well.

THE CUT Pig trotters

SERVES 4
PREP 20 mins, plus cooling   **COOK** 8½ hrs

4 front trotters, about 300g (10oz) each, tied in pairs with butcher's string

200ml (7fl oz) white wine

200ml (7fl oz) white wine vinegar

6 cloves

2 bay leaves

sprig of marjoram

4 tsp sugar

½ tsp ginger

2 garlic cloves, crushed

salt and freshly ground black pepper

25g (scant 1oz) fine breadcrumbs

1 Place the trotters in a large flameproof casserole. Pour the wine and vinegar over. Then add the cloves, bay leaves, marjoram, sugar, ginger, and garlic. Season with 2 teaspoons of salt and add just enough water to cover the meat. Bring to the boil.

2 Reduce the heat to a simmer, cover, and cook for 8 hours, topping with water as necessary. You can also cook the trotters in a slow cooker or in the oven at 150°C (300°F/Gas 2) for 8 hours.

3 Remove from the heat and leave to cool slightly. Remove the trotters from the cooking liquid and place on a large plate. Place another plate on top and press them together, to help the trotters retain their shape while cooling. Leave to cool completely. Preheat the oven to 190°C (375°F/Gas 5).

4 Remove the butcher's string carefully and separate the trotters. Sprinkle each trotter with the breadcrumbs and transfer to the oven. Cook in the oven for 30 minutes. Set the grill at its highest setting.

5 Remove from the oven and brown quickly under the grill. Season well. Strain the cooking juices and place in a large bowl. Taste and adjust the seasoning, if needed. Place the trotters on a large serving dish and serve with some of the strained cooking juices poured over.

SCRATCHINGS

The perfect snack to go with an aperitif, this delicious dish is made by drying and roasting pig skin.

THE CUT Pig skin

SERVES 8
PREP 15 mins, plus overnight drying
COOK 2 hrs

1.35–2kg (3–4½lb) pig skin

1 tbsp fine sea salt

1 Place the pig skin on a clean work surface and cut into 2cm (¾in) strips. Place the strips on a baking sheet and chill in the fridge overnight to help them dry out.

2 Preheat the oven to 150°C (300°F/Gas 2). Remove the baking tray from the fridge. Sprinkle the salt evenly over the pig skins and transfer the baking sheet to the oven.

3 Roast the skin in the oven for 1 hour. Then remove from the oven, turn it over, and return to the heat for 1 more hour, until crisp all over. Remove and drain on a plate lined with kitchen paper. Serve hot.

SPICY TWIST

For a variety of flavours, sprinkle with different spices, such as Chinese five-spice powder or paprika, after they come out of the oven.

OX CHEEKS WITH GREMOLATA

The rich flavour and gelatinous texture of this dish contrasts perfectly with the citrussy dressing.

THE CUT Ox cheeks

SERVES 4
PREP 30 mins   **COOK** 4½ hrs, plus resting

1kg (2¼lb) ox cheeks

salt and freshly ground black pepper

1–2 tbsp olive oil

1 tbsp butter

8 shallots

3 carrots, sliced thickly at an angle

500ml (16fl oz) beef stock

1 bay leaf

2–3 sprigs of thyme

FOR THE GREMOLATA

2 tbsp chopped flat-leaf parsley

1 garlic clove, finely chopped

grated zest of 1 lemon

1 Preheat the oven to 150°C (300°F/Gas 2). Season the ox cheeks well. Heat the oil in a flameproof casserole. Add the meat and cook until well-browned. Remove from the pan and set aside. Add the butter to the pan. Then add the shallots and carrots, and cook until browned.

2 Reduce the heat and return the meat to the pan. Pour in the stock and reduce the heat to a simmer. Add the herbs and cover with a disc of greaseproof paper, cut to fit snugly in the pan, to keep the moisture in. Cover and braise in the oven for 3½–4 hours. Check to make sure the liquid does not reduce too much and top up if necessary.

3 Remove the casserole from the oven. Leave the meat to rest in the liquid for at least 30 minutes. Meanwhile, for the gremolata, mix the parsley, garlic, and lemon zest in a bowl.

4 Remove the meat and vegetables with a slotted spoon. Strain the liquid into a separate pan and discard the herbs. Cook the sauce over a low heat to reduce a little. Taste and adjust the seasoning, if needed. Slice the cheeks and add to the sauce along with the vegetables to reheat. Remove from the heat. Sprinkle a spoonful of gremolata over the cheeks and serve with the shallots, carrots, and some of the sauce.

CASTILLIAN PIG TROTTERS

Ground almonds show a Moorish influence in this rich, flavoursome, and lightly spiced dish.

 **Pig trotters**

SERVES 4
PREP 30 mins   **COOK** 2½ hrs

2 onions

4 cloves

4 front trotters, split lengthwise

3 bay leaves

salt and freshly ground black pepper

1 tbsp lard

1 garlic clove, finely chopped

1 tbsp almonds, roughly chopped

1 tbsp flour

125ml (4¼fl oz) white wine

1 tsp hot paprika

2 carrots, diced

1 Stud 1 onion with the cloves. Wash the trotters thoroughly and place them in a large, lidded stock pot. Add the studded onion and bay leaves, and pour in just enough water to cover the meat. Bring to the boil.

2 Then reduce the heat to a simmer and season with salt and pepper. Cover and cook for 2 hours, until the meat is almost falling off the bone. Remove from the heat. Use a slotted spoon to lift the trotters out of the pot. Place them on a large plate, cover with foil, and set aside. Strain and reserve the cooking liquid.

3 Heat the lard in a shallow frying pan over a medium-low heat. Thinly slice the remaining onion. Add the sliced onion and garlic to the pan and fry until soft. Stir in the almonds and flour, and cook until lightly browned.

4 Add 500ml (16fl oz) of the strained cooking liquid to the pan. Then pour in the wine, stirring continuously to prevent the formation of lumps. Season with salt, pepper, and paprika.

5 Add the carrots and simmer for 10 minutes. Then gently place the trotters in the pan and simmer for a further 20 minutes. Remove from the heat. Serve hot with rice. It can also be chilled in the fridge overnight and reheated the next day.

BRAISED OXTAIL WITH CLEMENTINE

Oxtail is rich and robust, and braising it very slowly tenderizes it completely. The fruity sweetness and texture of prunes and clementines complement the meat well.

 **Oxtail**

SERVES 4–6
PREP 20 mins   **COOK** 3 hrs 15 mins

2 oxtails, about 1.35kg (3lb) each, cut into joints

salt and freshly ground black pepper

2 tbsp olive oil

2 red onions, sliced

3 garlic cloves, finely chopped

a pinch of dried chilli flakes

350ml (12fl oz) red wine

4 star anise

handful of black peppercorns

1 bay leaf

8 soft prunes, stoned and chopped

800ml (1½ pints) hot beef stock

4 clementines or 2 oranges, peeled and sliced into rings

small bunch of curly parsley leaves, finely chopped

1 Preheat the oven to 150°C (300°F/Gas 2). Season the oxtail with salt and pepper. Heat half the oil in a large flameproof casserole over a medium heat, then add the meat in batches and fry for 8–10 minutes until browned on all sides. Remove with a slotted spoon and set aside.

2 Heat the remaining oil in the casserole over a medium heat, add the onions, and cook for 3–4 minutes to soften. Stir through the garlic and chilli flakes, then pour in the wine and let it simmer for about 5 minutes until slightly reduced. Return the meat to the casserole and add the star anise, peppercorns, bay leaf, and prunes, and pour over just enough stock to cover the meat. Bring to the boil, then reduce to a simmer. Add the remaining stock, cover, and place in the oven for about 2½ hours. Check occasionally that it is not drying out, and top up with a little hot water if needed.

3 Then add the clementines or oranges, return the casserole to the oven, and cook, uncovered, for a further 30 minutes, until the liquid has thickened slightly and the meat has fallen off the bones. Stir occasionally to keep the oxtail moist and coated with the gravy. Remove from the heat. Remove and discard the bone, bay leaf, and star anise. Serve on a bed of pasta, sprinkled with some parsley.

VARIATION

Braised oxtail with Jerusalem artichokes Add 250g (9oz) Jerusalem artichokes, scrubbed or peeled and cut into chunks, and 2 sliced carrots to the mixture before cooking. Leave out the star anise, chilli flakes, and clementines. Add 1 tablespoon brandy with the red wine and cook as above. Serve spooned over fluffy mashed potatoes.

OSSO BUCO

Winter citrus lends a delicious fragrance to this Italian classic. Ask your butcher for a hind leg of veal as they are meatier than the front legs.

THE CUT Bone-in veal shin

SERVES 4–6
PREP 30–35 mins
COOK 1 hr 45 mins–2 hrs 15 mins

30g (1oz) flour, seasoned with salt and pepper

1.8kg (4lb) bone-in veal shins

2 tbsp vegetable oil, plus extra if required

30g (1oz) butter

1 carrot, thinly sliced

2 onions, finely chopped

250ml (9fl oz) white wine

400g can Italian plum tomatoes, drained and coarsely chopped

1 garlic clove, finely chopped

grated zest of 1 orange

salt and freshly ground black pepper

120ml (4fl oz) hot chicken or veal stock

FOR THE GREMOLATA

small bunch of flat-leaf parsley, leaves picked and finely chopped

grated zest of 1 lemon

1 garlic clove, finely chopped

1 Preheat the oven to 180°C (350°F/Gas 4). Place the flour in a shallow bowl. Add the veal pieces, toss to coat lightly, and shake off any excess.

2 Heat the oil and butter in a large flameproof casserole over a medium heat, add the meat (in batches and with extra oil, if necessary), and cook until well-browned. Transfer to a plate with a slotted spoon and set aside.

3 Add the carrot and onions to the casserole and cook, stirring occasionally, until soft. Add the wine and boil until reduced by half. Stir in the tomatoes, garlic, orange zest, and season. Place the meat on top and pour over the stock. Cover and put in the oven for 1½–2 hours until very tender. Check occasionally that it is not drying out, topping up with a little hot water if needed.

4 For the gremolata, mix the parsley, lemon, and garlic in a small bowl. To serve, place the veal on warmed plates, spoon the sauce on top, and sprinkle with the gremolata.

VARIATION

Osso buco with celery, leek, and almonds Prepare in the same way, but substitute 1 sliced leek for 1 onion, and add 2 chopped celery sticks to the mixture at the beginning of step 2. Use an Italian red wine, such as Chianti, instead of the white wine and add a pinch of sugar in step 3. Prepare the gremolata for garnish, but add a small handful of toasted, flaked almonds to the mix.

ROASTED VEAL BONE MARROW

Delicious and simple to prepare, bone marrow is best served with toast or as a side with beef or veal sauces.

THE CUT Veal bone marrow

SERVES 4
PREP 5 mins   **COOK** 30 mins

12 pieces veal bone marrow, 7.5cm (3in) each

green salad, to serve

handful of mixed herbs, finely chopped, to serve

1 Preheat the oven to 230°C (450°F/Gas 8). Place the marrow bones in a large roasting tin, making sure they are spaced well apart. Avoid using smaller pieces of marrow bones as it would be difficult to remove the marrow from these after roasting.

2 Transfer the roasting tin to the centre of the preheated oven. Roast the marrow bones for about 20 minutes, enough to loosen the marrow but not to melt it.

3 Remove from the heat and spoon the marrow out of the bones. Spread it on toasts and serve along with a crisp green salad and herbs. You can also add it to beef sauces and gravies to enrich their flavour.

HOME BUTCHERY

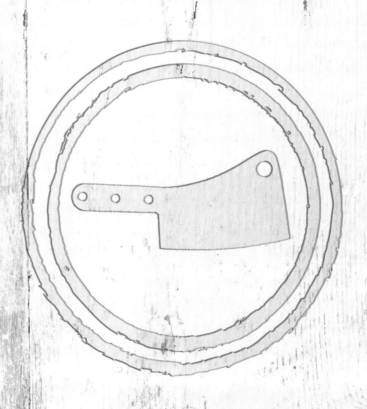

HOME BUTCHERY

CUTTING UP YOUR OWN MEAT IS FASCINATING. THE SKILLED ART OF BUTCHERY TAKES MANY YEARS TO ACQUIRE, AND IN EVERY REGION OF EVERY COUNTRY, BUTCHERS WILL TACKLE CARCASSES DIFFERENTLY. THIS IS A STEP-BY-STEP GUIDE TO SOME BUTCHERY BASICS.

OUR STARTER GUIDE shows some simple ways of breaking down carcasses into manageable cuts without the need for specialized large butchery equipment. There are many other cuts that can be produced; the more you trim and divide muscles, the leaner and smaller the pieces become.

USING OUR CUTTING GUIDE

Read through each section before starting, then decide which cuts you want to produce. This determines in which order you cut, or debone, the various parts. Some steps may need to be done in a different order to the sequence in which they are written. These choices are highlighted.

Whatever its size, the muscles are the same on every mammal, so some techniques, such as removing the forequarter, are common to all animals. The larger the animal, the more the muscles are divided, and the more the meat is taken off the bone. Small animals have more cuts left on the bone.

There are many examples online of how to cut meat and some are very helpful. Some demonstrations are aimed at wholesale butchers or chefs, who use different cuts to the home cook. Try to find examples that make retail cuts.

SAFETY

• Take care when handling and carrying heavy carcasses, so as not to cause injury.
• Make sure the table you plan to work on is solid and stable. Meat carcasses are heavy, and a wobbly table can be dangerous when sawing and chopping.

• Always point knives towards the floor when walking around; never point them outwards.
• Always wear a protective metal apron and a chain-mail glove, as some butchery procedures require the knife to be cut towards the body, and butcher's knives – and animal bones – are extremely sharp.
• Fat and scraps dropped onto the floor can make it very slippery.

HYGIENE

• Keep the temperature of the room as low as possible; use a natural draught if necessary. Keep all meat refrigerated when not cutting it up.
• Use fly coverings over open doors and windows, and an electric fly killer inside. Never leave meat uncovered. If possible, butcher meat during the winter, when there are fewer flies.
• Scrub hands and nails thoroughly before starting.
• Sterilize knives from time to time. Pour a kettleful of boiling water into a jug deep enough to hold the knives. Keep them in the hot water for a minimum of 2 minutes.
• When you've finished butchering, clean all surfaces and equipment. First use cool water to remove all blood and meat, then use hot water and detergent to remove fat. Rinse off detergent using sanitizer or a weak solution of bleach and water.

MAKING THE MOST OF YOUR MEAT

Many muscles can be improved and made suitable for flash-frying if they are thoroughly trimmed. Remove excess fat, but leave some to lubricate the meat.

Remove gristle, sinew, cartilage, and membranes from roasts and steaks, but some can be left on for slow-cooking cuts.

Dry-aged meat may have some dried, slippery, or even slightly mouldy parts on the edges; this is normal, but trim off these parts before you start.

EQUIPMENT

• **Sturdy table**
• **Large, heavy chopping board**
• **Boning knife** with thin, flexible blade
• **Steak knife** for cutting large slices
• **Sharpening steel**
• **Butcher's saw and sawblades**
• **Large containers and trays** for meat and trimmings
• **Covers** to prevent fly damage
• **Butcher's twine**
• **Skewers** to secure meat before tying

Protection:
• **Chain-mail glove:** worn on the hand not holding the knife
• **Metal apron:** essential for beginners as some movements require the knife to be moved or pointed towards the body
• **First-aid kit**

WHATEVER ITS SIZE, THE MUSCLES ARE THE SAME ON EVERY MAMMAL, SO SOME TECHNIQUES ARE COMMON TO ALL ANIMALS.

TOP TIPS

• Use the saw as little as possible; bone dust is gritty and it makes meat go off. When there is bone dust, brush it off.
• Use your fingers to feel for splinters of bone. The bones of small animals can easily shatter when sawn.
• When deboning meat, find the natural seams between the muscles with the tip of the knife and pull them apart by hand, using the knife to ease stubborn parts.
• Make use of gravity. If a joint can bend over the table edge, it makes cutting off large pieces easier.
• Put a thick damp towel under your cutting board to prevent it sliding about.
• When trimming, cut or scrape off all bloody meat, white bone sheath, bone splinters, excess fat, lymph nodes, gristle, and silver sinew.

USING KNIVES

The diagrams show how to hold the knife. For most processes it is held vertically and the wrist is articulated to move the knife. For slicing, the knife is held in the conventional fashion. Tilt the knife edge towards the bone to avoid slashing the meat. Never cut towards your hand.

When cutting a long length of meat, mark the initial cut and then deepen it with a stroking motion. Use this stroking motion to take meat off rib bones, too.

USING SAWS

Before using a saw, cut through as much meat as possible around the bone with a knife. Then open out the meat to expose the bone. As soon as the saw reaches the end of the bone, switch back to a knife to avoid tearing the meat.

TYING A JOINT

Two methods of tying a joint of meat are shown below. It helps to practise on a rolled-up tea towel. Butchers' elastic bands can be used instead of twine if necessary, but these are not recommended because, when removed after cooking, they flick fat and meat juices around.

Tying meat the butcher's way

This method produces the neatest joints, which can be divided into smaller joints or noisettes by cutting between the strings. This is the method used in "Roll and tie a joint" on page 299.

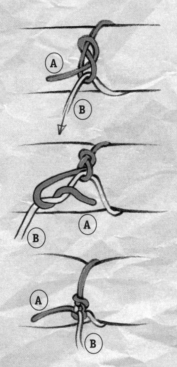

1 Slip the string under the meat and tie a slip knot loosely, as shown, in the centre of the meat. Leave 5cm (2in) on end A. Now lift up end B (as shown on p299) and gently tighten the knot against the meat. Once it is in the correct place, give it a tug to secure it.

2 Secure the tightened slip knot by making another simple knot: loop end B around end A and tighten. This ensures the knot cannot come undone.

3 The knot looks like this when finished. Trim the ends of the string. Continue tying strings around the meat, spacing them evenly. If the joint looks unstable, tie another string around from end to end.

Tying meat the "parcel" way

This method is easier than above, but it is less tidy and is of no use if the meat needs to be cut between the strings.

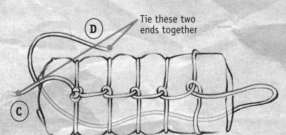

Tie these two ends together

1 Slip the string under one end of the joint and tie a slip knot (see step 1, above). Leave at least 10cm (4in) on end C.

2 Loop the string around the meat as shown, distributing the strings evenly as you go. Pass the string under the joint and tie it to the long end of the first knot.

PORK, LAMB, AND SMALL DEER

THE PRINCIPLES FOR BUTCHERING THESE THREE SPECIES ARE VIRTUALLY THE SAME – ANY EXCEPTIONS HAVE BEEN HIGHLIGHTED. THE DIAGRAMS SHOW A PIG BEING BUTCHERED; LAMB AND DEER ARE SLIMMER AND MORE ELONGATED, BUT ALL THE MUSCLES AND BONES ARE IN THE SAME PLACE.

CUT INTO PRIMALS

To make the carcass easier to handle, first divide it into three parts, or "primals": forequarter, middle or saddle, and back leg or haunch. The breastbone will already have been sawn open; if not, saw it open before starting.

REMOVE THE FOREQUARTER

PRELIMINARY STEP

For pork only, first cut off the head behind the jawbone and ears. Saw it in half or leave whole, as wished.

1 Open the chest cavity and count 5 ribs from the head end. Insert the knife through the flank at this point, and cut between the 5th and 6th ribs on both sides.

2 Turn the carcass over and continue to cut all the way up to the backbone, cutting through all the meat. Repeat on the opposite side.

3 Saw through the backbone to remove the forequarter. Scrape off the bone sawdust from the cut edges.

NOTE: Cutting between the 5th and 6th ribs leaves 8 ribs on the middle part for making a rack. Pork is sometimes cut between the 4th and 5th ribs, and lamb between the 6th and 7th.

DIVIDE THE MIDDLE FROM THE BACK LEGS

1 Feel for the hip bone and cut, from the flank edge, right through to the backbone. Repeat on the other side.

2 Counting from the leg (tail) end, cut between the 1st and 2nd lumbar vertebrae. Use a knife to cut through the cartilage disc of the backbone, being careful not to cut through the meat on either side. Cut the loin meat to remove the legs

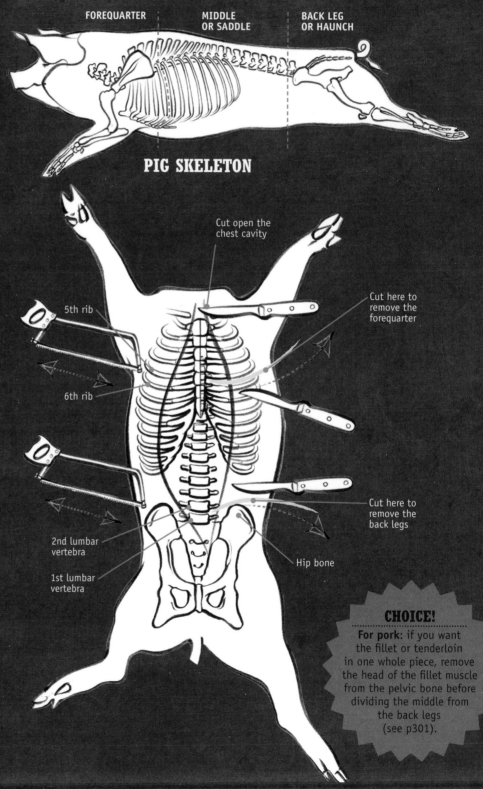

FOREQUARTER   MIDDLE OR SADDLE   BACK LEG OR HAUNCH

PIG SKELETON

Cut open the chest cavity

Cut here to remove the forequarter

5th rib

6th rib

Cut here to remove the back legs

2nd lumbar vertebra

1st lumbar vertebra

Hip bone

CHOICE!

For pork: if you want the fillet or tenderloin in one whole piece, remove the head of the fillet muscle from the pelvic bone before dividing the middle from the back legs (see p301).

THE FOREQUARTER

THERE ARE MANY WAYS OF PREPARING THE FOREQUARTER, especially with pork, and you can choose a combination of cuts, making bone-in cuts from one half and boneless cuts from the other. Lamb and small deer are cut more simply. Beef is usually entirely deboned.

SPLIT IN HALF

For both boneless and bone-in cuts, the forequarter needs to be halved and prepared. Scrape off any bone sawdust, as it makes the meat deteriorate more quickly.

PRELIMINARY STEPS

For lamb and small deer only, first saw 2–3cm (1–1½in) off the neck end and discard. Saw off the remaining neck ready to debone the meat for stew or mince, or into bone-in slices.

For pork, cut off the trotters.

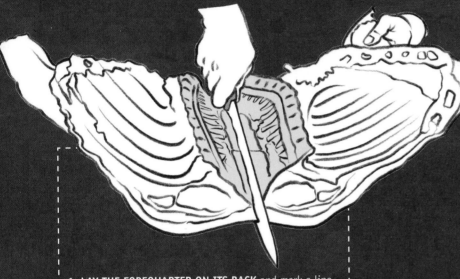

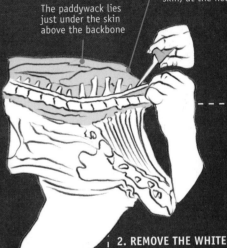

The paddywack lies just under the skin above the backbone

The fat lies between the ribs and the outer skin, at the neck end

1. LAY THE FOREQUARTER ON ITS BACK and mark a line down the centre of the backbone with your knife to use as a guide. Saw through the backbone, then cut through the meat on the other side to cut the forequarter in half.

2. REMOVE THE WHITE SPINAL CORDS as shown (this is only mandatory for lamb, but is desirable for other species). Cut out and discard the triangle of fat near the neck, which contains a gland. Remove the paddywack, a tough yellow piece of gristle.

MAKE BONE-IN CUTS

There are many different bone-in cuts. To make a **whole bone-in forequarter**, either with or without the shank, see below; to make **shoulder chops**, a **spare rib joint**, or a **whole bone-in shoulder joint**, see page 294.

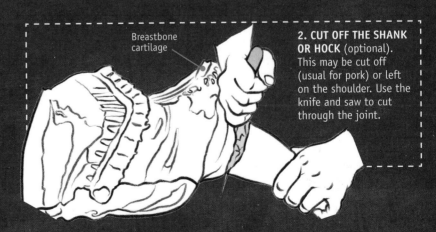

Breastbone cartilage

2. CUT OFF THE SHANK OR HOCK (optional). This may be cut off (usual for pork) or left on the shoulder. Use the knife and saw to cut through the joint.

1. TO MAKE A WHOLE BONE-IN FOREQUARTER JOINT, simply trim off the breastbone cartilage where it meets the ribs. In lamb, this is sometimes called a whole shoulder.

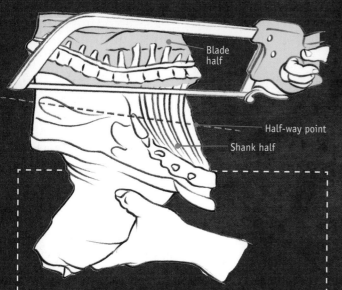

Blade half

Half-way point

Shank half

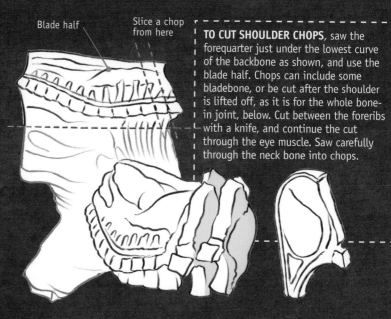

Blade half

Slice a chop from here

TO CUT SHOULDER CHOPS, saw the forequarter just under the lowest curve of the backbone as shown, and use the blade half. Chops can include some bladebone, or be cut after the shoulder is lifted off, as it is for the whole bone-in joint, below. Cut between the foreribs with a knife, and continue the cut through the eye muscle. Saw carefully through the neck bone into chops.

TO MAKE TWO HALF SHOULDER JOINTS, saw through the ribs at the half-way point. Cut through the meat and bone. Remove bone sawdust. The top part is the blade half and the other is the shank half (also called the hand and hock in pork).

TO MAKE FOREQUARTER SPARE RIBS. Cut the ribs off the breastbone and slice into spare ribs. The long neck vertebrae can also be sawn off the backbone to make "spare ribs".

TO MAKE A SPARE RIB JOINT, divide the shoulder as for chops (above). Cut through the meat until it hits the bladebone, then saw through the bladebone and cut through the remaining meat.

REMOVE THE PIECE OF BLADEBONE from the forerib joint as shown. Tie if wished.

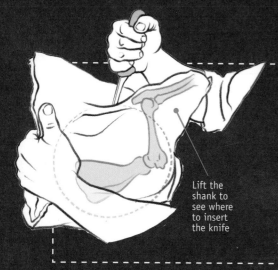

Lift the shank to see where to insert the knife

TO MAKE A WHOLE BONE-IN SHOULDER JOINT, lift off the whole shoulder blade. Lift up the shank and insert the knife where the meat stretches under the arm. Keep lifting the foreleg to help part the meat and, using the point of the knife, carefully pare away the shoulder from the forequarter (it is not attached by bones). Cut off the shank at the elbow joint if wished. Trim off excess fat if necessary.

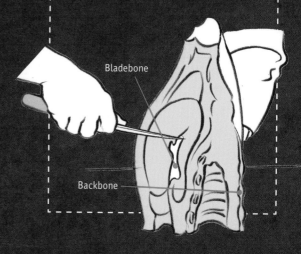

Bladebone

Backbone

DEBONE THE FOREQUARTER

To make steaks, rolled joints, diced stew, and mince, the shoulder needs to be deboned. Work from the inside of the carcass so the outside skin is left intact and is neat to roll. Leave the hock or shank bone on so it can be used as a lever.

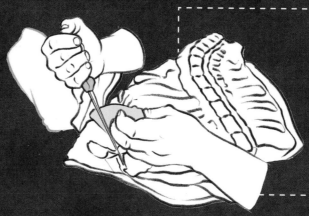

1. REMOVE THE RIBS AND BACKBONE: Starting at the breast edge, lift off the rib bones. Loosen the meat from the rib bones, then, keeping the knife tilted towards the ribs, scrape off the flank meat with a stroking motion, working down towards the backbone.

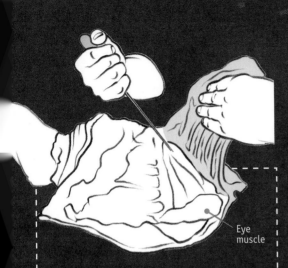

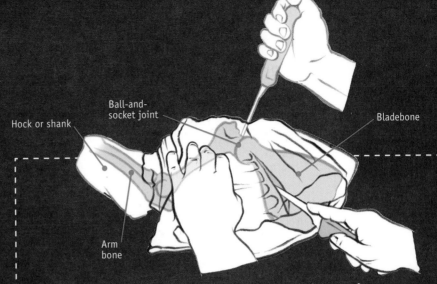

Hock or shank

Ball-and-socket joint

Bladebone

Arm bone

Eye muscle

2. ONCE YOU HAVE ENOUGH TO HOLD, pull the ribs up with a tugging motion. Gravity will help the knife to part the meat from the bone. Work carefully around the eye muscle meat to remove the backbone and ribs in one piece.

3. TAKE OUT THE BLADEBONE: With the hock or shank pointing away from you, insert the point of your knife, at 90°, down through the very centre of the shoulder (where the ribs ended) until you hit the ball-and-socket joint where bladebone meets arm bone. Note this mark. Now look for the edge of the bladebone where the forequarter was sawn off, and mark a line from here to the ball-and-socket joint. Cut down the inside edge of the bladebone with your knife. Keeping your knife edge tilted to the bone, scrape off the flesh on top of the bladebone until you reach the socket joint.

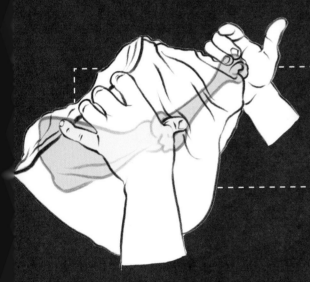

4. WHEN THE MEAT from on top of the bladebone is freed off, turn the shoulder over skin-side up. Hold the shank or hock and wiggle it until you can feel the joint between shank and arm bone moving. Pull the shank up towards you to pop open the joint.

Bladebone

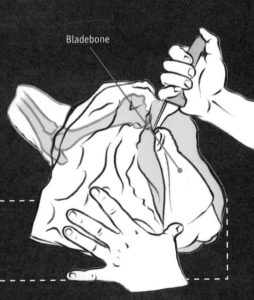

5. NOW WORK AROUND THE BLADEBONE to remove the meat from either side of the ridge. Pull out the bladebone, using your knife to free it off, if necessary.

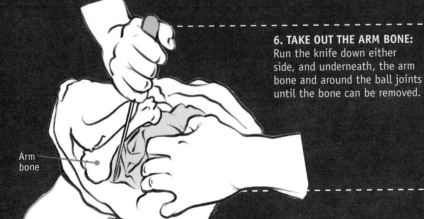

Arm bone

6. TAKE OUT THE ARM BONE: Run the knife down either side, and underneath, the arm bone and around the ball joints until the bone can be removed.

NOW YOU CAN...

- Trim off any surplus fat, gristle, and sinew.
- Cut shoulder steaks from the leanest, thickest parts.
- Carefully remove the eye muscle to produce a lamb or deer neck fillet, or a pork rib-eye joint.
- Roll into a shoulder joint (see p299).
- Dice into stew and use trimmings for mince.
- Saw off the soiled end of the shank or hock to cook it whole.
- Remove the shank meat and dice or mince it.

THE MIDDLE OR SADDLE

THIS SECTION, WHICH IS ALSO KNOWN AS THE LOIN, includes the finest meat on the carcass – the loin and the fillet or tenderloin. There is often a lot of fat on this part, although deer has less.

CUT OFF THE FLANK AND RIBS

The ribs may be cut at different lengths. To make a traditional saddle joint, see right.

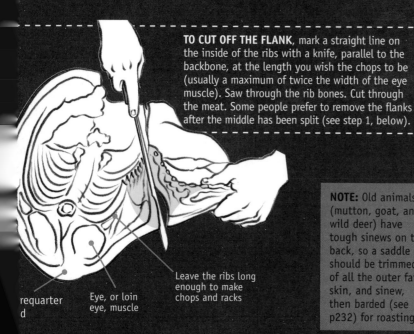

TO CUT OFF THE FLANK, mark a straight line on the inside of the ribs with a knife, parallel to the backbone, at the length you wish the chops to be (usually a maximum of twice the width of the eye muscle). Saw through the rib bones. Cut through the meat. Some people prefer to remove the flanks after the middle has been split (see step 1, below).

Forequarter end

Eye, or loin eye, muscle

Leave the ribs long enough to make chops and racks

NOTE: Old animals (mutton, goat, and wild deer) have tough sinews on the back, so a saddle should be trimmed of all the outer fat, skin, and sinew, then barded (see p232) for roasting.

MAKE A SADDLE JOINT

TO MAKE A SADDLE JOINT, cut off the flanks as shown, left, but closer to the eye muscle, as shown here. Leave whole for a long saddle joint, or cut off the carvery saddle end – it has no ribs and includes the fillet. Cut it off where the ribs end, as marked. To make double or Barnsley chops, cut slices straight across the carvery end of the saddle.

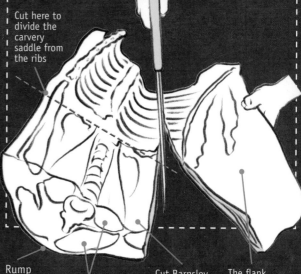

Cut here to divide the carvery saddle from the ribs

Rump end

The fillet and loin eye muscle are the two most tender cuts

Cut Barnsley chops from this end

The flank includes the spare ribs and belly

MAKE BONE-IN CUTS

These include loin and double loin chops, elegant rack roasts, and Barnsley chops (see above).

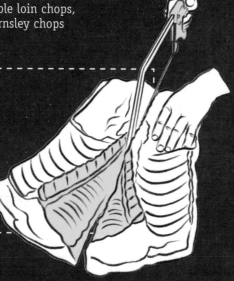

1. SPLIT THE SADDLE OR MIDDLE: Turn the saddle onto its back. Mark down the centre of the backbone with a knife to create a guideline. Saw down the centre to part the two sides, then cut through the remaining meat and fat with a knife.

2. REMOVE THE CHINE BONE (optional): This removes the sharp edges from chops and racks. Saw off the backbone at a 45° angle, starting at the ribs, until the bone is nearly cut through, then part the meat off the backbone with the knife at the cartilage. Be very careful not to cut into the meat. An alternative method, using a cleaver, is shown on page 193.

MAKE JOINTS, RACKS, AND CHOPS

TO DIVIDE THE BONE-IN LOIN INTO JOINTS, RACKS, CHOPS, OR DOUBLE LOIN CHOPS: Trim off excess skin, fat, and sinew, then cut between the ribs, using the point of a knife to find the gristle between the vertebrae. Cut down firmly with a large knife to break open the joint. Then cut through the meat. Alternatively, saw through the backbone, being careful not to cut the meat. See page 193 for instructions on French trimming chops and racks.

Loin joint

Rack joint

Loin chop or cutlet has a rib bone and no fillet

Double loin chop includes fillet

MAKE BONELESS CUTS

Once deboned, this section yields joints and steaks from the fillet, loin, and loin eye. Loin eye has all the external fat and sinew removed.

1. REMOVE THE FILLET OR TENDERLOIN (if not already removed): With the loin lying skin-side down, scrape the fillet away from the bone. Keep the knife close to the backbone. Trim off any silver sinews and the chain steak (a thin strip of meat that runs along the length of the fillet).

THE RIBS, BELLY, BREAST, AND FLANK

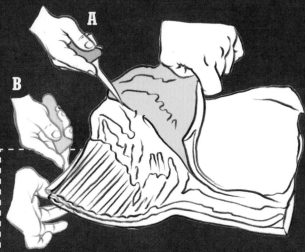

A

B

TO MAKE SPARE RIBS: Lift off the flap of flank (A) covering the rib ends and the ribs from the belly at the point where the ribs end. The ribs can be left as a set or cut into individual spare ribs.

TO MAKE BELLY, BREAST, AND FLANK CUTS: Alternatively, all the rib meat can be taken off the bone. Slip the knife under the rib bones as shown (B), and scrape off the meat. The belly, breast, and flank can be rolled and tied (see p299), sliced, minced, or made into bacon (see p21).

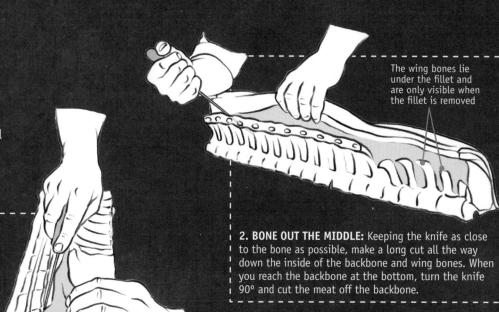

The wing bones lie under the fillet and are only visible when the fillet is removed

2. BONE OUT THE MIDDLE: Keeping the knife as close to the bone as possible, make a long cut all the way down the inside of the backbone and wing bones. When you reach the backbone at the bottom, turn the knife 90° and cut the meat off the backbone.

NOW YOU CAN...

Trim off excess skin, fat, and sinew, or leave it on if preferred. Then slice the meat into **loin steaks**, trimmed **loin eye steaks**, or **loin joints** as required.

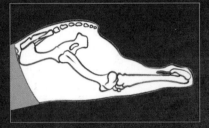

THE BACK LEG OR HAUNCH

WITH SMALL ANIMALS SUCH AS LAMB AND DEER, the leg or haunch is usually simply divided into bone-in joints, or even left whole. But it can also be deboned for rolled joints and steaks. Whole pork legs are used for hams and large roasts, but most are deboned for steaks and boneless joints. Page 303 shows how to debone and divide a leg.

SPLIT THE LEGS

Because of their shape, the legs can be difficult to hold steady while sawing them apart. If necesssary, wedge something under one side to secure it.

PRELIMINARY STEP

For pork only, cut off the trotters. (This may be done later if wished.)

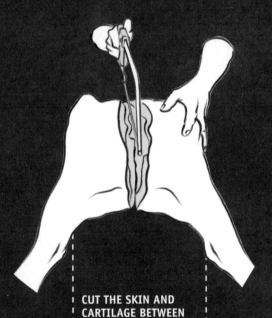

CUT THE SKIN AND CARTILAGE BETWEEN THE LEGS and through the pelvic bone. Cut or saw through the backbone and tail bones to part the legs.

MAKE BONE-IN JOINTS

With lamb and deer, the leg joint is often left whole with the chump or rump still attached; the pelvic bone can be removed for ease of carving. To do this, see "To remove the entire pelvic bone", below. Pork is more likely to be cut into smaller pieces.

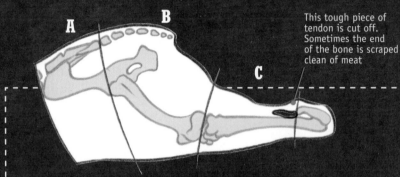

A B C

This tough piece of tendon is cut off. Sometimes the end of the bone is scraped clean of meat

THE LEG CAN BE CUT INTO SEVERAL BONE-IN JOINTS. The lines above indicate the usual cutting points. Part A is the chump end (to remove, see "To cut off the chump", opposite). It is not easy to carve because of the pelvic bone so is either deboned (see "To debone the chump", opposite), or cut into chops. Part B is the leg end. It is also easier to carve with the pelvic bone removed (see "To remove the entire pelvic bone", below). Part C is the shank or hock. It is often included with a leg of lamb or deer. The small, bony end part is usually removed in lamb and deer, and the tendon removed. To make bone-in leg steaks, cut slices of the leg including leg bone, and saw through the bone. Remove any sawdust.

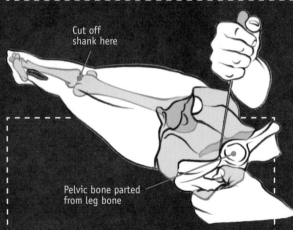

Cut off shank here

Pelvic bone parted from leg bone

TO REMOVE THE ENTIRE PELVIC BONE (aitch bone, hip, and tail bone): Remove the head of the fillet from the hip bone to expose it (see "To debone the chump", opposite). Work the tip of the knife around the aitch bone round to the ball-and-socket joint. Part the piece of connective gristle in the ball-and-socket joint. Work around the tail bone to free off the meat. Work around the pelvic bone and lift all the bones out. Trim off excess fat and skin.

TO REMOVE THE SHANK OR HOCK, without using a saw, feel for the halfway point at the hock (knee) joint and make a cut through the cartilage. Using the edge of the table, vigorously bend back the hock to crack open the joint, then cut through the connecting gristle. Cut through the meat to remove the hock.

Slice the shank into osso buco, saw off the soiled end to serve as a whole shank or hock, or debone and dice or mince the meat.

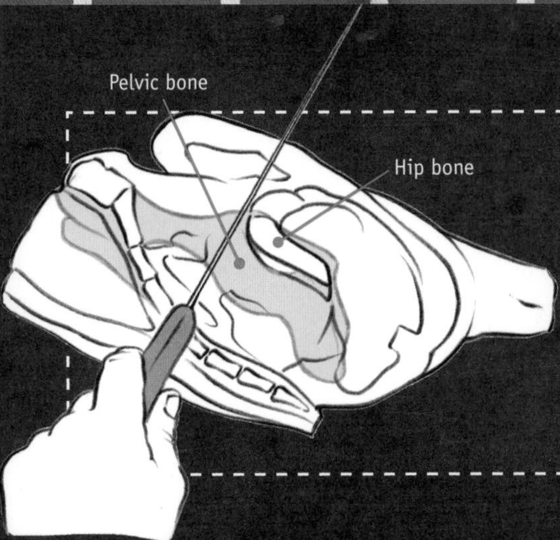

To cut off the chump image labels:

Pelvic bone

Hip bone

TO CUT OFF THE CHUMP, cut halfway between the pubic bone and the 1st lumbar vertebra (count from the tail end) at a 45° angle through the bone, then slice through the meat to remove the chump. Leave whole for a bone-in chump roast or, using the knife and saw, cut into slices for chump chops. Trim off any remaining flank as required.

MAKE BONELESS JOINTS

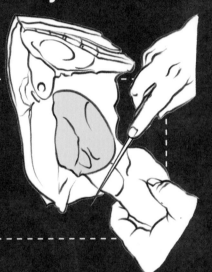

TO DEBONE THE CHUMP, take the fillet head off to expose the pelvic bone. Keeping the knife close to the bone, cut the bone out of the meat. Slice to make chump steaks, or roll and tie into a chump joint.

TO REMOVE THE LEG BONE, see page 303, steps 3–6. The boneless leg is now ready to roll and tie (see below). With the topside and leg bone removed, the deboned leg can be made into a large rolled joint, with or without the shank. Roll the topside into a smaller joint, or slice into leg steaks.

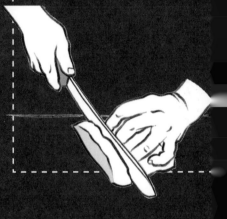

TO SLICE STEAKS, hold the piece of meat firmly down on the table, close to the edge where it will be cut, to prevent it moving. Cut even slices across the grain, using a large knife and long, smooth cutting strokes.

ROLL AND TIE A JOINT

Single muscles can be roasted without tying, although tying gives a better shape. Butchers' elastic bands may be used, but they are very messy to remove after cooking.

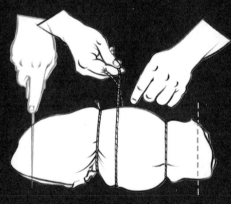

1. TO ROLL MEAT READY TO TIE INTO A JOINT: Make sure the meat is of an even thickness thoughout. Cut out muscles from thick parts and lay them into thin parts. If there is a large flap at one end, this makes it easier to roll (eg, when rolling loin, leave a flap of flank attached). Roll the meat as tightly as possible; if necessary, hold it in place with skewers.

2. TO TIE A JOINT: Make the first tie in the middle. Slip the string under the meat and tie a slip knot (see "Tying meat the butcher's way", p291, step 1). Pull the knot up over the meat as shown, then tug it down gently onto the meat. Now give another tug to tighten it. Then secure it with a simple knot (see p291, step 2). For a single-muscled joint, tie strings from the centre to the ends. For a multi-muscled joint, tie the second and third strings at either end and then fill in. This prevents the meat from slipping out. Slice off any untidy ends of the joint. If the joint looks unstable, tie some strings around from end to end to secure it while cooking.

BEEF AND LARGE DEER

THIS SECTION SHOWS HOW TO BUTCHER BEEF AND LARGE DEER CARCASSES. A FOREQUARTER OF BEEF IS TOO LARGE FOR DOMESTIC BUTCHERY. HOWEVER, THE PRINCIPLES OF CUTTING BEEF (AND LARGE DEER) ARE THE SAME AS FOR PORK, LAMB, AND SMALL DEER – SEE PAGES 293–5.

SEE PAGES 293–5

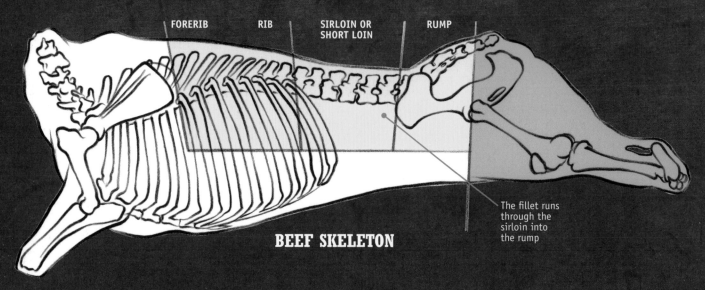

SIRLOIN OR MIDDLE (WITHOUT FLANK)

LEG, TOP BIT, OR HAUNCH

FORERIB   RIB   SIRLOIN OR SHORT LOIN   RUMP

The fillet runs through the sirloin into the rump

BEEF SKELETON

THE SIRLOIN OR MIDDLE (WITHOUT FLANK)

A SIRLOIN AND RIB OF BEEF is usually bought as a side (one half), without the flank. For deer, see page 296 for splitting the saddle and removing the flank. First, decide whether you want bone-in cuts or boneless cuts, or a combination. This determines in which order you butcher the meat.

Before starting, remove the kidney: turn the sirloin or saddle on its back and remove the large knob of kidney fat. Run the knife under the fat and pull the fat from the bone, taking care not to damage the fillet underneath. The kidney is embedded within the fat. Deer may have little or no fat around the kidney.

BONE-IN CUTS

Bone-in cuts include sirloin, rib, and forerib roasts, as well as T-bone and Porterhouse steaks. To make venison saddle joints, see page 296.

If the fillet or tenderloin is required as a whole piece, see "To remove the fillet", opposite, and cut out the whole fillet first. However, note that you will not then be able to cut a sirloin joint or T-bone steaks, as these cuts include the fillet muscle.

1. REMOVE THE RUMP FROM THE SIRLOIN: Cut off the rump where the curved set of tail bones changes into the larger back bones (lumbar vertebrae). Cut through the meat in a line that just misses the tip of the hip bone.

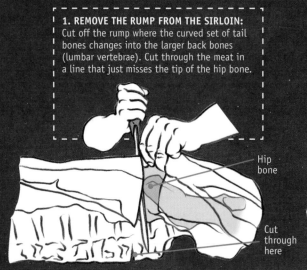

Hip bone

Cut through here

2. SAW THROUGH THE BACKBONE to part the rump from the loin, taking care not to saw into any meat. See opposite to debone the rump.

Push the meat apart to make it easier to cut

NOW YOU CAN...
PREPARE BONE-IN ROASTS AND STEAKS

SIRLOIN ROASTS
These have a portion of fillet so there is meat on either side of the backbone, which makes it more difficult to cut without damaging the meat. They have short wing bones rather than rib bones. Decide what size of roast is wanted, and use the knife to cut through the fillet and loin meat. Then part the meat and saw carefully between the vertebrae to cut off the joint.

SIRLOIN RIB, STANDING RIB, AND FORERIB JOINTS
These are cut from the front part that has rib bones but no fillet. Choose the number of ribs desired, and cut through the meat between the bones with a knife. Saw through the backbone, then cut through the loin eye muscle with a knife. This picture (see right, top) shows only three ribs, but if the whole sirloin and rib is longer, the forerib end may contain a small piece of bladebone cartilage, which should be removed. Remove the chine bone if wished (see p296, step 2), and also French trim the ends of the joint if wished (see p193).

PORTERHOUSE STEAKS
These steaks (see right, bottom) are cut from the sirloin where the rump was removed. They are cut to the full thickness of the first vertebra. T-bone steaks may be any thickness, but must include some fillet meat. To cut these steaks, slice through the meat on one side of the backbone and then cut on the other side of the bone. Part the meat slightly, then saw through the bone. This avoids having to saw into the meat.

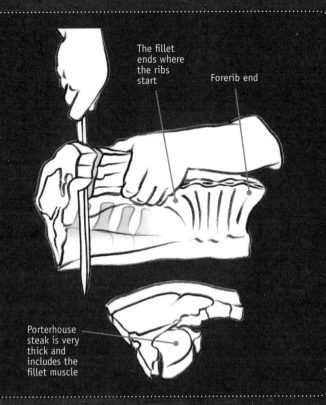

The fillet ends where the ribs start

Forerib end

Porterhouse steak is very thick and includes the fillet muscle

BONELESS CUTS

Boneless cuts include roasts and steaks cut from the boneless sirloin and loin eye, as well as fillet steak and roasts. Forerib cuts, such as rib-eye steak, are fattier.

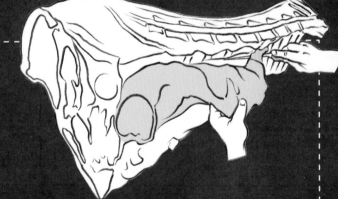

TO DEBONE THE RUMP:
Take out the fillet head that lies on top of the flat aitch bone. Then remove the bone – one of the most awkward bones. Follow the twisting contours, keeping the knife edge tightly against the bone to avoid slashing the meat. Trim the meat thoroughly, as the rump has a lot of fat and gristle.

NOW YOU CAN...
PREPARE RUMP CUTS

The meat can be used for a roasting joint, sliced into rump steaks, or used for stir-fries. The thinner pointed end is point steak. The thin muscle lying over the rump can also be removed and sliced into a cap of rump steak. Depending on how the carcass was cut, there may also be a part of the thick flank attached; this is the tri-tip.

TO REMOVE THE FILLET: Lay the loin on its back and start at the thin tapered end of the fillet. Keeping the edge of the knife close to the ribs, scrape the fillet off the bones with a stroking movement. At the point where the rib bones end, ensure that the knife does not slip into the loin muscle underneath. Once you reach the rump (if not already cut off), the fillet head (called the chateaubriand) divides into 2 muscles. It is partly embedded in the pelvic bone. Just keep scraping the fillet head out of the pelvic bone as cleanly as possible until the whole fillet is removed.

NOW YOU CAN... PREPARE FILLET CUTS

Remove the chain steak – a long, slightly ragged muscle on the backbone edge of the fillet that runs most of its length. Trim off fat, gristle, and any bone shards. The fillet can be cut into pieces for roasting, or sliced into steaks.

Wing bones

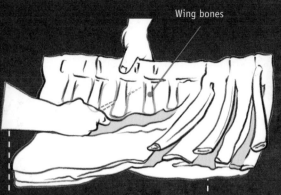

1. DEBONE THE LOIN: First free the rib and wing bones. With the loin lying ribs uppermost, slip the knife underneath the cut rib ends and start to cut the meat off the bones using a stroking movement ("stroke" the knife towards you at this point). Lift up the rib bones to make it easier to take the meat off them.

2. REMOVE THE RIBS AND BACKBONE: Once you meet the backbone (vertebrae), turn the knife downwards to keep taking the meat off the backbone. Watch out for the knobbly bits that stick out from the vertebrae. Remove all the bones from the loin.

NOW YOU CAN... PREPARE LOIN CUTS

First trim the loin. Turn the meat so the skin is uppermost and cut off about 2cm (1in) of the dried-up edge and the strip of gristle that runs along the backbone edge. Angle the knife upwards so that there is no danger of the knife making a downward cut into the eye muscle. Trim off excess fat. The boneless loin can be divided into joints or steaks as wished. The muscle cap over the front part of the rib-eye (from the part where the ribs were) can be taken off and used as a thin deckle steak. If wished, the skin, fat, and all silver skin can be removed to make fully trimmed loin-eye roasts or steaks.

THE LEG, TOP BIT, OR HAUNCH

THESE SPECIES ARE LARGE, so the back leg is rarely cooked whole, or even on the bone. The main butchery task in this section, therefore, is deboning and dividing the muscle blocks into manageable sections to make steaks, roasts, stewing meat, and mince.

DEBONE THE LEG AND DIVIDE INTO 3 MUSCLES

You will need to remove the remaining piece of hip bone and shank first, and then remove the leg bone so that the three main muscles can be divided.

Ball end of leg bone

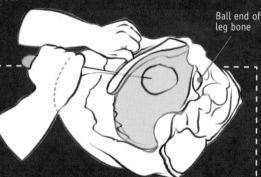

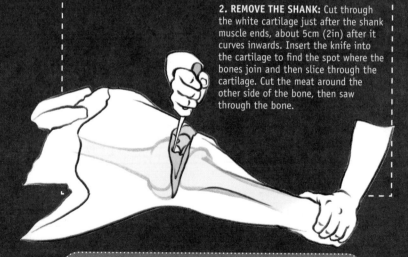

2. REMOVE THE SHANK: Cut through the white cartilage just after the shank muscle ends, about 5cm (2in) after it curves inwards. Insert the knife into the cartilage to find the spot where the bones join and then slice through the cartilage. Cut the meat around the other side of the bone, then saw through the bone.

1. REMOVE THE HIP BONE AND TAIL FROM THE RUMP END: Lay the leg with the hip bone uppermost. Scrape away any fat and the thin layer of meat from above the hip bone. (The diagram shows this fat and meat already removed, the bone exposed, and the large ball end of the leg bone visible.) Cut in behind the sawn bone edge, as shown, and work carefully around it, keeping the knife against the bone. To make it easier to see what you are doing, push the meat away from the bone as you work. When you reach the ball-and-socket joint, pull the hip bone backwards to expose the main tendon. You can use the steel to lever it back. Cut through the tendon and continue to cut round the hip bone until it can be removed.

NOW YOU CAN... PREPARE THE SHANK

For osso buco, cut through the meat around the bone in thick slices. Then saw through the bone. Remove the sawdust. Remove the thin, sharp bone next to the leg bone by feeling for it with your fingers, then work around it with your knife and remove. Discard the slices at either end. Alternatively, take all the meat off the bone then slice or dice it, or use it for mince or processing. The thick knuckle bone makes good gelatinous stock.

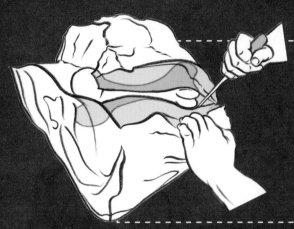

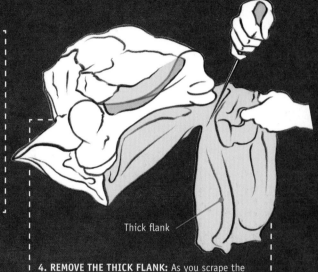

3. START DEBONING THE LEG:
Divide the topside muscle from the thick flank at the natural seam that runs diagonally from one end of the leg bone to the other. It is visible on deer, but in beef it is covered with fat. The seam runs at an angle so tilt the knife to cut between the muscles, right down to the bone. Work around the bone to divide the topside from the thick flank. Use the table edge to help part the muscles. Part the seam carefully all the way down to the leg bone.

Thick flank

5. REMOVE THE BONE:
Keeping the knife edge next to the bone, scrape the topside away until the two bone ends are freed. Then scrape off the silverside muscle from the underside of the leg bone until it can be lifted out.

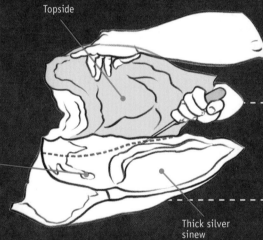

Topside

Silverside

Thick silver sinew

4. REMOVE THE THICK FLANK: As you scrape the thick flank off the leg bone, allow this muscle to bend over the edge of your cutting block, which makes it easier to see the thick silvery sheet of sinew on the silverside muscle. Part the thick flank from the silverside (located underneath the bone) by cutting it off at the kneecap cartilage, and set aside.

6. PART THE TOPSIDE FROM THE SILVERSIDE:
Look for the division between the topside (the cushion-shaped muscle on top) and the silverside. Using the point of the knife, carefully part these muscles and peel back the topside, as shown. Once the topside has been peeled right back, cut through the outer skin to remove it.

NOW YOU CAN... PREPARE BONELESS CUTS

TOPSIDE
The topside is roughly triangular in shape, with skin and fat on the outer edge and exposed meat on the cut sides. The thin outer cap of topside (or deckle) can be removed and used for frying steak. For boneless joints, cut the topside lengthways – with the grain – into several pieces, or slice it across the grain into steaks. Alternatively, it can be divided along the natural seam into a small and large muscle, which can be further divided if wished. Trim off excess fat and silver skin.

SILVERSIDE
The silverside has a thick, tough, silver sinew where it joins the thick flank. This must be removed. The silverside can be split into 2 separate muscles along the natural seam. The larger piece can be left as a joint or sliced into steak. The smaller muscle is called the salmon cut and makes a good joint, or can be cut into steaks. Trim off excess fat and silver skin.

THICK FLANK
Cut off the knee bone and gristle at the knuckle end. Lift off the thin cap of muscle that lies over the top. This is the tri-tip or cap of rump. The rest of the thick flank is made up of several muscles, which can be divided further if wished. It can be sliced thickly for braising steak, thinly for minute steak, or diced for stew. This muscle is very lean so makes extra-lean mince.

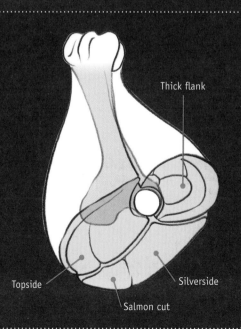

Thick flank

Topside

Salmon cut

Silverside

PLUCKING GAME BIRDS

WILD GAME VARIES IN THE WAY IT IS SHOT AND, IF IT IS BADLY DAMAGED, IT IS NOT WORTH PLUCKING THE WHOLE BIRD. INSTEAD, JUST REMOVE THE UNDAMAGED BREASTS. THE BIRD BEING PLUCKED IN THESE SEQUENCES IS A PIGEON.

SHOT DAMAGE

Look for signs where shot may have entered the flesh, and then try to locate the shot and remove it with a pair of tweezers. Often, a piece of feather will have been drawn into the hole with the pellet.

FEATHERS, BEAK, AND FEET

Tail and wing feathers are the toughest to remove. Waterfowl (duck and geese) have a layer of down underneath the feathers, which must be plucked after the feathers have been removed.

The bird's age affects how you prepare it. The beak and feet of a young bird are softer than on an old one and the feet can be easily torn off. Also, the spurs on a male bird are short and stubby on young birds, but long and pointed on older ones.

PREPARATION TIPS

If working inside, make sure there are no draughts that could blow the feathers around. If you prefer to sit, hold the bird on your knee and pluck straight into a box or bag. Ruffle the feathers a bit to make them stand up on end. This makes it easier to grasp a few at a time. Some people prefer to pluck the breast and back before the legs. Either way is suitable, although the breast has the most delicate skin so extra care is needed to avoid damaging the breast while plucking the legs.

EQUIPMENT

- **Poultry shears or other strong shears:** for cutting off the wings and feet.
- **Pair of pliers:** for grasping the tail and wing feathers.
- **Plastic bin bag or large cardboard box:** for plucking into and catching the feathers.
- **Small sharp knife:** for cutting through the skin.

REMOVING THE BREAST MEAT

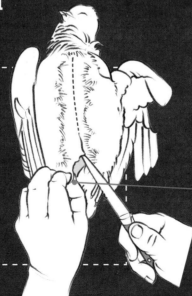

1. PLUCK A STRIP OF FEATHERS off the breast from vent to neck. This prevents the meat from getting covered in feathers. Insert a small knife just above the vent and, with the knife pointing away from the meat, cut the skin right up to the neck.

Lift the skin as you cut it to avoid slashing the meat

2. PULL THE SKIN BACK AS FAR AS IT WILL GO, right down to the legs and to the very end of the neck or wing end of the breast. Cut the breast down close to the breastbone. Turn it at right angles along the top of the chest cavity. Run the knife down the edge of the wishbone at the neck end and cut off the breast as far down towards the neck and wing as possible. The fillet (aiguillette) lies under the breast and should be removed with it.

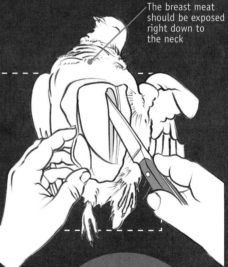

The breast meat should be exposed right down to the neck

TIP

There is a sinew attaching the aiguillette to the carcass. To remove the sinew, hold it between finger and thumb and hold the aiguillette in the other. Pull back the sinew to remove it. This is much easier to do while it is still attached to the carcass.

PLUCKING AND DRAWING

1. START WITH A LEG, beginning at the foot end. Hold the foot in one hand and, with the other, pull the feathers away from the direction in which they lie, using short sharp tugs so as not to tear the skin. If it looks as though the skin might tear (or has already torn), very carefully pull individual feathers the other way (in the direction they are lying) and, with your other hand, hold down the skin so it can't lift up and tear.

2. PLUCK THE BACK, then under the wings, the breast, and about 10cm (4in) of the neck. Pluck these feathers in the direction they lie as this skin is more fragile.

3. PLUCK UP TO THE FIRST WING JOINT: Take the rest of the wings off with poultry shears or other strong shears. Pull the wing and tail feathers out, one by one, in the direction of growth. Pliers are helpful. To remove tiny feathers and long hairs, hold them over a candle or gas ring to singe them off. Avoid singeing off too much feather or the bird will taste of burnt feathers.

On smaller birds, you can cut off the whole wing at the point where it meets the body

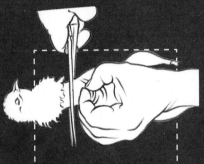

The crop contains the food the bird was eating

4. MAKE A CUT ALL THE WAY AROUND THE LEG at the foot joint, but only through the skin, not the meat or tendons. Bend the feet backwards and forwards (to loosen the tendons), then crack the joint until it snaps. Holding the drumstick in one hand, pull off the foot and the tendons from the leg. These may be tough.

5. CUT OFF THE HEAD. Pull the plucked skin towards the body so it is crumpled up. Then cut through the bone as close to the body as possible. You can fold the neck skin underneath for cooking.

6. FIND THE CROP AT THE HEAD END. Loosen it from the neck and body skin with your finger, pulling back the skin. The crop parts quite easily. Pull it out of the cavity and remove the gullet and windpipe as well.

Make the cut above the vent, not in it

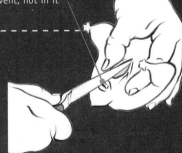

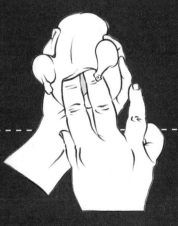

The gizzard is tough (see p267 for how to prepare it)

7. LOOK FOR THE VENT and make a shallow cut around it, ensuring that you do not pierce the gut. Make a small slit about 2–4cm (1–2in) long in the skin above the vent up towards the chest to make a small hole.

8. INSERT 2 FINGERS UNDER THE CHEST, right up to the diaphragm, and draw out the entrails. The gizzard will come out with the entrails; the heart and liver afterwards. The bird is now drawn. Pat the inside of the bird dry. If there has been any spillage of the gut contents, then run water through the cavity to clean it thoroughly.

SKINNING SMALL GAME ANIMALS

THE SAME METHOD CAN BE USED TO SKIN AND CLEAN A RABBIT, HARE, OR SQUIRREL (THE SEQUENCE BELOW SHOWS A RABBIT). FOR INSTRUCTIONS ON JOINTING A RABBIT OR HARE, SEE PAGE 233. SQUIRREL, BEING SO SMALL, IS OFTEN COOKED WHOLE OR SIMPLY DIVIDED INTO LEGS, SADDLE, AND SHOULDERS.

RABBITS AND HARES are easy to skin as the skin comes off readily. Squirrel skin, on the other hand, is tough to remove so more knife work is needed.

If you shoot your own rabbit, hare, or squirrel, make sure you empty its bladder as soon as it is shot. This keeps the carcass cleaner.

Skinning and cleaning can either be done on a table or the draining board of a sink. Alternatively, hang the carcass head down, with the back

legs tied apart. It's a good idea to put some newspaper on the floor or table as there may be drips.

If the animal has already been gutted, follow the procedure below as far as step 5, but take extra care when pulling off the skin so that the meat is not ripped off as well.

Use the point of your knife to start separating skin from meat. If the skin is very soiled, try to avoid it contaminating the meat. You will

need to trim off some of the edges of the stomach cavity and the cavity itself is more likely to be soiled, so take care not to contaminate the meat while working.

Keep the blood of a hare to thicken the sauce used during cooking. It collects in the chest cavity. Place a bowl underneath the chest and add a tablespoon of vinegar to the bowl. This will prevent the blood from coagulating as it drains into the bowl.

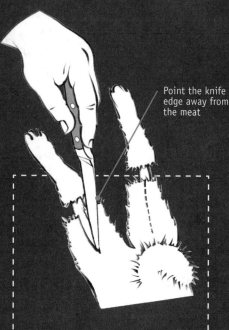

Point the knife edge away from the meat

1. CUT A RING AROUND EACH BACK LEG ABOVE THE HEEL, taking care to cut the skin only, and not the tendon. Cut around the front paws in the same way. Make a slit down the ouside of one of the hind legs from the heel to the base of the tail. Once you have inserted the point of the knife under the skin, keep the sharp edge pointing outwards and downwards (away from you) as you slide it under the skin. Cut the skin only, not the meat. Repeat with the other leg.

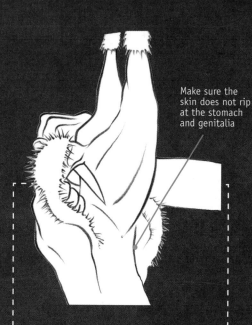

Make sure the skin does not rip at the stomach and genitalia

2. EASE THE SKIN AWAY FROM THE LEGS, using the point of the knife to nick any sinew that is tough or threatens to pull the meat off with the skin. Pull the skin off the leg downwards towards the tail and stomach. Repeat with the other leg. Make a slit in the fur at the base of the tail from leg to leg. Snap off the tail with your knife and make sure the skin is fully detached from the meat around the base of the tail. Ease off the skin around the genitalia; you may need to use the knife to sever the skin and avoid tearing the meat.

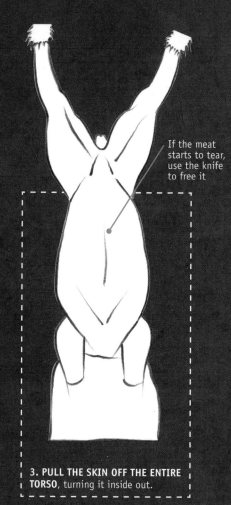

If the meat starts to tear, use the knife to free it

3. PULL THE SKIN OFF THE ENTIRE TORSO, turning it inside out.

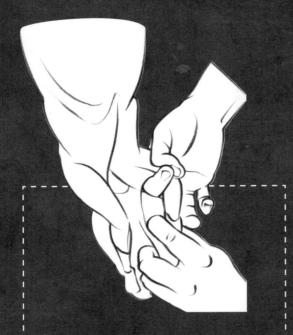

4. EASE THE FRONT LEGS OUT OF THE SKIN, using the elbows to pull them out. Continue to pull off the skin until the head or ears prevent it from going any further.

5. CUT OFF THE HEAD WITH A KNIFE. Then cut off the paws and feet. Bend them backwards to break the joint and use a knife to sever them. If the carcass is dirty at this point, wash it clean and pat dry before removing the guts.

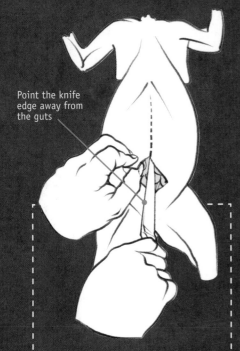

Point the knife edge away from the guts

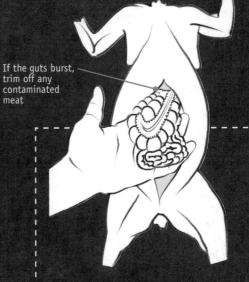

If the guts burst, trim off any contaminated meat

6. REMOVE THE GUTS by inserting the point of your knife into the bottom of the belly cavity and, lifting it upwards to avoid piercing the stomach contents, make a slit about halfway up to the chest.

7. INSERT YOUR FINGERS BETWEEN THE CHEST AND GUTS right up to the diaphragm, and gently pull the stomach contents out of the cavity.

8. CAREFULLY CUT THE GUTS AWAY around the anus. Discard the guts, genitalia, and bladder. Remove the heart, liver, and kidneys if wished. Without bursting it, cut off the bitter green gall bladder, attached to the liver. Pat the cavity dry. For hare only, place a bowl containing 1 tbsp vinegar underneath the chest cavity. Open the cavity and catch the blood in the bowl. Put the liver in the bowl with the vinegar and blood.

PREPARING AND MAKING SAUSAGES

Making your own fresh sausages is immensely satisfying and there are endless possibilities for flavour combinations. Omit the breadcrumbs and oatmeal if preferred, and vary the spices and herbs according to taste. If you experiment with new recipes, fry a small sample of the mixture first, taste, and adjust spicing accordingly.

EQUIPMENT

Apart from knives and chopping boards, you'll need one or two special items. Suppliers of ingredients and equipment can be found on the internet, as can second-hand equipment.

- **Mincer** or **grinder**. These can be hand-operated or electric, or you can use the grinder attachment for a food processor or mixer.
- **Large bowls** A plastic bowl, at least 5 litres (8¾ pints) capacity. Anything that can chip is dangerous for mixing raw meat.
- **Large, deep plastic tray** For mixing spices into meats, and receiving sausages after filling into skins. The deeper the tray, the easier it is to mix well.
- **Large funnel** A funnel must be fairly wide. You'll need a wooden or plastic stick to push the meat down into the skins.
- **Sausage filler**
- **Filling nozzles**

TABLE-TOP HAND MINCER
You can buy hand mincers that clamp on to a table, both with coarse and fine plates. Some can be used with nozzle attachments for filling.

FILLING NOZZLE
These are attachments for sausage-filling machines and mincers. Use different widths for the different sizes of skins. Two sizes will normally suffice.

SAUSAGE FILLER
Makes the job quicker and cleaner. Some food mixers have these as attachments.

MINCING PLATES
A coarse plate chops meat. A fine one produces tiny pieces; mincing twice gives a very smooth texture.

LARGE FUNNEL
A large funnel is useful for filling skins if you don't have a sausage filler.

HYGIENE AND HEALTH

CLEANLINESS It is crucial that everything is kept both clean and cold when making sausages, especially if the sausage is to be eaten uncooked. The more meat is chopped or minced, and other ingredients added, the more high-risk a product it becomes. Wearing food-grade plastic gloves helps to prevent contamination.

STORING AND COOKING TEMPERATURES
Try to work in as cold an environment as possible, and refrigerate your sausages to below 4°C (40°F). Thorough cooking to a minimum internal temperature of 75°C (165°F) will destroy harmful bacteria. Use a meat thermometer to check the temperatures.

INGREDIENTS

Almost any ingredient can be used to make sausages. Using the best quality ingredients possible will produce the finest sausages, and do make sure that all spices and herbs are as fresh as they can be, because they quickly lose their aromas and flavours as they age.

- **Meat** Shoulder is the preferred cut for sausages; it should be very fresh. Remove excess gristle and sinew, and any blood spots. If you do not have a mincer, buy minced meat and use it immediately.
- **Fat** This lubricates sausages and makes them taste good. Hard back fat is used for texture and in salamis; soft belly fat melts quickly, adding succulence. If no filler (see below) is used, the usual ratio is 1:4 fat to lean meat.

- **Spices** and **herbs** Use dried herbs for enhanced flavour and measure them accurately using one-third of the weight of fresh herbs.
- **Fillers** Using fillers makes sausages soft, and allows the fat content to be reduced. Use dried breadcrumbs, oatmeal, bulgur wheat, or rice. They should be as dry as possible.
- **Liquid** Adding some liquid (usually iced water) helps to ease sausagemeat into the casings and reduces air bubbles. Wine or fruit juice add different flavours. Wine vinegar helps to ferment sausages.

SAUSAGE SKINS

Also called "casings", sausage skins come in many widths. Natural skins make the best-quality sausages, as they are more resilient, easier to form into links, and do not toughen when cooked. They come either dry-salted or in brine and need soaking. They are sold in bundles and by length.

  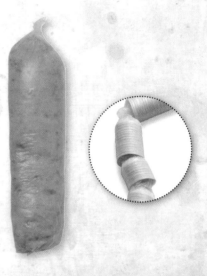

HOG CASINGS These are the most common kind of all. They are used to make chorizo, kiełbasa, and the thicker types of fresh or scalded sausages.

SHEEP CASINGS These are more expensive, but are thin, strong, and make the most tender eating. They are used to make slim fresh sausages and Frankfurters.

COLLAGEN CASINGS Made from reconstituted cow hide, these casings don't need soaking but are harder to make into attractive sausages. They can toughen up a bit on cooking.

PREPARING AND FILLING SKINS

When making sausages for the first time, it is far easier (and more fun) to have two people: one to turn the filler handle; the other to hold the skins while they are being filled. It does become easier with practice! Don't worry if your sausages are misshapen, they will still taste delicious.

 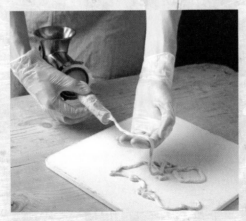 

1 Soak salted casings overnight, or brined casings for 30 minutes, then drain. Run fresh water through them. Tie a knot in one end. Keep in cold water.

2 Open the unknotted end and slip it over the nozzle, pulling up the rest onto the nozzle. Keep damp. Squeeze out extra air or they could burst when cooking.

3 Holding gently but firmly, push in the meat. If it bursts, break the sausage and re-knot the end. For links or cooked sausages, don't fill too tight or they will burst.

MAKING FRESH SAUSAGES

This sausage is best suited to grilling or frying. Use sheep casings if you would prefer to make thinner sausages. Wrap the sausages in cling film, in convenient one- or two-portion amounts, before freezing.

MAKES
2.5kg (5½lb)

SPECIAL EQUIPMENT
Large 5–6 litre (8¾–10½ pint) unbreakable mixing bowl

mincer

sausage filler

food-grade plastic gloves

INGREDIENTS
1.25kg (2¾lb) lean pork

500g (1lb 2oz) belly pork

500g (1lb 2oz) pork back fat

85g (3oz) salt

1½ tsp dried sage

1 tsp ground nutmeg

½ tsp ground ginger

180g (6oz) breadcrumbs or medium oatmeal

275ml (9¾fl oz) iced water

6m (20ft) of 28–35mm (¾–1½in) sheep or hog casings, soaked and one end knotted

1 Chop the meat and fat into chunks, and chill thoroughly. Mince the meat and fat through a coarse mincing plate on to a deep, wide tray, putting alternate pieces of meat and fat through the mincer.

2 Mix the salt, herbs, and spices with the breadcrumbs or oatmeal. Sprinkle this mixture over the minced meat and start to mix. Drizzle in the water and mix thoroughly to distribute the spices.

3 Test the mixture by making a small patty and cooking it in a frying pan. Taste to check if it is to your liking. If more spices are needed, add them to the mixture and mix well.

4 Mince the mixture through a fine mincing plate. Fit a skin on to the filler nozzle and fill the sausages (see p309). Do not fill the skin too tight, or it will burst when making links.

FORMING COILS

Forming a coil is most easily done with thin sheep casings. Start the coil in the centre and wind the sausage around to the desired width, keeping it tightly coiled. Secure with a skewer for cooking.

5 Twist the end of the sausage to close it. Decide on the length you want each sausage to be and pinch the length at that point, easing the meat away to form a gap in the casing.

6 Twist the casing twice between the sausages. Pinch the meat again to form the next sausage, but twist the casing in the opposite direction so that the sausages do not unravel.

FORMING RINGS

7 Continue along the length of the sausage skin. If air bubbles remain, pierce the skin at that point with a sterilized needle or toothpick. Check if any sausages are loosely filled. If they are, then push the meat away from the twist, and twist it again to tighten.

Leave 6cm (2½in) of empty skin at the end of each sausage and exclude all air. Make a knot at the end of each piece of skin. Bring the two ends together to form a ring, and tie them together. This shape is a common one for smoked sausages.

Entries in **bold** indicate ingredients.

ACKNOWLEDGMENTS

ABOUT THE AUTHOR

Nichola Fletcher MBE is regarded as one of the world's leading authorities on meat. She pioneered the UK's first venison farm with her husband John more than 30 years ago, and is a writer, consultant, speaker, and course leader on all things meat-related. She has co-authored eight books, including *Ultimate Venison Cookery* (2007) and DK's *Sausage* (2012). An award-winning food historian, Nichola lives in Scotland, where she was awarded an MBE for her services to the venison industry in the 2014 New Year Honours list.

ABOUT THE RECIPE WRITERS

Christopher Trotter is a food writer, restaurant inspector, food consultant, and author of several cookbooks including *The Whole Hog* (2010) and *The Whole Cow* (2013). He runs bespoke cooking classes and food tours around his native Scotland, and appears on radio programmes talking about seasonal food. He is currently on the committee of the Guild of Food Writers.

Elena Rosemond-Hoerr is a writer and photographer, and the author of the award-winning blog biscuitsandsuch.com and DK's *The American Cookbook* (2014). A confirmed lover of pie, she lives on the North Carolina coast with her husband and two dogs.

Rachel Green is an award-winning chef, food writer, food campaigner, and TV presenter. She is a farmer's daughter from Lincolnshire and her family have farmed in the county for 14 generations. Rachel has cooked for Her Majesty the Queen and 800 guests at the Savoy Hotel, London, and her TV appearances include *The One Show*, *Countryfile*, *World on a Plate*, *Kill It, Cook It, Eat It!*, *Farm of Fussy Eaters*, and *Flying Dishes*. www.rachel-green.co.uk

NICHOLA FLETCHER WOULD LIKE TO THANK:

Ralf Lautenschlaeger in Germany for his help with European meat cuts; Stephen Rimmer in São Paulo for his help on meat cuts in Brazil; The Q Guild, and Jonathan Crombie from Crombie's of Edinburgh for advice on the naming of meat cuts in Britain; John Fletcher for veterinary and animal welfare advice; David Stewart for providing game; Quality Meat Scotland for their meat cutting guides; The Balgove Larder, St Andrews, for allowing us to invade their butchery and take photographs of their meat being cut. Most of all, Nichola would like to thank Graeme Braid, their master butcher, for going the extra mile to advise us on the home butchery section.

DK WOULD LIKE TO THANK:

Charlotte Tolhurst for new recipe photography; Stuart West and William Reavell for additional photography; Sara Robin, Geoff Fennell, Kat Mead, and Penny Stock for photography art direction; Fern Greene, Nancy McDougall, Rob Morris, Rebecca Rautner, and Isla Mackenzie for food styling; Matthew Ford and Lucy Pedder for food styling assistance; Wei Tang, Linda Berlin, and Tamsin Weston for prop styling; Adam Brackenbury and Tom Morse for image retouching; Sonia Charbonnier for technical support; Juliet Percival for the butchery illustrations and animal artworks; Harriet Yeomans for designing the butchery section; Jane Bamforth, Anna Burges-Lumsden, Jan Fullwood, Chris Gates, Anne Harnan, and Sue Harris for recipe testing; Kathy Woolley, Nidhilekha Mathur, Divya Chandhok, and Charis Bhagianathan for editorial assistance; Vicky Read, Laura Buscemi, Sourabh Challariya, and Aparajita Barai for design assistance; Claire Cross, Dorothy Kikon, Ligi John, and Janashree Singha for proofreading; and Vanessa Bird for the index.

All photography and artworks © Dorling Kindersley